Lecture Notes in Computer Science 4934

Uwe Brinkschulte Theo Ungerer
Christian Hochberger Rainer G. Spallek (Eds.)

Architecture of Computing Systems – ARCS 2008

21st International Conference
Dresden, Germany, February 25-28, 2008
Proceedings

Volume Editors

Uwe Brinkschulte
Universität Karlsruhe (TH)
Institut für Prozessrechentechnik, Automation und Robotik
76131 Karlsruhe, Germany
E-mail: brinks@ira.uka.de

Theo Ungerer
Universität Augsburg
Institut für Informatik
86135 Augsburg, Germany
E-mail: ungerer@informatik.uni-augsburg.de

Christian Hochberger
Rainer G. Spallek
Technische Universität Dresden
Institut für Technische Informatik
01062 Dresden, Germany
E-mail: {christian.hochberger,rgs}@inf.tu-dresden.de

Library of Congress Control Number: 2008920680

CR Subject Classification (1998): C.2, C.5.3, D.4, D.2.11, H.3.5, H.4, H.5.2

LNCS Sublibrary: SL 1 – Theoretical Computer Science and General Issues

ISSN 0302-9743
ISBN-10 3-540-78152-8 Springer Berlin Heidelberg New York
ISBN-13 978-3-540-78152-3 Springer Berlin Heidelberg New York

Springer is a part of Springer Science+Business Media

springer.com

Printed in Germany

Typesetting: Camera-ready by author, data conversion by Scientific Publishing Services, Chennai, India
Printed on acid-free paper SPIN: 12227785 06/3180 5 4 3 2 1 0

Preface

The ARCS series of conferences has over 30 years of tradition in reporting top notch results in computer architecture and operating systems research. It is organized by the special interest group on "Computer and System Architecture" of GI (Gesellschaft für Informatik e.V.) and ITG (Informationstechnische Gesellschaft im VDE - Information Technology Society).

In 2008, ARCS was hosted by the Technical University of Dresden, which has one of the leading information technology schools in Europe. This year's special focus was on adaptivity and adaptive system architectures. A wide spectrum was covered from pre-fabrication adaptation of architectural templates to dynamic run-time adaptation of deployed systems. Like the previous conferences in this series, this year's event constituted an important forum for the presentation of computer architecture research.

The call for papers resulted in a total of 47 submissions from around the world. Every submission was reviewed by three members of the program committee or additional reviewers. The program committee decided to accept 19 papers, which were arranged into seven sessions with the result of a strong program. The two keynote talks by Theo Ungerer of the University of Augsburg and Chris Schläger of AMD Dresden focused our attention on the "Grand Challenges of Computer Engineering" and on the "Impact of Operating Systems on Modern CPU Designs (and Vice Versa)".

The organizers gratefully acknowledge the support of ACM, IEEE, IFIP TC10, CEPIS, and EUREL.

We would like to thank all those who contributed to the success of this conference, in particular the members of the program committee and the additional referees for carefully reviewing the contributions and selecting a high-quality program. Our Workshop and Tutorial Chair Andreas Koch did a perfect job in organizing the tutorials and coordinating the workshops. Our special thanks go to the members of the organizing committee for their numerous contributions as well as to Thomas B. Preußer for setting up the conference software and for designing and maintaining the conference Web site. We would also like to thank Julian Wolf for his thorough preparation of this volume.

We hope that all of the participants enjoyed a successful conference, made a lot of new contacts, engaged in fruitful discussions, and had a pleasant stay in Dresden.

December 2007

Uwe Brinkschulte
Theo Ungerer
Christian Hochberger
Rainer G. Spallek

Organization

Organizing Committee

General Chairs

Christian Hochberger	TU Dresden, Germany
Rainer G. Spallek	TU Dresden, Germany

Program Chairs

Uwe Brinkschulte	Universität Karlsruhe (TH), Germany
Theo Ungerer	Universität Augsburg, Germany

Workshops and Tutorials

Andreas Koch	TU Darmstadt, Germany

Program Committee

Nader Bagherzadeh	University of California, Irvine, USA
Michael Beigl	University of Braunschweig, Germany
Mladen Berekovic	IMAP, Belgium and Delft University of Technology, The Netherlands
Guillem Bernat	Rapita Systems and University of York, UK
Arndt Bode	Technical University of Munich, Germany
Koen De Bosschere	Ghent University, Belgium
Jiannong Cao	The Hongkong Polytechnic University, China
Francisco J. Cazorla	UPC, Barcelona
Alois Ferscha	University of Linz, Austria
Werner Grass	University of Passau, Germany
Jadwiga Indulska	University of Queensland, Australia
Wolfgang Karl	University of Karlsruhe, Germany
Spyros Lalis	University of Thessaly, Greece
Paul Lukowicz	University of Passau, Germany
Jianhua Ma	Hosei University, Japan
Erik Maehle	Universität zu Lübeck, Germany
Christian Müller-Schloer	University of Hannover, Germany
Burghardt Schallenberger	Siemens AG, München
Pascal Sainrat	Université Paul Sabatier, Toulouse, France
Hartmut Schmeck	University of Karlsruhe, Germany

Karsten Schwan	Georgia Tech, USA
Peter Steenkiste	Carnegie-Mellon University, USA
Lothar Thiele	ETH Zurich, Switzerland
Pedro Trancoso	University of Cyprus, Cyprus
Gerhard Tröster	ETH Zurich, Switzerland
Mateo Valero	UPC, Barcelona
Lucian Vintan	Lucian Blaga University of Sibiu, Romania
Klaus Waldschmidt	University of Frankfurt, Germany
Stephan Wong	Delft University of Technology, The Netherlands
Laurence T. Yang	St. Francis Xavier University, Canada

Additional Reviewers

Tanguy Risset
Dimitris Theodoropoulos
Julien Dusser
Andreas Hofmann
Akira Hatanaka
Jean-Philippe Diguet
Yoon Yang
Wen Hsiang Hu
Oliverio J. Santana
Filipa Duarte
Rubén González
Hans Vandierendonck
JungSook Yang
Mojtaba Sabeghi
Christine Rochange
Jun Ho Bahn
Pier Francesco Foglia
Joan Manuel Parcerisa
Liu Yang
Weigang Wu

Table of Contents

Invited Program

Part I Hardware Design

Part II Pervasive Computing

Part III Network Processors and Memory Management

Part IV Reconfigurable Hardware

Part V Real-Time Architectures

Part VI Organic Computing

Part VII Computer Architecture

Invited Program

Keynote: Grand Challenges of Computer Engineering

Theo Ungerer

University of Augsburg
Department of Computer Science, D-86159 Augsburg
ungerer@informatik.uni-augsburg.de

This talk presents the results of two years of discussions of distinguished members of the common Section on Computer Engineering of the two national German societies on Computer Science – the Gesellschaft für Informatik (GI) and the Information Technology Society (Informationstechnische Gesellschaft ITG). The target of the "Grand Challenges of Computer Engineering" initiative is to provide research orientation to industry and to academic researchers as well as to research funding agencies. Our topics were defined not from a sole scientific perspective but with the vision to identify research areas that will safeguard employment and create new jobs within the next ten to twenty years. We restricted our analysis to the area that we know – computer engineering.

In a series of workshops we agreed upon three exemplary Application Challenges in the domains smart machines and environments and eight more fundamental Grand Challenges that are shown in the figure below.

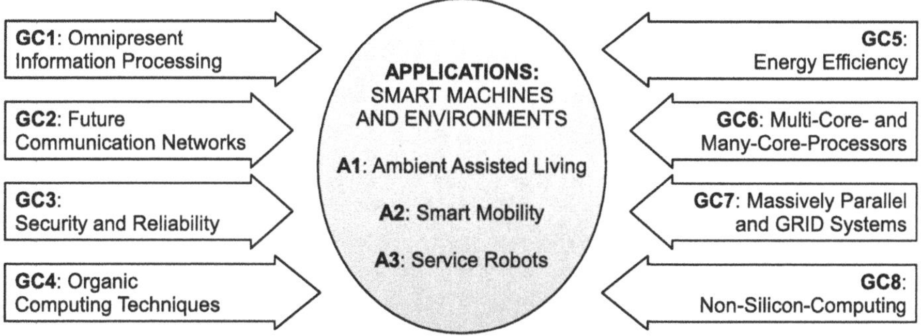

Fig. 1. Grand Challenges of Computer Engineering

More information is available at the websites of the Gesellschaft für Informatik GI[1] and of the Information Technology Society ITG[2].

[1] http://www.gi-ev.de/gliederungen/fachbereiche/technische-informatik-ti/fa-arcs/

[2] http://www.vde.com/VDE/Fachgesellschaften/ITG/Arbeitsgebiete/Fachbereich+6/Fachausschuss6.1.htm

U. Brinkschulte et al. (Eds.): ARCS 2008, LNCS 4934, p. 3, 2008.

Keynote: The Impact of Operating Systems on Modern CPU Designs (and Vice Versa)

Chris Schläger

Advanced Micro Devices Inc., Dresden
chris.schlaeger@amd.com

When the Mega-Hertz-race ended processor features started to dominate the marketing messages of the CPU vendors. This brought a noticeable change to the market. The continuous increase of clock frequencies and cache sizes made it easy both for the customer as well as the CPU manufacturer. These changes were easy to understand and communicate, and they were mostly invisible to the operating systems. In recent years, features such as 64-bit instructions, multiple cores, power management and virtualization support are the main selling factors. These features are visible to the OS and need to be supported by the OS to be exploitable.

The influence of the operating system interface of a CPU on its overall performance has grown tremendously. For AMD as a hardware vendor, this created a big challenge. The traditionally long feedback cycle between us and the OS vendors had to be shortened dramatically. Instead of relying on outside OS developers we had to bring OS development in-house. Even if that meant that we are developing something that we had no plans to ever sell. Pre-silicon hardware profiling with real work loads has become instrumental for the success of a CPU design.

The talk will describe the motivations for AMD to create the Operating System Research Center. It will also discuss how an in-house OS development can impact key design decisions for upcoming CPU architectures and how the CPU designers drive OS designs. It will also give an glimpse of the huge design space that CPU designers are faced with today. It will highlight some key design decisions and the impact on the success of the product. The talk will close with an outlook on features that may end up in future CPU generations.

U. Brinkschulte et al. (Eds.): ARCS 2008, LNCS 4934, p. 5, 2008.

Part I
Hardware Design

System Level Simulation of Autonomic SoCs with TAPES

Andreas Lankes, Thomas Wild, and Johannes Zeppenfeld

Institute for Integrated Systems, Technische Universität München
{andreas.lankes,thomas.wild,zeppenfe}@tum.de

Abstract. During the design process of modern SoCs (systems on chip), system architects require the support of design tools and methods that allow for a precise exploration of promising solutions. A trend towards autonomic SoCs is being proposed, in which a system's behavior is adapted at run time to improve reliability or power consumption. However, this opens ever more degrees of freedom in the definition of suitable architectures. Not only must the allocation and binding of resources and tasks be determined, but also the strategies by which an autonomic system adapts to changing working conditions. This paper presents an extension to the TAPES system simulator in order to support the evaluation of autonomic SoCs.

1 Introduction

The continued growth of chip complexity as described by Moore's law has enabled the integration of multiple components on a single chip, resulting in so-called systems on chip (SoCs). However, the design of SoCs is still a big challenge. Resource allocation, task binding, definition of memory and communication architectures etc. open up a huge design space that cannot be conquered by experience only. System architects therefore need the support of new methods and tools during the exploration process to identify promising solutions. In order to enable the interactive exploration of many alternatives, turnaround times should remain in a timeframe of minutes while maintaining a high level of accuracy.

In order to handle reliability problems associated with decreasing feature sizes and to provide more power efficient solutions, [1] proposes a paradigm shift in IC design towards autonomic SoCs, which ensure reliable systems in spite of design errors, manufacturing faults or soft errors. An autonomic SoC is a system that can adapt itself to changing conditions, including variations in the workload or the occurrence of errors. The autonomic system reacts to such changes by adapting its architectural parameters in accordance with a strategy designed to reach a predefined optimization target. Possible objectives include guaranteeing reliable system operation, maintaining a certain level of performance or minimizing the system's power consumption. Combinations of such goals are also possible.

The design of such autonomic SoCs not only consists in the definition of a suitable system architecture as is the case in conventional SoCs, but also in the specification of a strategy that allows reaching the optimization target using

U. Brinkschulte et al. (Eds.): ARCS 2008, LNCS 4934, pp. 9–22, 2008.

autonomic principles. Therefore, during the design phase of autonomic SoCs, the combined exploration of both architectural choices and system adaptation strategies must be supported by evaluation methods and tools. To the best of our knowledge there are currently no tools available which fulfill these requirements. The objective of this work is therefore to create a system level simulator that supports the simulation of autonomic SoCs.

The starting point for this work is the TAPES (Trace-based Architecture Performance Evaluation with SystemC) system level simulator, which enables fast and precise SoC performance analysis as part of the architecture exploration loop [2]. In this paper we present an extension of TAPES to support the simulation of autonomic SoCs. As one possible objective of such a system is the minimization of power consumption, the simulator's functionality to estimate the power consumption of the simulated system should be noted here. This power estimation functionality was presented in [3].

The paper is structured as follows: Section 2 presents related work regarding autonomic computing and performance evaluation of SoCs. Section 3 sketches the basic concepts of TAPES and the approach for extending it with support for autonomic systems. Section 4 describes implementation aspects and Section 5 shows an experiment with the extended simulator. Section 6 concludes this paper with possibilities for further improvement.

2 Related Work

Until recently, the focus for applying autonomic computing principles has mainly been at the system level, especially targeting the manageability of a system's software components [4]. For example, the CARUSO project [5] proposes the use of helper threads in a multi-threaded software environment to monitor an application and decide if various self-x strategies should be applied. These threads are responsible for dynamically adapting the system to changing operating conditions by making use of e.g. the system's reconfigurable hardware resources. The rising chip complexity has led to the necessity for similar approaches directly in the hardware components of a system [6]. Research has therefore been intensified to enhance SoC hardware with autonomic principles, for example [1], which proposes a new SoC architecture and design methodology to overcome the design gap inherent in SoC design. This approach is discussed in more detail below.

Methods and tools that support system designers in exploring the design space and help in evaluating architecture alternatives are the subject of intensive research. [7] gives a broad overview of methods used in architecture exploration. These range from analytic approaches to simulation based concepts. Examples for analytic performance evaluation are [8], which is based on Network Calculus and uses performance networks for modeling the interplay of processes on the system architecture, or SymTA/S [9], where formal scheduling analysis techniques and symbolic simulation are used for performance and timing analysis. In simulation based evaluation concepts, transaction level models (TLM, [10]) are widely used because they allow modeling computation and communication independently from each other and thus enable an easier modification of system architectures. SystemC [11] has gained wide acceptance as the language for this type of model. TLMs, however, are applied on different abstraction levels and for very different purposes [12]. The performance simulation part of StepNP, a network processor evaluation platform described in [13], uses a SystemC TLM that captures the complete system functionality, executed on an instruction set simulator. On the other end of the spectrum is the performance evaluation approach TAPES [2], which abstracts the functionality of SoC architecture components as processing latencies and captures their interaction on shared resources. The contribution of this paper is the enhancement of TAPES with autonomic principles for the simulation of time-variant systems. The details for capturing runtime modifications to system parameters in TAPES are described in the following section.

3 Concept

According to [1], an autonomic system can be split into two layers: the functional layer (FL) and the autonomic layer (AL). The functional layer corresponds to a non-autonomic SoC, with components refered to simply as functional elements (FEs). The AL, which can be compared to the vegetative nervous system of a human being, has the task of supervising and controlling the FL, and consists of multiple autonomic elements (AEs), each responsible for the supervision of a specific FE.

The two layers form a control loop (shown in Figure 1), which consists of the following three parts:

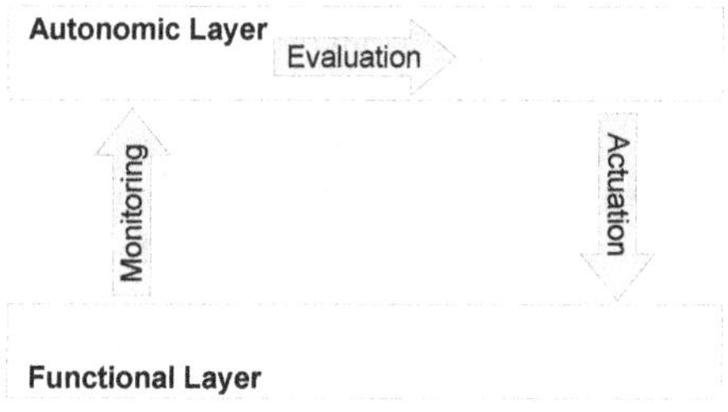

Fig. 1. Control loop between FL and AL

1. Monitoring: The AE is provided with information on the FE's state.
2. Evaluation: The AE applies the information provided by the monitor to a set of rules and decides if an adaptation of the FE is required.
3. Actuation: The AE adapts the FE according to the decisions made.

We assume the following metrics as possible inputs to the rule set of the autonomic element:

- Load and activity of the FEs

- Occurrence of errors in the FEs
- Memory usage and buffer fill levels

In opposition to load and usage values, the occurrence of errors, such as timing violations, must be modeled explicitly and cannot be extracted from the original TAPES model. The actions that can be taken as a result of the evaluation currently include the following:

- Deactivation and activation of CPUs and accelerators.
- Modifications to the clock frequency of CPUs and accelerators.
- Adapting supply voltages in accordance with clock frequency.
- Changing SoC bus properties (clock frequency, maximum burst length, utilized bus width).

Note that these lists are not exclusive. They can easily be extended by further metrics and actions as provided by a real system.

The TAPES simulator forms the basis for this work, and is extended according to the concepts presented above. In TAPES, architectural resources are treated as black boxes whose internal functionalities are abstracted as delays. They interact via transactions on a bus-based communication architecture (original simulation model shown in Figure 2). The number and type of resources can be configured in a flexible manner. The functionality is specified using so-called application traces, which encompass sequences of processing latencies interleaved with transaction calls corresponding to the communication with other resources. Transactions initiate the execution of traces in the target module and thus allow capturing the behavior of the complete system. Note that no application data is processed or exchanged in this simulation model. Only the required time for processing and data transfer is recorded.

To demonstrate the trace-based approach of TAPES, Figure 3 shows a small example of trace execution that captures the interaction of a CPU and an accelerator from the original simulation model shown in Figure 2. The CPU trace begins with processing data (DEL trace element, delay). This is followed by a write operation to the accelerator (BWS, bus write of specific length), which can be seen in the activity diagram of the write bus (pipelined bus). This transfer initiates the execution of a trace in the accelerator, which simulates the processing

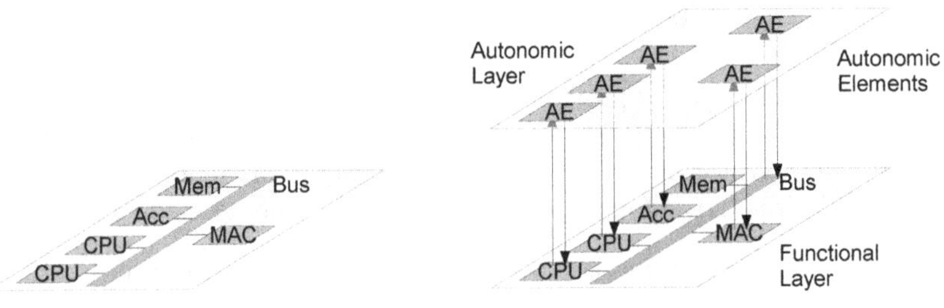

Fig. 2. Original and extended TAPES simulation model

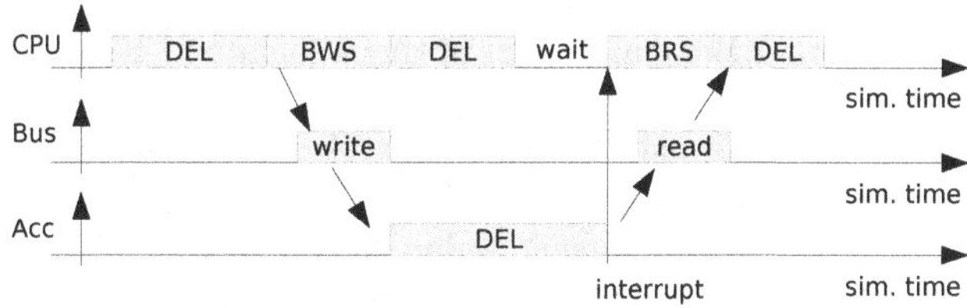

Fig. 3. Trace execution in CPU and Accelerator

of data (DEL) and afterwards issues an interrupt to the CPU (INT, interrupt). The CPU, which was originally simulating the processing of data (DEL), is now waiting due to a semaphore trace element (not shown) until the accelerator is ready to deliver its results. The interrupt causes the CPU to resume its trace execution with a read access to the accelerator (BRS, bus read specific length), followed by further processing of data (DEL).

The simulator provides information on the activities of system resources, data processing latencies, fill levels of internal buffers and even the power consumption of the simulated system. To explore different architecture variations, the application traces as well as the key parameters of the architecture can be freely configured. These include the number of CPUs, accelerators or memories, the clock frequency of individual components, buffer sizes and the width of the system bus.

4 Implementation

The original TAPES forms the basis of the functional layer of the extended simulation model, and is extended by an AL. In contrast to the functional elements which are abstracted by delays, the modeled autonomic elements are fully functional. As suggested in [1], the AL is composed of multiple AEs, each of which is associated with a single FE. The extended simulation model in Figure 2 shows the elements of both layers. Communication between AL and FL takes place only between associated AEs and FEs. An AE gathers information monitored from the corresponding FE and uses it to adapt the FE's behavior. Globally this means that the control loop between AL and FL is formed by multiple smaller control loops between individual FEs and AEs. To allow for global decisions, all AEs can communicate directly with each other.

Besides adding the AL to the simulation model, changes must also be made to the FL. In order to allow the monitoring shown in Figure 1, appropriate interfaces must be defined and implemented in the FEs. Similar interfaces are required for actuation. All modifications to the TAPES simulator (implemented in SystemC 2.2) described above are realized in a modular fashion, i.e. it is possible to compile the simulator both with and without the autonomic features.

4.1 Monitoring

In order to decide whether the parameters of the associated FE must be adapted, the AE requires information about the state of the FE. The associated exchange of data can be realized either using polling (the AE periodically checks the state of the associated FE), or by pushing (the FE actively transfers the data to its AE every time the state or a monitored value changes). Pushing is used for the current implementation, which constantly provides the AE with the current information on the FE. This allows strategies that react immediately on occurring events. Listing 1.1 shows the interface class used for this communication channel.

```
// interface class for an autonomic element of a module
class ae_module_if : public sc_interface {
    virtual void error_occurred() = 0;
    virtual void current_command(int command) = 0;
    virtual void fill_level(int queue, int fill_level) = 0;
};
```

Listing 1.1. Interface class for autonomic elements

Various types of data which are transferred over this interface were already detailed above (Section 3). The majority of this information is directly available from the FEs. For example, the load or activity of the FE can be derived directly from the object representing the currently executed trace element. However, the occurrence of errors, such as timing violations, must be modeled explicitly. For this purpose, one or more error models are added to the functional elements, allowing the combination of multiple error types. So far these models are very simple; they just read an error file that specifies the occurrence of errors. The sole purpose of modeling errors is therefore to simulate the reaction of the autonomic system, allowing AEs to take actions that potentially prevent the occurrence of further errors. The effects of errors on the functional level are not modelled, since the few clock cycles necessary for error correction are considered negligible on the system level.

4.2 Evaluation

Based on the information provided by the FE and the rules programmed into the AE, the AE decides whether the FE requires adaptation or not. If the information on the associated FE is not sufficient, an AE can access other AEs for information on their associated FEs. Most of the data provided by the FEs require processing before it can be applied to the rules that decide on the adaptation of the associated FE (see Figure 4). These rules define the strategy of the autonomic system. Currently the rules are hard-coded into the source code of the AEs. Consequently the exploration of different strategies requires recompilation of the simulator.

The processing necessary for the evaluation of data arriving from the FEs depends on the rules to be used. However, there are some basic processing steps

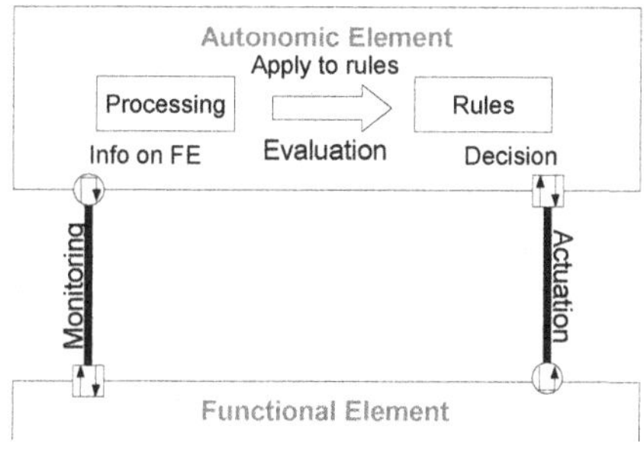

Fig. 4. Block diagram of an autonomic element (AE)

that are helpful for all types of rules. Examples of such processing steps are averaging over specified time periods, building up histories of values or counting events within time windows. In order to simplify and accelerate the implementation of these rules, components providing these basic processing steps are implemented. These processing components can be used in different combinations, for implementing the rules in the autonomic layer.

In the following paragraphs three basic rules are presented that can be realized using the processing components listed above. By combining these basic rules, more complex adaptation strategies for autonomic systems can be formed.

The fill level of a buffer and the knowledge of the receiving module of the buffered data, allows a prediction of the receiving module's future workload. By building up a history of buffer fill levels, it is possible to recognize trends of buffer usage. Such a rule can be extended by also supervising the activity of the receiver module mentioned above.

For an activity based rule it is best to look at the history of averaged busy or idle values of an FE (see Figure 5). To get a criterion for deciding if the throughput must be increased or decreased, ranges that change with the simulation time can be defined. In Figure 5 these ranges, which are opened up by a load interval and a time period, are called idle window and busy window. If the graph of the average load lies completely within the busy window, the condition for increasing the performance of the module is met. The same check can be performed for the idle window. By changing the height (i.e. load interval) and

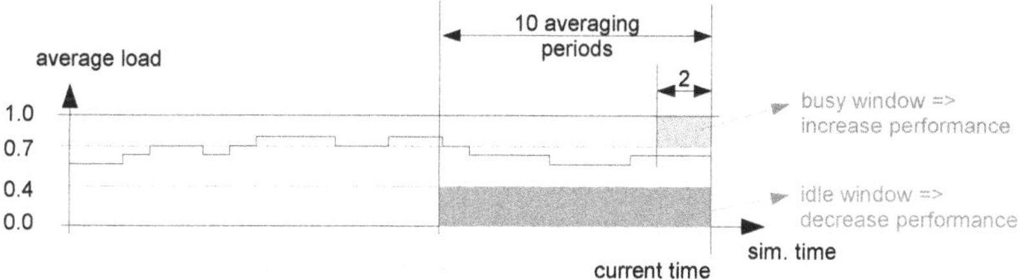

Fig. 5. Idle and busy window

width (i.e. the number of averaging periods) of these windows, the conditions can be parametrized.

As described above, an AE is notified about errors occurring in the associated module. If the frequency of error events exceeds a certain threshold, the AE can try to change parameters of the FE in order to reduce the occurrence of these errors. For example in order to counter too frequent timing violations in a real system's component, the AL could decrease the clock frequency or increase the supply voltage. In the simulation model the ability of the AE to influence the errors depends on the utilized error models. If an error file is used (i.e. the occurrence of errors is independent of the module's current parameters), the AE can only prevent errors by switching the associated module off.

4.3 Actuation

To enable the adaptation of an FE's architectural parameters, an additional communication channel is required between the AEs and their associated FEs. While introducing this interface (see Listing 1.2) between the AEs and FEs is fairly straightforward, providing a mechanism for changing FE parameters (i.e. changing the functional behavior of the FEs) at run time is much more difficult. First, a new parameter must be added to the FEs, allowing them to be activated or deactivated. For this purpose the parameter power state is introduced, which is tightly coupled with the power estimation functionality introduced in [3]. The possible power states are 'running', 'hot standby', 'cold standby' and 'dead'.

```
// interface class for a module (e.g. cpu, acc, ...)
class fe_module_if : public sc_interface {
   virtual void set_power_state(power_state state) = 0;
   virtual void set_clock_period(int clock_period) = 0;
   virtual void set_voltage(int voltage) = 0;
   virtual void set_execution_value(int exec_value) = 0;
};
```

Listing 1.2. Interface class for functional elements (e.g. CPU, ACC, ...)

State 'running' is the active state in which the FE can execute traces, i.e. process or transfer data. The other states are inactive states: 'hot standby' and 'cold standby' are sleeping modes, 'dead' represents a broken device that has permanently been shut down. While a resource is in an inactive state, it must be guaranteed that no execution of traces or data processing occurs. Furthermore, requests via point-to-point connections or the bus must be rejected by the module. When deactivating a module of a system, another resource has to take over its task of data processing. For example, if the CPUs of a network processor are supported by an accelerator for encryption and this accelerator is shut down, the CPUs must handle the encryption by themselves (i.e. in software).

For the simulation model, this means that the execution of the traces must be dynamic, allowing an adaptation when a resource is switched off. Unfortunately in the original TAPES simulator, the trace execution is static, requiring the introduction of a conditional trace element that allows branching in the execution of traces. This new IF trace element calls a specific trace depending on the state of a referenced FE. Besides the static trace execution of the original simulator, there is an additional problem when deactivating FEs. As in a real system, a module should only be switched off during simulation if it is not processing or transferring any data. Consequently it must be ensured that a module is turned off only if it is idle and contains no data.

When changing the clock frequency of a functional element, we must differentiate between modules and the bus model. In the modules the change of this parameter has an effect on the delay trace elements. As the delays of these trace elements is specified in clock cycles, the delays have to be rescaled when the clock frequency changes. Current executions of delay trace elements have to be aborted and the remaining delay has to be scaled according to the new clock period, before execution can be resumed. In the bus model the time required for arbitration and data transfer depends on the clock period. The clock period of the bus is assumed to be only adaptable between transfers. As the delay of a transfer is calculated anew for each transfer, the delay is always based on the current bus clock.

The voltage parameter of the modules, which is tightly coupled to the power estimation functionality described in [3], also has to be adaptable in order to be able to model dynamic voltage and frequency scaling (DVFS). As this parameter has no effect on the functional behavior of a module, no additional effort is required for enabling adaptation at runtime.

5 Experiment

One of the most important properties of autonomic computing is the increased reliability of such systems. This increase of reliability is achieved by the ability of these systems to adapt themselves at runtime to occurring errors, such as timing violations. In the following experiment the adaptation process of such an autonomic network processor architecture is investigated. The basic architecture of this network SoC is shown in Figure 6. It consists of one bus, three CPUs, two memory modules, one MAC-module for receiving and transmitting packets, a buffer manager that autonomously stores/retrieves packets and a queue manager. Listing 1.3 shows a section of the according system configuration file.

The task of this network processor is basic IP forwarding, which is assumed to require 560 cycles on a CPU for every packet [14]. The rate of the incoming traffic is 200 MBit/s, the size of each packet is 64 Bytes and a total of 4000 packets are simulated. In this example we want to model the occurrence of timing violations in the third CPU. Since we use the simple error model described above, the occurrence of these errors is specified in advance, as shown in Figure 6.

```
<!-- xml configuration file of simulation -->
<architecture>
    <resources>
        <!-- number of cpus -->
        <cpu>3</cpu>
        <!-- number of accelerators -->
        <acc>0</acc>
        <!-- number of memories -->
        <mem>2</mem>
        ...
    </resources>
    <cpu>
        <!-- base clock frequency of cpus in MHz -->
        <clock>500</clock>
    </cpu>
    <bus>
        <!-- clock frequency of bus in MHz -->
        <clock>100</clock>
        <!-- width of data busses in bits -->
        <bus_width>128</bus_width>
        <!-- max number of bus words per burst transfer -->
        <burst_length>8</burst_length>
        ...
    </bus>
    ...
</architecture>
<traffic>
...
```

Listing 1.3. Section of the simulated system's configuration file

For adaptation of the system at runtime there are two rules, programmed into the autonomic layer: The first rule regards the occurrence of errors in the CPUs. If there are more than two errors within a time window of 20 us in a CPU, it will be shut off. The second rule aims at keeping the CPUs' utilization at approx. 85%, by adapting clock frequency and voltage accordingly. For homogeneous traffic, a constant utilization of the CPUs results in a more or less constant

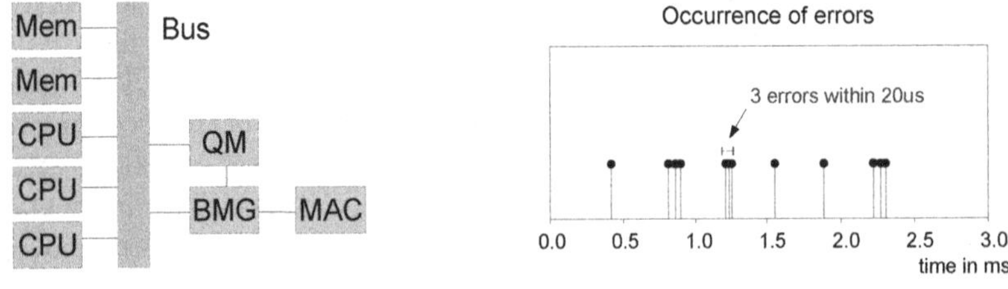

Fig. 6. Simulated network processor system and specified occurrence of errors

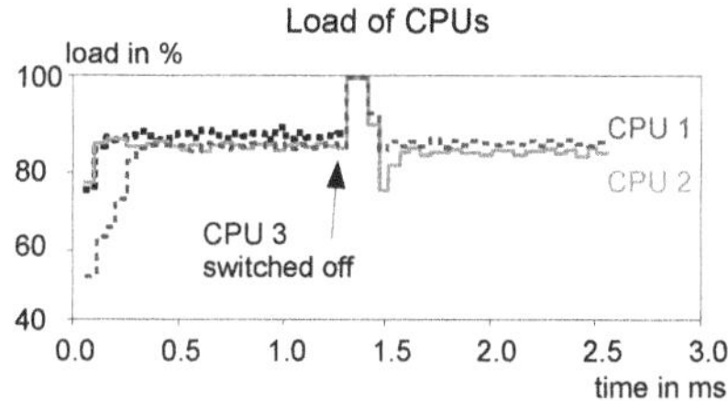

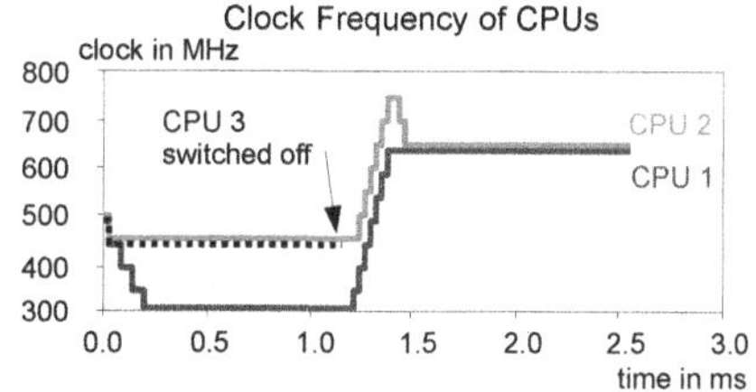

Fig. 7. Load and clock frequency of CPUs

packet output rate. According to the second rule, the clock frequency of the CPUs is reduced at the beginning, as depicted in Figure 7. Figure 6 shows the point in time at which the rule regarding the errors is met and the corresponding CPU is switched off (also visible in Figure 7). After shutting off the third CPU, the system reacts to the decrease in throughput by increasing the clock of the remaining CPUs.

The utilization of bus arbiter and read/ write buses are shown in Figure 8. Immediately after the deactivation of CPU 3, the load of the arbiter drops significantly. This decrease is caused by the missing arbitration requests of the deactivated CPU. With the increased clock frequencies of the remaining CPUs after the system's adaptation, the arbiter's load returns to the original level corresponding to the unchanged ingress load. The load of read and write buses are subject to the same variations.

The average fill level of the CPU queue in the buffer manager is shown in Figure 9. This queue stores the packet descriptors of packets waiting to be processed by the CPUs. The peak in the fill level of the CPU queue originates from the temporarily lower throughput of the processing resources (CPUs).

Figure 10 shows the packet latencies of the outgoing packets, the point in time at which the CPU is shut off can easily be recognized by the significant increase of the latency. However, the adaptation of the system, performed by the autonomic layer, makes sure that this increase is just temporary by raising the clock frequency of the remaining CPUs. Now that two CPUs have to keep up with the same rate of incoming packets as the three CPUs before, the processing of the packets has to be faster resulting in lower packet latencies. The point in time of the system's adaptation can also be seen in Figure 10 showing the

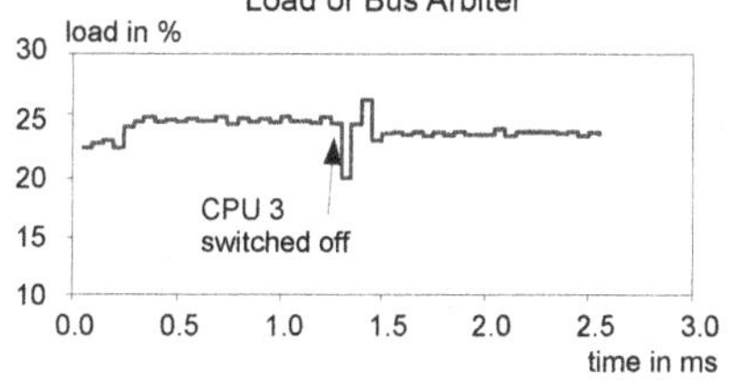

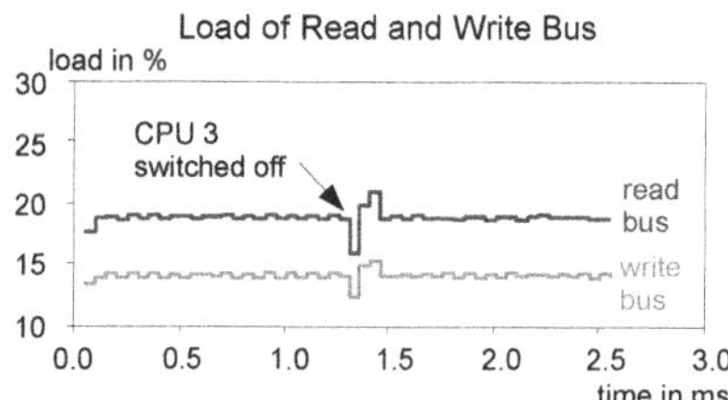

Fig. 8. Load of bus arbiter and read and write bus

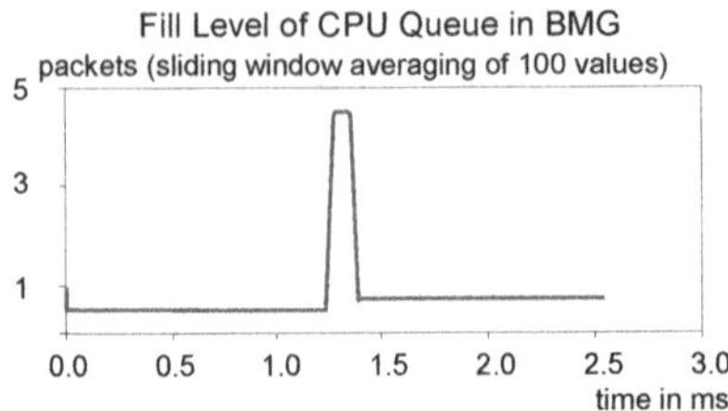

Fig. 9. Fill level of the CPU queue in the buffer manager

incoming and outgoing packet rates. The outgoing packet rate drops at first, after the third CPU has been shut off, but then recovers after the adaptation of the remaining CPUs' performance.

The power consumption diagram (Figure 11) of the autonomic network processor shows that the two CPUs require significantly more power to keep up with the incoming packets, than the three CPUs. This is due to the significantly increase of the CPUs' clock frequencies as well as the associated increase of the CPUs' supply voltage. The power values of the diagram are normalized to the mean power consumption of a non-autonomic network processor with the same basic architecture (3 CPUs @ 500 MHz) as the autonomic processor in this example.

Simulating the system presented above takes approx. 1 second on an Intel Pentium M 2.0 GHz with 1024 MB RAM running under LINUX (Kernel 2.6.20, gcc 4.1). However for a simulator used in architecture exploration not only simulation performance is relevant, but also the effort required for modeling the simulated systems. For setting up the basic architecture of the example above, the system's parameters have to be specified in the XML configuration file of the simulator. Creating the rules for adaptation of the system at runtime requires slightly more effort. The rules used in this autonomic system must be programmed into the AEs associated with the CPUs. This can be done using the basic components presented in Section 4.2. Since the rules are hard coded, a recompilation of the simulator is necessary. Once these rules are implemented, they can easily be varied by changing certain parameters of the processing components (e.g. averaging period, ranges, etc.).

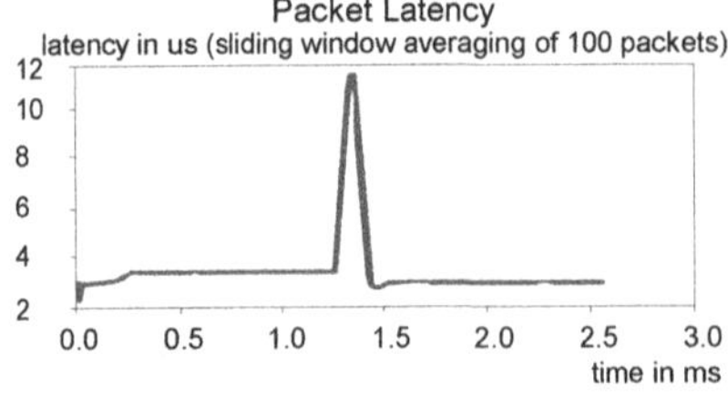

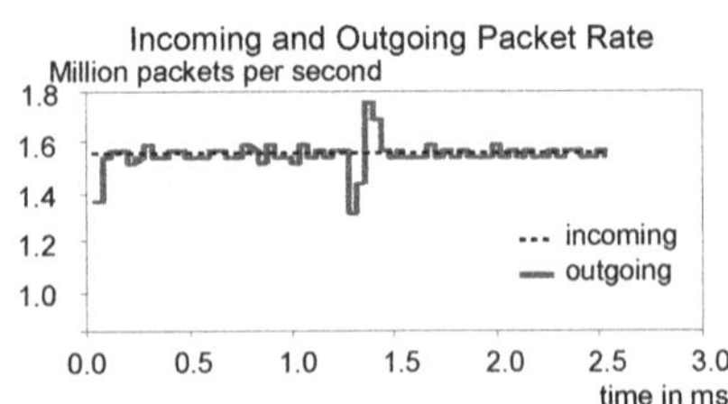

Fig. 10. Packet latencies and packet rate of incoming/outgoing packets

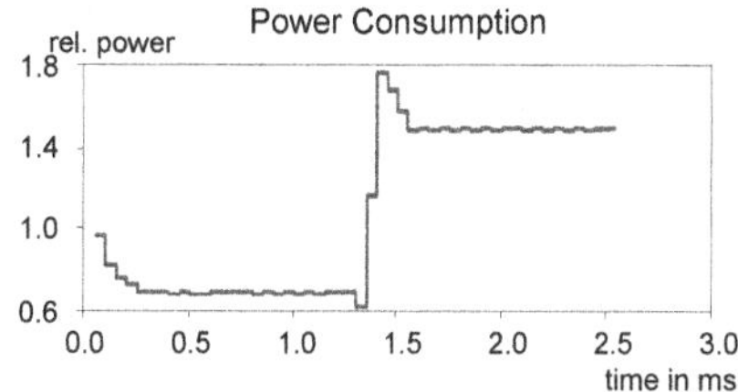

Fig. 11. Power consumption of simulated system

6 Conclusion and Outlook

The contribution of this paper is the extension of the TAPES system simulator, now providing the means to simulate autonomic SoCs. Such systems can adapt themselves to varying amounts of incoming traffic or occurrences of errors by changing their architectural parameters. The example in Section 5 shows that the extended simulator supports the investigation of strategies for autonomic SoCs. Evaluation of the simulated architectures is possible in terms of performance as well as of power consumption. Our experiment shows that due to fast turnaround times, an interactive exploration of autonomic architectures is possible.

Beyond the presented extensions to the simulator, additional enhancements can be made. The introduction of dynamic error models, in which the error rate depends on the current parameters of the corresponding FE, will enable an investigation of tradeoffs concerning power, performance and reliability. Secondly, the consideration of time penalties required to change module parameters will improve the accuracy of the simulation model. Finally, a simplified configuration of autonomic rules will avoid recompilation.

References

[1] Lipsa, G., Herkersdorf, A.: Towards a Framework and a Design Methodology for Autonomic SoC. In: The 2nd IEEE International Conference on Autonomic Computing (June 2005)

[2] Wild, T., Herkersdorf, A., Lee, G.-Y.: TAPES - Trace-based architecture performance evaluation with SystemC. Design Automation for Embedded Systems 10(2–3), 157–179 (2006)

[3] Lankes, A., Wild, T., Zeppenfeld, J.: Power Estimation of Time Variant SoCs with TAPES. In: DSD 2007: 10th EUROMICRO Conference on Digital System Design: Architectures, Methods, Tools, EUROMICRO, pp. 261–264 (August 2007)

[4] Kephart, J.O., Chess, D.M.: The Vision of Autonomic Computing. Computer 36(1), 41–50 (2003)

[5] Brinkschulte, U., Becker, J., Dorfmüller-Ulhaas, K., et al.: CARUSO - Project Goals and Principal Approach. In: Workshop on Organic Computing, GI Jahrestagung, Ulm (September 2004)

[6] De Micheli., G.: Robust System Design with Uncertain Information. In: MEMOCODE 2003: Proceedings of the First ACM and IEEE International Conference on Formal Methods and Models for Co-Design (MEMOCODE 2003), p. 283. IEEE Computer Society Press, Washington (2003)

[7] Gries, M.: Methods for evaluating and covering the design space during early design development. Integr. VLSI J. 38(2), 131–183 (2004)

[8] Thiele, L., Wandeler, E.: Performance Analysis of Distributed Embedded Systems. Embedded Systems Handbook (2005)

[9] Henia, R., et al.: System level performance analysis - the SymTA/S approach. IEEE Proceedings Computers and Digital Techniques 152(2), 148–166 (2005)

[10] Cai, L., Gajski, D.: Transaction level modeling: an overview. In: CODES+ISSS 2003: Proceedings of the 1st IEEE/ACM/IFIP international conference on Hardware/software codesign and system synthesis, pp. 19–24. ACM Press, New York (2003)

[11] SystemC Homepage, `www.systemc.org`

[12] Donlin, A.: Transaction level modeling: flows and use models. In: CODES+ISSS 2004: Proceedings of the 2nd IEEE/ACM/IFIP international conference on Hardware/software codesign and system synthesis, pp. 75–80. ACM Press, New York (2004)

[13] Paulin, P.G., Pilkington, C., Bensoudane, E.: StepNP: A System-Level Exploration Platform for Network Processors. IEEE Design and Test of Computers 19(6), 17–26 (2002)

[14] Ramaswamy, R., Wolf, T.: PacketBench: A tool for workload characterization of network processing. In: IEEE 6th Annual Workshop on Workload Characterization (WWC-6), Austin (October 2003)

Topology-Aware Replica Placement in Fault-Tolerant Embedded Networks

Thilo Streichert, Michael Glaß, Rolf Wanka, Christian Haubelt, and Jürgen Teich

Department of Computer Science 12
University of Erlangen-Nuremberg, Germany
{streichert,glass,wanka,haubelt,teich}@cs.fau.de

Abstract. Application details uncertain at design time as well as tolerance against permanent resource defects demand flexibility and redundancy. In this context, we present a strategy for placing replicas in embedded point-to-point networks where link as well as node defects may occur at runtime. The proposed strategies for replica placement are based on the partitioning of the network into biconnected components. We are able to distinguish between different replication strategies, i.e., active and passive replication. Our experimental results show that the reliability improvement due to the proposed replica placement strategies is up to 23% compared to a randomized strategy.

1 Introduction

Many networked embedded systems such as sensor networks or networks in the field of industry automation need to be flexible and extensible towards applications which are unknown at design time. In particular, new network nodes need to be integrated and new tasks are to be placed onto the computational resources in the network. On the other hand, such networks have to meet demands concerning reliability/availability at a minimum of additional monetary costs. But how is it possible to combine flexibility with reliability at a minimum of extra monetary cost? Traditional approaches try to treat transient and permanent faults by introducing spatial or temporal redundancy at design time or by applying coding techniques. In this contribution, we will propose an online methodology that replicates the tasks executed by the network nodes in order to tolerate permanent fail-silent faults of nodes and links. These replicated tasks will be dynamically placed onto network nodes using underutilized computational reserves. That is, we need not explicitly extend the network with a node and a spare node providing the same functionality. Instead, the functionality of a new node or a new application will be distributed over the network making use of free computational reserves in the network, i.e., reducing the amount of extra cost. Moreover, it is possible to tolerate several subsequent permanent defects.

Using a two-phase online methodology (Fig. 1), we are able to integrate new tasks into the network and to treat resource defects. After a defect of a node or link in the network, the online methodology tries to activate replicas and

U. Brinkschulte et al. (Eds.): ARCS 2008, LNCS 4934, pp. 23–37, 2008.

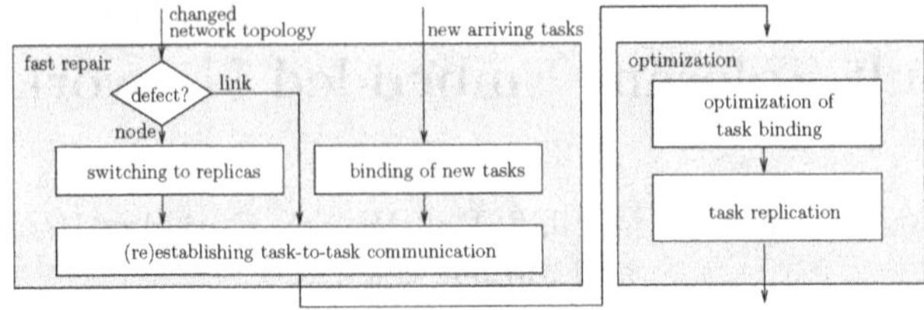

Fig. 1. In case of topology changes, the *fast repair* phase activates replicated tasks and reroutes the communication. If a new task arrives at one node in the network, the network decentrally tries to bind the task onto one of its network nodes. The optimization phase optimizes the binding of tasks and creates new replicas.

reroute the communication paths in a *fast repair* phase. The second phase called *optimization phase* tries 1.) to optimize the binding of the tasks and 2.) to place replicas in order to tolerate further resource defects. In this paper, we focus on the algorithmic aspects of placement of replicas in order to tolerate node or link defects.

As an introductory example, consider the networks and placement of tasks in Fig. 2. Two cases are shown which are completely different in their reliability. Both cases show a network with six nodes $n_1, \ldots, n_6$ and two communicating tasks t_1 and t_2, each having a unique replica t'_1 and t'_2, respectively. If in Fig. 2a) node n_2, node n_4 or the link (n_2, n_4) fails, the functionality fails as well because no connected component contains both tasks. In Fig. 2b) the placement of the replicas t'_1 and t'_2 differs such that each node and link defect, even n_2, n_4 as well as the link (n_2, n_4) may occur without loosing the functionality. Thus, the reliability of the entire network depends heavily on the placement strategy of replicated tasks and the underlying topology.

Therefore, we will study in this paper the impact of replica placement on the network reliability and in summary, the contributions are:

1. Novel heuristics for placing replicas are presented which are based on the partitioning of networks into so-called *biconnected components*.

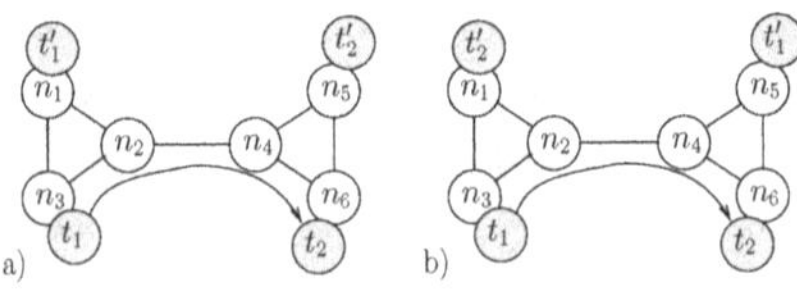

Fig. 2. In a) neither the nodes n_2, n_4 nor the link (n_2, n_4) must fail. Otherwise, the functionality provided by the communicating tasks t_1 and t_2 cannot operate any more. In b), the nodes n_2 and n_4 as well as the link (n_2, n_4) may fail without loosing functionality as the communication from task t_1 to t_2 may still be handled from replica t'_1 to t_2 or from t_1 to t'_2.

2. Differences for placing *passive replicas* and *active replicas* are analytically discussed and experimentally evaluated.
3. An experimental evaluation compares the presented heuristics with respect to resulting reliability properties.

The remaining paper is structured as follows: Sec. 2 presents the related work in the field of replica placement. Sec. 3 introduces our network model used throughout this paper. Sec. 4 focuses on the main contribution of this paper, i.e., on distributed replica placement techniques. The proposed replica placement approach is evaluated in Sec. 5.

2 Related Work

Replication has been a research topic in different areas, like distributed file servers, content delivery networks, and databases. In databases for instance, replication has been applied for performance reasons. In distributed systems, replication or redundancy is usually introduced for fault-tolerance reasons and obtained by replicating tasks or services as well as components or devices.

Independent of the kind of replication, i.e., active replication or passive replication, different strategies have been investigated for the placement of replicated tasks. In the field of *content-delivery networks*, data objects are replicated on servers in order to minimize the latency in case of an access by a client. A famous approach that minimizes this latency is the *Hot Zone* algorithm [12] which is derived from the *Hot Spot* [10] algorithm. The Hot Spot algorithm attempts to place replicas close to the clients generating the highest amount of traffic. N potential sites are sorted according to this amount of traffic and on the M sites with the highest traffic replicas are placed. The Hot Zone algorithm partitions the network into regions consisting of nodes with a low latency to each other. Then, the Hot Zone algorithm places replicas into the most active regions.

A very good overview of different placement strategies, objectives and application areas is given in [7]. The presented algorithms are executed in a centralized way with global knowledge. But interestingly, the authors of [7] see a strong relevance towards the research of distributed online-placement strategies which is the scope of this paper. They argue that distributed approaches overcome scalability problems of centralized approaches.

Heuristics which determine a placement of replicas in a distributed manner have been presented by Douceur and Wattenhofer. They studied placement strategies [4] based on hill-climbing algorithms which are applied in the distributed server-less file system Farsite [1]. The heuristics select replicas and swap their placement in order to iteratively increase their availability. In particular, one group of nodes contacts another group and each of it selects a file it manages. The groups then decide whether to swap the files or not. For the selection of files, three different strategies were applied: 1.) A *RandRand*-strategy swaps two randomly chosen files. 2.) A *MinRand*-strategy swaps between a minimum-availability file and any other file. 3.) A *MinMax*-strategy swaps between a minimum-availability file and a maximum-availability file. The swaps are only processed if they reduce the difference of the file availabilities.

In [3], a distributed algorithm with a loosely synchronized global database is presented which tries to take placement decisions of data objects into account by applying a randomized strategy. A more recent publication [9] proposes a so-called *sequential placement* strategy which determines a binding of a primary object with the help of a hash function calculated for that object. The idea of sequential placement is to place replicas close to each other such that failures can be detected and repaired very fast.

Unfortunately, all these heuristics fail in the context of embedded networks, since they consider only the availability of a single data object on its own. But, in the context of embedded networks an application consisting of distributed *communicating tasks* works only correctly if all tasks are available. Moreover, in the context of embedded systems based on point-to-point communication, there is a high risk that networks split up into two parts due to a defect. Therefore, in the following sections, we study novel heuristics for the placement and replication of communicating tasks.

3 Computational Model

The considered systems are specified by the *network model* which separates functionality from the network architecture. The network model consists of a *topology graph* and a *sensor-controller-actuator graph*. The third component of the network model is the set of mapping edges which denotes the binding possibilities of tasks onto network nodes. Hence, we model also heterogeneous nodes that cannot execute all tasks. The system model can be formally described as follows:

Definition 1 (Network Model). *The entire network model* $M(G^{\mathrm{tg}}, G^{sca}, E_{\mathrm{m}})$ *consists of a* topology graph G^{tg}, *a set of* sensor-controller-actuator chains G^{sca}, *and a set of* mapping edges E_{m}.

Definition 2 (Topology Graph). *The topology graph* $G^{\mathrm{tg}}(N^{\mathrm{tg}}, E^{\mathrm{tg}})$ *consists of network nodes* $n_i \in N^{\mathrm{tg}}$ *and edges* $e_i^{\mathrm{tg}} \in E^{\mathrm{tg}} \subseteq N^{\mathrm{tg}} \cup N^{\mathrm{tg}}$. *Edges* e_i^{tg} *between the network nodes are undirected.*

For modeling the functionality, we define a *sensor-controller-actuator graph.*

Definition 3 (Sensor-Controller-Actuator Graph). *The sensor-controller-actuator graph* $G^{sca}(T^{\mathrm{sca}}, E^{\mathrm{sca}})$ *consists of tasks* $t_i \in T^{\mathrm{sca}}$ *and edges* $e_i^{sca} \in E^{sca} \subseteq T^{\mathrm{sca}} \times T^{\mathrm{sca}}$ *represent the data dependencies between the tasks.*

Definition 4 (Mapping Edges). *The set of mapping edges* $E_{\mathrm{m}} \subseteq T^{s} \times N^{\mathrm{tg}}$ *relate vertices of the sensor-controller-actuator chains with the vertices of the topology graph. A mapping edge* $e_{\mathrm{m}} \in E_{\mathrm{m}}$ *starts at a vertex of the sensor-controller-actuator graph and ends at a vertex of the topology graph.*

A mapping edge $e_m \in E_m$ indicates the possible implementation of a task onto the corresponding resource. If a mapping edge $(t_i, n_i) = e_m$ is selected, the task t_i of the sensor-controller-actuator graph is executed at the corresponding node n_i. This will be also denoted with $t_i \mapsto n_i$ in the following.

In the following, we assume that at most two mapping edges e_m are selected, one for the task t_i and one for the replica t'_i. The replicas can be either active or passive and throughout the reminder of the paper, we define the property of active and passive replication as follows.

Definition 5 (Active Replica). *Active replicas t'_i are executed on a node in the same way as primary tasks t_i. Thus, the active replicas produce the same computational load c_i as the corresponding primary tasks t_i.*

Definition 6 (Passive Replica). *Passive replicas t'_i are not executed on a node, but stored in the memory of that node. In order to work like a primary task t_i, replicated tasks need to be activated. Thus, the passive replicas produce no computational load c_i unless they are activated.*

Furthermore, the replica placement methodology presented here is based on the following *failure model*:

Definition 7 (Failure Model). *Only one node or communication link may fail simultaneously and another subsequent defect of such a resource occurs after the methodology from Fig. 1 has been processed.*

Obviously, such a defect might result in a situation where more than one resource is inaccessible due to the decomposition of a network into two or more parts. But for the presented replica placement algorithms, this assumption is very important and typically, the execution time of the online methodology is much shorter than the time between two resource defects. Thus, this assumption does not reduce the applicability of the presented approach.

4 Topology-Aware Replica Placement

According to the overall methodology presented in Fig. 1, the placement of tasks and replicas is performed in two steps with competing objectives. The placement of tasks is executed with the objective to improve the performance of an application, i.e., reduce the traffic in the network and balance the load on the network nodes such that the task response times and the overhead due to context switches are reduced. Due to the fact that the run-time behavior is of major interest, the task placement is prioritized and executed at first. Afterwards, the replica placement phase places replicas onto the remaining computational resources in the network. That is, the replica placement phase assumes a fixed binding of tasks onto network nodes and each task already consumes a certain part of the computational capacity of its host network node. With the objective to increase the reliability of the entire functionality executed by the network, the placement strategy binds replicated tasks onto network nodes.

In embedded networks tasks might be inoperable because the communication partners are in separated connected components of the network after a resource defect. Therefore, a novel strategy is proposed which 1.) identifies network partitions that will under no circumstances split up into disjoint components under the above mentioned conditions and 2.) places replicas t_i' with respect to these partitions. These two parts are explained in the following subsections.

4.1 Identifying Network Partitions

With the help of our failure model, it is possible to identify network regions that will under no circumstance decompose. Such components are called *biconnected components* (e.g., see [2, Sec. 5.3]):

Definition 8 (Biconnected Component). *Let $G(V, E)$ be an undirected graph where V is the set of vertices and $E \subseteq V \times V$ is the set of edges e_i. Two edges e_i, e_j are said to be* biconnected *if $e_i = e_j$ or there exists a* simple cycle *containing both e_i and e_j. A simple cycle is a path consisting of vertices $v_k, v_l, \ldots, v_k$ where no vertex except v_k occurs twice. Each two distinct edges e_i and e_j are in the same set $E_s \subseteq E$ iff they are biconnected. All vertices $v_j \in V$ incident to the edges $e \in E_s$ belong to the set $V_s \subseteq V$. A maximal subgraph $G_s = (V_s, E_s)$ is called a* biconnected component.

For the following examinations, we define a set of nodes BCC_i containing only the nodes of a biconnected component G_s: $BCC_i = V_s$. In networks with several biconnected components, the following elements might occur which are critical with respect to the reliability of the network:

Definition 9 (Articulation Point). *An* articulation point *is a vertex whose removal disconnects the graph.*

Definition 10 (Bridge). *A* bridge *is an edge whose removal disconnects the graph.*

In Fig. 3 a network with six nodes $n_1, \ldots, n_6$ is shown. The biconnected components in this network are given by the sets $V_{s1} = \{n_1, n_2, n_3\}$, $V_{s2} = \{n_4, n_5, n_6\}$, and $V_{s3} = \{n_2, n_4\}$ with their corresponding edges. Biconnected components with more than two nodes have the important property that each node is connected to any other node in the same biconnected component via at least two disjoint paths. Thus, a node defect will result in a failure of the functionality of the defect node but the functionality of the other nodes within this biconnected component will not be inaccessible. In case of a link defect, no task bound onto nodes within the biconnected component will be inaccessible. Note that biconnected components with two elements are somehow an exception because a link between the two nodes might decompose the two nodes. On the other hand, a link defect in such a small biconnected component can be interpreted as a node defect. Hence, the biconnected component will shrink from a node's point of view but will not decompose. However, the articulation points in Fig. 3 are n_2 and n_4. If one of these nodes is faulty, the network is divided into two parts.

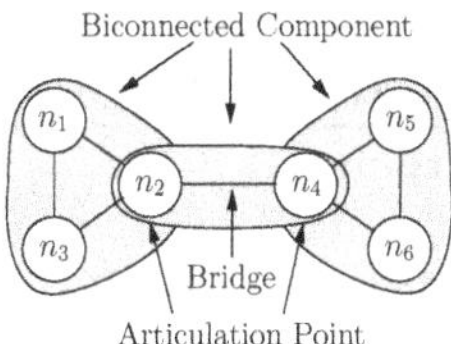

Fig. 3. Shown is a network with six nodes $n_1, \ldots, n_6$, with two articulation points n_2, n_4, one bridge (n_2, n_4), and three biconnected components given through their sets $V_{s1} = \{n_1, n_2, n_3\}$, $V_{s2} = \{n_4, n_5, n_6\}$, and $V_{s3} = \{n_2, n_4\}$ and corresponding edges

The same holds true for the bridge between the nodes n_2 and n_4. If the link has a defect, the network is divided, too.

Severl approaches for maintaining biconnected components exist: The first approach for finding biconnected components in undirected graphs is based on depth-first search. Such a sequential algorithm which solves the problem in $\mathcal{O}(n+m)$ time where n is the number of vertices in the graph and m is the number of edges has been presented in [6][2, Sec. 5.3]. If each node in the network knows about the topology and changes to the topology are immediately announced to each node in the network, this algorithm is applicable in our replica placement strategy. A very efficient approach has been presented in [13] which allows for adapting biconnected components after an edge insertion. Unfortunately, this approach is not applicable to our case because we consider link defects, i.e., edges are deleted but not inserted. The algorithms presented in [5] and [11] are distributed algorithms that solve the problem of finding biconnected components concurrently in dynamic graphs.

4.2 Replica Placement Algorithms

After the biconnected components are identified in the network, each node hosting tasks t_i searches for other host nodes for placing the replica t'_i. This search can be simply implemented with a sort of depth-first search. This search sends a message *msg* to one neighboring node. The message *msg* consists of two ordered lists *msg.visited* containing all visited nodes and *msg.backtracking* with nodes which will be visited again if a search in a certain network direction was not successful. Additional task parameters are stored in *msg.constraints* and contain the following information: 1.) required resources like computational capacity or dedicated I/O components and 2.) the current quality of the replica placement. Based on the information in *msg.constraints*, the receiver of the message *msg* can decide whether the replica will be accepted or not. If the receiver of *msg* accepts the new replica, it sends a message back to the former host node such that the task binaries can be transferred to the new host. In Alg. 1 the search strategy for nodes is presented which is locally executed at each network node.

In algorithm Alg. 1 line 10, the replicas are accepted by a receiving node iff certain constraints stored in *msg.constraints* are fulfilled. It has been mentioned that these constraints cover resource constraints like required computational

Algorithm 1. In order to search for nodes which may host a replica, this depth-first search algorithm processes messages *msg*.

```
if myNodeID in msg.visited then
    forall neighbors do
        if neighborID not in msg.visited then
            send msg to neighborID;
            return;
    delete myNodeID from msg.backtracking;
    send msg to last element of msg.backtracking;
else
    if msg.constraints are fulfilled then
        allocate resources for the replica;
        notify former replica host
        delete msg;
    else
        push back myNodeID to msg.visited;
        push back myNodeID to msg.backtracking;
        forall neighbors do
            if neighborID not in msg.visited then
                send msg to neighborID;
                return;
        delete myNodeID from msg.backtracking;
        send msg to last element of msg.backtracking;
```

capacity, necessary I/O components, etc. But it is also important that these constraints contain information about the current placement of the replicas. Therefore, criteria are explained in the following that allow for deciding whether the new replica placement is better than the current placement.

The first group of algorithms requires reliability values of computational resources in the network and respects these values during the placement process:

Max Rel: The *Max Rel* strategy tries to place tasks onto nodes with highest reliability as long as enough computational capacity is available and other resource constraints are not violated. The host node of the replica t'_i and its task t_i must not be the same. This strategy resembles the idea from [4] explained in Sec. 2. This strategy is considered as a reference here, and the next three approaches will be compared to it.

BCC Max1 Max Rel: The *BCC Max1 Max Rel* places a replica in a biconnected component where the most adjacent tasks are located, i.e., tasks the replica communicates with after activation of the replica. Within this biconnected component, the replica is placed onto the most reliable node. As before, the host node of the replica t'_i and its task t_i must not be the same.

BCC Max2 Max Rel: The *BCC Max2 Max Rel* places a replica in a biconnected component where the most tasks are located. In this case, data dependencies between tasks are not respected. Within this biconnected component, the replica is placed onto the most reliable node. Again, the host node of the replica t_i' and its task t_i must not be the same.

BCC Task Max Rel: The *BCC Task Max Rel* places a replica t_i' in a biconnected component where the corresponding task t_i must not be located in. The idea is to distribute the tasks and replicas over the biconnected components such that one component with the entire functionality survives. Within the biconnected component the replica is placed onto the most reliable node. If another biconnected component without the task t_i and a node with higher reliability is found the replica t_i' will be placed onto the new node. If only one biconnected component exists, the replica is placed onto the node with the highest reliability in this component.

In many cases, a network designer does not precisely know about the reliability of the applied communication or computational resources. Therefore, the following algorithms are investigated which do not require any reliability values, e.g., failure rates, of the resources:

Random: The *Random* strategy places a replica t_i' onto a randomly selected node which does not execute the task t_i. This strategy is just considered for comparison of our approaches.

BCC Max1: The *BCC Max1* strategy resembles the *BCC Max1 Max Rel* strategy, but instead of selecting the node with highest reliability an arbitrary node of the biconnected component is chosen.

BCC Max2: The *BCC Max2* strategy is also similar to the *BCC Max2 Max Rel* strategy, but neglects the reliability of the nodes.

BCC Task: The *BCC Task* strategy places the replica t_i' in the biconnected component next to the biconnected component hosting the task t_i. If only one component exists the replica t_i' is placed onto an arbitrary node.

The entire replica placement approach is a greedy strategy which places a replica onto a network node if it improves the current binding. Moreover, the approach runs asynchronously and concurrently in the network.

4.3 Computational Load of Active and Passive Replicas

Typically, the computational capacity in embedded networks is restricted and it might not be possible to execute the tasks and their replicas simultaneously (active replication). Instead, it is possible to keep replicas passively in the memory and activate them if the node executing the corresponding tasks will fail. In this case, it has to be assured that the computational capacity of each node is not exceeded after the replicas are activated. Therefore, we will consider two load scenarios here: 1.) tasks are actively replicated such that each replica requires memory as well as computational resources and 2.) tasks are passively replicated such that only memory but no computational resources are required (unless a node fails and the replica is activated).

In the following, we will formally describe the differences between active and passive replication in the context of computational load. For simplicity, we assume that each task can be executed by each node, i.e., other resource constraints than the computational power do not exist.

Definition 11 (Normalized Load Constraint). *Let the computational capacity of a node n_i be 1. Let $c_j \in \mathbb{R}^+$ be the real-valued fraction of the capacity of a task t_j consumed if executed by node n_i. All computational loads c_j of tasks executed by n_i must not exceed the capacity: $\sum_{t_j:t_j \mapsto n_i} c_j \leq 1$ $t_j \mapsto n_i$ means that task t_j is executed by node n_i.*

Definition 12 (Active Replication Constraint). *The sum of computational loads c_s of the tasks t_s or active replicas t'_s executed by node n_i must not exceed the capacity of n_i: $\sum_{t_s:t_s \mapsto n_i} c_s + \sum_{t'_{\tilde{s}}:t'_{\tilde{s}} \mapsto n_i} c_{\tilde{s}} \leq 1$*

By Def. 5, it is trivial that Def. 12 obeys Def. 11.

For the following considerations, we additionally assume that each node n_i knows whether a task t_x is executed by a node n_j in the same biconnected component ($n_i, n_j \in BCC_r$) or in a different biconnected component ($n_i \in BCC_r, n_j \in BCC_s$ with $BCC_r \neq BCC_s$). If the nodes n_i, n_j are in different biconnected components, the unique articulation point $n_k^{AP} \in BCC_r$ required for accessing BCC_s is also known by $n_i \in BCC_r$.

Definition 13 (Passive Replication Constraint). *Let c_x be again the normalized computational load of a task t_x and its passive replica t'_x after activation. Then, for a node n_i belonging to a biconnected component BCC_r ($n_i \in BCC_r$), the following equation must hold:*

$$\max\left(LR_{n_i}^{\mathrm{BCC}}, LR_{n_i}^{\mathrm{AP}}\right) + LT_{n_i} \leq 1 \tag{1}$$

$LR_{n_i}^{\mathrm{BCC}}$ denotes the load caused by the replicas placed onto node n_i. The replicas stem from the tasks of the nodes n_k within the same biconnected component than n_i where n_k is not an articulation point ($n_i, n_k \in BCC_r, n_k \notin BCC_s$ with $BCC_r \neq BCC_s$):

$$LR_{n_i}^{\mathrm{BCC}} = \max_{\substack{n_k \in BCC_r \\ \wedge n_k \neq n_i \\ \wedge n_k \notin BCC_s}} \Bigg(\sum_{\substack{t'_x:t'_x \mapsto n_i \\ \wedge t_x \mapsto n_k}} c_x \Bigg) \tag{2}$$

$LR_{n_i}^{\mathrm{AP}}$ denotes the load caused by the replicas placed onto node n_i. This time the replicas stem from the tasks of the nodes n_k which are not in the same biconnected component than n_i ($n_i \in BCC_r, n_k \notin BCC_r$):

$$LR_{n_i}^{\mathrm{AP}} = \max_{\substack{n_j^{AP} \in BCC_r \\ \wedge n_j^{AP} \neq n_i}} \Bigg(\sum_{\substack{n_k \in BCC_s \\ \wedge n_j^{AP} \in PATH(n_i, n_k) \\ \wedge BCC_r \neq BCC_s}} \sum_{\substack{t'_x:t'_x \mapsto n_i \\ \wedge t_x \mapsto n_k}} c_x \Bigg) \tag{3}$$

$PATH(n_i, n_k)$ denotes a set of nodes connecting $n_i \in BCC_r$ and $n_k \in BCC_s$. n_j^{AP} is an articulation point as defined in Def. 9.

$LT_{n_i}^{\mathrm{AP}}$ denotes the load caused by the tasks placed onto node n_i: $LT_{n_i} = \sum_{t_x:t_x \mapsto n_i} c_x$

Theorem 1. *If passive replication is applied then the passive replication constraint satisfies the normalized load constraint.*

Proof. The overall computational load of a node n_i is composed of three different loads: 1.) the load of replicas $t'_x \mapsto n_i \in BCC_r$ with $t_x \mapsto n_j \in BCC_r$ and $n_j \notin BCC_s$, 2. the load of replicas $t'_x \mapsto n_i \in BCC_r$ with $t_x \mapsto n_j \in BCC_s$ ($BCC_r \neq BCC_s$), and 3.) the load of tasks $t_x \mapsto n_i$.

1. Given are two different nodes n_k and n_i belonging to the same biconnected component $n_i, n_k \in BCC_r$ and n_k belongs to no other biconnected component BCC_s, i.e., n_k is not an articulation point. The tasks t_x of node n_k have replicas t'_x at node n_i which do not cause any computational load unless they are activated (see Def. 6). After a single defect of n_k, the other nodes n_j belonging to the same biconnected component $n_j \in BCC_r$ are still connected to n_i (see Def. 8). Thus, only the replicas t'_x of the tasks t_x of node n_k will be activated. Since each node n_k might fail and may have replicas t'_x of its task at n_i, the maximum computational load that will be added to the load of n_i after a defect of a node n_k has to be considered. This is $LR^{\text{BCC}}_{n_i}$.

2. Given are two different nodes n_k and n_i belonging to different biconnected component $n_i \in BCC_r$, $n_k \in BCC_s$ and $BCC_r \neq BCC_s$. BCC_r has one or more articulation points $n_j^{AP} \in BCC_r$. Since different biconnected components are connected via one unique articulation point n_j^{AP}, a single resource defect leads to a situation where all tasks t_x on n_j^{AP} and behind this articulation point are inaccessible. Thus, a failure of $n_j^{AP} \in BCC_r$ leads to a failure of all biconnected components BCC_s accessible via $n_j^{AP} \in BCC_r$. Since one resource may fail simultaneously, the network region accessible via another $n_l^{AP} \in BCC_r$ is still accessible in case of the a failure of $n_j^{AP} \in BCC_r$. Thus, network regions accessible via different articulation points $n_l^{AP} \in BCC_r$ fail exclusively from the point of view of a node $n_i \in BCC_r$. The maximal computational load at node n_i coming from a network region if $n_j^{AP} \in BCC_r$ fails is $LR^{\text{AP}}_{n_i}$.

The load caused at a node $n_i \in BCC_r$ due to a defect of $n_k \in BCC_r$ is either $LR^{\text{BCC}}_{n_i}$ or $LR^{\text{AP}}_{n_i}$. This depends on whether n_k is an articulation point or not. Thus, the maximum of $LR^{\text{BCC}}_{n_i}$ and $LR^{\text{AP}}_{n_i}$ will be added to the load of n_i.

3. Since all tasks t_x executed by n_i cause a computational load, the overall load caused by the tasks is the sum of the corresponding c_x.

As an example for the case covered by Eq. (1), consider the network in Fig. 4. The network consists of eight nodes partitioned into three biconnected components which are connected by two articulation points (n_2^{AP}, n_5^{AP}). The task binding is given and some of the replicas are already placed in the network Assume that node n_4 is asked whether it can host a passive replica of task t_5 by the algorithm shown in Alg. 1. The node n_4 need to know that they access nodes outside their own biconnected component via n_2^{AP} or n_5^{AP}. In detail, the nodes n_1 and n_3 can be accessed via a path containing articulation point n_2^{AP} whereas the nodes n_7 and n_8 can be accessed via a path containing articulation point n_5^{AP}. Thus, a defect of on single resource , e.g., n_2^{AP} or n_5^{AP}, can split the network such that either the left or the right biconnected component is not accessible from n_4. But, it is not possible that the left and right biconnected component will

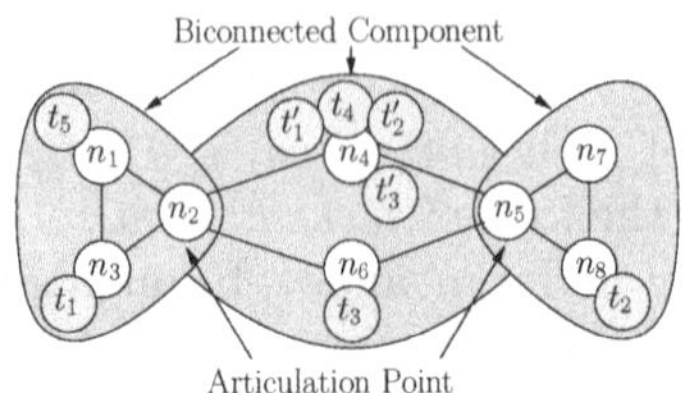

Fig. 4. The figure acts as an example for Eq. (3). From the point of view of node n_4, a single node defect might lead to failure of the functionality hosted in either the right biconnected component, the left biconnected component, or node n_6 but not all together.

become unaccessible from n_4 at the same time. If node n_6 fails no task hosted by other nodes will be inaccessible. Thus, node n_4 has to calculate:

$$LR_{n_4}^{\mathrm{BCC}} = \max(c_3), \quad LR_{n_4}^{\mathrm{AP}} = \max(c_5 + c_1, c_2), \quad LT_{n_4} = c_4 \tag{4}$$

If the following inequality holds true the replica of t_5 can be placed:

$$\max\left(LR_{n_4}^{\mathrm{BCC}}, LR_{n_4}^{\mathrm{AP}}\right) + LT_{n_4} \leq 1 \tag{5}$$

5 Experimental Evaluation

With the help of extensive Monte-Carlo simulations, the different strategies have been evaluated. For this purpose, we implemented a behavioral model of the network and each node as well as each link in the network has been annotated with a constant failure rate λ. Afterwards, the simulator randomly determines the defect time of each node and link using the inverse function of the reliability function $R(t) = e^{-\lambda t}$ [8]: $t = \frac{\ln R(t)}{-\lambda}$ Note that the random values for $R(t)$ are uniformly distributed. The resources are ordered according to their defect time t. Starting with the smallest defect time, the simulator removes at each defect time the corresponding resource from the network topology. After each removal of a resource, the online methodology (see Fig. 1) is processed and the simulator checks if the entire functionality is still operable. If this is not the case, the network has failed to operate. The defect time t of the last removed resource which led to a network failure is called the *time to failure* TTF. In order to determine the *mean time to failure* $MTTF$, the simulation is repeatedly executed and the average of all obtained TTF values is calculated.

For the experimental evaluation of our methodology, we generated different network system models and varied 1.) the number of mapping edges for each task and 2.) the failure rate of the links ($\lambda - Link$) and the failure rate of the nodes ($\lambda - Node$).

In the following figures, a relation of the failure rates is presented. A relation of the failure rates $\lambda - Node/\lambda - Link = 0.1$ denotes a case where $\lambda - Node$

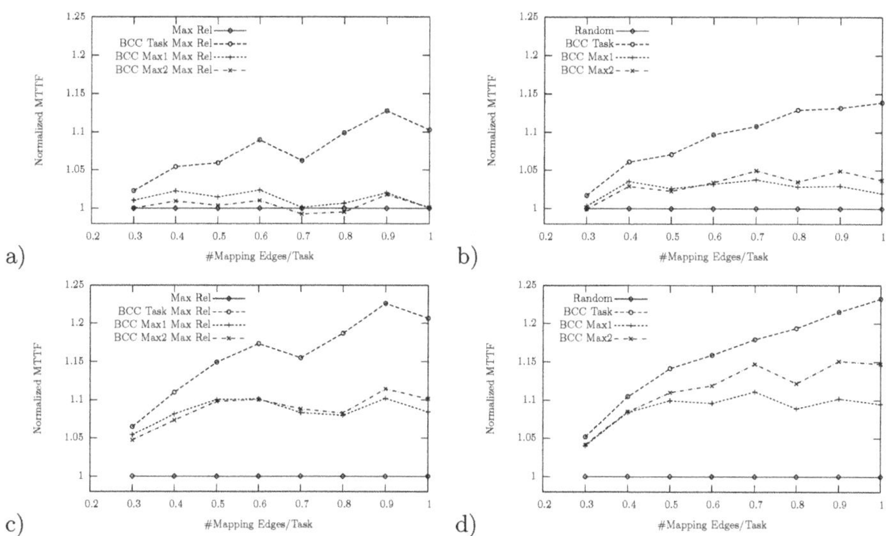

Fig. 5. Depending on the number of mapping edges per task, the reliability improvements a) compared to the reliability of the Max Rel strategy and b) compared to the Random strategy for active replication as well as c) compared to the reliability of the Max Rel strategy and d) compared to the Random strategy for passive replication are presented

varies between 0.0001 and 0.0009 and $\lambda - Link$ ranges from 0.001 to 0.009. The number mapping edges is normalized with the number of tasks, i.e., if $\#MappingEdges/Task = 0.3$, each task can be executed by 30% of the network nodes. If $\#MappingEdges/Task = 1$ each task can be executed everywhere in the network unless the nodes do not have enough computational resources. The computational power of all network node is normalized to one and the load of a task varies between 0.1 and 0.5.

At first, we consider the placement strategies where active replicas are placed in the network. We normalized the MTTF values obtained with the proposed strategies with the MTTF values of the reference strategies *Random* or $MaxRel$, respectively. Fig. 5a shows the normalized MTTF for active replication over the number of mapping edges per task where each node knows its failure rate. The same case is presented in Fig. 5b) but here, the nodes do not know about their failure rate. Fig. 5c),d) present the same results than Fig. 5a),b), but instead of placing active replicas, passive replicas are placed within the network.

As mentioned above, we also varied the failure rate of nodes and links. Therefore, the same results as in Fig. 5 and Fig. 5 are presented over the failure rate relation $\lambda - Node/\lambda - Link$ in Fig. 6. Fig. 6a),b) show the results for active replication while Fig. 6c),d) show results for passive replication.

Our test-cases show that the *BCC Task (Max Rel)* strategy outperforms the other distributed approaches to replica placement. Thus, a diverse placement

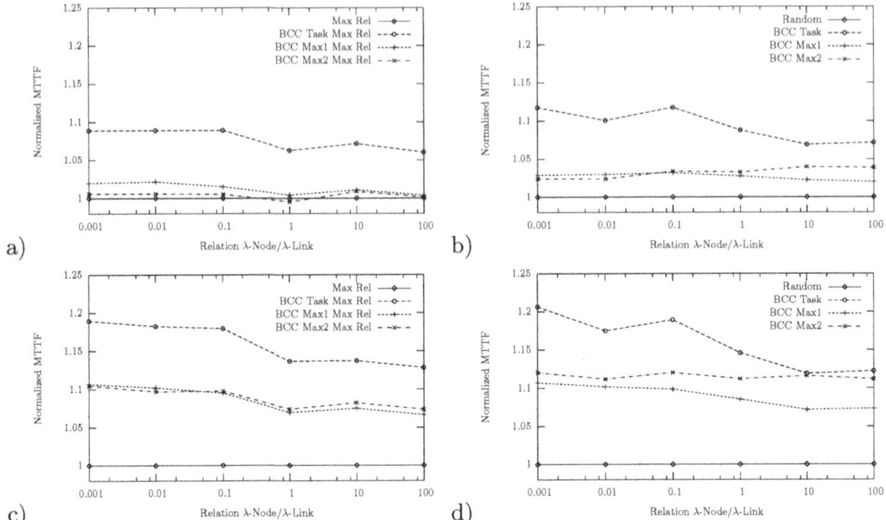

Fig. 6. Depending on the failure rate relation $\lambda - Node/\lambda - Link$, the reliability improvements a) compared to the reliability of the Max Rel strategy and b) compared to the Random strategy for active replication as well as c) compared to the reliability of the Max Rel strategy and d) compared to the Random strategy for passive replication are presented

of tasks and replicas in the network is better than cumulating tasks in certain biconnected components in the network. Comparing Fig. 5a) with Fig. 5c) and Fig. 5b) with Fig. 5d), respectively shows the impact of passive replication to tolerate permanent resource defects. In particular, passive replication together with the *BCC Task (Max Rel)* strategy leads to an improvement of the MTTF which is up to 10% higher than active replication. Of course, active replication has advantages concerning transient faults and fault reaction times, but due to the limited computational power of network nodes, passive replication is able to improve the availability of the entire network functionality.

Fig. 6 shows that the benefit of our topology-aware replica placement strategies decreases if network nodes are much more likely to fail than links between these nodes. This behavior is due to the fact that the network decomposes very fast, but no connected component is able to host all communicating tasks and the network functionality cannot be provided any more. In this case, the potential for increasing the MTTF compared to strategies without topology information is low. On the other hand, if the probability of a link defect is higher than the probability of a node defect, the network topology might become like a chain of biconnected node groups. In such a network topology, our strategies are aware of the node groups and are able to place tasks such that the MTTF is improved. Note that this latter case where the failure rate of a link is higher than the failure rate of a node is more realistic. Hence, our approach leads to a better improvement of the normalized MTTF for more realistic cases.

6 Conclusions

In this paper, we presented novel heuristics for placing replicated tasks in embedded networks. With the goal to increase the mean time to failure and hence the reliability of the network and to delay the failure of the network's functionality, different heuristics are proposed which are based on the partitioning of the network into biconnected components. Moreover, we discussed differences of active and passive replication and experimentally illustrated the impact of the passive replication on the mean time to failure. All in all, replica placement strategies based on biconnected components seem to be quite attractive, 1.) because they run in a distributed manner, 2.) they improve the mean time to failure, and 3.) they allow for distinguishing between active and passive replication.

References

1. Adya, A., Bolosky, W.J., Castro, M.: FARSITE: Federate, Available, and Reliable Storage for an Inclomplete Trusted Environment. In: Proceedings of the OSDI (2002)
2. Aho, A.V., Hopcroft, J.E., Ullman, J.D.: The Design and Analysis of Computer Algorithms. Addison-Wesley, Reading (1974)
3. Cuenca-Acuna, F.M., Martin, R.P., Nguyen, T.D.: Autonomous Replication for High Availability in Unstructured P2P Systems. In: 22nd IEEE International Symposium on Reliable Distributed Systems (2003)
4. Douceur, J.R., Wattenhofer, R.: Competitive Hill-Climbing Strategies for Replica Placement in a Distributed File System. In: Welch, J.L. (ed.) DISC 2001. LNCS, vol. 2180, pp. 48–62. Springer, Heidelberg (2001)
5. Hohberg, W.: How to find biconnected components in distributed networks. J. Parallel Distrib. Comput. 9(4), 374–386 (1990)
6. Hopcroft, J., Tarjan, R.: Algorithm 447: efficient algorithms for graph manipulation. Commun. ACM 16(6), 372–378 (1973)
7. Karlsson, M., Karamanolis, C., Mahalingam, M.: A Framework for Evaluating Replica Placement Algorithms. Technical report, HP Labs, HPL-2002-219 (2002)
8. Laprie, J.C.: Dependability: Basic Concepts and Terminology - In English, French, German, and Japanese. Springer, Heidelberg (1992)
9. Lian, Q., Chen, W., Zhang, Z.: On the Impact of Replica Placement to the Reliability of Distributed Brick Storage Systems. In: Proceedings of the 25th IEEE International Conference on Distributed Computing Systems (ICDCS 2005), pp. 187–196. IEEE Computer Society Press, Washington (2005)
10. Qiu, L., Padmanabhan, V.N., Voelker, G.M.: On the Placement of Web Server Replicas. In: Proc. of the IEEE INFOCOM conference, pp. 1587–1596 (April 2001)
11. Swaminathan, B., Goldman, K.: An Incremental Distributed Algorithm for Computing Biconnected Components in Dynamic Graphs. Algorith. 22(3), 305–329 (1998)
12. Szymaniak, M., Pierre, G., van Steen, M.: Latency-Driven Replica Placement. In: Proc. of the Symp. on Applications and the Internet (SAINT 2005) (2005)
13. Westbrok, J., Tarjan, R.E.: Maintaining Bridge-Connected and Biconnected Components On-Line. Algorithmica 7(1), 433–464 (1992)

Design of Gate Array Circuits Using Evolutionary Algorithms

Peter Bungert, Sanaz Mostaghim, Hartmut Schmeck, and Jürgen Branke

Institute AIFB, Universität Karlsruhe (TH), Karlsruhe Institute of Technology, Germany
{peter.bungert,sanaz.mostaghim, hartmut.schmeck,juergen.branke}@kit.edu

Abstract. In this paper, we study the design of combinational logic circuits using evolutionary algorithms. In particular, this paper is about fitness assignment methods and recombination operators for speeding up the optimisation process. We propose a new fitness assignment mechanism called MaxMin method and compare it with the straightforward method used in the literature. The results show significant improvements both in terms of computational time and quality of the solutions. Furthermore, a new cross-over operator called area cross-over has been introduced and compared with other typical operators. This operator is particularly designed for gate matrices where two rectangular logic blocks are exchanged between the individuals. We observe that the MaxMin fitness assignment as well as the area cross-over operator considerably improve the performance of the evolutionary optimisation.

1 Introduction

Two-dimensional arrays of gates are used in many devices like Field Programmable Gate Arrays (FPGA), Field Programmable Analog Arrays (FPAA) or memory chips. During circuit design, various aspects have to be considered, like few successive logical levels, a minimal number of gates or a high operation frequency. Here, we study combinational logic circuits without memory elements and aim at achieving an optimal circuit design for a given truth table by using evolutionary methods. The gates of such circuits may have different functionalities (types) such as AND, OR, XOR, NOT and Wire[1]. A circuit is optimal, if it 1) performs correctly as listed in the truth table and 2) has a maximum number of Wires, i.e., has a low number of AND, OR, XOR, or NOT gates. In general, these two optimisation goals are not conflicting and therefore it is not necessary to apply a multi-objective optimisation algorithm.

For this optimisation problem, we study Evolutionary Algorithms (EAs) which are known as powerful tools to solve a large range of optimisation problems [5]. Their use for the design of circuits has created the research area of "Evolvable Hardware", see e.g. [1,2,6,7,8]. In EAs, the evaluation mechanism and recombination operators have a great impact on the quality of the solutions. In this

[1] Wire is not a gate. It is a short circuit between input and output.

U. Brinkschulte et al. (Eds.): ARCS 2008, LNCS 4934, pp. 38–50, 2008.

particular application, finding an optimal design for a specific function gets very complicated as the number of inputs and outputs grows. Thus, it is of great importance to find a valid solution in a reasonable computational time.

In [7], Kalganova and Miller study EAs on combinational circuits where they introduce the geometry mutation operator and a new fitness evaluation mechanism to improve the quality of the solution. The geometry mutation changes the size of the matrix at random by adding or deleting a column or a row. This operator adds flexibility in the design but in order to ensure that the new generated solution with the new geometry represents a valid solution, a repair algorithm is applied. The fitness evaluation mechanism is applied in two levels. The first level is to obtain a correct design. As soon as a correct design has been achieved the second level is added in a way to maximise the number of not involved gates. Coello Coello et al. studied EAs and Ant Colony Optimisation for the automated design of such combinational circuits [2,3]. In a more recent work, Coello Coello and Aguirre [1] study a multi-objective approach where they treat each output value of the function's table as an objective. Hence the number of objectives increases exponentially with the number of inputs but as the objective values are binary (correct or not correct) a totally different multi-objective optimisation mechanism than the typical ones [4] has been introduced by them. Most of their work is based on typical evolutionary algorithms, they use operators and fitness assignment methods without considering the particular aspects of the problem. Here, we introduce new mechanisms in evolutionary algorithms which are particularly designed for the combinational circuit problem. We study a new fitness evaluation mechanism called MaxMin fitness assignment for finding the correct circuit in which we consider the number of correct outputs of each individual and also the difficulty of finding the correct outputs. If an output is found by a small number of individuals only, those individuals get a higher fitness value. This is compared with standard fitness assignment mechanisms on two examples and the new methodology is shown to have a great impact on the solutions and the computational time.

Furthermore, we study a novel cross-over operator (called area cross-over) which is designed particularly for a two-dimensional array of gates. We compare the area cross-over with the typical one-point and two-point cross-over operators and obtain results of better quality. The new methodologies are tested on two typical examples such as a full adder and a multiplexer.

This paper is structured as follows. In Section 2, we briefly describe logic gate arrays. Evolutionary algorithms and the new fitness mechanism and recombination operators are studied in Section 3. In Section 4, we examine and analyse the new approaches on two different examples. Section 5 is dedicated to conclusion and future work.

2 Gate Matrix

For the evolutionary design of combinational circuits the standard approach is to evolve configurations of a two-dimensional array of customisable logic gates and interconnections as shown in Figure 1. Circuits are composed from left to right, the n inputs are applied to the left and m outputs are taken from the right. Every matrix element consists of a single customisable gate representing one of the following types: AND, OR, XOR, NOT, and Wire. Wire is not a real gate. It directly connects the input to the output. In the cases of NOT and Wire where only one input is required, the first input is used.

In Figure 1, the gates are illustrated by the boxes indicated by g_{cr}. The indices c and r are the column and row indices representing the location of the gates. Each gate has two inputs (i_1, i_2) and one output, where I and O are the input and output vectors of the circuit. Connections are made by selecting one of the outputs from the previous column as the input for the next column. The functionality of the circuit can be described by a truth table as shown in Table 1. Obviously, this gate matrix could be viewed as a very specialised Field Programmable Gate Array.

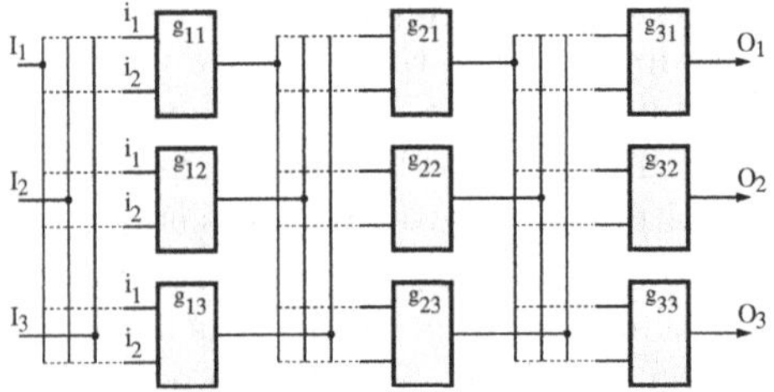

Fig. 1. Matrix representing a gate array circuit

Table 1. Representation of a function by a generalised truth table

I_1	…	I_n	$\hat{O}_1$	…	$\hat{O}_m$
0	…	0	$\hat{o}_{1,0}$	…	$\hat{o}_{m,0}$
0	…	1	$\hat{o}_{1,1}$	…	$\hat{o}_{m,1}$
⋮	⋱	⋮	⋮	⋱	⋮
1	…	1	$\hat{o}_{1,2^n}$	…	$\hat{o}_{m,2^n}$

For illustration, a full adder is used as one of our standard examples in this paper. The truth table and a correspondingly configured matrix for a full adder are shown in Figure 2 and Table 2. In the table, I_1, I_2 and I_3 are the inputs and the carry-in to the adder and the two outputs are indicated by $\hat{O}_1$ (sum) and $\hat{O}_2$ (carry-out).

Table 2. Truth table for a full adder circuit

I_1	I_2	I_3	$\hat{O}_1$	$\hat{O}_2$
0	0	0	0	0
0	0	1	1	0
0	1	0	1	0
0	1	1	0	1
1	0	0	1	0
1	0	1	0	1
1	1	0	0	1
1	1	1	1	1

Fig. 2. Matrix for a full adder circuit

3 Evolutionary Algorithms

In this section, we describe the evolutionary algorithm used to search for the optimal circuit for a given truth table. We assume a population of N individuals where each individual contains a chromosome representing the two-dimensional circuit (matrix of gates) as explained in Section 2. In more detail, every gate of the matrix is encoded as a triplet in which the first two elements are the inputs and the third one is the type of the gate. Figure 3 shows an example of a typical chromosome containing the triplets for representing each gate.

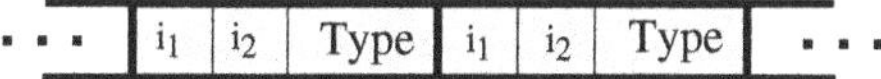

Fig. 3. Every gate encoded as a triplet in the chromosome

In order to evaluate the individuals, we compute their truth tables and compare these with the given truth table. The number of correct outputs characterises the degree of correctness. Together with the number of Wire-gates it determines the fitness of an individual. In the following, we study a straightforward fitness assignment mechanism and then introduce a new approach called MaxMin fitness assignment. For all our experiments, we use a generational algorithm with one elite individual.

3.1 Fitness Assignment

As mentioned before, the objective of the optimisation is to obtain a circuit computing the given truth table with a maximal number of wires. Therefore, the straightforward method for circuit evaluation is to compute two values [1,7]. The first is based on the correctness of the circuit, i.e., the number of correct outputs and the second relates to the number of Wires in the circuit. For a truth table as shown in Table 1 this leads to the following evaluation:

$$F_s = \sum_{i=1}^{m} \sum_{j=1}^{2^n} f_s(i,j) + W \quad \text{with} \quad f_s(i,j) = \begin{cases} 0 & \text{if } \hat{o}_{i,j} \neq o_{i,j} \\ 1 & \text{if } \hat{o}_{i,j} = o_{i,j} \end{cases} \tag{1}$$

where $\hat{o}$ and o are the desired and W denotes the total number of gates with the selected type as wire:

$$W = \begin{cases} 0, & \text{if circuit not correct} \\ \#\text{Wires in circuit}, & \text{if circuit is correct} \end{cases} \tag{2}$$

n and m are the numbers of in- and outputs, respectively.

The use of this value F_s in the selection scheme determines the fitness of individual s. The main issue in this evaluation scheme is that the individuals are evaluated with preference on the correctness of the circuit. Table 3 shows an example of a truth table of an individual for finding a full adder circuit. Since only 8 of the 16 output values are correct, wires are not considered and the evaluation leads to the value 8.

Table 3. Truth table decoded from an individual for the adder circuit. The values in parentheses show the correct outputs.

I_1	I_2	I_3	O_1	O_2
0	0	0	(0)	(0)
0	0	1	(1)	1
0	1	0	(1)	1
0	1	1	1	0
1	0	0	0	1
1	0	1	(0)	0
1	1	0	(0)	0
1	1	1	(1)	(1)

3.2 MaxMin Evaluation Mechanism

The straightforward evaluation explained in the previous section depends only on one individual and the number of its correct outputs. Here, we study a new method where we consider all of the individuals of a population. The main idea is to observe which output is correctly found by how many individuals. For instance, if an output has been found by all the individuals, it should not have the same influence as a **difficult** output which has been found by a small number of individuals only. Those difficult outputs should have more influence on the evaluation. Table 4 shows an example of 6 individuals for solving the full adder circuit problem.

Individuals and their corresponding 16 output values in their truth tables are shown in columns. $S_{i,j}$ in the last column shows the number of individuals which found the correct output for each row:

$$S_{i,j} = \sum_{k=1}^{N} f_s^{(k)}(i,j) \quad \text{with} \quad f_s^{(k)} = f_s \text{ of individual k} \tag{3}$$

For example, individuals 2 and 4 find the correct output (1,5), therefore we have a 2 in row 6 of the last column. In this table, the last two rows indicate the quality value with respect to the previous evaluation and the corresponding MaxMin quality (we explain this new evaluation later in this section). Here, we can observe that individuals 2 and 4 have the highest number of correct outputs, namely 8. Individual 6 has the lowest number of correct outputs (only 4), but three of these correct outputs do not appear in other individuals. Hence, this solution is interesting for the optimisation. The new evaluation scheme is designed to take such solutions into account. By using the MaxMin evaluation, individual 6 gets the highest value, namely 21. The MaxMin value $G_s^{(k)}$ for each individual is calculated as below:

$$G_s^{(k)} = N \times \sum_{i=1}^{m} \sum_{j=1}^{2^n} \frac{f_s^{(k)}(i,j)}{S_{i,j}} + W \tag{4}$$

Table 4. Truth table for $N = 6$ individuals. The values in parentheses show the correct outputs.

$O_{i,j}$	Ind_1	Ind_2	Ind_3	Ind_4	Ind_5	Ind_6	$S_{i,j}$
(1,0)	0	0	0	0	0	(1)	1
(1,1)	(1)	(1)	(1)	(1)	(1)	0	5
(1,2)	1	1	1	1	1	(0)	1
(1,3)	(0)	1	(0)	1	(0)	1	3
(1,4)	(1)	(1)	(1)	(1)	(1)	0	5
(1,5)	1	(0)	1	(0)	1	1	2
(1,6)	0	0	(1)	0	0	0	1
(1,7)	1	1	(0)	(0)	(0)	1	3
(2,0)	(1)	0	0	0	0	(1)	2
(2,1)	1	(0)	1	1	(0)	1	2
(2,2)	0	(1)	(1)	0	0	0	2
(2,3)	(0)	(0)	1	(0)	(0)	1	4
(2,4)	0	(1)	0	(1)	(1)	0	3
(2,5)	0	0	0	0	0	(1)	1
(2,6)	(1)	0	0	(1)	0	0	2
(2,7)	(0)	(0)	1	(0)	1	1	3
$F_s^{(k)}$	7	8	6	8	7	4	—
$G_s^{(k)}$	13.9	16.9	15.4	15.9	12.9	21	—

Here, as before, as soon as an individual finds the correct truth table, the term related to the number of Wires (eq. 2) is added. In this approach, we maximise the influence of the least solved (minimal) output, therefore we call it *MaxMin* method.

3.3 Recombination Operators

In this section, we study cross-over operators and introduce a new operator called area cross-over. Typical cross-over operators, like one-point, two-point and uniform cross-over have been used in the context of gate matrix design optimisation [1,7]. Obviously, as the individuals represent the gate matrix (see

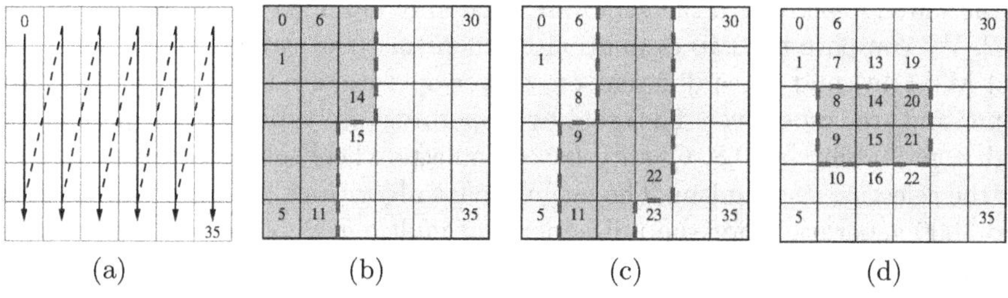

Fig. 4. (a) The string representing an individual is shown on a matrix. The figure illustrates the gate matrix where every box represents a gate. (b) Cutting point in one-point cross-over. (c) Cutting points in the two-point cross-over. (d) Cutting region of the area cross-over.

Section 2) and its geometry, the cross-over operators have a great impact on the new generated solutions. Figure 4a shows the string representing an individual on the gate matrix. If we apply, for instance, one-point cross-over to this individual, the cutting point is located in a random position as shown in Figure 4b. The two-point cross-over has two random cutting points as shown in Figure 4c.

In fact the cross-over operator exchanges two blocks of logical gates. Here, we design the area cross-over which exchanges two rectangular areas on the gate matrices of the two individuals. An example is shown in Figure 4d. The size of the area is selected at random by defining two random points for the upper-left and lower-right corners.

4 Experiments

In the experiment, we study two different circuits such as an adder and a 4–1–multiplexer. The adder circuit has been explained in Section 2 and is shown in Figure 5 (as a black box). For a correct circuit, 16 different outputs have to be tested. The multiplexer has 6 inputs and one output as shown in Figure 6. In this case, 64 outputs have to be tested.

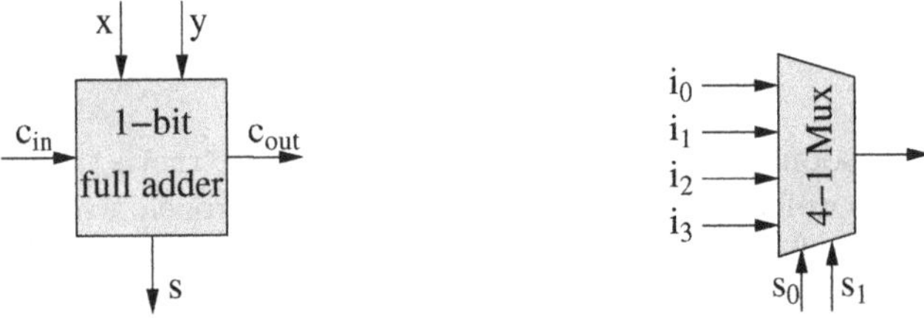

Fig. 5. A full adder

Fig. 6. A 4–1–multiplexer

We consider a matrix of 10×10 gates, i.e., 100 gates. For both the adder and the multiplexer problems, we apply an evolutionary algorithm as described in Section 3. We consider a population of 100 individuals. Mutation is applied to all of the individuals, where the genes are randomly modified with a probability of 0.02. We compare the two evaluation mechanisms (the straightforward method and MaxMin) and three different cross-over operators, namely one-point, two-point, and area cross-over. The cross-over operators are applied to the population with a probability of 0.8. Quality based roulette wheel selection has been used for the selection mechanism. The evolutionary algorithms has been run for 2000 and 3000 generations for the full adder and multiplexer problems, respectively, and results are averaged over 30 different runs.

4.1 Results

Figures 7 and 8 illustrate the quality values of the average and best solution (averaged over 30 runs) in all the generations. 1P, 2P and Area indicate the

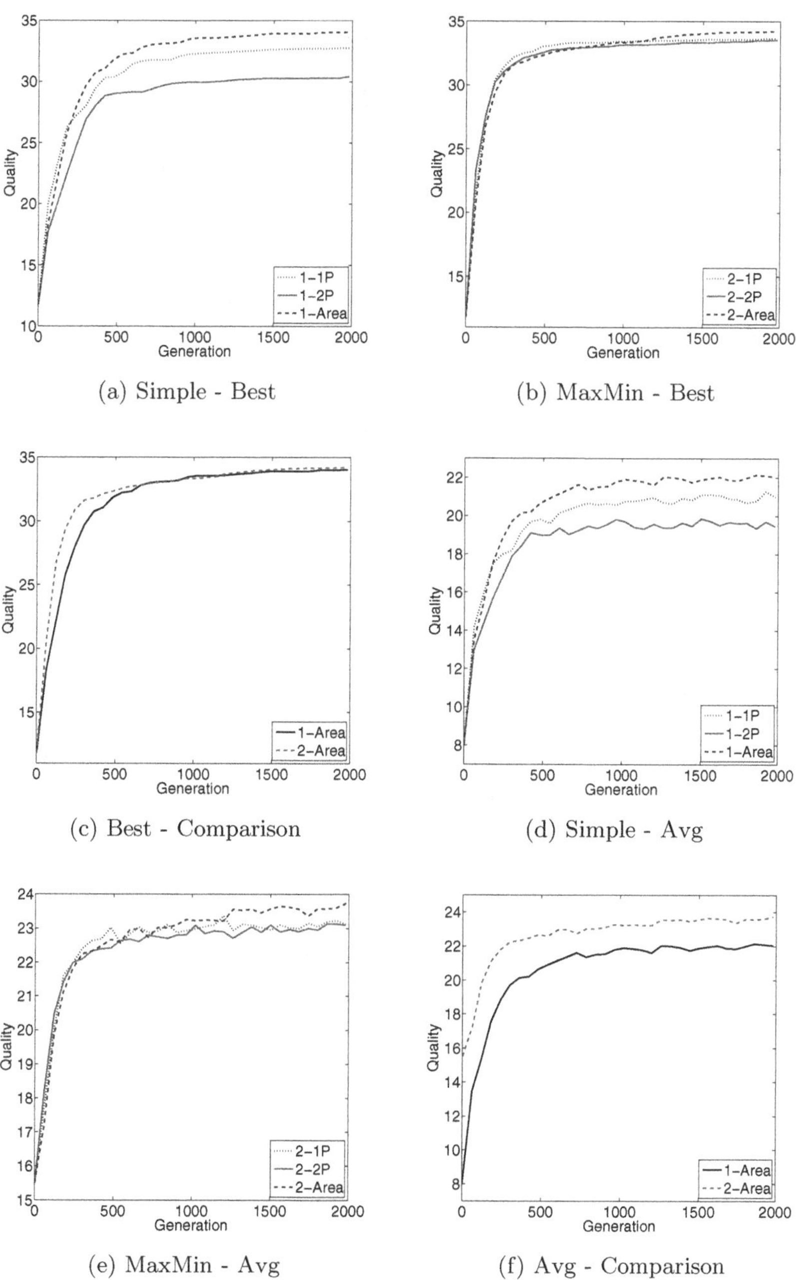

Fig. 7. Quality values over generations for the full adder circuit. (a)–(c) illustrate the best and (d)–(f) the average quality values of 30 runs.

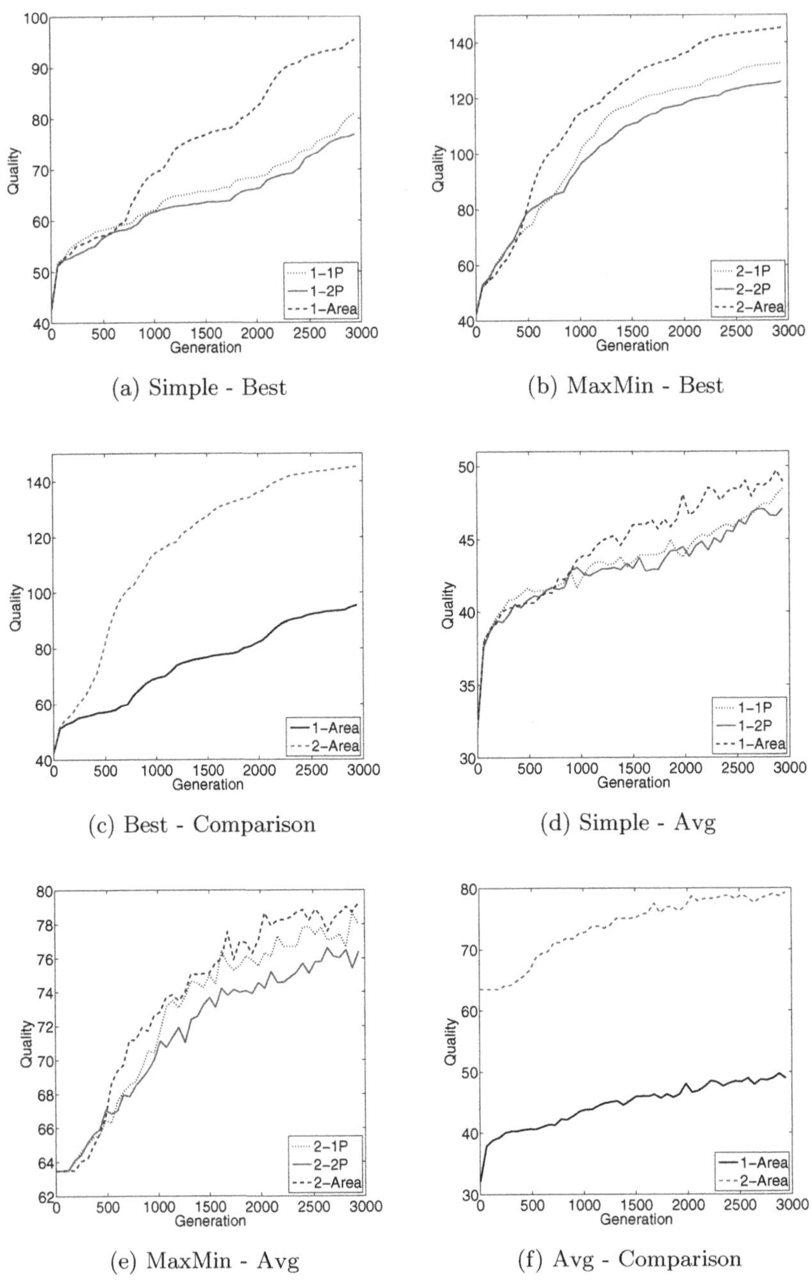

Fig. 8. Quality values over generations for the multiplexer circuit. (a)–(c) illustrate the best and (d)–(f) the average quality values of 30 runs.

one-point, two-point and area cross-over operators and 1 and 2 refer to the straightforward (simple) and the MaxMin evaluation mechanisms. The quality value in Figures 7 and 8 is the sum of the correct outputs – if justified because of a totally correct circuit – and the number of wires. The detailed values for some of the generations are shown in the Tables 5 and 6.

We observe that for both problems and both evaluation methods the area cross-over operator outperforms the one-point and two-point operators. Figures 7a, 8a, 7d, and 8d show that the quality values obtained by the area cross-over for the best as well as the average of the runs are higher than the two-point and one-point operators. This can be easily observed for the multiplexer problem where the optimal design of a multiplexer has more gates than the adder problem. The optimal design for the full adder problem contains 5 gates, while the multiplexer has about 11 gates. In the experiments, we also observe that the results of the two-point cross-over are worse than one-point cross-over. These results can be derived for the MaxMin evaluation as shown in Figures 8b, 7b, 8e, and 7e.

Furthermore, we compare the influence of the two evaluations mechanisms on the solutions. From Figures 7c and 8c, it can easily be concluded that the new MaxMin evaluation considerably improves the results. By considering the entire population during the evaluation, we achieve a better convergence rate.

For the analysis of the convergence rate and the computation time, we examine the number of generations that the different methods need to find a correct circuit. We test the two evaluation mechanisms and the three cross-over operators. As shown in Figures 9a and 9b the MaxMin evaluation (2) is able to find the correct circuits in a very small number of generations compared to the other method (1). Here, we can also see that the Area cross-over operator accelerates the convergence of the results and this operator together with the MaxMin method highly increases the convergence rate. This conclusion is valid for both test problems. In these figures, we observe that the standard error of 30 runs is lower for the MaxMin and the area cross-over cases than for the others.

Table 5. Quality values over the generations (adder)

	1 - 1-Point				**1 - 2-Point**				**1 - Area**			
Gen.	10	500	1000	2000	10	500	1000	2000	10	500	1000	2000
Avg.	10.52	19.73	20.65	21.09	10.39	19.01	19.56	19.57	10.95	20.78	21.54	21.92
σ	1.246	3.623	2.694	2.836	1.063	4.193	4.089	3.890	1.586	2.885	1.555	1.358
Best	14.20	30.40	32.28	32.74	13.86	29.02	29.96	30.52	14.06	31.96	33.56	34.06

	2 - 1-Point				**2 - 2-Point**				**2 - Area**			
Gen.	10	500	1000	2000	10	500	1000	2000	10	500	1000	2000
Avg.	15.54	22.89	22.87	22.95	15.61	22.56	22.70	23.07	15.54	22.62	23.08	23.44
σ	0.231	1.443	1.291	1.182	0.478	1.461	1.466	1.462	0.229	1.430	1.286	1.132
Best	14.24	33.02	33.42	33.66	14.64	32.66	33.16	33.54	14.18	32.42	33.34	34.26

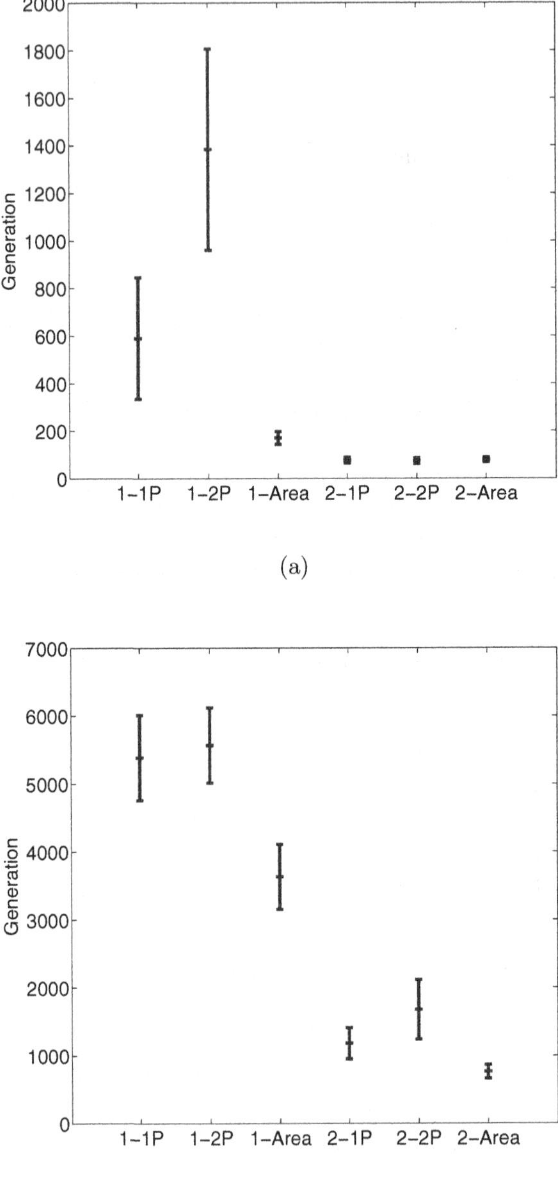

Fig. 9. Average value and standard error of the generation number where the respective method could find the correct circuit. (a) Full Adder and (b) 4–1–Multiplexer.

Table 6. Quality values over the generations (multiplexer)

	1 - 1-Point				**1 - 2-Point**			
Gen.	10	1000	2000	3000	10	1000	2000	3000
Avg.	34.12	42.74	44.13	48.67	32.89	43.22	43.66	47.10
σ	1.413	4.750	6.988	10.699	0.882	6.112	7.739	10.613
Best	47.30	62.03	68.60	82.53	46.53	61.60	66.27	77.03

	2 - 1-Point				**2 - 2-Point**			
Gen.	10	1000	2000	3000	10	1000	2000	3000
Avg.	63.50	72.23	76.68	77.99	63.51	70.54	73.98	75.51
σ	0.042	7.709	7.089	6.101	0.049	6.760	5.959	5.886
Best	46.50	99.73	123.50	132.80	47.63	96.03	117.70	126.03

	1 - Area				**2 - Area**			
Gen.	10	1000	2000	3000	10	1000	2000	3000
Avg.	35.38	43.70	46.87	48.12	63.49	73.22	77.49	78.49
σ	1.003	5.289	9.188	8.477	0.048	6.542	6.045	4.737
Best	47.30	69.17	82.37	95.77	46.73	114.50	136.17	145.47

5 Conclusion and Future Work

In this paper, we propose evolutionary algorithms for the design of combinational logic circuits. Particularly, we study different methods for improving the optimisation performance both with respect to solution quality and time. A gate matrix of logical gates is the basis of this design where the evolutionary algorithm is used to find the optimal types and connections between the gates. In this paper, a new population-based evaluation mechanism called MaxMin has been introduced. The MaxMin evaluation scheme maximises the influence of the solutions with correct outputs that had been found by a minimal number of individuals in the current population. Indeed, we observe that in many cases, due to some local optima, some of the outputs are very difficult to obtain. Therefore, those solutions which are able to find those outputs should influence the population (as done by MaxMin). This quality evaluation scheme is different from previously proposed methods and it is shown in this paper that it considerably improves the optimisation performance, having positive effects on the computation time, too.

Furthermore, we design a new cross-over operator for the gate matrix circuit representation in which we exchange two rectangular areas. This cross-over operator (called area cross-over) has been compared with other typical crossover-operators such as one-point and two-point. It is observed that the MaxMin evaluation in combination with the area cross-over operator significantly improve the solutions and the computation time. The new methods and the comparisons have been tested for the two test examples of full adder and multiplexer. For future work, we are interested to study the new methods on other more complex examples and on larger gate matrices than examined here.

References

1. Coello Coello, C., Christiansen, A., Hernández Aguirre, A.: Towards automated evolutionary design of combinational circuits. Comput. Electr. Eng. 7, 1–28 (2001)
2. Coello Coello, C., Hernández Aguirre, A., Buckles, B.P.: Evolutionary Multiobjective Design of Combinational Logic Circuits. In: Lohn, J., et al. (eds.) Proceedings of the Second NASA/DoD Workshop on Evolvable Hardware, pp. 161–170. IEEE Computer Society Press, Los Alamitos (2000)
3. Coello Coello, C., et al.: Ant colony system for the design of combinational logic circuits. In: Miller, J.F., et al. (eds.) ICES 2000. LNCS, vol. 1801, pp. 21–30. Springer, Heidelberg (2000)
4. Deb, K.: Multi-Objective Optimization using Evolutionary Algorithms. John Wiley and Sons, Chichester (2001)
5. Goldberg, D.E.: Genetic Algorithms in Search, Optimization, and Machine Learning. Addison-Wesley, Reading (1989)
6. Higuchi, T., Yao, X., Liu, Y.: Evolvable Hardware (Genetic and Evolutionary Computation). Springer, Heidelberg (2006)
7. Kalganova, T., Miller, J.: Evolving more efficient digital circuits by allowing circuit layout evolution and multi-objective fitness. In: Stoica, A., Lohn, J., Keymeulen, D. (eds.) NASA/DoD Workshop on Evolvable Hardware, pp. 54–63. IEEE Computer Society Press, Los Alamitos (1999)
8. Louis, S.J., Rawlins, G.J.: Designer genetic algorithms: Genetic algorithms in structure design. In: Belew, R., Booker, L. (eds.) International Conference on Genetic Algorithms, pp. 53–60. Morgan Kaufmann, San Francisco (1991)

Part II
Pervasive Computing

Direct Backtracking: An Advanced Adaptation Algorithm for Pervasive Applications

Stephan Schuhmann, Klaus Herrmann, and Kurt Rothermel

University of Stuttgart
Institute of Parallel and Distributed Systems (IPVS)
Universitätsstr. 38
70569 Stuttgart, Germany
{firstname.lastname}@ipvs.uni-stuttgart.de

Abstract. The adaptation of pervasive applications is in the focus of many current research projects. While decentralized adaptation is mandatory in infrastructureless ad hoc scenarios, most realistic pervasive application scenarios are situated in heterogeneous environments where additional computation power of resource-rich devices can be exploited. Therefore, we propose a hybrid approach to application configuration that applies centralized as well as decentralized configuration as appropriate in the given environment. In this paper we introduce the Direct Backtracking algorithm that represents an efficient way for centralized configuration and adaptation of pervasive applications in heterogeneous scenarios. In our evaluation, we show that compared with other centralized algorithms, our algorithm significantly reduces adaptation latency as it avoids unnecessary adaptations that arise in many other backtracking algorithms, without significantly increasing memory waste. This is achieved by introducing two mechanisms: 1. proactive backtracking avoidance and 2. intelligent backtracking.

1 Introduction

In recent years, automatic adaptation of pervasive applications that share the resources of different devices has become a research field of increasing interest. Besides our component system PCOM [1], many other research projects such as Gaia [2], Aura [3], or Pebbles [4] deal with this issue. Two fundamentally different approaches exist for adaptation of pervasive applications, namely distributed and centralized adaptation. The distributed approach is generally applicable in scenarios both with and without additional infrastructure. Unfortunately, this approach needs extensive communication between devices. Furthermore, it assumes a homogeneous environment and, thus, does not exploit additional computation power available on resource-rich devices.

Our work focuses on heterogeneous pervasive computing environments where resource-poor, potentially mobile devices as well as resource-rich infrastructure devices are present. Many of today's office or home scenarios satisfy these properties. In such scenarios, centralized adaptation can improve calculation speed

U. Brinkschulte et al. (Eds.): ARCS 2008, LNCS 4934, pp. 53–67, 2008.

and decrease communication overhead dramatically. Due to the wide range of different scenarios, we advocate a hybrid configuration approach that makes use of decentralized as well as centralized algorithms to exploit the resources present in the environment as effectively as possible.

In this paper, we present a new centralized configuration algorithm called *Direct Backtracking* (DBT) that can be employed on resource-rich devices to configure pervasive applications on near-by resource-poor devices. This complements our previous work on purely decentralized configuration [5] and enables a range of configuration solutions with different degrees of decentralization since both approaches may be combined to produce a hybrid configuration system.

We present two new innovative mechanisms in backtracking: 1. *proactive backtracking avoidance* and 2. *intelligent backtracking.* Both are used in our *Direct Backtracking* algorithm to reduce configuration latency and avoid thrashing effects (repetitive unnecessary reconfigurations) dramatically. In our evaluation, we show that *Direct Backtracking* displays vastly improved performance compared to its nearest competitor (Synchronous Backtracking) and, therefore, enables fast configurations and adaptations in much larger pervasive applications. We also show that increased memory consumption of our algorithm does not limit its general applicability in heterogeneous environments.

The paper is structured as follows: After a presentation of our system model in Section 2, we take a look on related work in Section 3. Then, we explain our algorithm in detail in Section 4. This is followed by an evaluation in Section 5. Finally, we recapitulate our work in Section 6 and give a short outlook on future works.

2 System Model

In many pervasive computing scenarios, a single device cannot provide the entire functionality required by an application because of limited resources. Thus, the main characteristic of a *pervasive application* is the fact that the required functionality is distributed among multiple devices which have to collaborate.

We assume a component-based software model, i.e. an application consists of *components* and each component *instance* requires a certain amount of resources. Figure 1 shows our application model. An application is represented by a tree of interdependent components that is constructed by recursively starting the components required by a root instance, the so-called application *anchor*.

A single component is resident on a specific device which is represented by a *container* that carries a unique identifier (ID). The number of components per container is not restricted. Interdependencies between components as well as resource requirements are described by directed *contracts* which specify the functionality required by the parent component and provided by the child component of this contract. A parent component may have an arbitrary number of dependencies. Our algorithm follows a depth-first search approach. This means that the algorithm proceeds from the top to the bottom of the tree and, within a sublevel of the tree, from left to right. If there exists more than just one

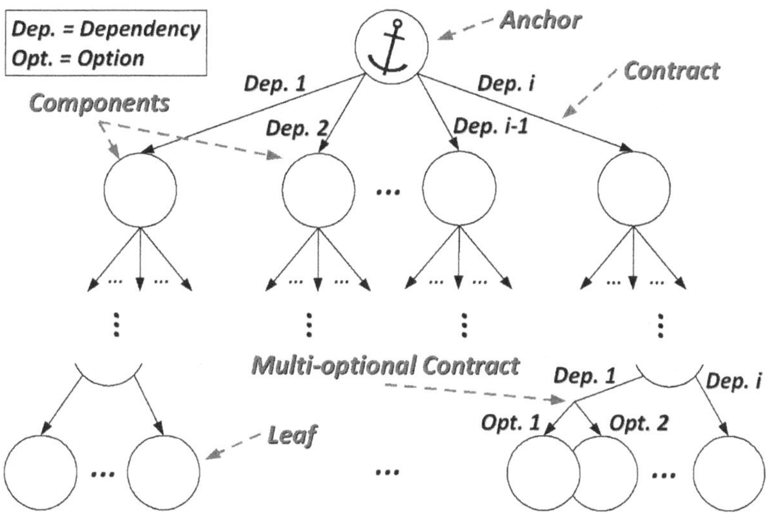

Fig. 1. Application model

component that provides the required functionality for a contract, the parent component can choose among several *options*. In the following, this is called *multi-optional contract*.

In a *configuration* process, the configuration algorithm tries to resolve all dependencies by finding a suitable component for each contract. Whenever the algorithm fails to find such a component for a contract (e.g., due to lack of resources), an *adaptation* process has to be initiated to resolve this conflict. Within this process, an instantiated component of another contract C has to be stopped to free resources, and another component that fulfills C's requirements with less resources has to be instantiated afterwards. If the algorithm does not consider whether the adapted contract requires the same resources as the contract which could not be fulfilled, it is possible that many adaptations are needless since they do not solve the conflict. So, the number of necessary adaptations increases which leads to additional configuration latency (time before the configuration is complete). This undesired effect is called *thrashing*.

As long as the anchor component is executed, its container ensures that dependencies are recursively resolved by binding adequate components to them. Since a parent component relies on its child components, it can only be instantiated if all of its children have been instantiated previously. An application is successfully started if all dependencies have been resolved so that for each contract, a suitable component which satisfies all requirements could be found.

We assume that a single device which performs centralized configuration and adaptation has collected relevant data beforehand using a specific protocol[1]. Thus, this device can create an internal representation of the application tree

[1] This protocol is not further described here since it does not affect adaptation aspects and does not produce considerable overhead.

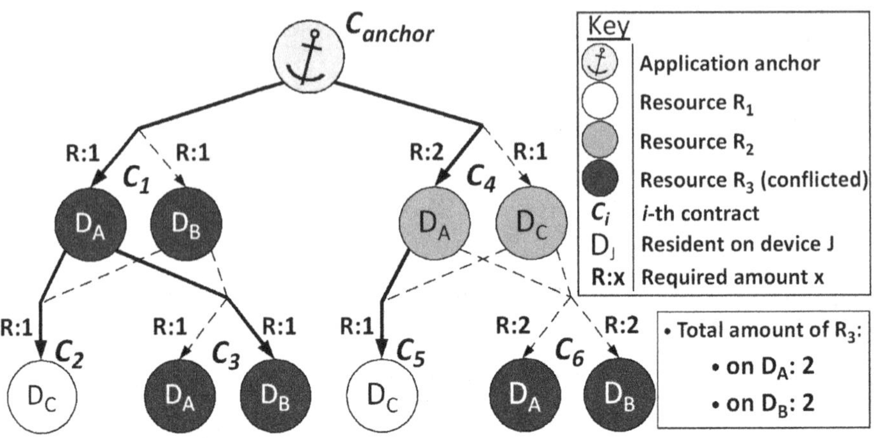

Fig. 2. Exemplary application tree

that comprises dependencies, components, and incorporated devices with their available resources. After a configuration is complete, another protocol has to distribute the results of the configuration to the respective devices.

2.1 Example

Figure 2 shows an exemplary application tree that consists of the anchor C_{anchor} and six contracts C_1 to C_6 whose dependencies have to be satisfied in order to start the application successfully. The contracts are ordered depth-first search like, according to the sequence of the algorithm. Hence, the algorithm starts the configuration process with C_1, and finishes with C_6. Contracts C_1, C_3, C_4, and C_6 are multi-optional, i.e. there exists more than one component that can satisfy the required functionality. The components are resident on three containers D_A, D_B, and D_C. The contracts can be satisfied by certain amounts of specific resources. For example, contracts C_1, C_3, and C_6 can be satisfied by R_3 which is available on containers D_A and D_B. Let us assume that enough resources of R_1 and R_2 are available on the containers and, thus, only R_3 can cause a conflict situation due to missing resources. Both D_A and D_B have two instances of R_3.

The thick lines show the components – resident on the denoted containers D_j – which were chosen by the algorithm for C_1 to C_5 and, thus, only C_6 has to be instantiated. In this situation, D_A as well as D_B have only one free resource of type R_3 left, but two resources are needed for every container to instantiate C_6. Therefore, none of the components can be instantiated for C_6 in this situation. Hence, an adaptation of the current configuration is inevitable.

As a concrete example, consider an instant messaging application that requires an input service, e.g. a keyboard or a touch screen, to write messages, and an output service to display messages. If there exists more than one input device, for instance, these devices represent several options of a multi-optional contract.

An adaptation is necessary, for instance, if the current output device becomes unavailable. Another example is a pervasive presenter [6] whose functionality of displaying presentation slides is provided by the cooperation of distributed devices.

The example described above could illustrate a similar presentation application, where resource R_3 represents display devices. D_A and D_B both have two displays. Displays are needed for different tasks within the application, e.g. to show images, videos, or presentation slides and, thus, are required in multiple contracts. Additionally required input and output devices like microphones or loudspeakers are represented by the other resources R_1 and R_2. Due to different properties of the resources, e.g. the maximum output volume of a loudspeaker, it is possible that different amounts of specific resources are required within a contract, as it can be seen for contract C_4.

3 Related Work

The adaptation of tree-based applications can be mapped to a Constraint Satisfaction Problem (CSP) [5]. In case of a fully distributed application configuration, this problem can be solved by distributed algorithms from the domain of Artificial Intelligence [7]. Due to their decentralization, these algorithms cause huge communication overhead for resolving dependencies between components. In case of n devices that are involved in the application configuration, the worst-case amount of messages to be sent is $O(n^2)$. In centralized algorithms, every involved device has to send only one message to the configuration device to inform this device about its available resources, which leads to a worst-case message amount of only $O(n)$. Furthermore, distributed algorithms do not take special care of resource-rich devices that are present in heterogeneous environments.

Thus, we concentrate on centralized backtracking algorithms in this paper. A survey of these algorithms is given by Baker [8]. The simplest centralized backtracking algorithm is *Synchronous Backtracking* (SBT) [9]. SBT executes a depth-first search in the application tree and has one huge drawback concerning adaptations: Since it does not consider the cause of a backtracking process and tries to adapt the first possible multi-optional contract, it suffers from thrashing. Especially for huge applications with many multi-optional contracts, this leads to an enormous overhead and, thus, increased latency.

Several approaches exist to avoid this thrashing effect. *Synchronous Backjumping* (SBJ) [10] searches for a multi-optional contract if it depends on the same kind of resource as the contract that was the reason for backtracking. It does not adapt contracts that are independent of the backtracking cause. This helps to reduce thrashing, but it cannot avoid it completely since SBJ does *not* keep previous intermediate results for subsequent adaptations. Furthermore, SBJ builds up a stack during backtracking. This causes additional computation overhead.

Dependency-Directed Backtracking (DDB) [11] solves the problem of thrashing by storing a set of so-called *nogoods* which are partial configurations without a solution for the complete application. Therefore, it can avoid infeasible solutions subsequently. The drawback of DDB is its enormous memory consumption since an ever-increasing set of nogoods has to be stored on a stack.

An advanced approach to remove thrashing completely without excessive waste of memory is *Dynamic Backtracking* (DyBT) by Ginsberg [12]. Similar to SBJ and DDB, this algorithm immediately moves to a point which conflicts with the latest assignment in case of a conflict. DyBT neither forgets intermediate values, nor is it memory-intensive since it does not rely on a stack. It is an iterative algorithm that stores a set of so-called *culprits* which represent forbidden assignments. DyBT does not only retain the chosen value for a contract C, but also the culprit set of C. If the instantiation of a component for a contract fails, the algorithm can easily decide which of the formerly configured contracts conflict with this contract and directly jump back to them.

However, DyBT changes the order of contracts to resolve conflicts. This is not an option in our problem of tree-based application configuration since parent-child relationships and differences in resource consumption are encoded in the order of contracts. This order needs to be preserved to ensure useful configurations. So, DyBT cannot be used for configuration of tree-based pervasive applications.

Direct Backtracking proceeds similar to DyBT in general, but in addition, it also adapts the adherent subtree of a component during an adaptation process. Thus, Direct Backtracking does not need to perform any changes in the order of components. Moreover, our algorithm applies two intelligent mechanisms that render the configuration process more efficiently.

4 The Direct Backtracking Algorithm

In Section 4.1, the general configuration process of Direct Backtracking is described. This is followed by the main contribution of this paper which are two additional mechanisms of Direct Backtracking: a proactive mechanism to avoid backtracking that is described in Section 4.2, and an intelligent backtracking mechanism to handle conflict situations without thrashing which is presented in Section 4.3. Finally, Section 4.4 presents an example for the adaptation process.

4.1 General Approach

Figure 3 illustrates DBT in C-like pseudo code. DBT includes five different functions: *start*, *create*, *started*, *stopped*, and *backtrack*.

The *start* function initiates the configuration process and calls the *create* function to resolve the first dependency of the anchor. Thereby, the function `getChild(i, j)` returns the j-th option of the i-th dependency of the current component. The selection of an option in case of a multi-optional contract is performed within the function `determOption()`. This is carefully made to decrease the number of conflict situations that make a backtracking process inevitable. This fundamental mechanism of DBT is described in detail in Section 4.2.

If there are enough resources available to resolve a dependency within the *create* function, two possibilities exist:

1. The component to be started represents a leaf of the tree. In this case, the *started* function is called subsequently to indicate this instantiation of a leaf component to its parent component.
2. The component to be started represents an inner node (i.e., no leaf of the tree). In this case, the *create* function is called recursively to instantiate the components on the next lower level of the tree.

If not enough resources are available to instantiate a component at the moment, the *stopped* function is called to indicate a resource conflict situation to the parent component. In this case, DBT at first tries to instantiate the next component option. If no further option exists, a *backtrack* process has to be initiated.

```
function start(Component anchor):
      create(getChild(0, determOption())); // see Sect. 4.2 for determOption()
end function;  // start

function create(Component comp):
      if (enoughResourcesAvailableForInstantiation())
            if (leafReached()) // leaf component can be started
                  started(comp.getParent());
            else  // try to instantiate first child component
                  create(comp.getChildComp(0, determOption()));
            end if;
      else  // component could not be instantiated
            stopped(comp.getParent());
      end if;
end function;  // create

function started(Component comp):
      if (unresolvedDependencyLeft())  // try to instantiate next dependency
            create(comp.getChild(comp.getDependency() + 1, determOption());
      else  // all dependencies resolved
            if (anchorReached())
                  terminateSuccessfully();  // configuration complete
            else  // indicate instantiation to parent component
                  started(comp.getParent());
            end if;
      end if;
end function;  // started

function stopped(Component comp):
      if (alternativeComponentAvailable())
            create(comp.getChild(comp.getDependency(), determOption()));
      else  // backtracking necessary
            Contract btContract = findBacktrackContract(); // see Sect. 4.3
            if (btContract == null)
                  terminateUnsuccessfully(); // no suitable contract found
            end if;
            Instance toStop = btContract.getInstance();
            Component toStart = determineAlternativeComp(btContract);
            backtrack(toStop, toStart);
            create(comp.getChild(comp.getDependency(), comp.getOption());
      end if;
end function;  // stopped

function backtrack(Instance toStop, Component toStart):
      stopSubtreeInstances(toStop); stopInstance(toStop);
      startInstance(toStart); startSubtreeInstances(toStart);
      return;
end function;  // backtrack
```

Fig. 3. Direct Backtracking

This function at first stops the adherent subtree of the selected backtracking component C_1, then stops C_1 itself, and instantiates another component C_2 and the previously stopped subtree components. C_2 has been determined before within `findBacktrackContract()` that is further described in Section 4.3. Afterwards, DBT retries to instantiate the component which could not be instantiated previously. The algorithm terminates within the *started* function when the anchor is reached and all dependencies of the anchor have been resolved.

4.2 Proactive Backtracking Avoidance

In case of a multi-optional contract for a certain dependency, the selection of a component has to be made cautiously in order to avoid conflict situations right from the start and reduce the number of situations in which backtracking is necessary. For this purpose, Direct Backtracking contains a proactive mechanism which carefully selects the component option to be instantiated in order to avoid backtracking.

Within multi-optional contracts, options are ordered in a list according to the container ID, i.e. a component on a container with a lower ID has higher priority for the configuration algorithm. If there exist multiple options for a specific dependency on one container, they are additionally ordered according to their resource consumption: The component with least resource requirements has highest priority.

Direct Backtracking performs the following steps on the ordered list of options in the given order:

1. Initially, DBT selects the first component option in the list to be instantiated, i.e. the highest-priority component.
2. If the currently selected option consumes the total free amount of a resource R, the algorithm scans the ordered list of options for alternative components. If there exists a component on another container whose instantiation would still leave some amount of R unused on this container, DBT adjusts the selected option in order to decrease the potential for future conflicts. This adjustment of the option to be instantiated is performed to the highest-prior component that fulfills the above condition of leaving some amount of R unused.
3. For the currently selected option, DBT verifies that there are enough global resources remaining to fulfill all missing contracts in theory after the initialization of the chosen component C. This means that there have to exist at least i free components among **all** devices with sufficient resources to fulfill the i dependencies of the application that have not been resolved yet. Otherwise, C is not instantiated at this moment as this would yield a future inevitable backtrack process. In this case, the algorithm selects the next lower-prior option in the ordered list and continues with step 2.

If none of the options can be instantiated, a backtracking is necessary. DBT's intelligent backtracking process is described in the next subsection.

4.3 Intelligent Backtracking

In case of a conflict situation, if none of the possible components for a contract C could be instantiated, a backtracking has to be initiated. Thus, another contract that can be adapted must be found. In many situations, there is more than just one candidate for an adaptation. In such a case, DBT performs an intelligent backtracking by carefully selecting a contract whose components can be adapted with little overhead.

First, let us assume that the components of C which could not be instantiated due to a shortage of a specific resource R form a set of components $S_1 = \{Cmp_1, Cmp_2, ..., Cmp_i\}$. If C is *not* multi-optional, S_1 includes only one component. Now, DBT determines the set $D_s = \{D_1, D_2, ..., D_j\}$ of containers which host at least one component that is included in S_1, i.e.

$$(\exists k, j : k \in \{1, ..., i\} \wedge l \in \{1, ..., j\} \wedge Cmp_k \in D_l) \Rightarrow D_l \in D_s \qquad (1)$$

Subsequently, DBT determines another set, S_2. This set contains those multi-optional contracts for which a component is currently instantiated that is resident on one of the containers included in D_s. Furthermore, only those contracts are included in S_2 for which an alternative component on another container Ctr exists that can be instantiated *now* due to sufficient uninstantiated amount of R on Ctr. The contracts in S_2 are ordered in descending order according to the amount of R that is consumed by the instantiated component. This means that the instantiated component which consumes the largest amount of R is at the beginning of the list because its termination would cause a considerable deallocation of resources. This helps to decrease the number of needless adaptations which would have to be revised later. If only one suitable component exists, the backtracking target is found and the adaptation process can be initiated.

In case of more than one suitable backtracking targets that consume an identical amount of R, an additional selection criterion is necessary for weighting them according to their suitability for adaptation. Since adaptation is simpler for contracts with small adherent subtrees (as the subtree also has to be adapted), DBT selects the component C that has least descendants (number of all child components down to the leaves) and, hence, is closest to the bottom of the tree. Thus, contracts with little adaptation overhead are preferred. In case of multiple contracts with a subtree of the same size, the algorithm selects the one with the highest priority, i.e. the one with lowest index.

If the resource conflict cannot be solved by adapting the first contract in S_2, DBT tries to solve it by adapting the second contract in S_2, and so on. If the conflict cannot be solved by adapting any contract included in S_2, this indicates that there are not sufficient resources in the environment. Thus, the algorithm terminates unsuccessfully within the *stopped* function and informs the user of this failure.

4.4 Example for Adaptation Process

Now let us revisit the example presented in Section 2.1 to see how the intelligent backtracking mechanism of DBT performs in practice. In the situation depicted in Figure 2, Direct Backtracking recognizes that the conflict arises for R_3. S_1 consists of the two possible components of C_6. These components are resident on D_A and D_B. Thus, we have a set $D_s = \{D_A, D_B\}$. Both of these devices lack one instance of resource R_3. According to the procedure described in Section 4.3, DBT identifies C_1 and C_3 as possible contracts for adaptation. The currently instantiated components of C_1 and C_3 both have allocated an identical amount of one instance of R_3. Hence, the subtree criterion has to be taken into account and C_3 is elected for adaptation because it has no adherent subtree which would cause additional adaptation effort. Thus, DBT directly backtracks to C_3, stops the instantiated component on D_B, instantiates the component on D_A, and returns to C_5. Now, DBT is able to instantiate the component on D_B to fulfill C_6, as sufficient free resources are available. Subsequently, the entire application is successfully instantiated.

In the same situation, Synchronous Backtracking would at first try to adapt contract C_4 which is the next higher-priority multi-optional contract above C_6. But since C_4 depends on a different resource, this adaptation of C_4 does not solve the problem. So, SBT has to initiate another backtracking process which would adapt C_3 as the next higher-priority multi-optional contract. This second adaptation would resolve the conflict.

Since SBT always performs backtracking stepwise to the previous contract in the tree, and because of the useless adaptation of C_4, the backtracking function is executed multiple times, while for DBT, only one direct backtrack to C_3 is necessary. Hence, due to its intelligent backtracking mechanism, DBT performs adaptation of this exemplary application with less overhead and, thus, much faster than SBT does. As DBT additionally avoids backtracking processes in many situations due to the proactive mechanism described in Section 4.2, DBT's benefit even increases in many resource-constricted environments.

5 Evaluation

This section presents our evaluation results. We simulated the algorithm on a discrete event PCOM simulator.

We compared Direct Backtracking to Synchronous Backtracking (SBT), the centralized version of Asynchronous Backtracking [7] that was used previously for distributed application configuration [5]. We chose to compare DBT to SBT as this is the best centralized algorithm that is applicable to the problem of adapting pervasive applications without excessive memory waste and computation overhead. As already mentioned in the related work section, a comparison of Direct Backtracking to Dynamic Backtracking (DyBT) is not possible since DyBT changes the order of the contracts to resolve conflicts, which is not an option here.

5.1 Experimental Setup

The simulated environments are constructed as follows to support various different scenarios: We create an application that consists of n instances by adding

n components to a binary application tree. Then, we create one container and place the anchor on it. For the remaining (n-1) components, we create $m \leq n$ containers and place the components on those containers in a round robin manner. Then, we artificially create conflicts by replicating k random components and by increasing their resource needs to two without increasing the available resources on the containers. Thus, increasing k will lead to a higher potential for conflicting selections during automatic configuration as it increases the number of multi-optional contracts.

Now, we varied the height h of the binary tree from two, where an application consisted of only $2^3 - 2 = 6$ components (excluding the anchor component), up to ten, which leads to $2^{11} - 2 = 2046$ components. For each tree height, we varied the number k of replicated components and ran 10000 simulations.

Regarding real-life pervasive scenarios, environments typically exist of many different devices with distinguished functionalities. They can be homogeneous as well as heterogeneous. Frequently, devices with similar or even the same functionality are available. This means that applications which use this functionality also include multi-optional contracts.

Hence, it can be seen that the assumed simulated setting is realistic for pervasive computing environments.

5.2 Evaluation Results

We evaluated the algorithm on a common desktop PC[2] and compared our algorithm to Synchronous Backtracking, especially concerning the aspects of *configuration latency*, *communication overhead*, *success quota*, *memory overhead* and *size of the source code* and got following results:

- **Configuration latency:** The main goal in the development of an advanced centralized configuration algorithm was the reduction of the configuration latency that is noticeable for the user. Figure 4 shows DBT's latency for three different heights of the binary tree and, thus, different application sizes. The graph shows the latency relative to the respective SBT performance. Thus, values above 1.0 indicate a DBT performance that is worse than that of SBT, while values below 1.0 indicate better performance. It can be seen that especially for a huge number of multi-optional contracts, there is an immense improvement when using DBT since it performs proactive backtracking avoidance, intelligent backtracking, and avoids thrashing by considering the cause of a backtrack. The figure also shows that the relative performance of DBT even increases with increasing application size. According to this figure, DBT induces just about 4.2 % of the latency of SBT if an application consists of 62 contracts, whereas 14 contracts are multi-optional. Nevertheless, it must be mentioned that for small fractions of multi-optional contracts, SBT performs better than DBT by up to 20 %. This is because of DBT's additional checks for avoiding conflict situations and the process of storing the backtracking causes. Since absolute latencies were very small in

[2] PC with Dual Core Processor (2.2 GHz), 2.0 GB of RAM.

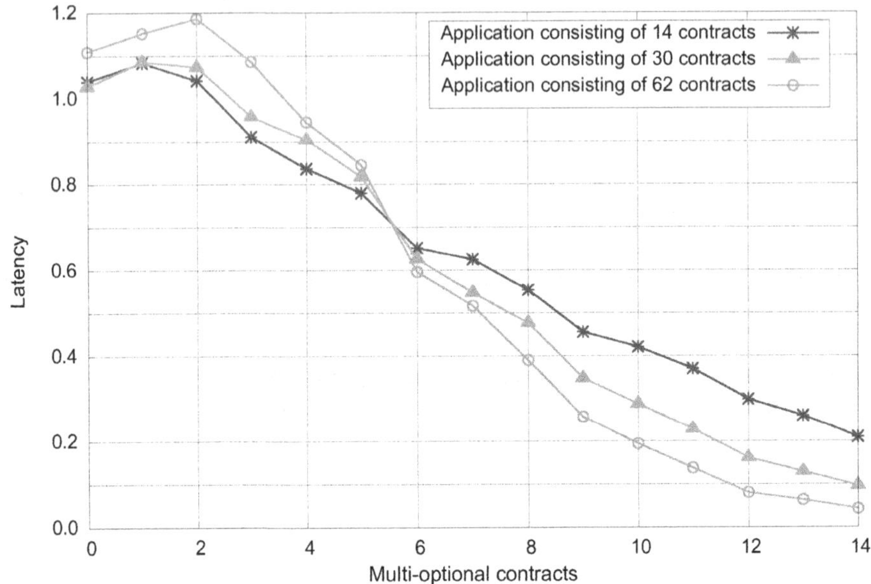

Fig. 4. Configuration latency of DBT (compared to SBT references)

those cases (in the range of few milliseconds), this overhead can be neglected. With increasing tree height, the *crossover point*, which represents the fraction of multi-optional contracts for which DBT starts to outperform SBT, exponentially decreases, as it can be seen in Figure 5. This means that for huge applications, even if just a small amount of contracts is multi-optional, DBT is the better choice regarding configuration latency.

- **Communication overhead:** Compared to the other centralized backtracking algorithms presented in Section 3, no additional communication overhead arises during runtime of our algorithm.
- **Success quota:** The scenarios have been created in a way that at least one valid configuration exists for each scenario. In every single simulation run, both SBT and DBT terminated successfully with a valid application configuration.
- **Memory overhead:** Compared to SBT, DBT needs to store additional information about arising conflicts, especially the contract chosen for adaptation and the contract to which the algorithm has to return after an adaptation has been performed. We measured the average random access memory consumption of the algorithm on a common desktop PC and compared it to SBT. While memory consumption of SBT was almost independent from the application size and the number of conflicts (the standard deviation was below 2 % in all runs), the overhead of DBT increased with the application size and the number of multi-optional contracts, but remained within acceptable limits. The average memory overhead of DBT varies between 8.0 % for applications

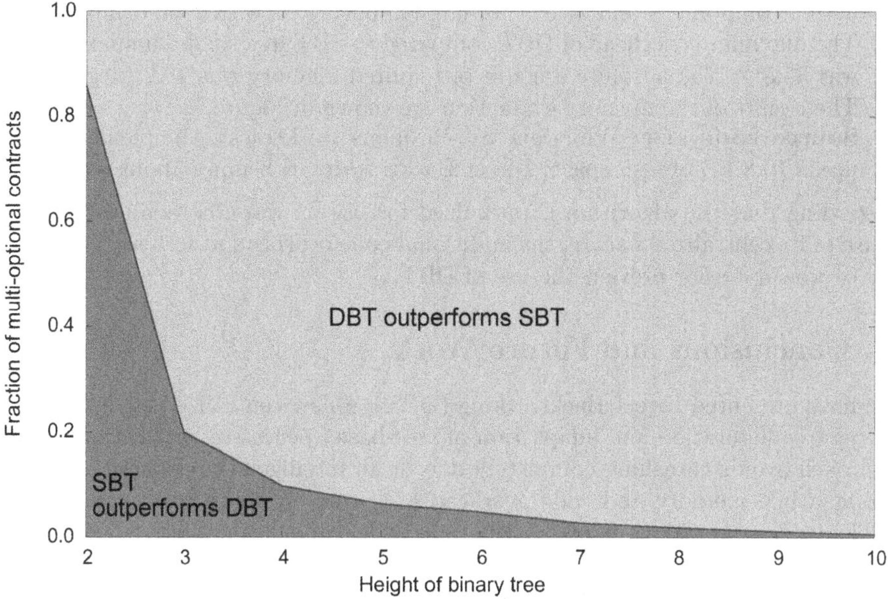

Fig. 5. Crossover points

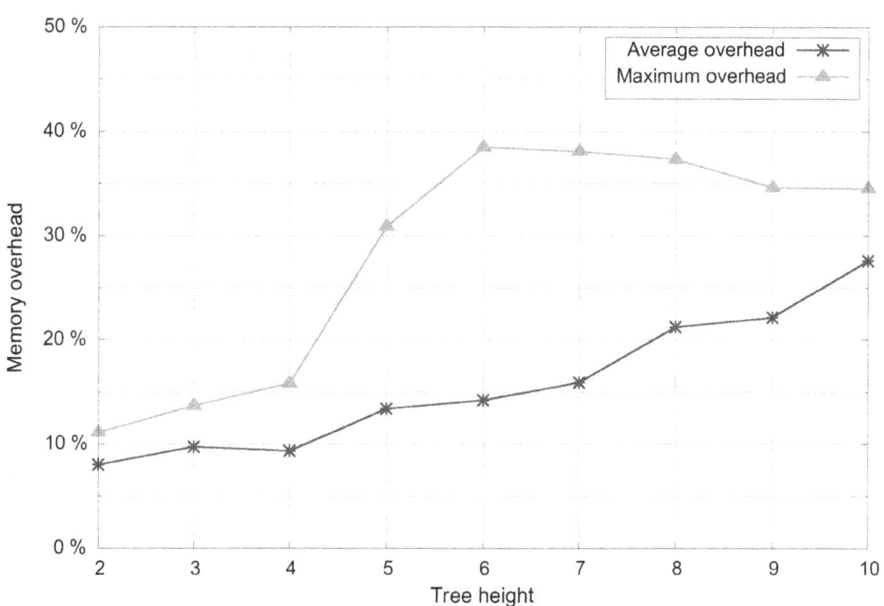

Fig. 6. Memory overhead of Direct Backtracking

with 6 components and 27.6 % for large applications with 2046 components. The maximum overhead of DBT compared to SBT in a single simulation run was 38.5 %, the absolute amount of required memory was 19.2 Megabytes. The results of the memory evaluation are shown in Figure 6.
- **Source code size:** While our Synchronous Backtracking implementation needs 10.8 kB of disk space, Direct Backtracking consumes about 96.9 kB.

Regarding that the algorithm is optimized for use on resource-rich devices because of its centralized nature, the additional code overhead as well as the memory overhead do not prevent the use of DBT.

6 Conclusions and Future Work

We have presented Direct Backtracking (DBT), a new centralized algorithm for efficient configuration and adaptation of tree-based pervasive applications. Our approach avoids thrashing completely due to an intelligent backtracking mechanism, while memory and code overhead are of acceptable size. Furthermore, DBT avoids adaptations in many situations as it employs a proactive backtracking avoidance mechanism.

We have shown that DBT significantly outperforms Synchronous Backtracking (SBT) for applications with various sizes, and especially for huge scenarios with many multi-optional components where it causes less than 5 % of SBT's configuration latency. The small latency overhead of up to 20 % for scenarios with a low fraction of multi-optional contracts can be neglected since absolute latencies for these applications were very small. The additional memory and code overhead of DBT is not significant as the algorithm is designed for centralized configuration on resource-rich devices.

Our future work concentrates on the efficient support of hybrid configuration and adaptation in homogeneous as well as heterogeneous environments by introducing a clustering scheme. Within each cluster, the cluster heads configure applications in a centralized way, while the different cluster heads perform distributed configuration among each other. Direct Backtracking will be used as efficient centralized algorithm for configuration and adaptation on the cluster heads.

Acknowledgement

This work is funded by the German Research Foundation within DFG Priority Programme 1140 - Middleware for Self-organizing Infrastructures in Networked Mobile Systems.

References

1. Becker, C., et al.: PCOM - A Component System for Pervasive Computing. In: Proceedings of the 2nd IEEE International Conference on Pervasive Computing and Communications (PerCom 2004), Orlando, USA (2004)
2. Román, M., et al.: Gaia: A Middleware Infrastructure to Enable Active Spaces. In: IEEE Pervasive Computing, pp. 74–83 (October-December 2002)

3. Sousa, J.P., Garlan, D.: Aura: an Architectural Framework for User Mobility in Ubiquitous Computing Environments. In: Proceedings of the 3rd Working IEEE/IFIP Conference on Software Architecture, August 2002, pp. 29–43. Kluwer Academic Publishers, Dordrecht (2002)
4. Saif, U., et al.: A case for goal-oriented programming semantics. In: UbiSys 2003: Workshop on System Support for Ubiquitous Computing at UbiComp 2003, Seattle, USA, pp. 1–8 (2003)
5. Handte, M., Becker, C., Rothermel, K.: Peer-based Automatic Configuration of Pervasive Applications. In: IEEE International Conference on Pervasive Services 2005 (ICPS 2005), Santorini, Greece (2005)
6. Handte, M., et al.: 3PC/MarNET Pervasive Presenter. In: 4th IEEE International Conference on Pervasive Computing and Communications (PerCom 2006), Pisa, Italy (2006)
7. Yokoo, M., et al.: The Distributed Constraint Satisfaction Problem: Formalization and Algorithms. IEEE Transactions on Knowledge and Data Engineering 10(5), 673–685 (1998)
8. Baker, A.B.: Intelligent Backtracking on Constraint Satisfaction Problems: Experimental and Theoretical Results. PhD Thesis, University of Oregon (March 1995)
9. Brito, I., Meseguer, P.: Synchronous, asynchronous and hybrid algorithms for DisCSP. In: Workshop on Distributed Constraints Reasoning (DCR 2004), Toronto, Canada (September 2004)
10. Gaschnig, J.: A general backtrack algorithm that eliminates most redundant checks. In: International Joint Conference on Artificial Intelligence, Menlo Park, p. 457 (1977)
11. Stallman, R.M., Sussman, G.J.: Forward Reasoning and Dependency-Directed Backtracking in a System for Computer-Aided Circuit Analysis. Artificial Intelligence 9, 135–196 (1977)
12. Ginsberg, M.L.: Dynamic backtracking. Journal of Artificial Intelligence Research 1, 25–46 (1993)

Intelligent Vehicle Handling: Steering and Body Postures While Cornering

Andreas Riener, Alois Ferscha, and Michael Matscheko

Johannes Kepler University Linz, Institute for Pervasive Computing,
Altenberger Str. 69, A-4040 Linz, Austria
Tel.: +43/732/2468-8555, Fax.: +43/732/2468-8524
{riener,ferscha,matscheko}@pervasive.jku.at

Abstract. Vehicle handling and control is an essential aspect of intelligent driver assistance systems, a building block of the upcoming generation of *"smart cars"*. A car's handling is affected by (*i*) *technological* (engine, suspension, brakes, tires, wheels, steering, etc.), (*ii*) *environmental* (road condition, weather, traffic, etc.), and (*iii*) *human* (attentiveness, reactiveness, driver agility, etc.) factors, and their mutual interrelationship. In this paper we investigate on how a driver's endeavor for precise steering interferes with lateral acceleration while cornering. Depending on the steering ratio and the cruising speed, we identify that the readiness of a driver to compensate lateral forces exhibits counterintuitive characteristics. A driver body posture recognition technique based on a high resolution pressure sensor integrated invisibly and unobtrusively into the fabric of the driver seat has been developed. Sensor data, collected by two 32x32 pressure sensor arrays (seat- and backrest), is classified according to features defined based on cornering driving situations. Experimental results verify an increased readiness to compensate lateral acceleration with increasing driving speed, but only beyond a certain driver specific "break even" point. Above intelligent driver assistance, e.g. to improve steering precision, to reduce or avoid over-steer or under-steer, or to proactively notify electronic stability control (ESC), our results also encourage for new modalities in driver-to-car and car-to-roadside interaction.

Keywords: Embedded Systems, Intelligent Driver Assistance Systems, Vehicle Handling, Car and Road Safety, Sitting Postures, Pattern Recognition.

1 Motivation

Increasing car and road safety, reducing driver distraction and enhancing driving comfort are the major reasons for transferring ubiquitous and pervasive computing applications into the automotive domain. Research, development and engineering efforts towards these goals are, popularly speaking, often motivated to establish a new generation of "smart cars". Of particular interest towards this

U. Brinkschulte et al. (Eds.): ARCS 2008, LNCS 4934, pp. 68–81, 2008.

vision are driver assistance systems that help to relieve the driver from manipulative and cognitive load while driving, questing for new modalities in driver-to-car (D2C) and car-to-roadside (C2R) interactions.

Steering, as one of the most crucial manipulative and cognitive issues in car handling challenges the driver with a complex, multidimensional interaction process. Both, driver experience and the contextual setting (like road and traffic conditions, weather, sight, etc.) determine car handling performance. Hence, in order to investigate on vehicle handling and driver engagement, dynamic models have to developed which are capable of real time driver activity recognition and multi-sensor based context recognition. An interesting aspect of such a model is the impact of the cruising speed onto the driver comfort. This paper, in particular, addresses a thorough investigation of the potential correlation among cruising speed while cornering against the driver's body posture as an expression of his or her feeling comfortable. The analysis in this paper is hence motivated by the following hypotheses:

(i) Cruising speed and body posture while cornering seems to be correlated, as observations from various driving situations suggest.
(ii) Increasing lateral acceleration while cornering directs to a higher level of driver stress and thus, to an escalating risk of operating errors.
(iii) The time gap between a change in body posture and the corresponding steering activity depends on the level of driving experience, and tends to zero for a professional driver on a familar driving route.
(iv) The risk of casualities in road traffic can be reduced if the inter-relations between driver's body posture and cruising speed in cornering driving situations are evidenced.

Intelligent driver assistance could relieve the driver from the above noticed manipulative and cognitive issues by adaptively controlling the vehicle before activities from the driver actually take place. This would also support efforts of official authorities like governments and international policy makers to make driving more safe, for instance as mentioned in the European Road Safety Action Programme[1].

In this work we investigate on our hypotheses from the following two points of view (see Fig. 1 for an illustration of our assumptions):

(i) While cornering at low speed the driver has low or moderate ambition to compensate centripetal force.
(ii) In high speed cornering situations the readiness to compensate lateral forces is high.

We presume that our hypothesis establishes a qualitative attribute which can be used for enhance intelligent driver assistance, e.g. to improve steering

[1] Saving 20.000 lives on our roads - a shared responsibility. European Road Safety Action Programme. URL: `http://ec.europa.eu/transport/roadsafety_library/rsap/rsap_en.pdf`, visited Sept. 30, 2007.

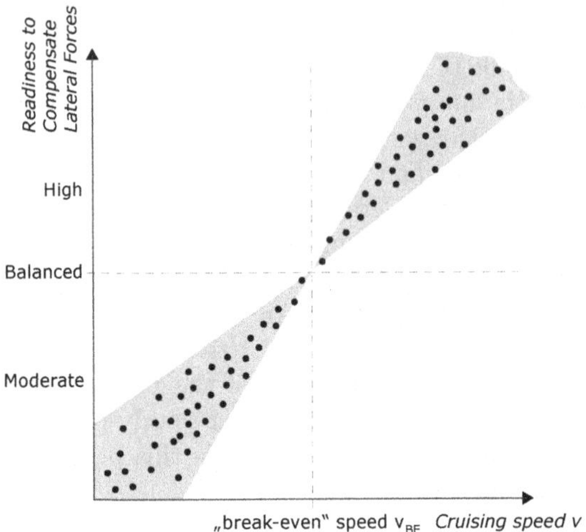

Fig. 1. Hypothesis on correlation between body posture and cruising speed

precision, to reduce or avoid over-steer or under-steer, or to proactively notify ESC. To this end we built up an experimental system in a car, recording a variety of parameters like vehicle speed, steering angle, and body posture. During system design we decided to integrate additional sensors (GPS-sensor, accelerometers, videocameras, ECG device, etc.) to improve measurement results, increase redundancy and to create a more general environment, also fitting demand for further experiments. Vehicle-specific data is gathered via the OBD-interface[2]. For body-posture capturing several techniques are available. However, most of them require a person to wear one or more sensors or even put markers on its body [1]. To avoid technology obtrusiveness as far as possible in our experiments, we used a passive method for measuring body-postures by inspecting pressure patterns on driver's seat and backrest, dynamically collected from two force sensor arrays (FSA). Our data acquisition system operates fully implicit, meaning that it needs no active participation of the driver, and therefore leads to no auxiliary user-distraction.

The rest of this paper is structured as follows: Section 2 motivates systems design and hardware selection, section 3 starts with a description of hardware assortment and discusses questions regarding data acquisition and processing. Section 4 describes our experimental testbed and mentions the features, extracted from the various sensors and utilized for data processing and analysis. Results of the experiment are announced in section 5. Section 6 concludes our findings on our research hypothesis and suggests future work.

[2] On-Board Diagnostics (OBD) is referring to a vehicle's self-diagnostic and reporting capability. OBD field descriptions can be amongst others found at: `http://www.obd2crazy.com/techstd.html`, visited Sept. 24, 2007.

2 Driver Assistance Systems

A multitude of enabling systems for vehicles has been presented in the last years, e.g. electronic anti-theft devices, rain-sensors for automatically controlling the windscreen wipers, ABS and ESP systems, navigation systems, parking assistance systems, cruise control systems[3], etc. All of them senses vehicle and environmental parameters, but there is only minor work on assistance systems considering the driver (or passengers) of a vehicle [1][p.29].

Contemporary systems primarily operate on speech ([2], [3]) or vision (face-tracking, iris-scan or eye-tracking) recognition methods ([4], [5]). Each sense has its benefits and drawbacks [6][p.374], especially speech modality has been early considered as the most convenient in-car interaction modality because it is both hands-free and eyes-free – this means that the hands can be kept on the steering wheel and the eyes can be kept on the road [2][p.155]. Later research revealed that speech recognition failed on its potentials, especially in the car domain, because voice is influenced by a multitude of parameters, including user characteristics like age, gender, mental workload, emotional stress, etc. In addition, ambient noise is responsible for distortion of spoken instructions [6][p.368]. Finally, voice interaction may distract the user from the driving task [2][p.156] and hence increasing safety hazards.

In-car driver observation has been studied in [7] and [8], introducing a system to predict driving maneuvers before they are actually induced by the driver. This system video-captures the surrounding traffic, the driver's head position and viewpoint, and integrates this information with other real-time data acquired from the car, such as brake, steering wheel angle, speed and acceleration throttle signals.

Latest results come from more user-centered approaches like body posture analysis systems as presented in [9] (color and thermal infrared video-based system for real-time 3D tracking of body parts), [10] (vision system for tracking roads, pedestrians and obstacles as well as the driver inside the car and try to predict her intentions), [11] (side-mounted camera to detect safe and unsafe periods of driver activity on it's profile or silhouette) or [12] (stereo and thermal infrared video capturing inside the car with the aim of increasing safety from airbags). Cheng and Trivedi present in [1] a video-tracking system based on markers to identify slow turns from the driver. A detailed survey about human tracking and pose estimation, considering aspects like active/passive sensors, different estimation models, etc., is given in [13], [14].

[15] considers not only the potential of driver assistance systems to alert the driver in critical situations, but annotates also additional distraction and annonyance if the driver is already aware of the situation (with the option that the driver disables the system...). They presented a "predictive" braking assistance system based on a color camera for head tracking, a infrared camera for tracking

[3] Robert Bosch GmbH, URL: `http://rb-k.bosch.de//de/service/produktuebersicht/produktuebersichtsicherheit.html`, visited Oct. 3, 2007.

driver's feet and onboard vehicle sensors (CAN-bus[4]) for inspecting wheel speed, acceleration, brake pedal pressure, etc.

There is still tremendous potential for innovative driver assistance systems, especially if not based on video- or infrared-cameras for person tracking and activity identification. Our approach is a passive one, inspecting sitting postures from pressure mats, attached to driver's seat and backrest, and enriched with onboard vehicle data acquired via the OBD-interface.

3 Experimental Setup for In-Car Context Capturing

For implicit and passive data acquisition in our experimental setting (see Fig. 2) we are basically interested in pressure forces, acquired from the vehicle seat. In favour we used force sensor arrays (FSA), interconnected to a notebook computer via USB interface. The utilized sitting posture system is robust, universal (it could be used in any type of car for arbitrary style of sitting or driving) and needs no active participation of the driver. To increase system stability and performance, additional sensors (as described in paragraph 4.1 below) are taken into consideration.

For data acquisition, the "FSA Dual High Resolution System" from Vistamedical[5] has been adopted. It allows for recording of the loads on a thin flexible sensor-mat, consisting of piezoresistive sensors. The matrix provided by the $1,09mm$ thick mats is formed by 32 rows and 32 columns of sensors, each covering a range of 0 to $26,67kPa$[6], and measuring an entire area of $430 * 430mm^2$ (our tests have shown, that this size is almost sufficient, only exceptionally heavy persons exceed the area). Each of the 1.024 sensors covers an area of $7.94mm^2$, the inter-sensor distance is $5.74mm$ [17]. The sampling/update rate of the two mats is generally below 1 second each (although sometimes connection errors lead to a slight delay).

Software Portion: The FSA-system is shipped with a software package for recording sensor data to a file system, but it is not suited for direct integration into the evaluation environment. In order to adapt to the specific needs of the experiments, a data collection and evaluation application had to be implemented on top of this system. Communication with the data collection box is established through the OLE[7] components included in the FSA software package. For that we had to extend the open source OLE framework included in the

[4] Controller Area Network is a communication system, originally developed by Intel Corporation and Robert Bosch GmbH, for connecting electronic control units in vehicles, URL: `http://en.wikipedia.org/wiki/Controller_Area_Network`, visited Nov. 27, 2007.

[5] Vista Medical Europe, URL: `http://www.vistamedical.nl`, visited Oct. 2, 2007

[6] Technical description of the mat system indicates a range from 0 to 200 mm_{Hg}. Since kPa is a more proper SI unit, all $Torr$ or mm_{Hg} values are conversed.

[7] Object Linking and Embedding is a distributed object system and protocol by Microsoft.

Eclipse[8]/SWT[9] packages. Acquisition of data from additional sensors has been partly integrated into that application, but most of them were collected from modified individual software components. All of them were time-synchronized one against the others (accelerometer and OBD recording software had been extended to store an extra timestamp in their data files, all other sensors came with a dedicated timestamp-field in their datafile format).

Reference Weight: For the analysis of the correlation between body posture and cruising speed it is necessary to determine the driver's weight inside the car (or on the driver's seat respectively). After pressure mat calibration we applied a reference weight to it: One person with given weight was placed onto the seat and 100 consecutive readings from the mat have been performed. The mean value of the accumulated pressures has been set as reference factor for further weight estimations as shown in equations (1) and (2).

$$\overline{pressure} = \frac{1}{100} \sum_{j=1}^{100} \sum_{i=1}^{1024} sensor_i \tag{1}$$

$$factor_{pressure} = \frac{weight_{real}}{\overline{pressure}} = \frac{74.80kg}{176.589} = 0.4235 \tag{2}$$

Nevertheless, the weight of a test subject could not be exactly calculated from the sum of weights of all charged individual sensors by reason of unbalanced load sharing and "dead space" between the sensors.

4 Evaluation with Experienced Drivers

4.1 Experimental Testbed

Restriction "Turns": In common road traffic we can distinguish between a number of different types of turns, e.g. right-angled streets or crossings, freeway entrance and exit ramps, U-turns, banked corners or "normal" curves. In this work we are focussed on driving situations while cornering left or right in curves with different radii. As for experimental evaluation, a field study was conducted in the driving safety center "Wachauring" near Krems, Austria[10] on a specified race course with a length of about 1,150 meters. Beside pressure values from the two force sensor mats (as described above in section 3) we used a number of additional sensors to get a reliable measurement environment. This gives us the opportunity for meaningful interpretations.

(i) An OBD-interface was used to acquire the following vehicle-specific data: Cruising speed (km/h), Engine RPM (rpm), Engine Load (%), Throttle

[8] Eclipse is an open-source, platform-independent software framework

[9] The Standard Widget Toolkit (SWT) is a graphical toolkit for the Java platform.

[10] URL: `http://www.oeamtc.at/netautor/pages/resshp/anwendg/1104290.html#`, visited Sept. 24, 2007.

Fig. 2. Experimental Setting on the "Wachauring" near Krems, Austria

Position (%), Coolant Temperature (°C), Intake Air Temperature (°C), Air Flow (gm/sec.), and a number of motor-specific data (fuel trim, various sensor voltages, etc.). For the actual experiment we examined only vehicle speed as relevant parameter.

(ii) A wireless 3-point ECG device "Heartman 301" from Heartbalance AG[11] was used to record driver's vital data (heart frequency, heart rate variability, etc.). (The results analyzing the influence of a users vital data and our findings coming from the respective ECG pattern analysis are reported elsewhere.)

(iii) A GPS receiver XGPS BT-929 with SiRF Star III chipset, mounted nearby the rear window, was used to get precise vehicle positions. GPS time field was consulted as external synchronization basis.

(iv) Acceleration and centrifugal forces were acquired with inertiacube high-precision accelerometers[12], placed on each axis of the vehicle.

(v) Videostreams from three Sony DCR-HC96E camcorders were used for visual examination of results.

The test-drivers involved in the experiments are very renowned and championship winning rallye drivers (Max Lampelmaier and Hannes Danzinger). They received instructions from the research groups staff, and were fully aware about the purpose of the experiments.

4.2 Gathering Data from On-Board Sensors

Data from different types of sensors had been recorded including timestamps for synchronization purposes. In a preprocessing step, data in different sensor

[11] Heartbalance AG, URL: `http://www.heartbalance.com/`, visited Sept. 30, 2007.

[12] Inertiacube3 from Intersense, URL: `http://www.isense.com/products.aspx?id=44&`, visited Sept. 30, 2007.

Table 1. Tabular specification of features

Time	FSA11	FSA12	...	FSA44	Accelerometer1			v	GPS ϕ	GPS λ
ms	kPa	kPa	...	kPa	x	y	z	km/h	GRD	GRD
540,687	5.444	19.144	...	0.000	-2.195	7.427	-3.456	118.648	1,519.736	4,812.780
540,890	5.420	19.026	...	0.004	-1.698	9.657	-0.201	119.528	1,519.739	4,812.781
541,109	10.086	24.365	...	0.004	-1.466	8.422	0.101	120.477	1,519.472	4,812.782
541,640	12.104	28.130	...	0.020	-0.368	8.729	3.824	122.778	1,519.778	4,812.786
541,828	12.081	28.277	...	0.000	-3.925	8.606	-3.213	123.593	1,519.751	4,812.786
...	...	...	...	...	...	...	...	...	...	...

records were time-aligned and filtered to meet the formats of the statistical analysis toolset.

The following list indicates the table-structure of all utilized characteristics used in the actual experiment (Measurement unit in brackets): (i) Time (ms), (ii) to (xvii) FSA11, FSA12, ..., FSA44 (kPa), (xviii) to (xx) Accelerometer-data in x, y, and z (m/s^2), (xxi) cruising speed (km/h), (xxii) GPS data latitude ϕ (GRD) and (xxiii) GPS data longitude λ (GRD). Table 1 shows five data sets out of the entire data table of 3,786 rows as presented in Fig. 7.

Accelerometer: Intersense accelerometers provide data at a high resolution of 180hz. The car itself acts as reference coordinate system, consequently all accelerometer-readings (which came in x, y, and z) had to be normalized against the vehicle coordinate system (x-coordinate is in vehicles direction of motion, y is oriented in the right angle of x, z face upwards). For our calculations, only the one accelerometer mounted on the left, front of the car has been utilized.

The normalized data stream from the accelerometer is synchronized against mat data, acquired at a maximum of 10Hz, and then smoothed with a ramp function. The new value for a_{i_ramp} is calculated from the original value a_i and the 8 sensor values aside this reading. Perhaps, using a gauss bell-shaped function instead of the actual used one, could improve results.

$$a_{i\_ramp} = \frac{0,2 \times a_{i-4} + 0,4 \times a_{i-3} + 0,6 \times a_{i-2} + 0,8 \times a_{i-1}}{5} + \frac{a_i}{5} + \frac{0,8 \times a_{i+1} + 0,6 \times a_{i+2} + 0,4 \times a_{i+3} + 0,2 \times a_{i+4}}{5} \quad (3)$$

Pressure Mats: FSA11, FSA12, FSA13, ..., FSA44 indicate the fragments of pressure-regions from the pressure mat (see Fig. 3) to give an estimation for the direction of leaning. Each value stands for the sum of 64 sensor values in the specified region. In the presented experiment two vertical regions *left* and *right* (e.g. *left* as combination of the 8 left squares indicated by the dashed rectangle in Fig. 3) had been distinguished.

Ideally, disjunction between the regions *left* and *right* should not be exactly at the middle of the mat, but at the midpoint between the pelvic bones. But previous tests showed, that there is almost no difference between the absolute middle of the mat and the midpoint calculated from the pelvic bones – therefore exact calculation of regions based on pelvic bones had been ignored in the current test.

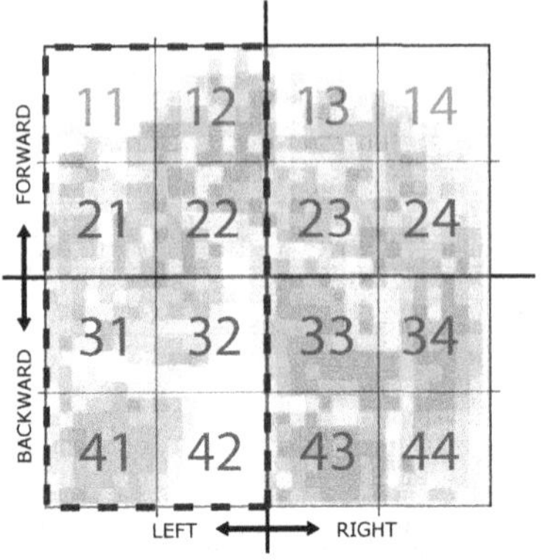

Fig. 3. Fragmentation of pressure mat to indicate direction of leaning

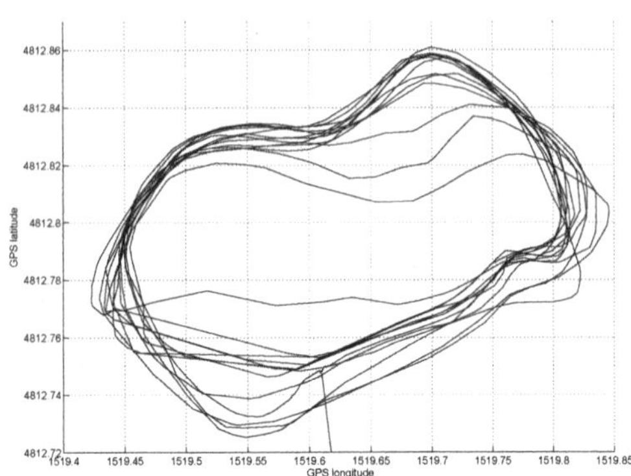

Fig. 4. GPS trace of a test run on the "Wachau-ring"

Since the mat sensors are intended to reason about the various "leaning" postures, we define *lean left* as a deviation from the initial symmetric pressure distribution (indicating an up-right sitting position of the driver). Analogously, *lean right* is a deviation of the sitting pressure distribution towards the right. (Formally, *left* and *right* are with respect to the vehicles direction of motion (x-axis). If the (dynamically evaluated) total pressure on the *left* side of the mat is higher than the pressure on the *right* side ($pressure(right) - pressure(left) \in [-50, 0[$), this stands for an inclination of the driver to the *left*), and vice versa (thus, $pressure(right) - pressure(left) \in]0, 50]$ means an inclination to the *right*).)

Speed sensor: Vehicle speed has been acquired via OBD-interface[13]. Due to rather poor update rate of this sensor – values are delivered only all 4 to 6 seconds –, speed is lineary interpolated between 2 readings.

GPS sensor: Fig. 4 shows the GPS trace of one test run. The direction of driving on the course was counter-clockwise, implicating 4 left-curves and a slight "s-shaped" turn in one lap. Each has a length of about 1,150 meters and a lap-time of $\approx$ 38 seconds (and therefore average speed of $\approx 108 km/h$). Test runs (as well as recordings) started at the service garage. The straight line, starting from the bottom of the diagram, indicates the initial transfer to the route.

5 Results

The results from some of the experiments are presented in the plots from Fig. 5 to Fig. 10. The plots basically contain three variables: acceleration force (acc_y) in the range $[-20, 40] m/s^2$, vehicle speed (v) in the range $[0, 125] km/h$ and

[13] OBD ElmScan5 USB with ELM327 chipset, URL: `http://allobd.com/proddetail.asp?prod=ST-DElmScan5_usb`, visited 27. Sept. 2007.

mat pressure on the left or right side of the mat (direction of inclination) (pr_{right_norm}) in the range $[-50, 50]$. A wide solid line illustrate the acceleration force, a small dotted line stands for the vehicle speed, and a small solid line represents the normalized pressure on the mat. (Acceleration force can also be interpreted as steering ratio.)

The findings from the experimental data can be summarized as follows:

(i) Fig. 5 shows a short experiment of approx. 300 seconds (or 5 minutes). The first 120 seconds were used for driver enrolment. After that the vehicle began to move to the test track where the test run started. The experiment stopped after finishing 3 laps. Acceleration force $\neq 0$ was recognized in periods where the vehicle moves. In parking positions, driver's normalized pressure indicates inclining to the right, probably influenced by a talk with the co-passenger.

(ii) Fig. 6 shows interesting features for a more elaborate test run. The additional vertical solid lines indicate recurrence of laps (12 laps could be identified). Lap time is almost constant, at least for the last 7 laps, which is a qualitative indicator for an experienced driver on the race course.

(iii) Fig. 7 is a magnification of Fig. 6 by factor 4 to allow for a better interpretation. It shows nearly 4 complete laps of the experiment. Lap time varies between $38,046ms$ and $39,766ms$ (the variance is small which refers to a professional driver, as already mentioned above).

(iv) Fig. 8 shows approx. 10 minutes of an experiment, considering only passages with vehicle-speed below the break-even speed v_{BE}. The weight-dependent value for the current driver (with weight (w_D)) therefore had to be found. In this experiment with race-driver Hannes Danzinger we calculated this value as beeing $\approx 75km/h$. (The euclidean distance between acceleration force and normalized mat pressure is smallest at this speed. Evaluations has been done for speed values from 0 to 120 km/h in steps of 1 km/h).
Of course, relationship of leaning and driving also depends on the geometry of the curve. Lower speeds at a tight turn could probably directs to the same result than high-speed driving in a wider turn or in a banked curve. In future experiments, break-even speed v_{BE} needs to be dynamically actualized according to the curve parameters.
For low-speed cruising below v_{BE} we can identify a inverse correlation between acceleration force and mat pressure (respective body pressure). Furthermore, we can see that the values for acceleration force are mostly below zero – this means that this turns are left-ones. Because they are driven at low-speed, the consequence is, that all of this turns are sharp-edged ones. In contrast p_{right_norm} is frequently above zero, an indicator for driver's direction of inclination toward right.

(v) Contrasting the observations from Fig. 8, Fig. 9 shows the interrelationship between acceleration force and body postures only during high-speed driving sections, Fig. 10 is a magnification of Fig. 9 by approximately a factor of 10 and can be interpreted as follows: Cornering here shows significant

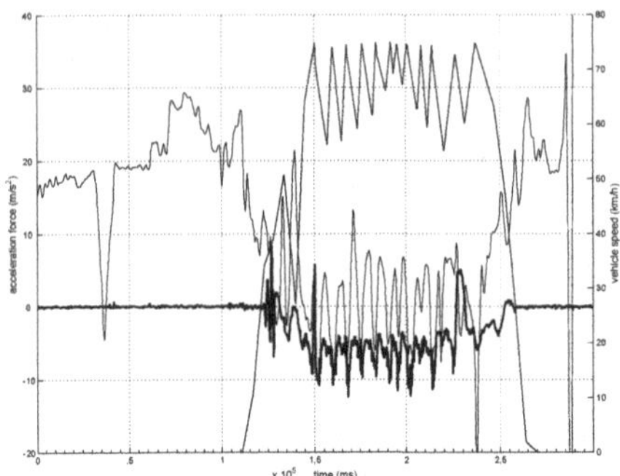

Fig. 5. Recorded body movements on the seat mat at the first minutes of the experiment (vehicle starts to move after 120 seconds)

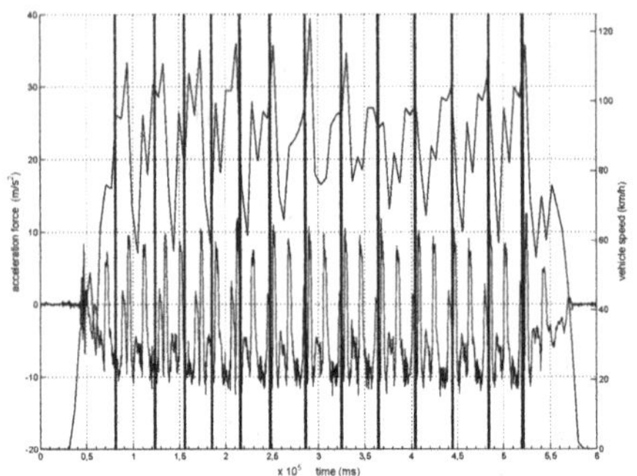

Fig. 6. A whole test run (vertical solid lines show recurrence of laps). Constant lap time (at least from the 5th lap) is an indicator for an experienced driver.

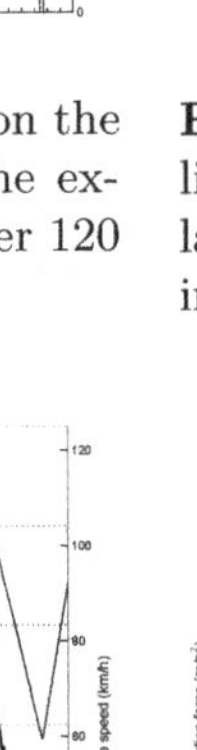

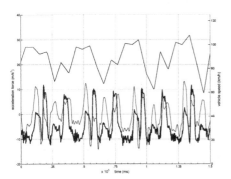

Fig. 7. Apparent resemblance of acceleration force and body posture for ≈4 laps, or 2.5 minutes

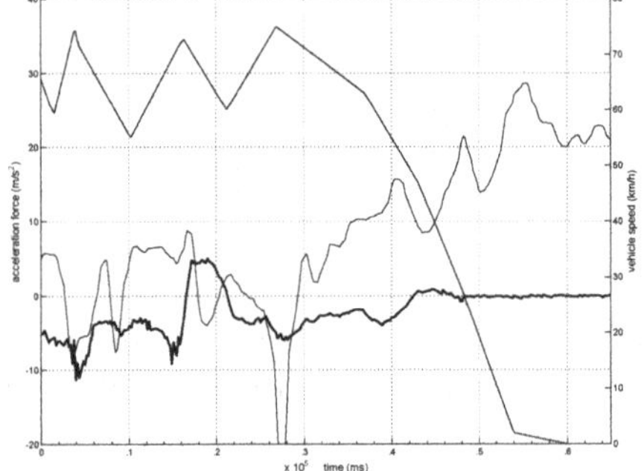

Fig. 8. Inverse correlation between acceleration force and persons bearing on low-speed cruising below v_{BE} ($75km/h$)

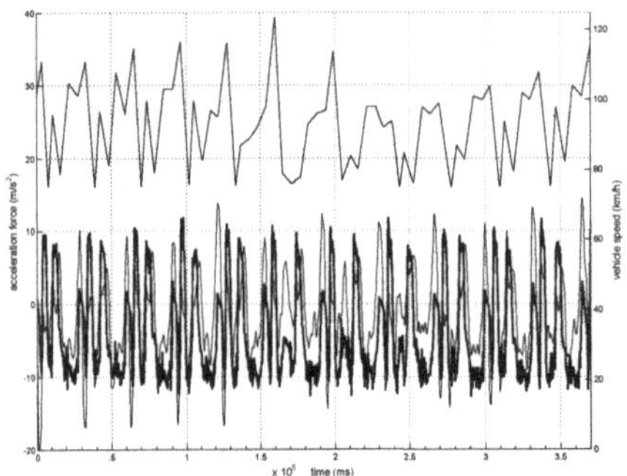

Fig. 9. High correlation of acceleration force and body posture while driving with high speed (above $75km/h$)

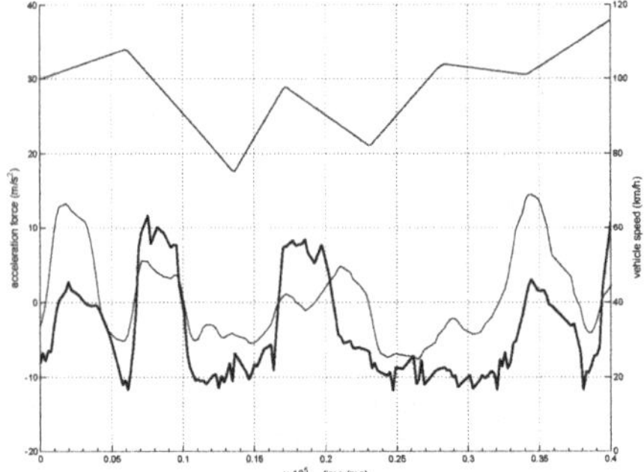

Fig. 10. Detail view of an arbitrary 40 seconds clipping of Fig. 9. shows the congruence between steering ratio and body posture

correlation between vehicles acceleration force and persons sitting attitude. Shape and peaks of the variables acc_y and pr_{right_norm} are similar.

6 Conclusions

In this paper we attempted at the hypotheses that a driver's readiness to compensate lateral acceleration when cornering correlates with the driving speed. To reason upon this hypotheses, we have developed an experimental sitting posture recognition testbed: a real-time data acquisition system in a car and a off-line evaluation environment. Experiments were conducted and preliminary evaluations confirmed our research hypothesis: Low speed cornering is attempted with moderate readiness to compensate centripetal force (see Fig. 8), while high speed cornering leads to a increased readiness to compensate lateral forces (see Fig. 9, 10).

The discovered correlation between steering ratio and body posture opens up the opportunity for a number of intelligent vehicle control add-ons. Amongst others, we identify the following:

(i) **Adaptive steering angle when cornering:** Similar in design to the AFS (Adaptive Frontlight System) we can think of an adaptive, intelligent steering wheel with the objective to provide the driver with the best possible steering behaviour by varying the influence of the steering ratio depending on context, like for example vehicle speed and the driver's readiness to compensate lateral forces.

(ii) **Adaptive chassis frame:** Adjust the chassis configuration from soft to tough suspension, according to driver's body postures on the mats. In a car race, body postures while cornering are completely different from postures exhibited during a family trip, even if the other parameters (steering ratio, curve radius, vehicle speed) are equal.

(iii) **Prevent wheels from spinning when accelerating or cornering (TCS):** Traction control systems are systems designed to prevent from loss of traction. Body postures could affect a new generation of traction control systems adhering to excessive postures like frequent left/right inclining. Hard steering maneuvers could proactively control the TCS in order to improve prevention from losing traction.

(iv) **Prevent wheels from blocking/locking (ABS/ESC):** Anti-lock braking systems prevent wheels from locking while braking in order to improve on maintaining steering control. Electronic stability control (ESC) is one step beyond ABS and contains additional sensors (steering-wheel angle sensor, gyroscope) to prevent the car from over-steering or under-steering. Again, deriving action or maneuver intent from the driver's body posture could improve on the performance of these systems by just giving them information way before the action is induced. The vehicle could already learn about potential hazards the driver is facing, but not explicitly expressing via the vehicle instruments (brake, steering wheel).

Finally, beyond intelligent vehicle handling, our preliminary results encourage to investigate on new modalities in driver-to-car and car-to-roadside interaction as well as for improvements of driver assistance systems (enhanced steering precision, reduced or avoided over- or under-steering, proactively notifications of electronic stability control, etc.).

As the next steps in the line of our investigations we aim at validating the existence of a break-even speed v_{BE} with further test runs involving different drivers, different driving situations, different types of vehicles, and different driving purposes. In particular are we interested in an evaluation of the influence of driving experience (e.g. newly licenced driver, professional driver, race driver, etc.) on both, break-even speed and body postures.

Acknowledgements. We would like to acknowledge the valuable help and support by Max Lampelmaier and Hannes Danzinger, both professional championship winning race drivers, for their serving as test-persons in all our experiments, and for the proliferation of a rich body of knowledge from professional race driving.

References

1. Cheng, S.Y., Trivedi, M.M.: Turn-intent analysis using body pose for intelligent driver assistance. IEEE Pervasive Computing 5(4), 28–37 (2006)
2. Graham, R., Carter, C.: Comparison of speech input and manual control of in-car devices while on the move. Personal and Ubiquitous Computing 4(2/3) (2000)
3. McCallum, M., et al.: Speech recognition and in-vehicle telematics devices: Potential reductions in driver distraction. International Journal of Speech Technology 7(1), 25–33 (2004)
4. Stallkamp, J., et al.: Video-based driver identification using local appearance face recognition. In: Workshop on DSP in Mobile and Vehicular Systems, Istanbul, Turkey, Interactive Systems Labs, Department of Computer Science, TU Karlsruhe, Germany, p. 4 (June 2007)
5. McCall, J., Trivedi, M.M.: Driver Monitoring for a Human-Centered Driver Assistance System. In: HCM 2006: Proceedings of the 1st ACM international workshop on Human-centered multimedia, pp. 115–122. ACM Press, New York (2006)
6. Erzin, E., et al.: Multimodal person recognition for human-vehicle interaction. IEEE MultiMedia 13(2), 18–31 (2006)
7. Oliver, N., Pentland, A.: Graphical models for driver behavior recognition in a smartcar. In: Proceedings of the IEEE Intelligent Vehicles Symposium, pp. 7–12 (October 3–5, 2000)
8. Oliver, N., Pentland, A.P.: Driver behavior recognition and prediction in a smartcar (2000)
9. Cheng, S.Y., Park, S., Trivedi, M.M.: Multiperspective thermal ir and video arrays for 3d body tracking and driver activity analysis. In: CVPR 2005: Proceedings of the 2005 IEEE Computer Society Conference on Computer Vision and Pattern Recognition (CVPR 2005) - Workshops, p. 3. IEEE Computer Society Press, Washington (2005)
10. Trivedi, M.M., Gandhi, T., McCall, J.: Looking-in and looking-out of a vehicle: Computer-vision-based enhanced vehicle safety. IEEE Transactions on Intelligent Transportation Systems 8(1), 108–120 (2007)

11. Veeraraghavan, H., et al.: Driver activity monitoring through supervised and unsupervised learning. In: Intelligent Transportation Systems, 2005. Proceedings, pp. 580–585. IEEE, Los Alamitos (2005)
12. Trivedi, M.: Occupant posture analysis with stereo and thermal infrared video: Algorithms and experimental evaluation (2003)
13. Moeslund, T.: Computer vision-based human motion capture – a survey (1999)
14. Moeslund, T.B., Granum, E.: A survey of computer vision-based human motion capture. Computer Vision and Image Understanding: CVIU 81(3), 231–268 (2001)
15. McCall, J.C., Trivedi, M.M.: Human Behavior Based Predictive Brake Assistance. In: Intelligent Vehicles Symposium, pp. 8–12. IEEE, Los Alamitos (2006)
16. Park, S., Trivedi, M.: Driver activity analysis for intelligent vehicles: Issues and development framework (2004)
17. Hermkens, J.: Tools for Professionals: FSA documentation. Vista Medical Europe B.V., Industrieterrein 40, NL-5981 AK Panningen, The Netherlands (August 02, 2006)

Part III

Network Processors and Memory Management

A Hardware Packet Re-Sequencer Unit for Network Processors

Michael Meitinger, Rainer Ohlendorf, Thomas Wild, and Andreas Herkersdorf

Technische Universität München, Arcisstraße 21
80290 Munich, Germany
michael.meitinger@tum.de

Abstract. Network Processors (NP) usually are designed as multi-processor systems with parallel packet processing. This parallelism may lead to flows with packets out-of-order when leaving the NP system. But packet reordering has a bad impact on network performance, especially when using the dominating TCP protocol. In this paper, we describe a Hardware Re-Sequencer Unit for Network Processors. Incoming packets will be tagged in the ingress path, preserving the packet order with flow granularity. An Aggregation Unit reorders the packet flows in the egress path if needed. In contrast to most other solutions the way of the packet through the NP system is dispensable, which enlarges design freedom in terms of e.g. load balancing. After explaining the general concept, a SystemC model is presented. Simulation results are used for dimensioning and a proof of concept with real traffic traces. General aspects concerning the implementation are discussed.

1 Introduction

In modern networks line speeds are growing and with it also the processing power needed for packet processing. Among all possible solutions Network Processors promise the best tradeoff between performance and flexibility. To handle the processing load all commercial Network Processors pursue a multi-core solution [1] for parallel packet processing.

Additionally, the processors (sometimes called microengines or processing engines (PE)) often support multithreading. This optimizes the resource utilization since a PE can continue working on another packet while waiting for memory or coprocessor access replies, for example. So if no special scheduling mechanisms are used, the packets can get allocated to different threads in different PEs. Since processing times can differ due to different resource access times, the packet order cannot be guaranteed.

But packet reordering can have a great impact on the overall network performance. Here, packet reordering means that packets of a flow are out-of-order. A flow, in turn, is defined by its IP 5-tuple (IP source and destination address, source and destination port number and transport layer protocol number). Especially the dominating TCP protocol is sensitive to packet reordering. If packets are out-of-order, this may lead to retransmission since late packets may be seen as being lost. Measurements on an IXP2400 [2] have shown, that the retransmission rate in a 10-hop network due to

U. Brinkschulte et al. (Eds.): ARCS 2008, LNCS 4934, pp. 85–97, 2008.

packet reordering is 10% and more if there are no order ensuring mechanisms. This can result in a significant network performance reduction of up to 60% in packet throughput [3].

There are several attempts to reduce packet reordering as far as possible. The most usual approaches are described in detail in the next chapter. The rest of the paper is structured as follows: in chapter 3 we present the general concept of our Hardware Re-Sequencer Unit. In chapter 4 our SystemC model is introduced and simulation results are presented. In chapter 5 we discuss some implementation aspects before concluding our work.

2 Related Work

As described before, packet reordering may be a problem for network performance. Although it is not mandatory to guarantee flow-based packet order in IP based Ethernet networks, it can be crucial for service quality.

Basically there are two different approaches. Most implementations try to guarantee packet order by using an appropriate scheduling mechanism. Every packet of a flow is processed by the same PE. Since there is no parallel processing within this flow, there is no possibility for packet reordering. The flows still must be distributed among the different available PEs. This is usually done by calculating a hash value based on the IP 5-tuple. The calculated hash value can be directly used as an index for the PE that should be used. Results have shown that using a CRC16 produces a very well balanced distribution of flows on the possible numerical range [4]. Nevertheless, since there are typically many flows with low activity and some flows with very high activity, the PE load may be unbalanced, resulting in an inefficient use of processing power. Therefore if some very active flows are aggregated an overload situation for a single PE may occur.

To prevent this situation, Dittmann [5] uses a dynamic configuration. Instead of using a small hash value directly as a static PE index, a larger hash value is used as an ID which is associated to a PE by a lookup table. The association between ID (representing a flow bundle with the same hash value) and PE now can be changed by dynamically changing the table entry. Newly activated IDs (i.e. IDs that have been inactive for some time) are mapped to the PE with the smallest queue at the moment. But flow bundles are also switched in overload situations which may lead to packet reordering. This drawback is accepted for the benefit of performance.

Shi [6] reduces this drawback by not shifting flow bundles randomly between PEs, but by identifying very active flow bundles with high packet rates. It is argued that much less flows must be shifted since the effect on the PE load for the highly active bundle is much greater now. The effect of packet reordering is therefore also lower, albeit still possible.

Nevertheless, in all schemes the granularity of load balancing depends on the activity of single flows. In some cases this will lead to an inefficient load distribution among all available PEs. Especially the bulk of non state-dependent packets (e.g. only IP forwarding) can be sprayed on all PEs for an optimal load balancing. That is why Wu [7] reconstructs the packet order per flow after spraying the packets on all available threads by a dispatcher for processing. A Content Addressable Memory (CAM) stores all active flows. When a packet arrives it is first checked if there are already packets of that flow in the system or if a new CAM entry has to be created. A second memory structure organizes the associated waiting queue by creating a centralized linked list recording the original flow sequence. Flags indicate if a packet has already been processed (set by the thread that is processing the packet) and if it is the first packet in the linked list of a flow, i.e. the first packet that should be sent out after processing. An egress scheduler checks all the packet entries for packets that can be transmitted in a round robin manner. When all packets of one flow have left the system, the CAM entry is deleted again. The use of the CAM enables a true flow solution without any hash value and resulting collisions. Nevertheless the number of total packets that can be managed at the same time is limited to the number of threads on the PEs and the threads are blocked as long as the processed packets are waiting for transmission.

3 Resequencing Concept

In our concept we want to combine the advantages of both basic approaches (scheduling and re-sequencing). Basically we are following the same approach as Wu [7] with the packets being re-sequenced after processing, enabling to spray packets of a flow among multiple PEs. Nevertheless in contrast to Wu [7] we are able to combine our approach with an additional scheduler to keep the ability for a dedicated scheduling of certain classes of packets. Additionally, we overcome basic drawbacks of [7], mainly the inefficient and limiting central management of all packets and the usage of a CAM which may be resource-intensive, especially for a high number of flows in the system at the same time. That is why we split our approach in two independent hardware entities as shown in Figure 1:

- An Ingress Tagger calculating an ID by hashing the IP 5-tuple and assigning a consecutive sequence number per ID, storing the input order of a packet flow bundle.
- An Aggregation Unit, checking the packet sequence. Out-of-order packets are stored in a buffer memory and re-sorted before transmission.

Since the re-sequencing information (ID and sequence number) is traveling with the packet through the system (for example as an additional header in front of the packet) there is no need for a centralized management. Additionally, we are hardly limited by

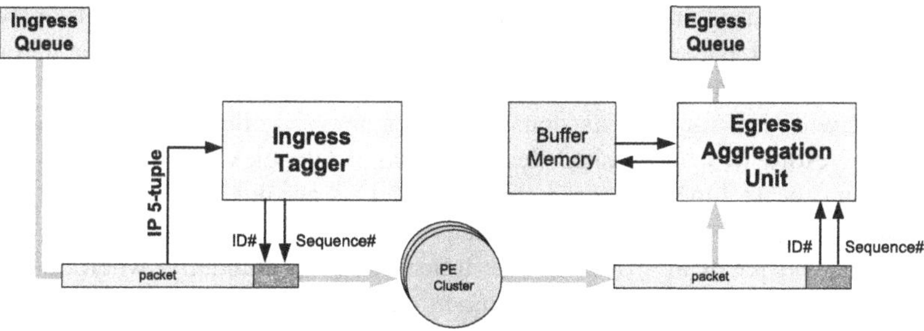

Fig. 1. Packet Re-sequencer Unit in a NP system

a maximum number of packets that are in the system at the same time. The only critical factor is the size of the buffer memory connected to the Aggregation Unit which depends on the degree of packet reordering. This will be examined using our SystemC model, presented in the next chapter.

By using a hash-based approach we can prevent the need of the resource-intensive CAM. Instead, we make use of conventional and comparatively cheap SRAM for flow information storage.

3.1 Ingress Tagger

The Ingress Tagger creates a flow ID and a sequence number for each incoming packet (see Figure 2a). The flow ID is calculated using a hash function on the IP 5-tuple. Each hash function that will distribute all possible flows evenly over the available hash value range is suitable. For every ID a counter stores the actual sequence number which is incremented when an associated packet arrives. The ID (hash value) and sequence number (counter value) is added to the IP packet. In our FlexPath NP system [8] this information is kept in a packet descriptor, a packet tag traveling through the system that contains packet information like the packet data memory pointer. Depending on the current system implementation, this information could generally also be added as an additional internal header in front of the packet.

The width of the hash value may be adapted on the particular system and requirements. On the one hand, the more bits are used for the flow ID, the more counters are needed, as the number of counters is the power of two of the bit width. On the other hand the probability of a collision of active flows on the same hash value is rising with a smaller hash bit width. The effects of these collisions are investigated using the SystemC model in the next chapter.

3.2 Egress Aggregation Unit and Buffer Memory

The Aggregation Unit as the counterpart of the Tagger is placed in the egress path and working in a similar way. Again there is a counter for each ID indicating the next sequence number to be transmitted (see Figure 2b). Based on this sequence number, the Aggregator decides on each packet arrival if it is really the next packet that should be sent out. Out-of-order packets must be stored in the buffer memory until all missing packets have passed.

This strategy is sufficient as long as (i) the buffer memory can hold enough packets for complete reordering and (ii) no packets are being lost within the PE cluster, which may be the case if packets are discarded due to IP checksum errors or a routing lookup miss. Since these packets already have passed the Ingress Tagger, the Aggregation Unit will wait for packets that will never arrive. Following packets with the same ID therefore will be blocked, leading to high latencies and a growing buffer. We thus want to use timers to make sure that packets are not waiting too long in the buffer. After a certain time, a packet that is still missing is defined as lost and all packets in the buffer of this flow will be transmitted. Additionally, when reaching a certain queue size, a missing packet is again defined to be lost, making sure that a queue of a very active flow is not getting too big.

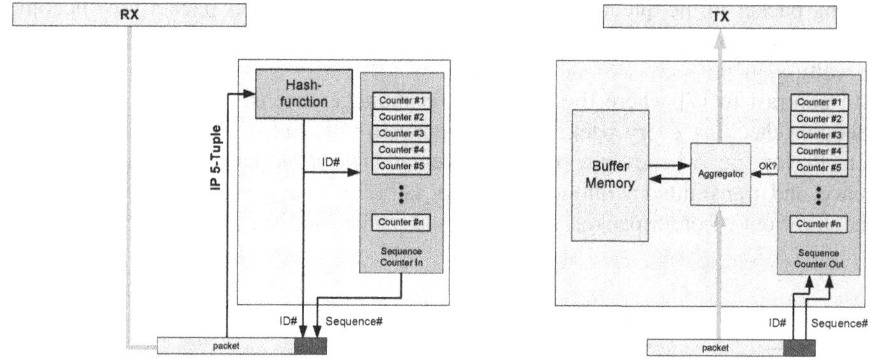

Fig. 2. Ingress Tagger (a) and Aggregation Unit block diagram

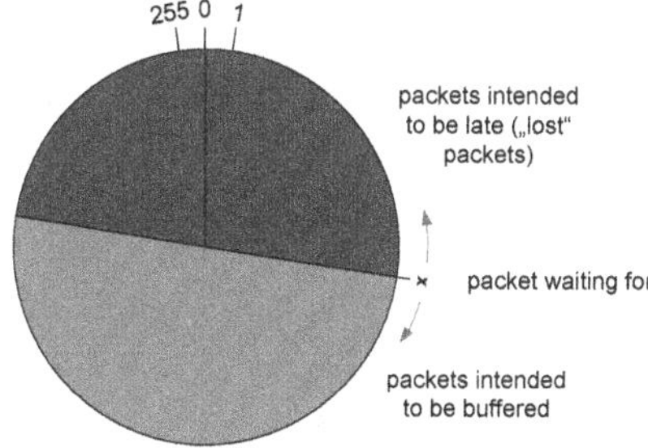

Fig. 3. Sequence number wrap-around and late packet definition (8 bit example)

Care must be taken of packets arriving after being classified as lost. Since the sequence number is wrapping-around after its highest value these packets might be seen as future packets and not as ones that already should have passed. A solution is to separate the sequence number range in two halves, separated by the next expected sequence number. Packets with a sequence number lower than the expected one (upper half of the circle in Figure 3) will be seen to be late and will pass immediately. The other packets will be treated as out-of-order packets and buffered if needed. The sequence number range must be chosen large enough.

The buffer structure is a critical parameter in the system. It must be large enough to hold all packets for re-sequencing. Since we do not store the whole packet, but only the already mentioned packet descriptors in our FlexPath NP system [8], the size of one buffer cell can be limited to 128 bit per packet. The packet data itself stays in the NP's main memory. When the whole packet must be stored, buffer dimensioning is more critical because of the different packet sizes.

The queues may be arranged as ring buffers. Pointers can link a flow ID to one of the queues for re-sequencing (compare Figure 4a). When a packet with the expected sequence number arrives (e.g. ID#3, packet #4 in Figure 4a) at the aggregator, all consecutive and already present packets will be sent out after this packet (compare Figures 4a and b). The queue starting pointer of the ring buffer will be updated. Packet transmission stops either when the queue is transmitted completely or when a missing packet in the queue is reached (ID#3, packet #6). This packet now becomes the next expected packet and the following packet (packet #7) now is the new head of the waiting queue.

In contrast to [7] where the transmission management is done by a round robin scheduler checking every packet for transmission possibility, our approach is totally event driven, i.e. whenever a packet arrives at the egress path it is checked for sequence and transmitted without delay if possible. Management and storage is only needed for out-of-order packets and not for all packets in the system.

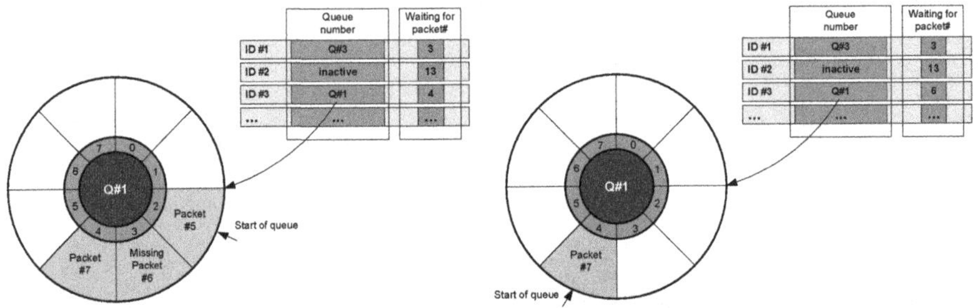

Fig. 4. Queuing example before (a) and after (b) transmission of packet #4 and #5

4 SystemC Simulations

4.1 Simulation Setup

For proof of concept and dimensioning issues, we have implemented a SystemC model of a simple Network Processor containing several processing units and our Packet Re-Sequencer Unit (see Figure 5).

For packet stimuli we use the pcap file format [9] which is a standard in packet capturing. Real pcap traffic traces are available for download [10][11][12], recorded for example on an internet backbone router, but packet files can also be generated artificially. This enables a stimulation of our system with realistic and representative traffic.

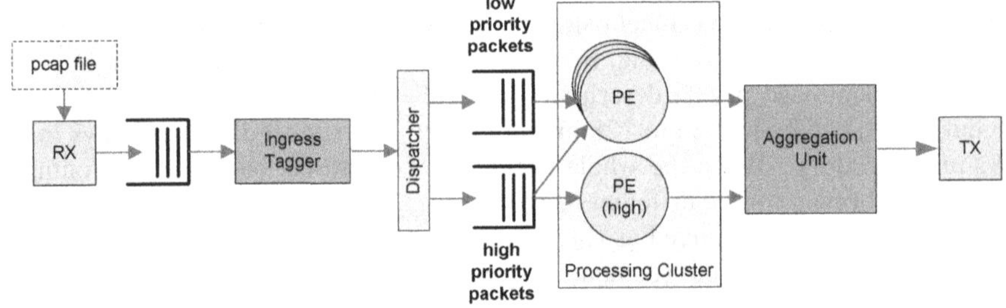

Fig. 5. SystemC simulation model

The pcap format contains packet data (often limited to the headers), packet information like packet size and a timestamp. Based on these timestamps and the packet data, the RX-module creates the packets and sends them to the system. A speedup factor enables a faster replay for higher data rates, if needed.

After the ingress queue the packets are marked by the Ingress Tagger. We calculate a 16 bit hash value based on the IP 5-tuple which can be reduced afterwards by cutting the most significant bits from the calculated hash value. The resulting bit width is defined by a special parameter. The hash function is a 16 bit sum up of the 5-tuple with a 3 bit shift after each summation. Measurements on a trace file have shown that this kind of hash value really creates a balanced distribution of the flows on the available hash values.

A dispatcher separates the high priority packets (IP Type of Service field > 0) from the low priority packets. Whereas the ingress queue may throw away packets if full, the following queues will give a backpressure if needed. So no packets can be lost by the queues after tagging. The low priority packets will then be processed by a PE cluster. For our simulations we have used 8 PEs with a random processing latency of 20-60 μs. The latency is saved for each flow, so that every packet of a flow has the same latency but with a random jitter of ±5%, representing random effects like memory accesses, bus load etc. About 5% of the flows have a higher latency of up to 112 μs based on the packet length. Additionally, there is one reserved PE for high priority packets. If this PE is still busy when another high priority packet arrives, it will be processed by the next free PE (high and low priority PEs). The processing time of the high priority packets is set to 20-60 μs again with a jitter of ±5%.

Due to the different processing times in the PE cluster packet reordering may occur. The packets are re-sequenced by the Aggregation Unit before transmission.

With this setup we try to represent a realistic NP with a throughput of approximately 1 Gbps (depending on the current random processing times).

4.2 Trace File

For the first simulations we have chosen a trace file of a 100 Mbps trans-pacific line with an average speed of 13.89 Mbps and a standard deviation of 1.10 M [10]. Overall the trace file has a record time of 15 minutes with about 3 million packets. Since the approximately 14 Mbps in average are not enough to stress our system, we have set the built-in speedup factor to 70. That raises our input data rate to 972 Mbps in average, whereas the simulated time is reduced to less than 13 seconds. This enlarges the processing load and thus the probability of packet reordering as a kind of worst case scenario. In fact, the peak data rates will exceed the Gigabit limit which leads to packet loss. This is not typical for a normal NP operation but stresses the conditions for dimensioning.

4.3 Simulation Results

Using this setup we have investigated the behavior of our system for different hash function bit widths.

In all cases the output throughput was about 906 Mbps, i.e. our PE cluster was at least temporarily in overload, leading to a packet loss rate of 9%.

In Figure 6 the collision rate is given depending on the hash bit width. A collision means that a packet is mapped to a hash value with at least one packet of a different flow but the same ID processed and managed by the Re-Sequencer Unit at the same time. A collision does not necessarily lead to a drawback by means of performance and latency although it may. Problems may arise if a flow with a short processing time and a flow with a long processing time collide. Because of the short processing time the packets of the first flow may overtake the other packets in the NP system. Because of the same ID the Re-Sequencer Unit will force all of these packets to leave the system in input order, leading to a needless delay and a higher resource usage because of the buffering. For 8 bit the collision rate is up to 4% and declines strongly with increasing bit width. For 12 bit it is already below 0.3% and for 16 bit the rate is approaching zero (0.01%).

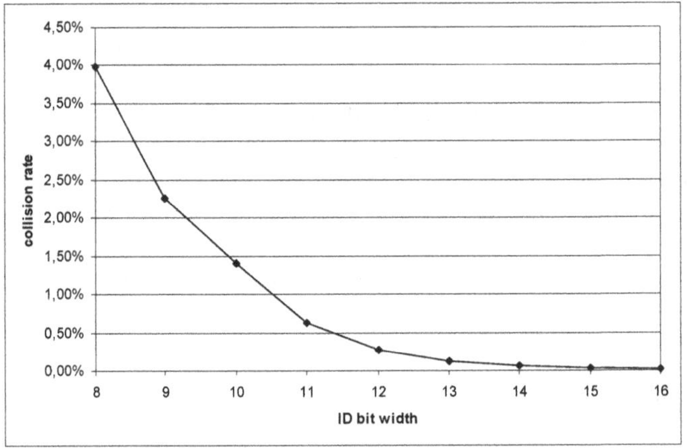

Fig. 6. Collision rate depending on ID bit width

To investigate the effect on the latency we measured the rate of packets stored temporarily in the egress path to get re-sequenced (see Figure 7). For wide hash values as seen before, the collision rate is practically equal to zero, so we have a constant packet part of 2.8% which is out-of-order after the PE cluster due to different processing times. Superimposed are the effects of collisions especially for lower bit widths, which raise this value up to 3.6% for 8 bit. The average Aggregation Unit buffer queuing delay for out-of-order packets rises from 10μs (16 bit) up to 11.8μs (8 bit). The maximum delay stays almost constant at 115μs for all cases.

Another interesting issue is the buffer size needed for re-sequencing. In all cases there were no more than 16 packets buffered in the egress path at the same time.

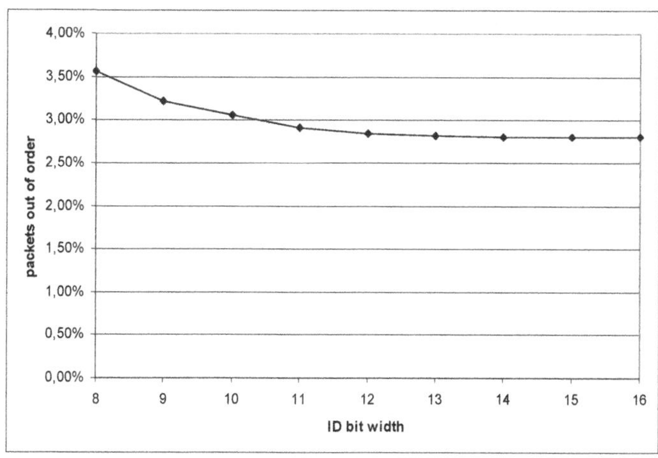

Fig. 7. Percentage of packets needed to be re-sequenced depending on ID bit width

When reducing the effect of collisions by using at least 11 bit hash values, no more than 10 packets were buffered to enable a complete re-sequencing.

On average, the effect of collisions seems to be negligible, at least for wide IDs. Nevertheless there are some cases where the latency of a single packet is important, especially with respect to Quality of Service (QoS). High priority packets might experience a large latency due to collisions. That is why we separated the high from the low priority packets by reserving one bit from the ID indicating a low or high priority packet. Now high priority flows can only collide with other high priority flows. As expected the collision rate for high priority packets is much lower since there are much less packets (see Figure 8). Only 1.8% of all packets have a high priority. For the low priority packets, things get a bit worse, since there is now one bit less for the hash function. Almost the same number of packets (98.2%) now must be spread among a smaller range. The collision rates are now quite the same when compared to the reference ID with one bit less, but the same hash size.

When investigating the number of out-of-order packets after processing (Figure 9), we see that the high priority packets are hardly affected by the hash value. The values are a bit lower (about 2.5%), mainly due to the usual in-sequence processing by one reserved PE. The low priority packets again suffer from the reduced hash value size.

The average buffer queuing delay for the low priority out-of-order packets again is comparable to those already measured with the same hash size and stabilizing for higher bit widths (12 bit and more) at 10µs in average. The high priority packets have a lower latency again due to their usually in-sequence processing. So the average delay for out-of-order packets is 7.6µs with a maximum of 54µs, both nearly stable for all bit widths. Again the buffer size needed is in the range of 10-15 packets.

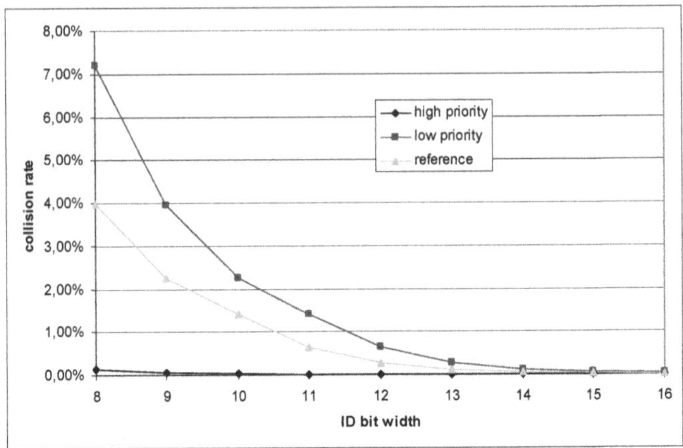

Fig. 8. Collision rate with priority bit

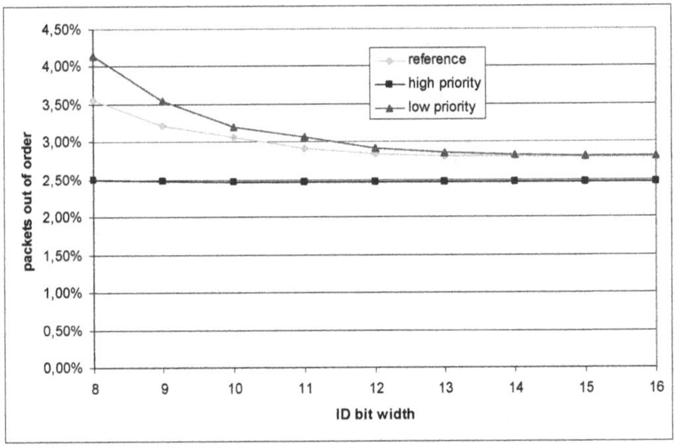

Fig. 9. Percentage of packets needed to be re-sequenced with priority bit

Based on the results a 12 bit flow ID with one bit reserved for low/high priority resolution seems to be a good solution. It is a good tradeoff between resource utilization and performance. The effects of collisions are very low to negligible. The next step now is to verify this design decision on a broader set of trace files. We have used some additional trace files and compared the results in Table 1. Besides a second trans-pacific link we have tested another oc-48 backbone node. Samples 4 and 5 derive from the University of North Carolina and contain the in- and outbound traffic of the university's border gateway to the internet. All samples had been scaled using the speedup factor to reach approximately gigabit speed on average.

All results assert the usefulness of our concept. For all simulations full packet re-sequencing can be sustained with a buffer size of no more than 12 cells.

Table 1. Simulation results for different traffic trace files (ID bit width 12, incl. priority bit)

Trace file	1	2	3	4	5
Source	[10]	[10]	[11]	[12]	[12]
Link	100 mbps	150 mbps	oc-48	oc-3	oc3
Type	Backbone	Backbone	Backbone	Border inbound	Border outbound
Orig. average data rate [Mbps]	13.89	118.07	121.31	19.26	30.54
Packets [million]	3.1	18.1	11.3	17.5	18.0
Orig. trace time [s]	900	900	300	3305	3308
Speedup factor	70	9	8	50	33
Sim. in data rate [Mbps]	972	1062	970	963	1008
Out data rate [Mbps]	906	1047	820	924	1007
Packet loss in PE Cluster[%]	9.3	1.8	14.4	4.6	0.05
coll. rate (low) [%]	0.62	0.45	0.73	0.58	0.42
coll. rate (high) [%]	0.002	0.006	0.038	0.21	0.20
Packets ooo after PE Cl. [%]	2.91	2.64	0.83	1.87	0.97
Max. buffer size (total)	10	12	12	12	9
Max. buffer size per queue	10	12	12	12	9
Max.# of active queues	3	4	3	5	4
Max.# of packets in System	28	25	29	27	27
Max.# of packets of one flow (ID) in System	19	20	18	17	20
Max.# of active flows in System	20	19	20	21	21

5 Implementation

At the moment, the implementation on a FPGA development board is in progress. Based on the simulation results, we have chosen a 12 Bit ID with 1 bit priority field. We are using an 8-bit sequence number. Since the simulations showed no more than 20 packets of one ID in the system at the same time (compare table 1), this gives a more than comfortable security margin to prevent problems due to wrap-around effects. By this decision it should be always possible to decide if a packet with a given sequence number is a still missing packet or a future packet. For the given bit widths we need a total of 8 KB on-board SRAM to store the counter values of ingress and egress part.

As the number of flows that has to be re-sequenced at the same time is limited to 5 in the simulations (see Table 1) we have decided to implement 8 re-sequencing queues with a maximum buffer length of 32 entries, based on the maximum simulated queue size of 12 entries per flow with a comfortable security margin. Since the memory usage of 8x32x128bit = 4 KB on-board SRAM is quite low, we have decided to use static queues instead of dynamic ones organized with a linked list. The management overhead for dynamic queues seems to be too high in this case. Nevertheless for different application scenarios with more and/or larger queue sizes, this may also be an option.

Again this shows the advantage of our concept compared to [7]. Since the percentage of out-of-order packets is small, most flows are still in sequence when leaving the PE cluster. Re-sequencing queues are only needed for flows with out-of-order packets, which was limited to 5 in the simulations. In a CAM solution an entry for every active flow in the PE cluster (maximum of 21 in the simulations) is needed. Every entry must have 104 bit, which is the size of the IP 5-tuple. So, in our concept the dimensioning is only influenced by the percentage of out-of-order packets. In [7] it is dominated by the number of flows in the system, even when in-order. This usually correlates with the number of packets. That means that for larger systems with more PEs, hardware accelerators etc., our approach should also scale better.

Despite the fact that the simulation results are very encouraging, it cannot be made sure, that in a worst case scenario the overall buffer size is sufficient to store all waiting packets. If the number of packets of all queues waiting in the buffer reaches the memory size limit, all the packets will be sent out. Despite the fact, that this is a degradation in terms of quality of service and packet reordering should be avoided, this behaviour is acceptable in rare cases and covered using TCP/IP. Retransmission of packets might be the case.

Packets that will end at the NP (i.e. with the NP's IP address) and control packets (ARP, ICMP) will not be managed by the Re-Sequencer Unit. These packets will be tagged with flow ID #0, indicating that they should not be managed. This requires that the other IP packets are not tagged with #0 (which must be considered in the hash function). Additionally, these packets must be identified at the ingress path. In our FlexPath project we use the Pre-Processor for this job. If not available, this must be implemented in the Ingress Tagger. In the PE cluster generated packets (like ICMP message) will also get ID #0, which ensures that they will be sent out immediately without buffering.

6 Conclusion

In this paper we have introduced a Hardware Re-Sequencer Unit for use in Network Processors. In difference to most implementations using a special scheduling we improve the freedom of packet distribution on parallel working processing units. The Re-Sequencer Unit guarantees that packet order is preserved reliably. The use of a hash function to calculate a flow ID in contrast to using the 5-tuple reduces design complexity while still enabling a high degree of Quality of Service. Simulations with SystemC indicate that our unit works well in most cases. Extreme situations like packet loss or a very high packet reordering are absorbed by a fail-safe implementation preventing the system from buffer overrun and disproportional packet latencies.

The next step now is to implement the design on a Xilinx Virtex-4 FPGA platform. As soon as our demonstrator runs, we will validate the simulation results under real conditions.

Acknowledgements

We would like to thank the German Research Foundation (DFG) for co-funding the FlexPath NP project in which this work has been done.

References

1. Shah, N.: Understanding Network Processors. Berkley Technical Report (September 2001)
2. Govind, S., Govindarajan, R., Kuri, J.: Packet Reordering in Network Processors. In: IPDPS 2007 (May 2007)
3. Laor, M., Gendel, L.: The Effect of Packet Reordering in a backbone Link on Application Throughput. IEEE Network (September/October 2002)
4. Cao, Z., Wang, Z., Zegura, E.: Performance of Hashing-Based Schemes for Internet Load Balancing. IEEE INFOCOM, Tel Aviv, Israel (March 2000)
5. Dittmann, G., Herkersdorf, A.: Network Processor Load Balancing for High-Speed Links. SPECTS 2002 (2002)
6. Shi, W., MacGregor, M.H., Gburzynski, P.: Load Balancing for Parallel Forwarding. IEEE Transactions on Networking 13(4) (August 2005)
7. Wu, B., et al.: A Practical Packet Reordering Mechanism with Flow Granularity for Parallelism Exploiting in Network Processors. In: IPDPS 2005(2005)
8. Ohlendorf, R., Herkersdorf, A., Wild, T.: FlexPath NP - A Network Processor Concept with Application-Driven Flexible Processing Paths. CODES+ISSS, Jersey City, USA (September 2005)
9. Libpcap homepage, http://www.tcpdump.org
10. MAWI Working Group Traffic Archive, http://tracer.csl.sony.co.jp/mawi/
11. CAIDA, traces of OC48 link at AMES Internet Exchange (AIX) (April 24, 2003), accessed via DatCat – Internet Data Measurement catalog, http://imdc.datacat.org
12. University of North Carolina at Chapel Hill, border link traces (September 25, 1999) accessed via DatCat – Internet Data Measurement catalog, http://imdc.datacat.org

Self-aware Memory: Managing Distributed Memory in an Autonomous Multi-master Environment

Rainer Buchty, Oliver Mattes, and Wolfgang Karl

Universität Karlsruhe (TH) – Institut für Technische Informatik (ITEC)
Lehrstuhl für Rechnerarchitektur und Parallelverarbeitung
Zirkel 2, 76131 Karlsruhe, Germany
{buchty,mattes,karl}@ira.uka.de

Abstract. A major problem considering parallel computing is maintaining memory consistency and coherency, and ensuring ownership and access rights. These problems mainly arise from the fact that memory in parallel and distributed systems is still managed locally, e.g. using a combination of shared-bus- and directory-based approaches. As a result, such setups do not scale well with system size and are especially unsuitable for systems where such centralized management instances cannot or must not be employed. As a potential solution to this problem we present SaM, the Self-aware Memory architecture. By using self-awareness, our approach provides a novel memory architecture concept targeting multi-master systems with special focus on autonomic, self-managing systems. Unlike previous attempts, the approach delivers a holistic, yet scalable and cost-friendly solution to several memory-related problems including maintaining coherency, consistency, and access rights.

1 Introduction and Motivation

An increasing problem in parallel, distributed system is how to assign and manage memory resources. Traditionally, this is done through a layered approach where local memory is managed per node. Locally, memory is typically attached using a shared bus, where appropriate coherency protocols (such as MESI) are applied; above node level, directory-based methods are employed to enable coherency and consistency. Virtualization of the memory subsystem, i.e. forming a system-wide, eventually shared, distributed memory resource from the individual local memory entities, and securing access rights in such systems require further assistance, typically realized through additional, OS-assisting software layers, or underlying virtualization and abstraction layers.

This strategy becomes increasingly performance-hampering: bus-based methods are hardly applicable beyond dual-core systems as they require bus systems running at a multiple of the required access speed, hitting technology boundaries. Likewise, in directory-based systems the directory itself and its connection, i.e. network, speed, and latency, become a bottleneck.

U. Brinkschulte et al. (Eds.): ARCS 2008, LNCS 4934, pp. 98–113, 2008.

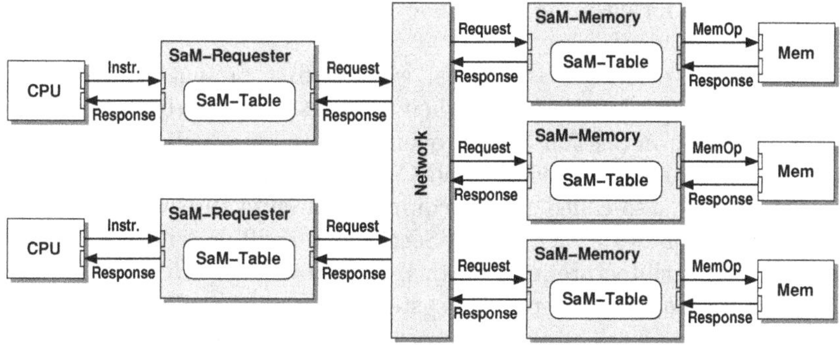

Fig. 1. Structure of SaM

With the rise of multicore and upcoming manycore architectures, we already observe a shift in computer architecture: instead of traditional bus-based approaches, these systems feature NoC-based interconnection between the individual cores and memory where each core not necessarily has exclusive access to local memory. Examples for such architectures are e.g. MIT RAW [20] and the late Intel Polaris being part of Intel's Tera-scale computing program [9].

Our work is motivated by a special kind of NoC-connected SoC architecture, the Digital On-demand Computing Architecture for Real-time Systems (DodOrg) [2]. DodOrg comprises a heterogeneous grid of processing elements, memory, and I/O cells. The processing cells can be e.g. standard CPU, DSP, or programmable logic (FPGA) cells [16]. DodOrg employs techniques derived from so-called organic or autonomic computing. Hence, no central management instances or supervising OS are used. Instead, a lightweight control loop for autonomous task-to-cell assignment and system surveillance is employed [3,4].

A memory management system fitting into such a system therefore also has to act autonomously and without external assist by e.g. OS and higher software layers. Since DodOrg was designed with focus on embedded real-time systems, this must not induce significantly raised hardware costs.

The aforementioned memory management problems arise from the fact that also in distributed systems memory is typically exclusively assigned and physically connected to a single processor, becoming the "housekeeper" of its assigned entity. Combination of these individual memory entities into a global shared memory resource requires the described multi-layer approach to ensure consistency, coherency, and uphold access rights. Depending on the target platform, such an approach is, however, not applicable.

In our paper, we describe a novel memory architecture concept, dubbed Self-aware Memory (SaM), targeted at distributed multi-master systems. Unlike previous attempts, the approach delivers a holistic, yet scalable and cost-friendly solution to several memory-related problems including coherency, consistency, access rights. This is achieved by employing so-called self-awareness so that the memory subsystem essentially becomes self-managing. As a beneficial side-effect, this also reduces complexity on hardware and software level as previously required instances for ensuring consistency, coherency, and access rights are no longer necessary in SaM.

This paper is structured as follows: we will first present related work in Section 2, where we shortly discuss their benefits and drawbacks. To further motivate our work, in Section 3 we provide a short introduction into an application scenario, our Digital on-Demand Computing Architecture for Real-time Systems (DodOrg), a so-called organic computing architecture which inspired the development of Self-aware Memory. In Section 4 we will present our SaM architecture concept, architecture implications, and show how such a setup matches the architecture requirements parallel systems in general, and specifically of architectures like DodOrg. The existing prototype, current work, and initial results derived from the prototype are shown in Section 5. The paper is concluded with Section 6.

2 Related Work

In the past multiple concepts for a different usage of the memory in a system were explored. With Intelligent RAM (IRAM) [13], Processing in Memory (PIM) [17], Parallel Processing In Memory (PPIM) [15] and some other related projects, computation of simple instructions is sourced out into small processing elements integrated in the memory modules. FlexRAM [10] is another PIM-based architecture; it features a programming concept called CFlex [6]. All these approaches share the same concept, i.e. offloading computation into memory and therefore saving expensive transfer time from memory to processor and back. Although these concepts are coined *intelligent memory*, this solely reflects the processing "intelligence". These concepts are all based on a static architecture and do not expose any flexible or autonomous behavior.

Active Pages [12] are another concept for relocating processing of instructions to the memory. In contrast to the aforementioned approaches, Active Pages are based on so-called RADram (Reconfigurable Architecture DRAM) which means, that the logic functions integrated in the memory can be changed during the execution. This gives the possibility to specifically adjust the logic to the requirements of an executed program. The system is flexible, so the same hardware can be used for more varying systems leading to lower costs. Another advantage is that Active Pages integrates in normal systems by using the same interface as conventional memory systems, hence, it is not replacing conventional architectures. Active Page functions are invoked through memory-mapped writes. Synchronization is accomplished through user-defined memory locations.

A special kind of connecting memory to a system of several processors exists in the *parallel sysplex architecture* of IBM mainframe computers. The so-called *coupling facility* [14,7] is a central memory concurrently used from all subsystems. It ensures the integrity and consistency of the data. This is achieved through a special processor with attached memory, which is connected to all processing elements of the sysplex configuration.

In contrast to this different projects, we introduce *Self-aware Memory* (SaM) – a memory system with autonomous, intelligent, self-aware and self-managing memory components. SaM features an easy to use memory concept in a shared memory system which adopts the four basic Self-X principles of Autonomic Computing [8]. By handing over memory control from the operating system to the self-managing and software-independent hardware, SaM is fully transparent to the programmer, i.e. no dedicated program support is required and is extraordinarily well-suited for parallel and distributed systems. SaM therefore lays the foundation for scalable, flexible on-demand computing systems.

3 The DodOrg Hardware Architecture

SaM was inspired by the requirements of the Digital On-demand Computing Architecture for Real-time Systems (DodOrg). DodOrg comprises a grid of individual nodes called Organic Processing Cells (OPCs) featuring peer-to-peer (P2P) connection of the cells [2]. Using a biologically inspired method, these cells individually announce their suitability for processing tasks leading to a decentralized, flexible, and fault-tolerant task distribution. As an effect of that method, closely collaborating tasks typically are executed on neighboring cells leading to the formation of so-called organs, i.e. clusters of cells performing a meta-function.

Because of the dynamic behavior of this task allocation and organ formation, traditional memory management techniques are not applicable. Instead, a similarly flexible approach – SaM – was required, which does not only account for the specific DodOrg requirements but also integrates nicely into the hardware and communication infrastructure offered by the DodOrg architecture.

4 Self-aware Memory (SaM)

Key problem of shared memory in parallel, distributed systems is its construction from several local memory entities, requiring several layers of management ranging to enable coherence and consistency, and enforcing access rights. Hence, in SaM local memory no longer exists. Instead, the memory is turned into an active, self-managing component interconnected through a network infrastructure spanning on-chip and off-chip communication.

In traditional systems memory management, consistency, and coherency are maintained by dedicated units embedded into a CPU's memory management unit, assisted by additional software layers. Within the focus of SaM, self-managing means, that these issues are handled by the memory itself.

This is already very beneficial for parallel and distributed systems, because now the management is no longer done by the individual processing units. No additional hardware or software overhead is required on a processor's side. Hence, scalability of a system is effectively decoupled from the number of processors and solely dependent on the capabilities of the used interconnection network and memory entities.

As a side effect of the self-managing aspect, the entire memory subsystem is effectively abstracted and treated as a single virtual memory entity, i.e. a uniform memory view is achieved and individual parameters or access methods of the attached memory are hidden. Because of the self-managing aspect, it is furthermore possible, to alter this memory entity by adding, removing, or replacing individual memory units. Hence, in contrast to similar concepts as outlined in Section 2, SaM is entirely transparent to the programmer, i.e. no dedicated programming technique such as e.g. with FlexRAM [1] is required.

Such behavior is eminent for the creation of dynamic, flexible systems ranging from traditional fault-tolerant systems to currently researched autonomous and organic systems like the aforementioned DodOrg architecture. With the abstraction of the memory hardware, the programmer has only to provide the desired memory capacities and capabilities such as size and access speed. Likewise, the OS only needs to support respective calls, translating the program calls to appropriate SaM protocol messages.

The implications of the SaM concept are that private local memory no longer exists, but only a globally shared memory resource. Hence, a processor does not have private access to an associated local memory as it is the case in traditional computer systems and prior to use, any memory (besides a required bootstrap memory) must be allocated first from the memory subsystem.

Given this basic introduction into SaM, we will in the following describe the design considerations, anatomy, and use of a SaM-based system, and demonstrate how SaM integrates into the DodOrg architecture framework.

4.1 Architectural Considerations

Driving force behind the design of our SaM concept was to provide a scalable, flexible infrastructure at minimal costs and software overheat – not only within the scope of our DodOrg project, but also for current and future parallel & distributed systems. In the following, we'd therefore like to address certain design aspects and their outcome with respect to system design.

Communication and Scalability. Memory allocation within SaM requires at least three steps: first, the processor is sending out its request where it specifies size and access parameters. The memory subsystem will then answer with an according offer, leading to one or more responses depending of size and current usage of the memory subsystem. From this choice, a best-fit selection is made and the associated memory region is selected and subsequently gets assigned to the requester.

To save bandwidth and communication efforts, we propose different scenarios for such a request and its appropriate answer: for a first-time request, the request is sent out as a broadcast to the network. Associated time-to-live or number-of-hops can be used to limit the broadcast's range. From the memory subsystem then only positive answers are sent back. A timeout mechanism ensures that this request phase will always terminate, even when no positive answer is received, e.g. in case requested access times and/or latency cannot be met.

Such an allocation process can be viewed best as a brokering system where a processor advertises its requirements and gets one or more offers from the memory subsystem. The processor then evaluates these offers and acknowledges fitting ones; finalizing, the memory subsystem grants these acknowledged memory regions and also stores ownership and access rights. CPU-wise, the only information stored is the translation table, i.e. which (virtual) memory addresses map what memory entities and addresses within those entities.

It is also possible to send direct requests to individual memory entities. This may be used in case when it is already known that a specific entity can provide desired resources, so that the initial broadcast and brokering phase is not required. Freeing memory or updating rights and ownership will typically use direct communication with the affected memory entities.

In addition, a multicast scheme – one message addressing several entities – and the aforementioned servicing, i.e. sending out the message only to the service node which then distributes it to its sub-nodes, are possible.

To further improve scalability and reduce communication, SaM specifically supports servicing: for instance, in a tree-like memory structure the root node will represent the entire tree and act as the sole communication partner between the requesting processor element and the underlying memory hierarchy.

The SaM approach therefore scales well with the overall communication capacity within a parallel computer system. Because the memory subsystem is fully decoupled from the system's processing elements, it is especially well suited for systems where processing capabilities are dynamically added, removed, or replaced. Using a metrics-based classification and a unified memory protocol provides an abstract, uniform view of the memory subsystem.

Processor Impact. Although – by design of SaM – a processor does know neither size nor structure of the attached SaM memory subsystem, memory allocation and rights management works similar to conventional memory: the processor needs to allocate a memory region of desired size and assign desired access parameters (code or data segment, access rights). In conventional systems this is typically handled by OS functions and, on hardware level, assisted by the processor's MMU.

Within SaM, the task of memory allocation and management becomes a function of the memory itself. To support this allocation process, we define a set of processor instructions supporting the new allocation and management process such as memory allocation and deallocation, or rights assertion. These solely interact with the SaM-Requester, anything else is handled transparently within the SaM infrastructure. In conventional systems, similar processor support exists, e.g. using machine status registers and supervisor-level instructions.

For a minimal setup, at least two instructions for allocating and freeing memory regions are required, possibly complemented by an additional instruction supporting re-sizing and re-allocation. To enable a shared memory system, another instruction for later access right change is required. Additional instructions providing additional guidance to the memory subsystem might be introduced, but are not mandatory.

These instructions carry required parameters such as size and mandatory access speed for a requested memory region in case of memory allocation.

4.2 Composition of a SaM-Enabled System

With SaM, the memory-modules are no longer directly associated to a single processor but are part of a network. This network may be an exclusive memory network or embedded into existing connection resources, forming a virtual memory network.

To achieve this, every memory entity is connected to a component called *SaM-Memory* managing the connected memory and serving as an interface to the memory network. Several different memories may coexist in the system, each of them connected through an own SaM-Memory component to the network.

Processors (or any other memory-accessing entity) are likewise attached to the memory network through a similar component called *SaM-Requester*. SaM-Requester manages the memory accesses of a processor and handles the overall access protocol of SaM. It also generates request messages to the memory subsystem and processes the answers from the affected *SaM-Memory* components.

Both, SaM-Memory and SaM-Requester, employ dedicated units called *SaM-Table* for storing internal information regarding memory allocation and ownership, and hold information about their corresponding address space. A SaM-Table therefore is basically a list of entries for address translation plus additional housekeeping data for memory management and access security.

The network used for communication within the SaM infrastructure is not specified; this was done deliberately to not restrict the usage of SaM to a special type of network. While this leaves the most freedom for the implementer, of course performance issues must be taken into account so that no performance bottleneck arises from choosing the wrong network infrastructure.

In the following subsections we will present the individual components, their integration into existing systems, and how memory access in a SaM-enabled system takes place.

4.3 SaM-Table

As mentioned before, the SaM-Table component is used to store the management data for individual memory segments accessed via SaM-Requester and SaM-Memory. Per used (i.e. allocated and assigned) memory segment, it contains an entry consisting of several parameters which are used to associate memory regions and access rights.

In our current setup, each SaM-Table entry consists of ID, Segment, Address, Length, Security, and Usage. Depending on whether the SaM-Table is used in a SaM-Requester or a SaM-Memory, the parameters have slightly different meanings, but for ease of development the overall structure remains identical.

For *SaM-Memory*, the ID field contains the network address of the owner, i.e. the originally requesting processor or, more precisely, its associated SaM-Requester. The Segment field contains an assigned identifier value; the Address and Length fields store start address and length of the assigned memory region, whereas the Security field stores the requested access rights such as e.g. exclusive or shared access, read-only or read/write access. The Usage field denotes whether an entry is valid or not.

When used within a *SaM-Requester*, the ID field contains the network address of the assigned memory entity (SaM-Memory). The Segment field will hold the aforementioned identifier value which is returned during the memory allocation process. In the Address field, the start address of the assigned memory segment in the processor's logical address space is saved. Length and Access right fields stay identical.

Take notice of the fact that the effective physical memory address is neither stored in the SaM-Table of the SaM-Requester. The actual place of the segments are defined by the network address of the SaM-Memory and the segment number. For the communication between SaM-Requester and SaM-Memory, solely the addresses of the underlying network are used. The translation between these different address spaces is done by the SaM-Requester and SaM-Memory with the data of the SaM-Tables.

4.4 SaM-Requester

From a processor's point of view the whole memory is abstracted and perceived as a single memory entity; neither size of existing memory resources nor the actual hardware structure of the memory subsystem is visible to the processor. To achieve that, every processor has its own logical address space which is managed by the *SaM-Requester*.

This unit basically performs address translation from local, logical address space of the connected processor into the distributed SaM memory space, i.e. which chunk of of the local address space maps to what physical memory location. Hence, SaM-Requester may be considered a (partial) replacement for a CPU's memory management unit. The management data is stored within the SaM-Requester's associated SaM-Table.

For allocating new memory space, it generates a request and sends it to the network. After that, it processes the received answers and reacts on them in a way which is defined in its implemented algorithms. For managing the logical address space and the allocated segments it uses a SaM-Table to store the data in it. In different implementations there could be various algorithms to manage the SaM-Table and optimize the usage of the address-space [19]. Which one of them is the best often depends on the underlying structure of the system.

Since this allocation process takes a certain time, a defined time window is opened during which answers to an allocation request are accepted. Upon positive answer by the memory subsystem, SaM-Requester will assign the offered memory region to a new segment of the processor's logical address space. If no suitable memory area is offered or if the request times out, this is signalled to the processor which then enters an appropriate handler.

4.5 SaM-Memory

SaM-Memory is the vital component for creating an abstract and uniform memory access regardless of the attached memory's type or access parameters and therefore providing additional memory management functionality. This is done by actively managing the attached memory, hence, SaM-Memory requires detailed knowledge about that memory, like size, usage, access parameters, and physical condition. To keep track of these parameters, monitoring capabilities are required.

SaM-Memory answers incoming requests generated by a SaM-Requester on the basis of the current memory status as stored in the associated SaM-Table. If an incoming allocation request can be fulfilled, SaM-Memory sends back a positive answer and assigns the new segment to the requesting processor's corresponding SaM-Requester. Likewise, read/write accesses, access right updates, or deallocation are processed. Typically, SaM-Memory will not respond to requests it cannot fulfill; however, this behavior is configurable so that it e.g. may offer insufficient resources for an incoming request, or sending out negative answers to requests instead of leaving them unanswered.

For a more detailed description of memory access we would like to refer the reader to the following section.

4.6 Memory Access in SaM

As said before, the SaM memory infrastructure may well consist of a variety of individual memory entities scattered among one or more memory interconnection networks. Naturally, these individual entities expose different size and access parameters, such as access time and latency. Hence, memory allocation requires additional guidance to account for the described memory subsystem heterogeneity. For memory allocation therefore not only the requested amount of memory must be provided, but also additional requirements such as maximum tolerated latency, or minimal block-size of individual memory chunks.

This request is directed to the memory subsystem, where it is evaluated and answered appropriately. This answer is then processed by the requesting entity and acknowledged accordingly so that the memory subsystem will then reserve a selected memory region and apply the specified access rights, so that for subsequent memory accesses an automatic access right checking can be performed and only rightful accesses take place.

In a system containing more than one memory units, a single request will therefore result in several answers. From these answers a best-fitting choice is selected which may lead to a requested memory size being assembled from individual offered chunks.

This memory layout is then stored on the requester's side and acknowledged to the offering memory entities, which in term mark the corresponding memory regions as used, and assign ownership and access rights accordingly.

Subsequent memory accesses then directly take place between the accessing entity and the addressed memory. If allocated memory is no longer used, it can be freed by the owner, the corresponding memory unit(s) will then unlock the affected memory regions so that they can be offered to further allocation requests.

Supervision of Memory Accesses. One big advantage of SaM is the implicit enforcement of memory access rights. On each memory access, the addresses will be checked two times: first, a processor's request is checked by its associated SaM-Requester. This unit will already reject accesses which do not comply with data stored in its SaM-Table, e.g. in case the memory is not allocated at all or if accesses beyond an allocated segment occur. Hence, it is ensured that spurious, maybe malicious accesses of a single processor are already stopped at the source and do not even enter the memory network.

A second check takes place at the addressed memory unit where the access is matched against boundaries of the accessed segment, ownership, and access rights stored in the corresponding SaM-Memory's SaM-Table. This ensures that only rightful accesses are actually performed.

So far, this does not protect against devices which generate malicious access messages; because of the high level of abstraction, SaM can be easily enhanced by additional cryptographic methods such as hashing and signing to enable proper identification and authorization of incoming requests. Because this extra functionality will be embedded into SaM-Memory and SaM-Requester, no software overhead is required.

Shared Memory and Rights Management. To enable shared memory in parallel systems, fine-grained rights management is required to control the memory accesses. Traditionally, this is done by the combination of software handlers (shared access over a network) and hardware (MMU managing local memory accesses). While this scheme can be used with SaM, it is unnecessarily complex and does not make use of the specific features of the SaM concept.

As mentioned before, within SaM a processor first allocates desired memory regions through its associated SaM-Requester. If that memory region is to be shared with other processors, then the Security fields of the affected memory units, i.e. their corresponding SaM-Memory component, have to be adjusted.

As of now, the simple case was implemented where a memory is either private to a single processor or completely shared. To fully accommodate for the requirements of parallel systems, however, a more fine-grained method is required where individual access rights can be assigned to each processor and memory region. We are currently evaluating the options, how these increased functionality will be implemented into SaM.

4.7 DodOrg Integration

The SaM extensions, i.e. SaM-Requester and SaM-Memory with their according SaM-Tables, will be unique to the cell-specific part as they are only required for memory cells and cells with memory-access capabilities such as processor or DSP cells.

SaM does not require any alteration of the cell-uniform communication infrastructure of DodOrg cells. Virtual links, already provided by that infrastructure, greatly enhance SaM's performance as they enable direct communication between corresponding SaM-Requesters and Memories over the P2P network at guaranteed communication times.

5 Results

To show the basic functionality of SaM, we designed and implemented a prototype using the United Simulation Environment (UNISIM) [5]. UNISIM consists of a modular simulator and a library of predefined modules. Using these predefined and additional user-programmed modules, a simulator framework is programmed which is then compiled into an executable simulation application by the UNISIM compiler.

The simulated hardware is divided into several components to ease development of complex simulation engines, hence, each implemented by an own module with well-defined interfaces enabling to simply replace modules or make further use of them in other simulations.

5.1 Simulation Setup and Results

Our prototype simulator consists of a variable number of processors equipped with SaM-Requester units and memory entities with their according SaM-Memory units connected by a network. The prototype therefore also reflects the basic structure of the DodOrg architecture, i.e. the connection of cells using a communication infrastructure. The P2P nature of DodOrg's communication infrastructure is not visible to the running application and abstracted on hardware level, hence, restricting our SaM prototype to a globally shared communication resource is a valid simplification for evaluating our SaM concept.

As a processor core we chose the DLX core which is provided together with UNISIM. This core was extended in two ways: first, the processor model was extended by dedicated functions for memory allocation and freeing. Second, the SaM requester component was implemented, providing the required interfacing to the communication infrastructure, most notably the memory allocation and access protocol. Likewise, we extended a UNISIM-provided memory model by the SaM memory component.

All SaM components are interconnected via a simple full-duplex communication model. The prototype offers the possibility to simply test and typical conflicts of concurrent memory accesses from different cores. The progress of requests and accesses of segments can be visualized and the limitation of the network can be made visible.

The prototype is set up in a parameterizable and scalable way, so that any number of processor and memory cores can be generated.

Aim of the described prototype is to properly evaluate the basic concept, i.e. to not only demonstrate the basic functionality, but also determine the overhead introduced by the new memory protocol and also addressing the question of real-time behavior. We therefore concentrate on the aspects of memory access, i.e. the eventual amount of overhead introduced by allocation and read/write accesses.

In order to test different scenarios of memory accesses, we developed a set of test programs as shown in Table 1, each demonstrating certain features and testing the behavior of SaM. Because of the additional, SaM-specific commands

Table 1. Memory-related test programs performed on the prototype

Test Program	Performed Test
`request.s`	Basic request to two memory segments
`read_write.s`	Simple read and write to and from a memory segment
`mult_req.s`	Multiple requests to different memory components
`req_eject1.s`	Memory request rejected without reaction of the program
`req_eject2.s`	Abort of program after rejected memory request
`inv_access.s`	Invalid memory accesses
`inv_br_acc.s`	Invalid memory access due to wrongly calculated branch address

used for memory allocation, the test programs were written in assembly language and translated into their binary representation using a patched DLX assembler.

Depending on the test scenario (function test vs. performance evaluation), these test programs were either executed on a single or all processors of the simulation model and the simulation output was logged and analyzed, proving the theoretically predicted behavior.

Only during the allocation process exists an overhead which directly corresponds with the used allocation procedure. Two basic approaches exist, which are round-robin and broadcast. For our prototype, we implemented the round-robin allocation procedure and were able to observe the expected behavior: in best case, the first addressed SaM-Memory will be able to fulfill the request and sending back an acknowledgement message, hence, no subsequent requests are sent. This scenario is comparable to memory allocation within a processor's local memory where a request either succeeds or fails.

If the first addressed memory cannot fulfill the request, the next in the queue of the round-robin mechanism is used. For every try, another message has to be sent to the memory and back to the requesting CPU. In worst case, the allocation request therefore needs to be subsequently re-sent to all other memory cells until the allocation either succeeds or fails. Hence, if n memory entities exist, it takes a maximum amount of time of $2 * n * \lambda_{net}$ for the allocation process to finish, where λ_{net} is the time for sending a message over the network. After that the request is rejected. In general, a request can be completed in $i * 2 * \lambda_{net}$, where $1 \leq i \leq m$ is the first memory which can fulfill the request. Simulation showed this expected behavior.

Therefore, request time is limited by the time for the transfer of the request over the network and the number of components. Bandwidth problems might arise when multiple users access a shared communication infrastructure, e.g. a shared bus. To account for that, the used communication infrastructure was a simple shared bus model. If no other component wants to access the bus, it can be used directly, otherwise the bus can be accessed by the components in a round-robin order.

Under most pessimistic assumptions, i.e. a fully occupied bus, the maximum waiting time for an individual access is $2 * k * \lambda_{net}$, with $0 \leq k < n$ being the number of components with pending bus requests and having higher access priority, i.e. their requests being performed before the actual request.

This leads to a worst-case time of $(2 * n * \lambda_{net}) * m$ for an allocation request to finish – as also attested by the simulation infrastructure – in case the bus is fully used with $k = n-1$ pending requests being executed prior to the current request, and none or the very last memory element, i.e. $i = m$, in the round-robin queue being able to fulfill the request. This extreme case, however, should not occur very often in practice as it would indicate a severe mismatch between required and provided bus bandwidth.

Once, memory is already assigned, subsequent accesses do not impose any overhead, because the read/write message can be directly sent to the corresponding memory component. To find the memory assigned to a given memory section, the SaM-Requester performs a lookup in the corresponding SaM-Table; likewise, the addressed memory will match the request against its own SaM-Table to ensure access rights. This will not contribute significantly to access latency, as such mapping and checking is conventionally done by the CPU's memory management unit. No external overhead takes place, hence, like in conventional systems, data access time is solely limited by the communication network's bandwidth and the addressed memory's access latency.

The tests performed did not only cover individual allocation and access scenarios, but we also addressed interference issues resulting from several simultaneous or colliding requests, and parallel accesses from different processors. We could demonstrate that not only the spreading or interleaving of allocated segments over different memory components works well, but we furthermore could verify the proper functioning of the SaM protocol with regard to memory allocation and access.

Allocation requests can be accomplished up until no more space is left in the memory subsystem, otherwise a defined error code is sent back to the processor in case the desired amount of memory is not available. Like in conventional approaches, this error code is then processed by the respective application.

Memory accesses may only be performed by the CPU holding appropriate access rights. Neither should accesses to un-allocated memory enter the network, nor should the memory itself answer illegitimate accesses. The first case is handled by the SaM-Requester, which will not forward accesses for which no corresponding entry exists in its SaM-Table. Likewise, SaM memory will match incoming read/write accesses against its SaM-Table to either fulfill this request, or send out a negative acknowledge.

5.2 Simulation Conclusion

The simulation prototype clearly confirmed our theoretical assumptions regarding the SaM protocol overhead, worst-case timing behavior, and proved the overall functionality of the SaM concept. Overhead only takes place for allocation and deallocation (freeing) of memory. In our prototype, we chose a simple-to-implement Round-Robin allocation procedure where a SaM-Requester will sequentially address all present memory modules with the current allocation request and directly receive the individual module's answer. Once the request is satisfied, no more allocation messages are generated.

The drawback of this method is that it only works on enumerated systems where all memory modules are known such as e.g. on a single DodOrg hardware chip. We are currently investigating broadcast-based methods which do not rely on an upfront enumeration.

Once the allocation process is finished, subsequent memory accesses do not carry additional overhead and are also independent of the chosen allocation strategy; regarding memory read/write accesses, SaM is therefore not introducing any more overhead.

Already this simple prototype shows the beneficial effects of introducing self-managing features into the memory subsystem: any number of memories can be shared by any number of processors without requiring an additional software level to ensure access rights in this distributed system. SaM is completely software- and OS-agnostic and therefore especially suitable for heterogeneous systems employing several, or – in the case of dedicated hardware accelerators – no operating system at all.

We further can show that any individual access to the SaM network has a guaranteed upper bound dictated by the network traversal time and distance (number of hops) between requesting and memory unit. This effect is not SaM-specific but a general effect of any communication. However, this information is vital for further work on the communication protocol as we can safely introduce time-out intervals for allocation and access messages when switching to a more sophisticated communication infrastructure model, and also use such information for answering allocation requests and autonomous optimization processes.

5.3 Current Development

Ongoing development of the simulation prototype targets protocol refinements, extended monitoring capabilities for improved measurements, and presentation and visualization of the simulation process.

The protocol is currently extended beyond simple allocation and access to also include assignment of access rights. With the introduction of more sophisticated monitoring and detailed communication infrastructure models we then will be able to perform detailed simulations of life-like systems where network-induced side-effects such as race situations between different messages might occur.

We then will target the introduction of high-level self-managing aspects such as autonomous memory layout optimization (defragmentation), access optimization through autonomous migration and replication of data, which in term require to address consistency and coherency aspects.

6 Conclusion and Outlook

SaM provides a promising way to deal with memory resources in dynamic parallel systems: within SaM, no central memory management unit is required. Instead, the memory itself manages allocation, ownership, and access rights easing the construction of scalable parallel computing systems. Single memory entities therefore are treated in a uniform way, regardless of their type: any memory entity is only classified by its core parameters such as memory capacity, access time, and access latency. The used communication protocol was specifically designed with respect to scalability and minimal communication overhead.

So far, we successfully implemented memory allocation and access rights enforcement. Ongoing and future work specifically addresses the exploration of further self-organizing features such as autonomous de-fragmentation, swapping, or reaction to changed memory capacities and access parameters.

With a refined simulation prototype, more detailed simulations of network infrastructures systems, also including cascading structures, will be possible. The memory components may be connected to more than one network and build a hierarchical structure. With autonomous extension of services – comparable to the self-extending services in JINI [11,18] – services of not directly connected components could be used by the processors.

References

1. Fraguela, B., et al.: Programming the FlexRAM parallel intelligent memory system. In: Proceedeings of the 2003 ACM SIGPLAN Symposium on Principles of Parallel Programming (PPoPP 2003), pp. 49–60 (June 2003)
2. Becker, J., et al.: Digital On-Demand Computing Organism for Real-Time Systems. In: Karl, W., et al. (eds.) Workshop Proceedings of the 19th International Conference on Architecture of Computing Systems (ARCS 2006), GI-Edition Lecture Notes in Informatics (LNI), vol. P81, pp. 230–245 (March 2006)
3. Brinkschulte, U., Pacher, M., Renteln, A.: Towards an Artificial Hormone System for Self-Organizing Real-Time Task Allocation. In: Obermaisser, R., et al. (eds.) SEUS 2007. LNCS, vol. 4761, Springer, Heidelberg (2007)
4. Buchty, R., Karl, W.: A Monitoring Infrastructure for the Digital on-demand Computing Organism (DodOrg). In: de Meer, H., Sterbenz, J.P.G. (eds.) IWSOS 2006. LNCS, vol. 4124, p. 258. Springer, Heidelberg (2006)
5. European Network of Excellence on High-Performance Embedded Architecture and Compilation (HiPEAC). UNISIM: UNIted SIMulation Environment
6. Fraguela, B.B., et al.: Programming the flexRAM parallel intelligent memory system. In: Programming the flexRAM parallel intelligent memory system, pp. 49–60. ACM Press, New York (2003)
7. Greis, W.: Die IBM-Mainframe-Architektur. Open Source Press (2005)
8. Horn, P.: Autonomic computing manifesto - ibm's perspective on the state of information technology. IBM Research (October 2001)
9. Intel Corp. Intel Tera-scale Computing. (2007), `http://techresearch.intel.com/articles/Tera-Scale/1421.htm`
10. Kang, Y., et al.: FlexRAM: Toward an advanced intelligent memory system. In: International Conference on Computer Design (ICCD 1999), pp. 192–201. IEEE Computer Society Press, Washington (1999)
11. Kumaran, S.I.: JINI technology. Prentice-Hall, Englewood Cliffs (2002)
12. Oskin, M., Chong, F., Sherwood, T.: Active pages: A computation model for intelligent memory. In: Proceedings of the 25th Annual International Symposium on Computer Architecture (ISCA 1998). New York, June 27–July 1. ACM Computer Architecture News, vol. 26,3, pp. 192–203. ACM Press, New York (1998)

13. Patterson, D., et al.: A case for intelligent RAM. IEEE Micro 17(2), 34–44 (1997)
14. Raften, D.: System-managed cf structure duplexing. IBM e-server zSeries (June 2004)
15. Rangan, K., Abu-Ghazaleh, N., Wilsey, P.: A distributed multiple-SIMD processor in memory. In: 2001 International Conference on Parallel Processing (ICPP 2001), pp. 507–516. IEEE Computer Society Press, Washington (2001)
16. Schuck, C., Lamparth, S., Becker, J.: artNoC - A novel multi-functional router architecture for Organic Computing. In: 17th International Conference On Field Programmable Logic and Applications (August 2007)
17. Sterling, T., Brockman, J., Upchurch, E.: Analysis and modeling of advanced PIM architecture design tradeoffs. In: SC 2004 Conference CD, Pittsburgh, PA. IEEE/ACM SIGARCH (November 2004)
18. Inc Sun Microsystems. Jini architectural overview. Technical White Paper (1999)
19. Tanenbaum, A.S.: Modern Operating Systems, 2nd edn. Prentice-Hall, Englewood Cliffs (2001)
20. Taylor, M.B., et al.: The Raw Microprocessor: A Computational Fabric for Software Circuits and General Purpose Programs. In: IEEE Micro (March/April 2002)

Part IV

Reconfigurable Hardware

Dynamic Reconfiguration of FlexRay Schedules for Response Time Reduction in Asynchronous Fault-Tolerant Networks

Robert Brendle, Thilo Streichert, Dirk Koch, Christian Haubelt, and Jürgen Teich

Department of Computer Science 12
University of Erlangen-Nuremberg, Germany
robert.brendle@web.de, {streichert,dirk.koch,haubelt,teich}@cs.fau.de

Abstract. In this paper, we present fault-tolerance strategies for implementing passive replication techniques in networked embedded systems based on TDMA-communication such as FlexRay busses. In particular, we assume that processes are replicated at different nodes for tolerating node failures. Hence, if one node fails another node can execute the process and requires the bandwidth for transmitting those messages created by the process over the bus medium. Two concepts are introduced to solve this problem: 1.) to replicate not only the processes but also the messages and to reserve the required bandwidth a priori at design time or 2.) to reconfigure the TDMA-schedule and assign the bandwidth dynamically to the nodes. Obviously, reserving bandwidth for each failure case might lead to a huge overhead and to long response times. Therefore, we provide different reconfiguration strategies for the recently developed FlexRay bus. Moreover, the timing behavior as well as the implementation overhead are evaluated with the help of an experimental setup consisting of five FlexRay nodes.

1 Introduction

Automotive embedded networks typically consist of heterogeneous *electronic control units* (ECUs) which are networked in order to sense and control their environment in an efficient manner. In contrast to other sensor networks which connect different control units via dedicated point-to-point links, the automotive domain mainly applies shared busses for establishing the communication among ECUs. These busses can be either master-slave busses like the local interconnect network (LIN) [1] or multi-master busses like CAN [2], TTP [3], or FlexRay [4]. While CAN uses a priority based arbitration mechanism of the bus which allows a fast access of high priority massages to the bus, TTP and FlexRay are TDMA-based communication protocols, i.e., certain messages are only allowed to be transferred in dedicated time slots. These slots belong to a static bus schedule which is repeated periodically. Thus, a networked embedded system has a scheduler at the sending ECU, one schedule for the communication and a scheduler for the receiving ECU. Regarding these different schedules, networked

U. Brinkschulte et al. (Eds.): ARCS 2008, LNCS 4934, pp. 117–129, 2008.

embedded systems can be further classified into *synchronous* and *asynchronous* systems, i.e., systems where the schedules are synchronized or systems where the schedules are executed independently in an asynchronous manner. Obviously, the synchronization of different schedules is not only a technical problem but also an algorithmic problem and a matter of future work. Nowadays, asynchronous networks are state-of-the-art. In asynchronous systems, no synchronized schedules need to be determined and the synchronization of different ECUs, gateways, and busses, running at different speeds is not necessary. Here, we consider automotive networks which are based on the FlexRay protocol where all ECUs and the bus run in an asynchronous manner.

Another important aspect of such embedded networks is fault tolerance. Different fault tolerance techniques for tolerating *permanent*, *transient*, or *intermittent faults* are applied in such networks. In this contribution, we focus on permanent faults which are typically handled by redundancy, i.e., processes are replicated at different ECUs in the network and if one ECU fails another ECU will execute the functionality. Obviously, this migration of processes from one node to another has an influence on the bus schedule. As an exemplification, consider Fig. 1 which shows two systems each with four nodes $n1,\ldots,n4$ and a corresponding bus schedule consisting of one TDMA cycle. The nodes host processes $p1,\ldots,p4$ and each process sends a message $m1,\ldots,m4$. In order to tolerate defects, the processes are replicated on a neighboring node, i.e., process $p4$ is replicated at node $n3$, process $p3$ is replicated at node $n2$, and so forth. Assuming, for example, that node $n3$ fails during operation would lead to a situation where the node $n2$ requires bandwidth for transmitting message $m3$ of the replica $p3'$ and message $m2$ of the process $p2$. In the system shown in Fig. 1a), message $m3$ of replica $p3'$ will be transferred in slot $s7$ and $m2$ in $s2$. Thus, not only the processes need to be replicated but also the slots in the bus schedule. This case is shown in Fig. 1a) where the slots required for the replicated processes are statically assigned to the nodes. In Fig. 1b), the same system is shown as in Fig. 1a) but the assignment of slots to nodes is different. Here, it is assumed that the bus schedule can be reconfigured, i.e., if a node fails, another node will execute those processes of the defect node and gets the slots of the failed node. For example, if node $n3$ fails, node $n2$ will send the message $m3$ of replica $p3'$ in slot $s3$ instead of the additional slot $s7$. Hence, the dynamic reconfiguration of bus schedules and the dynamic assignment of slots to nodes avoids the need of reserving bandwidth in the TDMA schedule. This has a great advantage with respect to the communication latency. In Fig. 1a), the worst case communication latency is 8 slots, while the worst case communication latency in Fig. 1b) is only 4 slots.

This motivating example leads to the contributions of this paper: In order to reduce the communication latency, we studied the capability of dynamically assigning slots to nodes in a FlexRay-based network. For this purpose, different platform-dependent and platform-independent solutions will be presented. In particular, we provide solutions suitable for the E-Ray communication controller by Bosch [5] and the MFR4200 by Freescale [6]. Moreover, the advantages and drawbacks as well as the reconfiguration times for the different proposed

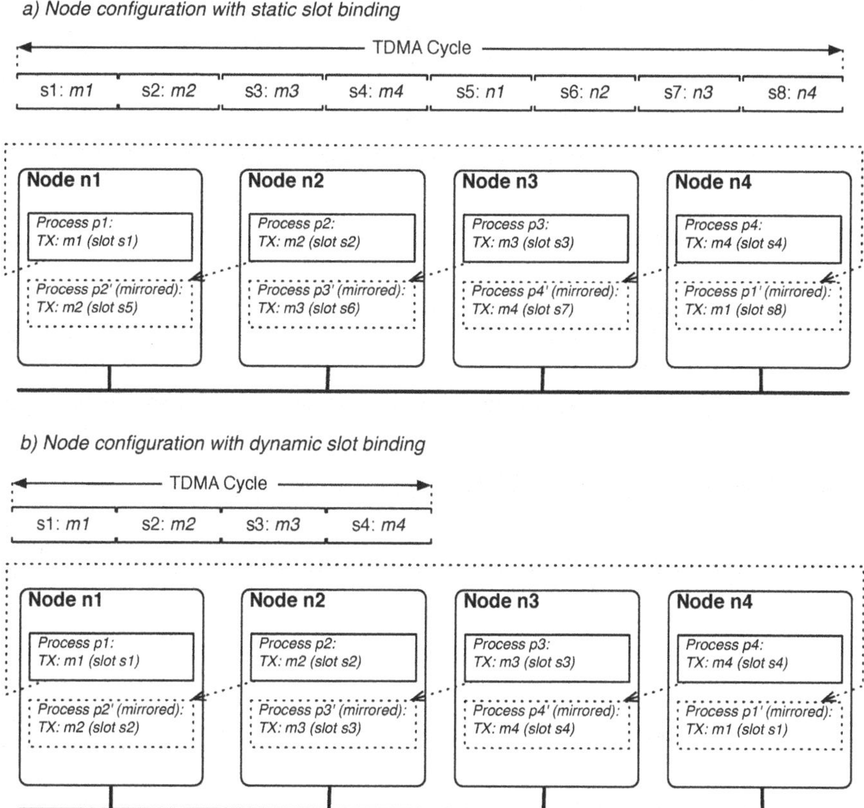

Fig. 1. a) Typically, time slots are statically assigned to nodes and messages of redundant tasks are sent redundantly. b) If slots can be assigned dynamically to nodes, the response time will decrease.

solutions will be discussed. With the concepts and results of this paper, it is Possible to build up efficient networked embedded systems using passive replication [7] for processes with data dependencies.

The structure of the paper is as follows: In Sec. 2, we give an overview about the academic research in the field of fault tolerance and parameter determination for TDMA-based busses. Afterwards, we briefly introduce the FlexRay protocol (see Sec. 3) which is inevitable for the understanding of the following sections. Sec. 4 proposes four different strategies for dynamically assigning bandwidth to nodes. These four strategies are evaluated and discussed in Sec. 5.

2 Related Work

Recently published research work focuses on the analysis and optimization of the FlexRay protocol. In [8], the authors present a methodology for analyzing the real-time behavior of systems using the static and dynamic part of the FlexRay protocol. Based on this analysis methodology, Pop et al. present in [9] heuristics for determining the global parameters of the FlexRay bus which are suitable for asynchronous networks, i.e., networks where nodes are not synchronized to the bus schedule. The methods for analyzing and optimizing the bus-based system are based on the assumption that processes are statically bound to the nodes in the system. Thus, passive replication as presented in Fig. 1b) is not considered.

In another interesting publication [10], the same authors propose a methodology for designing and scheduling time-triggered systems such that these systems are able to tolerate transient faults. For this purpose, the design methodology decides about the kind of redundancy, i.e., spatial or temporal redundancy and determines a schedule according to real-time constraints. Although reconfiguration strategies of the bus schedule can be combined with the methodology presented in [10], the reconfiguration capability of busses is not studied in [10].

3 Basic Principles of the FlexRay Protocol

FlexRay is a cycle-based protocol. Each cycle consists of four segments: 1.) a static segment, 2.) a dynamic segment, 3.) a symbol window, and 4.) the idle time. While the static segment and the network idle time are required for a correct network configuration, the dynamic segment and the symbol window are optional. The duration of each segment is defined by a certain number of so-called *macro ticks*. These are the smallest common time unit. A macro tick consists of a variable number of *micro ticks* which varies between the nodes and depends on the oscillators of the nodes. Due to the accuracy of the oscillators, the length of a micro tick varies. Therefore, a time synchronization algorithm determines in each cycle the duration of a macro tick in micro ticks. In Fig. 2, such a cycle with its four segments is presented and explained in more detail in the following:

- **Static Segment.** In the *static segment* of the FlexRay protocol, the data is transmitted using a *time division multiple access* (TDMA) scheme. The static segment consists of a constant number of equal slots of a fixed length. Each slot is assigned to exactly one sending node in each cycle which is denoted with a *Frame-ID*.
- **Dynamic Segment.** The *dynamic segment* is designated for transferring event triggered messages. It consists of a fixed number of *mini slots*. The length of a message for the dynamic segment may vary within certain bounds and is always a multiple of a mini slot. Each node which eventually sends a message in the dynamic segment has one or more *Frame-IDs*. The Frame-IDs are equivalent to a priority necessary for the bus arbitration. At the beginning of the dynamic segment, the node with the lowest Frame-ID is allowed to access the bus. In order to notify the other nodes in the network how long the bus will be occupied, the node sends the message length at the beginning of the transfer. If no message needs to be transferred by the node,

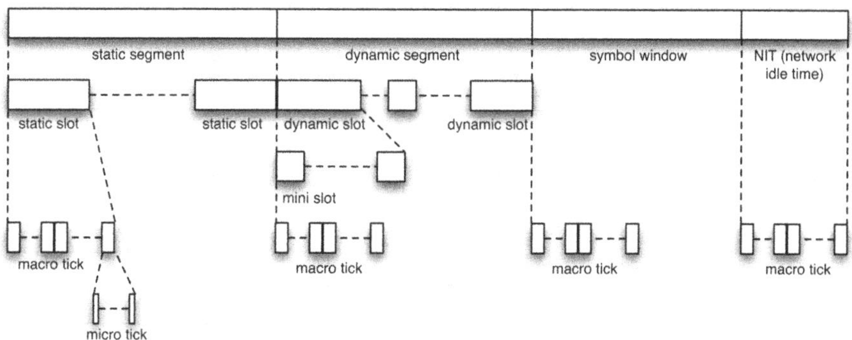

Fig. 2. Structure of a FlexRay cycle [4]

one mini slot will be wasted and in the next mini slot, the node with next higher Frame-ID may send a message.
- **Symbol Window.** The *symbol window* is necessary for the network management. For example signals like *wake up* or *sleep* messages can be transferred for controlling each single node.
- **Network Idle Time.** The network idle time is necessary for the time synchronization in order to correct the global time base. Moreover, it might be necessary for node internal processes which do not send messages via the bus.

4 Dynamic Reconfiguration of the Slot Distribution

Assuming that processes are passively replicated in order to tolerate defects of nodes, this section proposes four strategies for the dynamic assignment of bandwidth to nodes. With these strategies, alternatives to an a priori reservation of bandwidth are given that reduce the response time in asynchronous bus-based systems.

4.1 Complete Reconfiguration

In the start-up phase, the communication controller of each single node passes different operating states before it is ready to send and receive messages. In one of these states, the communication controller is configured with the necessary parameters for the arbitration of the bus according to the given bus schedule. This configuration state is always executed after reset. Thus, one obvious strategy to reconfigure the message buffers is 1.) to modify the configuration data in the memory, 2.) to reset the communication controller, and 3.) to load the modified configuration data to the controller. As an example for this strategy refer to Fig. 3. In Fig. 3a), three nodes $n1, n2, n3$ are shown. Node $n1$ executes process $p1$ which periodically sends its message $m1$ in the slot $s2$ of the static segment. Process $p3$ at node $n3$ sends a message $m5$ in aperiodic rounds in the dynamic segment of a cycle. The main focus is set on process $p2$ running at node $n2$.

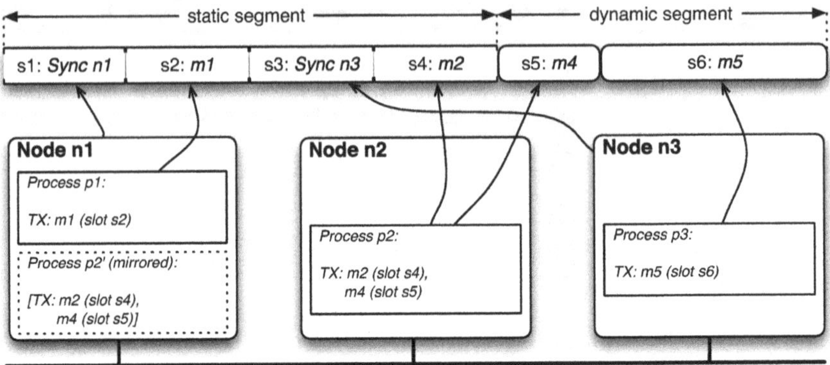

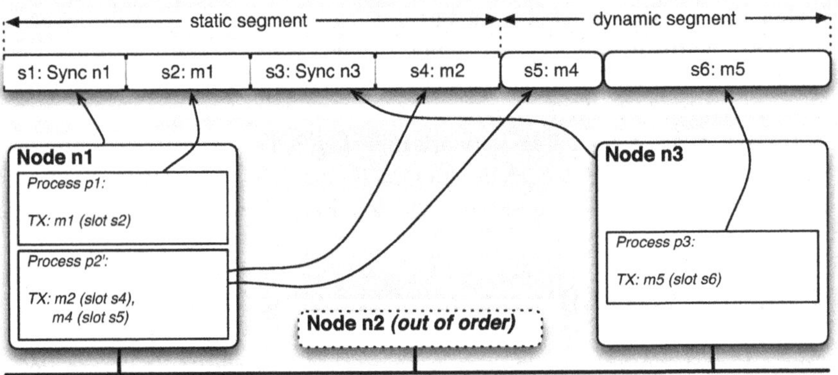

Fig. 3. Example for a complete reconfiguration

A replica of this process $p2'$ is bound onto node $n1$. The process $p2$ sends message $m2$ in the static segment and message $m4$ in the dynamic segment. While node $n2$ is active and has not failed, the replica $p2'$ sends no messages.

After node $n2$ has failed (cf. Fig. 3b)), the communication controller of node $n1$ will be reset for allocating the transmit buffers for slot $s4$ and $s5$. Afterwards, the new configuration data for the required slots $s4$ and $s5$ is loaded to the controller. Due to this reset and configuration procedure, node $n1$ loses its synchronization with the bus. Hence, node $n1$ needs to be reintegrated into the network. During this time, all processes executed on this node lose their ability to communicate with the network. The other nodes in the network are not necessarily affected by the reset of the controller. In the example shown in Fig. 3, the network needs to be initialized completely because node $n3$ receives no *sync messages* and halts itself. As soon as node $n1$ has finished its reconfiguration, the network will be restarted and the processes $p1, p2$, and $p3$ can transfer their messages in their former slots.

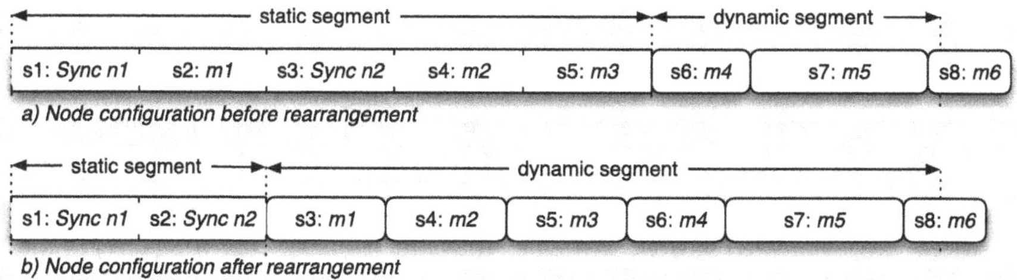

Fig. 4. FlexRay schedule a) before and b) after the adaptation for the partial reconfiguration in the dynamic segment

4.2 Partial Reconfiguration in the Dynamic Segment

In order to avoid a reset of the communication controller in case of a reconfiguration, it would be necessary to reassign the transmit buffer at runtime. Although the FlexRay specification [4] does not explicitly specify a reconfiguration of transmit buffers for the static and dynamic segment, some communication controllers like the MFR4200 by Freescale [6] support this reconfiguration at least in the dynamic segment. This leads to the idea to send all messages in the dynamic segment which might be sent by another node after a node failure. Due to the different bus arbitration in the dynamic segment, it is inevitable to respect the following constraints:

- Since low priority messages in the dynamic segment might not be sent, it is necessary for a guaranteed transmission of messages to assign one of the highest priorities to shifted messages. Moreover, the length of the dynamic segment needs to be long enough.
- If a message in the dynamic segment will not be sent, the time between two messages is not deterministic any more, i.e., the time interval decreases. This might lead to problems if a time limit needs to be satisfied for node-internal computation. In order to avoid this problem, the messages can be transmitted in a *continuous send mode*, i.e., a message is read non-destructively from the message buffer and sent in each cycle, no matter if the message has changed.

In Fig. 4, two schedules are shown: a) before, and b) after shifting messages to the dynamic segment. The messages $m1, m2$, and $m3$ as well as the synchronization messages of the nodes $n1, n2$ will be transferred in the static segment at first. The dynamic segment is used for sending the messages $m4, m5$, and $m6$. Note that message $m6$ can only be transmitted if $m4$ or $m5$ will not be transferred. Otherwise, the time for the dynamic segment is not long enough.

After shifting the messages $m1, m2$, and $m3$ to the dynamic segment, only the synchronization messages of node $n1, n2$ are sent in the static segment. Following the upper constraints, the messages $m1, m2$, and $m3$ have the highest priority and the length of the dynamic segment is enlarged.

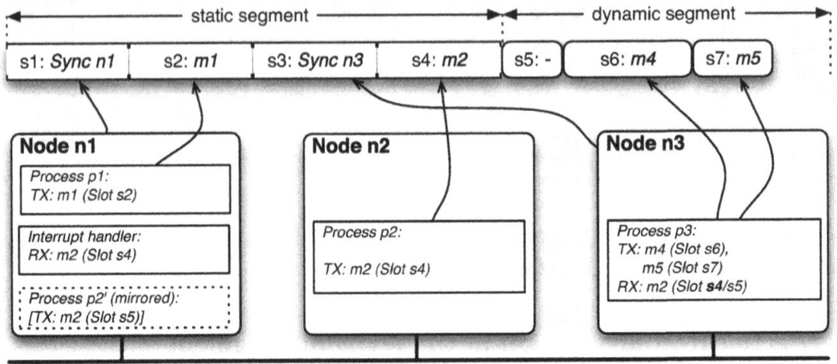

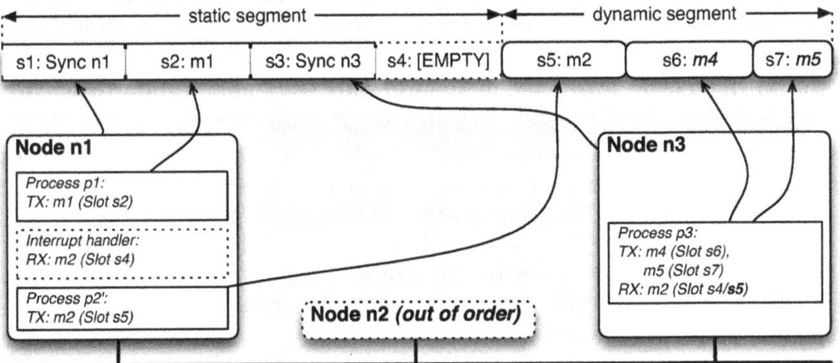

Fig. 5. Example for handling a node defect by using secondary receive buffers

4.3 Reconfiguration with Secondary Receive Buffers

Another possibility is to assign secondary receive buffers in the dynamic segment at design time to the nodes. If a node or process, respectively, does not receive a message in its primary receive buffer, it will be possible to receive a message in the secondary receive buffer.

In order to illustrate this strategy, Fig. 5 presents again a network with three nodes and three processes. Node $n1$ hosts the process $p1$ and the replica $p2'$ of process $p2$ which runs at node $n2$. This process transmits the messages $m4, m5$ and receives the message $m2$. Message $m2$ will be received either via the primary receive buffer in slot $s4$ or via the secondary receive buffer in slot $s5$. Furthermore, node $n1$ executes an interrupt handler triggered by the communication controller in order to activate $p2'$ in case of a node defect of $n2$. Here, node $n1$ checks whether message $m2$ of process $p2$ has been sent in slot $s4$ of the static segment. As soon as the defect of node $n2$ has been detected, node $n1$ starts with the activation of replica $p2'$. A reconfiguration of the communication controller is not necessary in this case because node $p2'$ does not transmit its message in slot $s4$. Instead, the secondary receive buffer of process $p3$ in slot $s5$ is used. Thus, a process migration is realized without the need to reconfigure each controller.

4.4 Partial Reconfiguration of the Static Segment

Since the current FlexRay specification [4] does not prohibit a reconfiguration of the communication controller at runtime, it might be possible to reassign message buffers of the static segment after a defect of a node. Interestingly, the E-Ray controller by Bosch opposed to the MFR4200 does not prohibit this reconfiguration. In combination with the previous strategy which uses secondary receive buffers to transmit messages of the replicas, the time between a defect and the termination of the reconfiguration can be drastically reduced.

As a scenario, consider the case shown in Fig. 6. The binding of the processes $p1, p2, p3$ as well as the binding of replicas $p1'$ and $p2'$ onto the nodes $n1, n2, n3$ is the same as before. Starting from the initial configuration in Fig. 6a), node $n2$ fails. After such a failure, the reconfiguration of the communication controller is processed in two phases (see Fig. 6b),c)): In the first phase (see Fig. 6b)), message $m2$ will be sent by replica $p2'$ in the secondary slot $s5$, while the communication controller of node $n1$ starts configuring a message buffer for slot $s4$. The process $p1$ is not affected by this reconfiguration, but the message $m2$ delays the messages $m4$ and $m5$ in the dynamic segment. As soon as the reconfiguration is finished, message $m2$ can be sent in its original slot $s4$ in the static segment. Note that the secondary slot in the dynamic segment still occupies one mini slot each cycle. This is shown in the configuration in Fig. 6c).

5 Experimental Evaluation and Discussion

In order to evaluate the timing behavior of the reconfiguration strategies of the FlexRay bus, we set up a network of four FlexRay nodes [11] and a PC equipped with a FlexRay diagnostic card acting as a fifth FlexRay node. The timing evaluation has been done 1.) with the help of a monitoring software [12] sniffing at the bus and 2.) with the help of timers which were triggered when entering and leaving a certain reconfiguration phase.

Complete Reconfiguration. The main advantage of this strategy is the flexibility of the reconfiguration, i.e., after a reset, all message buffers can be reconfigured and assigned to the nodes. Unfortunately, a reset disturbs the communication of all processes hosted at that node. The duration is critical for the correct operation of the network and denoted with t_{reconf}. It is composed of three time values: $t_{reconf} = t_{reset} + t_{config} + t_{integrate}$.

- The time value t_{reset} denotes the time interval from starting a software routine that wants to reset the communication controller until entering the reset state of the communication controller. In our experimental setup, we measured a reset time of $t_{reset} = 0.1ms$.

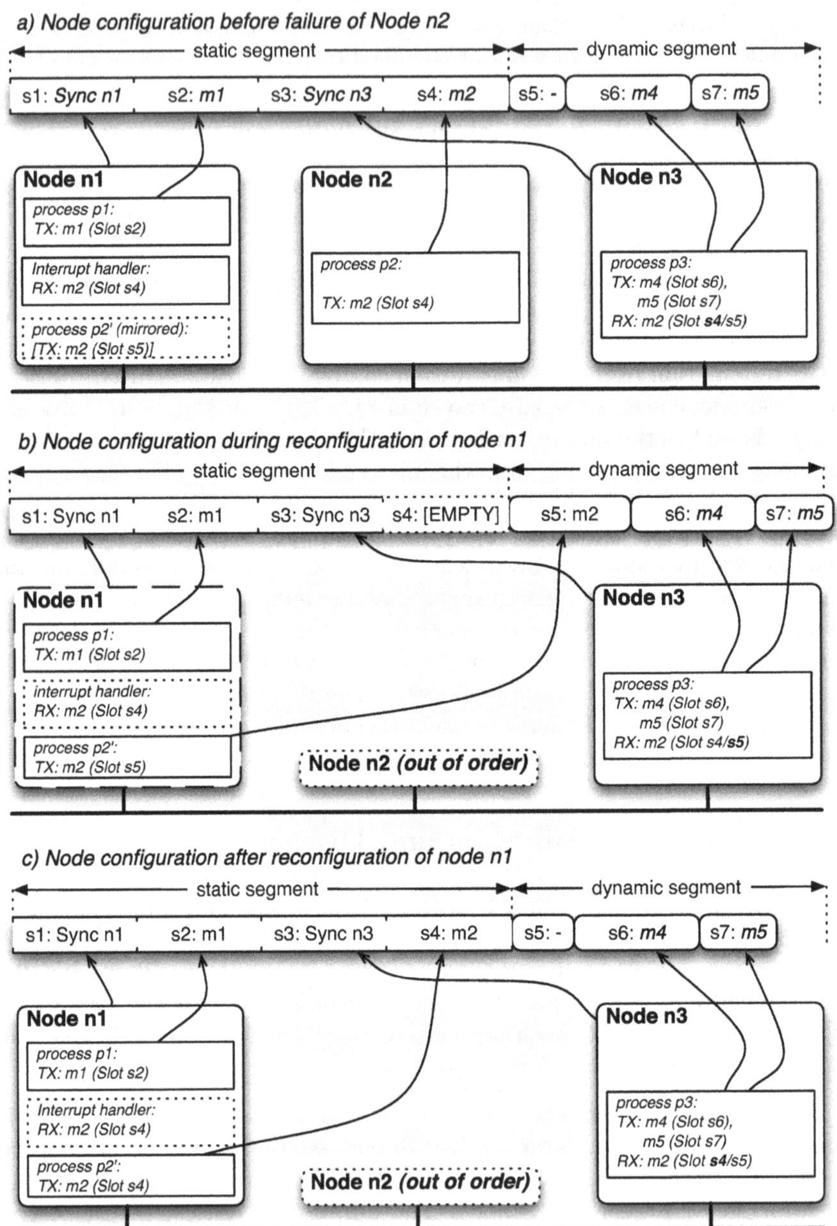

Fig. 6. Example for the hybrid approach of using secondary receive buffers and partially reconfiguring the static segment

- The time value t_{config} is the time which is required to load the new configuration to the communication controller. With our experimental setup, we measured a configuration time of $t_{config} = 4.4ms$.
- The last time value $t_{integrate}$ depends on the global parameters of the FlexRay network. It denotes the time to reintegrate a node after a reset, i.e., to synchronize the local communication controller with the other controllers. In general, the time for reintegrating a node into a running network lasts five bus cycles, two cycles for synchronizing the internal clock with the network and three cycles to check the correct synchronization of the clock with the network. Normally, the reintegration phase does not start with the beginning of a cycle. Thus, another cycle has to be considered for the worst case integration time. Note that the specification limits the cycle length to 16ms.

Partial Reconfiguration in the Dynamic Segment. At design time, this strategy demands the reservation of message buffers which can be used in case of a defect. These buffers will be reconfigured at runtime, i.e., they will be assigned to a new slot in the dynamic segment. This time for reassignment of message buffers to slots determines the latency for reconfiguration. It is obvious that the latency may vary with this method because it depends on the number of message buffers which need to be reassigned. Therefore, we determined the reconfiguration time with one message buffer using our experimental setup which is $t_{reconf} = 450\mu s$. Due to this short reconfiguration time, it might be possible to 1.) detect a missing message in the static slot, 2.) to reconfigure the transmit buffer in the dynamic segment, and 3.) to send the message in the dynamic segment by a replicated process within the same cycle. Thus, no extra delay caused by the reconfiguration would affect the operation of the system.

Reconfiguration with Secondary Receive Buffers. Since this strategy does not reconfigure the communication controller, no cycle gets lost until the first message will be sent by the replica. Note that this strategy causes problems concerning the message order and the time between two messages. Although the messages will be sent in the same cycle, they will be sent at a different point of time within this cycle. Moreover, a certain bandwidth will be unused before and after a node defect. In the static segment, some slots remain unused after a node defect, but additional bandwidth is required in the dynamic segment of the protocol. Otherwise, low priority messages can be displaced by the high priority messages of the replica. Also, exactly one mini slot needs to be reserved for the fault case.

Partial Reconfiguration of the Static Segment. While the previous three strategies can be implemented for the MFR4200 communication controller by Freescale as well as the E-Ray controller by Bosch, the partial reconfiguration is only possible with the latter controller. Due to the switching between two configurations, at most one cycle gets lost. This is due to the configuration mechanism of the E-Ray controller. In each cycle, the communication controller checks the configuration for a certain number of future slots. For example, in slot s16, the message buffer will be checked for the slots s24 to s31. If the message buffer for slot s20 will be reconfigured at this time, the reconfiguration is valid in the next cycle.

Table 1. Time for Reconfiguration

Reconfiguration Strategy	Time for Reconfiguration	Overhead
Complete Reconfiguration	$4.5ms + [5, 6) \cdot$ cycle length (determined for MFR4200)	++
Partial Reconfiguration in the Dynamic Segment	$450\mu s$ (determined for MFR4200)	++
Reconfiguration with Secondary Receive Buffers	(no reconfiguration necessary)	-
Partial Reconfiguration of the Static Segment	$[0, 1) \cdot$ cycle length (determined for E-Ray)	++

By combining the *partial reconfiguration of the static segment* and the *reconfiguration with secondary receive buffers*, it is possible to bridge the reconfiguration time of the static segment. In this case, no message will get lost within a cycle and the order of messages as well as the time between two messages will be the same before and after reconfiguration.

The different reconfiguration strategies differ in their implementation and timing behavior. Table 1 summarizes and compares the timing behavior as well as the implementation overhead.

6 Conclusion and Future Work

In this contribution, we presented different strategies for reconfiguring FlexRay schedules in order to reduce the message transfer latency or the cycle length, respectively. Such techniques are essential for building fault-tolerant systems using passive replication. Furthermore, we implemented the proposed strategies for a network consisting of five FlexRay nodes and evaluated the timing behavior of the reconfiguration process.

In the next step, we are planning to consider synchronous systems where the node schedules are synchronized to the bus schedule. This next step reveals two problems: 1.) the technical problem of synchronizing the nodes and 2.) the algorithmic problem of determining a global schedule for the bus and the nodes.

References

1. LIN-Subbus: Local Interconnect Network, `http://www.lin-subbus.org/`
2. CAN: Controller Area Network, `http://www.can.bosch.com/`
3. Kopetz, H., Grünsteidl, G.: TTP - A Time-Triggered Protocol for Fault-Tolerant Real-Time Systems. In: Proceedings of the 23rd IEEE International Symposium on Fault-Tolerant Computing (FTCS-23), Toulouse, France, pp. 524–532 (1993)
4. FlexRay Organization Consortium, `http://www.flexray.com`
5. Robert Bosch GmbH: E-Ray User's Manual, Rev. 1.2.3, 8 (2006)
6. Freescale Semiconductors: MFR4200 Data Sheet, Rev. 1, 12 (2006)

7. Wiesmann, M., et al.: Understanding Replication in Databases and Distributed Systems. In: Proceedings of the 20th International Conference on Distributed Computing Systems, EPFL Lausanne, ETH Zürich, pp. 184–191 (January 2000)
8. Pop, T., et al.: Timing Analysis of the FlexRay Communication Protocol. In: Proceedings of ECRTS Euromicro Conference on Real-Time Systems (2006)
9. Pop, T., et al.: Bus Access Optimisation for FlexRay-based Distributed Embedded Systems. In: DATE 2007: Proceedings of the Conference on Design, Automation and Test in Europe (2007)
10. Izosimov, V., et al.: Design optimization of time-and cost-constrained fault-tolerant distributed embedded systems. In: DATE 2005: Proceedings of the conference on Design, Automation and Test in Europe, Washington, DC, USA, pp. 864–869. IEEE Computer Society Press, Los Alamitos (2005)
11. TZM - Technologie Zentrum Mikroelektronik, http://www.tzm.de
12. Vector Informatik, http://www.vector-informatik.com

Synthesis of Multi-dimensional High-Speed FIFOs for Out-of-Order Communication

Joachim Keinert[1], Christian Haubelt[2], and Jürgen Teich[2]

[1] Fraunhofer Institute for Integrated Circuits IIS,
Am Wolfsmantel 33, 91058 Erlangen, Germany
Joachim.Keinert@iis.fraunhofer.de

[2] Hardware/Software Co-Design, Department of Computer Science,
University of Erlangen-Nuremberg,
Am Weichselgarten 3, 91058 Erlangen, Germany
{haubelt,teich}@cs.fau.de

Abstract. Due to increasing complexity of modern real-time image processing applications, classical hardware development at register transfer level becomes more and more the bottleneck of technological progress. Modeling those applications by help of multi-dimensional data flow and providing efficient means for their synthesis in hardware is one possibility to alleviate the situation. The key element of such descriptions is a multi-dimensional FIFO whose hardware synthesis shall be investigated in this paper. In particular, it considers the occurring out-of-order communication and proposes an architecture which is able to handle both address generation and flow control in an efficient manner. The resulting implementation allows reading and writing one pixel per clock cycle with an operation frequency of up to 300 MHz. This is even sufficient to process very huge images occurring in the domain of digital cinema in real-time.

1 Introduction

With increasing capacities of *Field Programmable Gate Arrays (FPGAs)*, more and more complex applications with growing demands can be realized. This can also be observed in the domain of digital image processing where new standards and algorithms offer powerful functionality at the price of huge complexity. JPEG2000 [1] for instance is a new compression technique which is currently introduced in the domain of digital cinema. However, its huge computational requirements and algorithmic complexity together with the large image sizes attaining up to 4096×2140 pixels constitute severe challenges for a real-time implementation.

As this complexity is more and more difficult to cope with by a low level description like classical *Register Transfer Level (RTL)* source code in VHDL, high level synthesis is considered to play an important role in future system design. Whereas transformation from sequential C-code into a parallel hardware implementation requires complex extraction of the contained parallelism, data flow

U. Brinkschulte et al. (Eds.): ARCS 2008, LNCS 4934, pp. 130–143, 2008.

descriptions like *Synchronous Data Flow (SDF)* [2] or *Kahn Process Networks (KPN)* [3] offer a natural representation of the inherent coarse grained parallelism. For this purpose, the system is composed into a set of *actors* representing processes which are interconnected by *edges* modeling communication.

In classical one-dimensional data flow, this communication is realized by help of *FIFOs* which transport data elements, also called *tokens*, from a *source* actor to the corresponding *sink*. Image processing algorithms however work on multi-dimensional arrays of pixels where the order by which the data is produced and consumed might differ (*out-of-order communication*). FIFOs however only support strict in-order communication. Thus, the necessary pixel reordering either has to be hidden in the actor or leads to complex system descriptions. In both cases, analysis and optimization being important in order to achieve high-performance implementations are difficult.

In order to alleviate this situation, multi-dimensional data flow models of computation like *Windowed Synchronous Data Flow (WSDF)* [4] have been proposed. They take explicitly into account that a written or read token is part of a whole array. This geometric information allows describing out-of-order communication without hiding information in the actors. Consequently, the latter one is explicitly available for analysis [5] and optimization. This however also means that communication edges cannot be realized anymore by simple one-dimensional FIFOs. Instead, *multi-dimensional FIFOs* [6] have to be deployed which directly support out-of-order communication.

This paper focuses on the hardware implementation of such a FIFO in order to contribute to a synthesis path from multi-dimensional data flow descriptions to FPGA solutions. In particular, it shows how the occurring out-of-order communication can be solved efficiently. Thanks to its explicit modeling, different optimizations like relative address generation and fast flow control can be performed. Special care is taken, that also applications processing very huge image sizes in real-time can be taken into account. As a key result, an architecture is proposed which can read and write one token per clock cycle at frequencies up to 300 MHz, thus being sufficient to process images with 4096×2140 at 30 frames per second.

The remainder of this paper is as follows. After a comparison of our approach with related work in Section 2, Section 3 introduces the out-of-order communication which we want to handle. Section 4 then presents a hardware architecture for the corresponding multi-dimensional FIFO. The two major challenges, namely address generation and flow control, are discussed in Sections 5 and 6. Section 7 finally presents the results obtained by our implementation.

2 Related Work

As the handling of today's system complexity is a major challenge for future technological progress, communication generation for hardware implementations is an important topic in many research approaches. Ref. [7] for instance investigates for SDF graphs, how to efficiently transport huge amounts of data by splitting the FIFO functionality into an FPGA internal pointer transport and an external background memory for data storage. *SA-C* [8] allows generating hardware accelerators for sliding window algorithms described by special loops. *IMEM* [9] describes chains of local image processing algorithms and permits for efficient synthesis of the underlying FPGA-internal memory structures. *ADOPT* [10] investigates incremental address calculation when accessing multi-dimensional arrays. All these approaches pay no special attention to out-of-order communication and the resulting scheduling challenges.

Ref. [11] describes the communication techniques deployed for translating sequences of loop nests into parallel hardware implementations using the *DEFACTO* compiler. Different degrees of communication granularity are supported, ranging from individual pixels to complete images. A granularity however is only allowed, if production and consumption is performed in the same order. Furthermore, for chip-internal communication, huge amounts of data are transmitted in parallel requiring large register banks.

ESPAM is another loop-oriented design flow which takes out-of-order communication into account [12,13]. Ref. [12] proposes to use a *Content Addressable Memory (CAM)* storing the data values and an associated valid-bit. Whereas this leads to the smallest achievable memory size, CAMs are very expensive in terms of required hardware resources. Furthermore, the dynamic memory allocation requires two clock cycles per write and four clock cycles per read due to polling of the valid bit. One clock cycle is specified as 40 ns. Ref. [13] deploys a normal RAM. The address generation bases on a hyper-rectangle comprising all simultaneously *life* data elements. As in [12], a valid-bit is used to decide whether the required data element or free space is available. A write operation takes two clock cycles, a read three clock cycles, each having 10 ns.

In comparison with these approaches, the multi-dimensional FIFO we propose offers the typical status information like *full* and *empty* signals, as well as the amount of available data elements on the read side and free spaces on the write side. Thus, no valid-bit is necessary and the source resp. sink can determine very quickly whether a write or read is possible. As extremely huge image sizes shall be processed, a static memory allocation is preferred against CAM which is considered as being too expensive. The addressing scheme does not base on a hyper-rectangle, but instead linearization in production order is applied as this has come out to be more efficient for our applications [5]. In order to achieve sufficient throughput, we require that each clock cycle a pixel can be read and written simultaneously. Pipelining helps to achieve high synthesis frequencies. Finally, communication on pixel granularity is allowed independently on the production and consumption order.

3 Out-of-Order Communication

Out-of-order communication is a phenomenon which can be observed in various image processing applications. Many camera sources for instance deliver the images in a raster-scan order line by line, while the JPEG2000 compression standard [1] allows cutting these images into sub-images, so called *tiles*, which are then processed sequentially. Similar situations occur, when composing the code-blocks for entropy encoding or re-ordering the 8×8 blocks obtained from a JPEG decoder into a raster-scan order suitable for display devices. In all cases, the order by which the data elements are produced and read differs.

Figure 1 exemplarily shows the JPEG2000 tiling operation. The input image is generated line by line in raster scan order whereas the sink reads the tiles sequentially and applies the compression algorithm. In order to support this operation, the source and sink shown in Fig. 1(a) cannot be connected any more by a classical one-dimensional FIFO. Instead, the FIFO has to perform a data re-ordering and is called *multi-dimensional*, because it is aware of the token position in the multi-dimensional array. It is parameterized with the image size and the *execution order* of both the sink and the source. The latter one is described by dividing the array into a hierarchy of (hyper-)rectangles which are written and read in raster-scan order [5]. In Fig. 1 for instance, the source generates the complete image in raster scan order, whereas from the sink's point of view it is divided into six blocks forming the tiles.

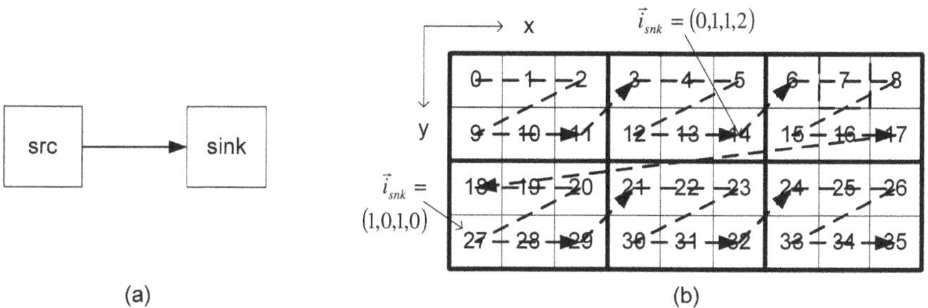

Fig. 1. JPEG2000 tiling. (a) shows the data flow graph, (b) the consumption and production order. The latter one is indicated by increasing numbers, the dashed lines illustrate the read order. Each rectangle corresponds to a pixel.

The multi-dimensional FIFO hence has two different tasks, namely (i) correct flow control and (ii) association of a memory cell to each data element. In other words, the FIFO has to figure out, whether there is enough space to accept the next token produced by the source and whether the data required next by the sink is already available. Especially, if the tiles are huge sized, this decision must be performed on the granularity of pixels instead of tiles, as the latter one would lead to a significant increase in delay and buffer size. For each written and read data element, the multi-dimensional FIFO has to derive the memory address of the FIFO buffer where the corresponding token is stored.

In the next section, a hardware architecture of the multi-dimensional FIFO is presented which fulfills these tasks.

4 HW-Architecture of the Multi-dimensional FIFO

As FIFOs have turned out to be an efficient medium for data transport and synchronization, the multi-dimensional FIFO shall provide a similar interface: Full and empty signals indicate whether the next token can be written or read. Fill-level indicators show the amount of tokens which can be read by the sink (*rd_count*) and written (*wr_count*) by the source before the FIFO gets empty or full. Moreover, it shall be possible to read and write one token per clock cycle.

Figure 2 shows the corresponding hardware architecture. It consists of two major parts, the memory where the tokens are stored and which can be both FPGA internal or external, and the controller. The latter one is responsible for the fill-level control and the address generation. For this purpose, it needs to know the current position of the source and sink actors in the processed image. This information is kept by so called *iteration vectors* $\boldsymbol{i}_{\mathbf{src}} \in I_{\text{src}} \subset \mathbb{N}^{n_{\text{src}}}$ and $\boldsymbol{i}_{\mathbf{snk}} \in I_{\text{snk}} \subset \mathbb{N}^{n_{\text{snk}}}$ where I_{src} and I_{snk} are sets of indices with dimensions n_{src} and n_{snk} respectively. For the tiling shown in Fig. 1, $\boldsymbol{i}_{\mathbf{src}} = (y_{\text{src}}, x_{\text{src}})$ is a two-dimensional vector indicating the row y_{src} and the column x_{src} of the next pixel to produce. $\boldsymbol{i}_{\mathbf{snk}} = (ty_{\text{snk}}, tx_{\text{snk}}, ry_{\text{snk}}, rx_{\text{snk}})$ has four dimensions and specifies the tile coordinates $(ty_{\text{snk}}, tx_{\text{snk}})$ and the position $(ry_{\text{snk}}, rx_{\text{snk}})$ relative to the tile borders of the next pixel to read (see Fig. 1).

The possible vector values are given by the image and tile extensions as well as the number of tiles. For Fig. 1, this leads to $\mathbf{0} \leq \boldsymbol{i}_{\mathbf{src}} \leq \boldsymbol{i}_{\mathbf{src,max}} = (3, 8)$ and $\mathbf{0} \leq \boldsymbol{i}_{\mathbf{snk}} \leq \boldsymbol{i}_{\mathbf{snk,max}} = (1, 2, 1, 2)$. Each time the *wr_en* signal or the *rd_nxt* signal is set to one, the corresponding iteration vector is updated by a simple lexicographic increment:

$$\langle \boldsymbol{i}(t+1), \boldsymbol{e_j} \rangle = \begin{cases} (\langle \boldsymbol{i}(t), \boldsymbol{e_j} \rangle + 1) \bmod (\langle \boldsymbol{i}_{\mathbf{max}}, \boldsymbol{e_j} \rangle + 1) & if\, C1 \\ \boldsymbol{i}(t) & otherwise \end{cases} \quad (1)$$
$$C1 : \forall j < k \leq n : \langle \boldsymbol{i}(t) - \boldsymbol{i}_{\mathbf{max}}, \boldsymbol{e_k} \rangle = 0$$

Example 1. Suppose, that the sink in Fig. 1 currently is processing pixel number 14 corresponding to an iteration vector of $\boldsymbol{i}_{\mathbf{snk}} = (0, 1, 1, 2)$. Applying equation (1), the iteration vector of the next sink invocation is given by $\text{succ}(\boldsymbol{i}_{\mathbf{snk}}) = (0, 2, 0, 0)$. In other words, the sink starts the third tile by processing pixel 6.

5 Address Generation

For each token which is written into the FIFO or read from it, the corresponding memory address has to be derived. For this task, we use linearization in production order, as investigations in [5] have shown, that this leads to good memory efficiency. This means that the generation of the source addresses is very simple, because for each produced source pixel, the write address has simply to be increased by one. If the latter one exceeds the available buffer size B which can be selected by the user, then a simple wrap around to the address zero has to be performed.

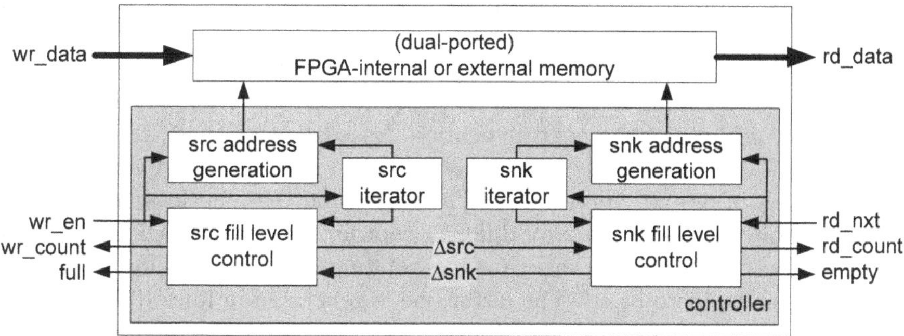

Fig. 2. Hardware architecture of the multi-dimensional FIFO

The determination of the read address is unfortunately more complex because of the occurring out-of-order communication. Due to the linearization in production order, we first need to calculate the producing source invocation from which we can then derive the memory address. Although it is easily possible to establish the corresponding mathematical relations (see also Section 6.1) we observed, that their solution in general requires several multiplications or even integer divisions[1]. As especially the latter ones are very expensive in hardware and both require in general several clock cycles, we invented another approach which for practical applications came out to work very well.

We observed in fact, that relative address generation is efficiently possible despite out-of-order communication. Take for instance the example given in Fig. 1. Due to the linearization in production order, the address of a data element simply corresponds to the number of the producing source actor invocation which is represented by Arabic numerals in Fig. 1. If we now follow the sink invocations in the order indicated by the dashed flashes, we can observe, that the address of the accessed data element can be easily derived from the address of the previous invocation. In the concrete example, the address increment simply amounts one, as long as we stay in the same line of the same tile. If we move to the next line in the same tile, the address is increased by seven. Moving to the next tile in horizontal direction means an address decrement of eight and so on. In other words, relative address generation is easily possible by simply taking the value of the sink iteration vector into account which tells us the current position of the sink actor.

As however we want to process very huge images, we cannot just synthesize a look-up table which associates to each sink iteration vector the corresponding address offset, as this would be extremely expensive in terms of hardware resources and synthesis time. Instead, we have to group as many identical address offsets as possible.

---

[1] Whereas for the example in Fig. 1 multiplications are sufficient, the re-ordering of blocks into a simple raster scan order requires indeed integer divisions.

Figure 3(a) shows the pseudo-code for the corresponding algorithm generating nested if-then-else statements expressing the correct address increment. It is started with $j = 1$ and obtains a table $T : I_{\text{snk}} \rightarrow \mathbb{Z}$ which assigns to each sink invocation $\boldsymbol{i}_{\text{snk}}$ the address increment $T(\boldsymbol{i}_{\text{snk}})$ required in order to calculate the data element address of the next invocation. Based on this table, the algorithm groups identical address increment values in order to obtain a compact representation in form of nested conditionals. Therefore, line (05) checks whether there exist two table entries which only differ in coordinate j and which do not have the same value. If this is the case, a corresponding distinction in form of a conditional has to be introduced. The latter one is generated in lines (06) and (08), whereas line (02) outputs the assignment of the result variable *addr_inc*.

In part (b) of Figure 3, the code generated by the above algorithm for the tiling example in Fig. 1 is print off. As it can be seen, the number of required if-statements is much smaller than the number of pixels forming the image. They can hence be efficiently synthesized in hardware.

```
(00) create_cond(j,c){
(01)   if j = $n_{\text{snk}} + 1$
(02)     →addr_inc := $T(\boldsymbol{c})$
(03)   else
(04)     for $\langle \boldsymbol{c}, \boldsymbol{e}_j \rangle = 0 : \langle \boldsymbol{i}_{\text{snk,max}}, \boldsymbol{e}_j \rangle - 1$
(05)       if $\left\{ \begin{array}{c} \exists \boldsymbol{k}_1, \boldsymbol{k}_2 \in I_{\text{snk}}(j, \boldsymbol{c}), \\ \langle \boldsymbol{k}_1, \boldsymbol{e}_j \rangle = \langle \boldsymbol{c}, \boldsymbol{e}_j \rangle, \\ \boldsymbol{k}_2 = \boldsymbol{k}_1 + \boldsymbol{e}_j : \\ T(\boldsymbol{k}_1) \neq T(\boldsymbol{k}_2) \end{array} \right\}$
(06)         →IF i_snk[j]<=$\langle \boldsymbol{c}, \boldsymbol{e}_j \rangle$
(07)         create_cond(j+1,c);
(08)         →ELSE
(09)       end if
(10)     end for
(11)     $\langle \boldsymbol{c}, \boldsymbol{e}_j \rangle = \langle \boldsymbol{i}_{\text{snk,max}}, \boldsymbol{e}_j \rangle$;
(12)     create_cond(j+1,c);
(13)   end if
(14) }
```

(a)

```
IF i_snk[2]<=1
 IF i_snk[3]<=0
  IF i_snk[4]<=1
   addr_inc := 1
  ELSE
   addr_inc := 7
 ELSIF i_snk[4]<=1
  addr_inc := 1
 ELSE
  addr_inc := -8
ELSIF i_snk[3]<=0
 IF i_snk[4]<=1
  addr_inc := 1
 ELSE
  addr_inc := 7
ELSE
 addr_inc := 1
```

(b)

Fig. 3. (a) Coding of the address offsets by nested conditionals. The resulting code output is indicated by the "→"-sign. $I_{\text{snk}}(j, \boldsymbol{c}) = \{\boldsymbol{i}_{\text{snk}} \in I_{\text{snk}} \mid \forall 1 \leq k < j : \langle \boldsymbol{i}_{\text{snk}} - \boldsymbol{c}, \boldsymbol{e}_k \rangle = 0\}$. (b) shows the (reformatted) code generated by the algorithm for the example given in Fig. 1. *Else*-statements immediately followed by an *if*-statement are replaced by *elsif*-constructs.

The next section shows, how based on the introduced memory model, efficient flow control can be realized. In other words, we want to solve the question when the source or sink can be executed.

6 Fill-Level Control

Whereas for one-dimensional FIFOs, the fill-level control is rather easy to implement, the out-of-order communication makes this task more challenging. Consider for instance once again the tiling operation illustrated in Fig. 1. Then it can be easily recognized, that each of the first three source invocations immediately allows the sink to execute once. The source invocations 3-8 however do not allow the sink to continue, because due to out-of-order communication, the latter one requires the data element produced by source invocation 9. On the other hand, once the sink has processed pixel 11, it can immediately continue with pixels 3-5 without waiting for the source, because they are already available.

A similar reasoning is valid for freeing buffer elements and hence for the question, whether the source can still execute or has to wait due to a full buffer. Because of the linearization in production order, pixels stored in the buffer can only be freed in the same order in which they have been produced. In other words, in Fig. 1 it is not possible to discard data elements 9-11 before 3-5, because otherwise we would get holes in the address space which would be too complex to handle in hardware. This however also means, that no buffer elements can be freed, when the sink processes pixels 9-11. On the other hand, when discarding pixel 8, also pixels 9-14 can be freed because they have already been processed.

This example clearly shows, that in contrast to one-dimensional FIFOs it is not sufficient anymore to count the tokens stored in the buffer in order to derive whether the source or the sink can execute. Consequently, in the architecture shown in Fig. 2, both the source and the sink fill level control modules contain their own counters indicating the number of possible source resp. sink invocations. Both are initialized with the correct values during startup. If neither initial tokens nor virtual border extension [4] occurs, the sink counter is set to zero and the source counter equals the buffer size. Each time the source or sink fires, the corresponding counter is decreased by one. Additionally, whenever the source executes, it communicates the number of additional sink invocations to the sink-level fill control and vice-versa.

The next subsection will show how the corresponding values can be derived.

6.1 Invocation Number Calculation

In order to determine the possible number of source and sink invocations, we need to know the additional possible sink invocations $\Delta snk\,(\boldsymbol{i_{\mathbf{src}}})$ resulting from the source invocation $\boldsymbol{i_{\mathbf{src}}}$ as well as the number of additional source invocations $\Delta src\,(\boldsymbol{i_{\mathbf{snk}}})$ due to execution of $\boldsymbol{i_{\mathbf{snk}}}$.

Both questions can be answered by help of a Parametric Integer Program (PIP) [14] which minimizes a system of linear inequalities in the sense of the lexicographic order $\prec$. The latter one establishes an order on $\mathbb{Z}^n$ and is defined as following:

$$\mathbb{Z}^n \ni \boldsymbol{i_1} \prec \boldsymbol{i_2} \in \mathbb{Z}^n$$
$$\Leftrightarrow \exists k, 1 \leq k \leq n : \langle \boldsymbol{i_1}, \boldsymbol{e_k} \rangle < \langle \boldsymbol{i_2}, \boldsymbol{e_k} \rangle \wedge \forall 1 \leq j < k : \langle \boldsymbol{i_1} - \boldsymbol{i_2}, \boldsymbol{e_j} \rangle = 0$$

For example, $\boldsymbol{i_1} = (1,1,1,2) \prec \boldsymbol{i_2} = (1,2,0,0)$. Due to our definition of the iteration vectors (see Section 4), $\boldsymbol{i_1} \prec \boldsymbol{i_2}$ also means, that $\boldsymbol{i_1}$ is executed before $\boldsymbol{i_2}$.

By help of a particular parametric integer program, we can now calculate $\Delta src\left(\boldsymbol{i_{snk}}\right)$. Given for instance the current sink iteration $\boldsymbol{i_{snk,0}} \in I_{\text{snk}} \subset \mathbb{N}^{n_{\text{snk}}}$, then the following PIP searches for the lexicographically smallest source iteration $\boldsymbol{i_{src}} \in I_{\text{src}} \subset \mathbb{N}^{n_{\text{src}}}$ whose data elements are still required[2]:

$$\min_{\prec}\left(\boldsymbol{i_{src}}\right) \tag{2}$$

$$\boldsymbol{i_{src,max}} \geq \boldsymbol{i_{src}} \geq \mathbf{0} \tag{3}$$

$$\boldsymbol{i_{snk,max}} \geq \boldsymbol{i_{snk}} \geq \mathbf{0} \tag{4}$$

$$\boldsymbol{i_{snk}} \succeq \boldsymbol{i_{snk,0}} \tag{5}$$

$$\underbrace{M_{\text{src}} \cdot \boldsymbol{i_{src}}}_{(a)} - \underbrace{M_{\text{snk}} \cdot \boldsymbol{i_{snk}}}_{(b)} = \mathbf{0} \tag{6}$$

$$\boldsymbol{i_{snk,max}} \geq \boldsymbol{i_{snk,0}} \geq \mathbf{0} \tag{7}$$

$\boldsymbol{i_{snk,0}}$ is considered as the PIP parameter whose possible range is specified by the *context* [14] in equation (7). Equation (6) describes the data element mapping. Part (a) calculates the coordinates of the pixel produced by the source invocation $\boldsymbol{i_{src}}$, part (b) the pixel coordinates accessed by the sink iteration $\boldsymbol{i_{snk}}$. Together, they establish a relation between the sink iteration $\boldsymbol{i_{snk}}$ and the corresponding source iteration $\boldsymbol{i_{src}}$ producing the required data element. Working on m-dimensional images, M_{src} is an $m \times n_{\text{src}}$ matrix, M_{snk} an $m \times n_{\text{snk}}$ matrix. For the example given in Fig. 1, we have

$$M_{\text{snk}} = \begin{pmatrix} 0\,3\,0\,1 \\ 2\,0\,1\,0 \end{pmatrix},\ M_{\text{src}} = \begin{pmatrix} 0\,1 \\ 1\,0 \end{pmatrix}.$$

Equations (3) and (4) specify the possible iteration range. Equation (5) finally takes care, that only sink iterations which do not occur before $\boldsymbol{i_{snk,0}}$ are taken into account. This relation can be transformed into a simple inequality as required for PIPs by establishing the following order:

$$O_{\text{snk}}\left(\boldsymbol{i_{snk}}\right) = \left\langle \boldsymbol{i_{snk}}, \boldsymbol{o_{snk}} \right\rangle$$

$$\left\langle \boldsymbol{o_{snk}}, \boldsymbol{e_j} \right\rangle = \prod_{k=j+1}^{n_{\text{snk}}} \left(\left\langle \boldsymbol{i_{snk,max}}, \boldsymbol{e_k} \right\rangle + 1\right),\ 1 \leq j \leq n_{\text{snk}}$$

It can be easily seen, that $\boldsymbol{i_{snk}} \succeq \boldsymbol{i_{snk,0}} \Leftrightarrow O_{\text{snk}}\left(\boldsymbol{i_{snk}}\right) \geq O_{\text{snk}}\left(\boldsymbol{i_{snk,0}}\right)$. Equation (5) can hence be replaced by

$$O_{\text{snk}}\left(\boldsymbol{i_{snk}}\right) \geq O_{\text{snk}}\left(\boldsymbol{i_{snk,0}}\right) \tag{8}$$

The overall system of inequalities thus searches the earliest source iteration (Eq. (2)) whose produced data element is required by a sink invocation $\boldsymbol{i_{snk}}$

[2] We do not detail border processing or initial tokens in this paper.

(Eq. (6)) which occurs not before $\boldsymbol{i}_{\mathbf{snk,0}}$. In other words, let $\boldsymbol{i}_{\mathbf{src}} = f(\boldsymbol{i}_{\mathbf{snk,0}})$ be the solution of the above PIP. Then we know, that all data elements produced before $f(\boldsymbol{i}_{\mathbf{snk,0}})$ are not required anymore and can be discarded. If we now solve the same PIP for the successor of $\boldsymbol{i}_{\mathbf{snk,0}}$, we can derive the number of additional data elements which can be discarded after execution of $\boldsymbol{i}_{\mathbf{snk,0}}$and hence the number of additional possible source invocations:

$$\Delta src(\boldsymbol{i}_{\mathbf{snk,0}}) = O_{\mathrm{src}}(f(\mathrm{succ}(\boldsymbol{i}_{\mathbf{snk,0}}))) - O_{\mathrm{src}}(f(\boldsymbol{i}_{\mathbf{snk,0}})) \ .$$

$O_{\mathrm{src}} : I_{\mathrm{src}} \rightarrow \mathbb{N}_0$ is a function which enumerates all source invocations as shown in Fig. 1. A similar reasoning can be performed for $\Delta snk(\boldsymbol{i}_{\mathbf{src}})$.

6.2 Solution of the PIP

Solutions of parametric integer programs can be expressed symbolically by help of nested conditionals. The latter ones can be obtained by help of the PIP-library [15] which can solve parametric integer programs as those presented in the previous section. However, in practical implementations, we observed severe difficulties. First, the expressions returned by the PIP-library are extremely complex. Although we succeeded to perform various simplifications, for some examples they stayed unsuitable for a hardware implementation. Secondly, even for very small image sizes, we observed sometimes a tremendous calculation effort and extremely huge memory requirements. Even worse, sometimes the PIP-library failed completely.

Consequently, we have elaborated an alternative approach to solve the above parametric integer program. It allows to derive $f(\boldsymbol{i}_{\mathbf{snk,0}})$ by help of simulation and bases on the buffer analysis presented in [5]. Whereas this does not allow for symbolic solutions, it can process very huge image sizes in reasonable time. As a result, we obtain a table $T : I_{\mathrm{snk}} \rightarrow \mathbb{N}_0$ which assigns to each sink iteration the resulting number of additional source invocations. By help of the algorithm shown in Fig. 3, this table can be coded as nested conditionals which can be efficiently synthesized in hardware.

6.3 Elimination of Modular Dependencies

Whereas for the example given in Fig. 1 determination of $\Delta\mathrm{src}(\boldsymbol{i}_{\mathbf{snk}})$ by the above approach does not cause any difficulties, $\Delta\mathrm{snk}(\boldsymbol{i}_{\mathbf{src}})$ shows inherent modular dependencies. This is because the number of additional possible sink invocations depends on the tile structure. Consider for instance the first row of tiles in Fig. 1. Then for all tiles except the last one, we observe that whenever the source has generated the last pixel of a tile, the sink can not only read this pixel, but also all lines of the next tile except for the last line. Hence, in order to determine the value of $\Delta\mathrm{snk}(\boldsymbol{i}_{\mathbf{src}})$, the multi-dimensional FIFO has to know whether the source has produced the last pixel of a tile. Mathematically, this is nothing else than checking whether

$$\langle \boldsymbol{i}_{\mathbf{src}}, \boldsymbol{e}_{\mathbf{1}} \rangle \bmod 2 = 1 \tag{9}$$

$$\langle \boldsymbol{i}_{\mathbf{src}}, \boldsymbol{e}_{\mathbf{2}} \rangle \bmod 3 = 2 \tag{10}$$

Unfortunately, this modular dependency increases the complexity of the resulting hardware implementation. As the nested conditionals generated by the algorithm shown in Fig. 3 do not contain any modulo function, they are translated into a possible huge amount of conditions. Equation (10) for instance can be represented by $\langle \boldsymbol{i}_{\mathbf{src}}, \boldsymbol{e}_{\mathbf{2}} \rangle = 2 \vee \langle \boldsymbol{i}_{\mathbf{src}}, \boldsymbol{e}_{\mathbf{2}} \rangle = 5 \vee \ldots$. This however increases the required resources for a hardware implementation. Furthermore, even if the conditions included a modulo function, this would not help much, as its hardware realization is expensive too.

Fortunately, the situation can be easily improved by replacing $\boldsymbol{i}_{\mathbf{src}}$ with a four dimensional vector: $\boldsymbol{i}^*_{\mathbf{src}} = \left(y^*_{\mathrm{src},1}, y^*_{\mathrm{src},2}, x^*_{\mathrm{src},1}, x^*_{\mathrm{src},2}\right)$ with $\mathbf{0} \leq \boldsymbol{i}^*_{\mathbf{src}} \leq (1,1,2,2)$. This removes the modular dependencies, because they are now already occurring in the source iterator. In other words, equation (10) for instance can be replaced by $x^*_{\mathrm{src},2} = 2$ which can be efficiently represented in hardware.

7 Results

In order to verify our concept of the multi-dimensional FIFO, we have implemented it in VHDL and verified its functional correctness by help of different Modelsim simulations. In order to get an idea about the achievable speed, we have furthermore synthesized several configurations of the out-of-order communication shown in Fig. 1. As we want to process very huge images in real-time, we have written the VHDL code in such a way, that critical operations can be pipelined over several clock cycles. For instance, we allow the calculation of Δsnk and Δsrc to take several clock cycles as this does not violate our requirement to process one pixel per clock cycle. Additionally we have realized a pipelined memory access as it is found in many high-speed memories: As for high frequencies it is impossible to retrieve the desired data word within one clock cycle, the interface is designed in such a way, that the memory controller can issue one read request per clock cycle while it might take more than one clock cycle until the requested data word effectively arrives. We deploy the same principle for the sink address generation. Whereas both the sink address generation and the data access might take more than one clock cycle, we have designed the FIFO interface in such a way, that the sink can issue one read-request per clock cycle.

Tab. 1 shows the hardware results obtained after place-and-route with the Xilinx ISE 8.2 tools. Two different configurations are tested, using a big and a small tile size. The latter allows using internal block ram (BRAM) as FIFO buffer, whereas this is infeasible for the big tile size. In the latter case, we assume an external memory by assigning the address bits to FPGA pins. Note that an external memory controller is not taken into account, because the generation of FPGA output signals and sampling of FPGA input signals significantly complicates the achievement of high frequencies due to tight phase requirements. As however the proposed multi-dimensional FIFO is independent of the applied memory controller, the latter one is omitted in order to avoid influence on the synthesis timing.

Table 1. Achievable frequency and required hardware resources after place-and-route for an image size of 4096 × 2140 pixels

Tile size	Virtex4 LX25-12			Virtex2 XC2V6000-6		
	MHz	FF	LUT	MHz	FF	LUT
128 × 5 (BRAM)	300	503 (2%)	719 (3%)	193	503 (1%)	719 (1%)
128 × 5 (ext.)	300	471 (2%)	717 (3%)	195	471 (1%)	717 (1%)
1024 × 1070 (ext.)	262	612 (2%)	988 (4%)	174	612 (1%)	989 (1%)

As it can be seen, the proposed architecture for the multi-dimensional FIFO achieves both for recent and older FPGA technology very good operation frequencies. In the case of a Virtex4 device, the frequencies are even sufficient to process an image with 4096 × 2140 pixels at more than 30 frames per second which is a considerable throughput. Moreover, even with a Virtex2, 20 frames per second are possible. Nevertheless, the resource consumption is acceptable, needing not more than 1% of a Virtex2 6000 and not more than 4% of a Virtex4 LX25 which is a rather small chip.

Table 2 shows the overhead caused by the support of out-of-order communication. It compares the developed multi-dimensional FIFO with an ordinary FIFO generated by the *Xilinx CORE Generator* [16]. In order to allow for a fair comparison, the multi-dimensional FIFO is configured in such a way that data production and consumption occur in the same order and can thus be realized by an ordinary FIFO. Both FIFOs dispose of the same amount of memory equaling 16384 items. The multi-dimensional FIFO is synthesized in two variants. One uses the same pipeline settings required to achieve the high synthesis frequencies of Table 1. The second takes into account, that identical consumption and production order is less complex than out-of-order communication. Hence, less pipeline steps are required. Nevertheless, as expected, the multi-dimensional FIFO in both cases requires more resources and the achievable frequency is smaller than for the CORE Generator FIFO. We identified as underlying reason the address calculation which is more complex for out-of-order communication compared to an ordinary FIFO. Consequently, the VHDL implementation needs to deploy more complex logic structures. Unfortunately, the synthesis tool is not able to remove this complexity even when the multi-dimensional FIFO is configured for identical consumption and production order. Consequently, a possible optimization strategy for complete systems is to replace multi-dimensional FIFOs with ordinary ones if no out-of-order communication is required.

However, whenever this is not possible like for the example shown in Fig. 1, our implementation proves to achieve high throughput with acceptable resources. Thanks to our static compile time analysis, we achieve higher synthesis frequencies compared to [12,13] (see Section 2). Furthermore, our implementation does not need any valid-bit and allows one read and write access per clock cycle which is not possible in [12,13]. On the other hand, as [12] uses dynamic memory allocation, it has an increased flexibility and possibly better memory utilization.

Table 2. Comparison of the multi-dimensional FIFO for out-of-order communication with an ordinary FIFO generated by the Xilinx CORE Generator for a Virtex4 LX25-12 device

	Frequency (MHz)	FF	LUT
Multi-dimensional, heavily pipelined	300	259	431
Multi-dimensional, less pipelined	305	212	395
CORE Generator	394	89	114

8 Conclusions

Due to the increasing complexity of modern image processing applications, classical hardware description at register transfer level gets more and more inadequate. Modeling by help of multi-dimensional data flow and providing efficient means for the required synthesis is one possibility to alleviate the situation, because the application is described at a higher level of abstraction.

The paper in hand contributes to this new methodology by providing an efficient and fast implementation of a multi-dimensional FIFO which allows for out-of-order communication. The latter one is required by different applications like JPEG2000 or JPEG. As a major contribution, this paper presented an architecture which is able to read and write one pixel per clock cycle. Usage of linearization in production order leads to memory efficient solutions and trivial source address generation. Determination of the corresponding sink address is more challenging due to the occurring out-of-order communication, but can be efficiently solved by relative address calculation. In order to solve the question, how often the source or sink can still be fired before the FIFO gets full or empty, a parametric integer program can be established. For its solution, two different approaches are available, namely by help of the *piplib* library and by simulation. Especially the latter allows to process huge images. The obtained synthesis results prove, that a very huge throughput can be achieved allowing to process images with 4096×2140 pixels in real-time.

References

1. ISO/IEC JTC1/SC29/WG1: JPEG 2000 Part I Final Committee Draft Version 1.0, N1646R (March 2002)
2. Lee, E.A., Parks, T.M.: Dataflow Process Networks. Proceedings of the IEEE 83(5), 773–801 (1995)
3. Kahn, G.: The semantics of a simple language for parallel programming. In: Proceedings of IFIP Congress 74, Stockholm, Sweden, pp. 471–475 (August 1974)
4. Keinert, J., Haubelt, C., Teich, J.: Modeling and analysis of windowed synchronous algorithms. In: ICASSP2006, vol. III, pp. 892–895 (2006)
5. Keinert, J., Haubelt, C., Teich, J.: Simulative buffer analysis of local image processing algorithms described by windowed synchronous data flow. In: IC-SAMOS, pp. 161–168 (July 2007)

6. Keinert, J., et al.: Actor-oriented modeling and simulation of sliding window image processing algorithms. In: Proceedings of the 2007 IEEE/ACM/IFIP Workshop of Embedded Systems for Real-Time Multimedia (ESTIMEDIA 2007), pp. 113–118 (2007)
7. Ko, D.I.: System Synthesis for Image Processing Applications. PhD thesis, University of Maryland (2006)
8. Draper, B., et al.: Compiling and optimizing image processing algorithms for FPGAs. In: Proceedings of Fifth IEEE International Workshop on Computer Architectures for Machine Perception, pp. 222–231(September 11–13, 2000)
9. Norell, H., Lawal, N., O'Nils, M.: Automatic generation of spatial and temporal memory architectures for embedded video processing systems. EURASIP Journal on Embedded Systems 2007, pages 10 (2007)
10. Miranda, M., et al.: ADOPT: Efficient hardware address generation in distributed memory architectures. In: ISSS 1996: Proceedings of the 9th international symposium on System synthesis, p. 20 (1996)
11. Ziegler, H.E., Hall, M.W., Diniz, P.C.: Compiler-generated communication for pipelined fpga applications. In: DAC 2003: Proceedings of the 40th conference on Design automation, pp. 610–615. ACM Press, New York (2003)
12. Zissulescu, C., Turjan, A., Kienhuis, B., Deprettere, E.: Solving out of order communication using CAM memory; an implementation. In: 13th Annual Workshop on Circuits, Systems and Signal Processing (ProRISC 2002) (2002)
13. Zissulescu, C., Kienhuis, B., Deprettere, E.: Communication synthesis in a multiprocessor environment. In: International Conference on Field Programmable Logic and Applications, pp. 360–365 (August 2005)
14. Feautrier, P.: Parametric integer programming. Operationnelle/Operations Research 22(3), 243–268 (1988)
15. `http://www.piplib.org/`
16. Xilinx: CORE Generator, `http://www.xilinx.com/`

A Novel Routing Architecture for Field-Programmable Gate-Arrays

Alexander Danilin[1], Martijn Bennebroek[2], and Sergei Sawitzki[1]

[1] NXP Semiconductors
Corporate Innovation and Technology, Research Division
High Tech Campus 32
5656AE Eindhoven, The Netherlands
{Alexander.Danilin,Sergei.Sawitzki}@nxp.com
[2] Philips Research Europe
High Tech Campus 5
5656AE Eindhoven, The Netherlands
martijn.bennebroek@philips.com

Abstract. A novel routing fabric is introduced that offers high flexibility at significantly lower silicon cost compared to routing fabrics currently incorporated in Field Programmable Gate Array (FPGA) devices, IP cores, and IP-core wrappers. This fabric is entirely constructed from multiplexers and unidirectional point-to-point connections, controlled by configuration bits. Key in optimizing its efficiency is to derive an appropriate connectivity pattern between logic blocks. Although this problem is complex in general, three guidelines have been identified to define suitable patterns. For a fabric connecting 4-input Look-Up-Tables, area savings of 60% are demonstrated when routing applications from the MCNC benchmark set. The use of multiplexer-based routing is not limited to these basic logic blocks only, so the potential of its usage for more complex logic blocks is illustrated as well. Benefits in timing closure, performance, and power are briefly discussed.

1 Introduction and Previous Work

Reconfigurable logic offers great flexibility with respect to standard-cell logic though at significant area, power, and delay penalties. The main culprit is the configurable routing fabric that consumes most of the silicon area and, even worse, is often not utilized efficiently when mapping applications. Therefore, academic and industrial effort has been and still is devoted to further improve routing fabrics traditionally in stand-alone devices but, more recently, also in embedded IP cores and IP core wrappers. Most commercial Field Programmable Gate Array (FPGA) devices, including the recent families of Xilinx and Altera, use a Manhattan routing fabric [1] schematically depicted in Fig. 1. Such routing fabrics are also known as mesh-based [1] or island-style [2]. Here, logic blocks are connected by connection boxes to adjacent horizontal and vertical routing channels.

U. Brinkschulte et al. (Eds.): ARCS 2008, LNCS 4934, pp. 144–158, 2008.

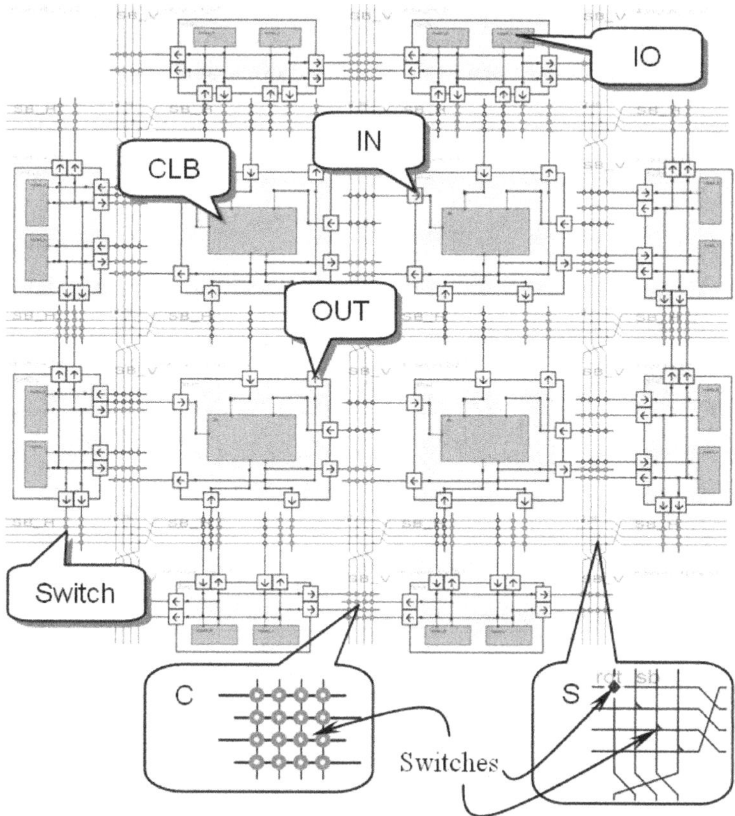

Fig. 1. Diagram of Manhattan routing fabric. C — connection block, S — switch block.

The wire segments in a channel can be of various lengths, from short (spanning a single or few logic blocks) to medium (four to sixteen logic blocks) and long (spanning half a die or even a full die). Switch boxes are located at the channel intersections to enable wire segments to be connected in any direction, horizontally or vertically, and thereby to route signals between any logic and/or IO blocks in the two-dimensional array. The main challenge in designing (Manhattan) routing fabrics is to achieve routability for a wide variety of applications with a minimum of routing resources such that the utilization density of logic blocks is maximized (whereby signal speeds and power consumption are still acceptable). In reality, Manhattan routing fabrics are designed based on best practices and incorporate a wealth of routing resources that dominate the FPGA area. For example, in [1] it is reported that 84% to 92% of the FPGA area is consumed by the routing fabric. The FPGA architectures studied in [1] contain logic blocks with clusters of six 4-LUTs. For FPGA architectures containing simpler logic blocks, the area consumption may become even more extreme and (for one of the FPGA architectures discussed later in this paper with only a single 4-LUT logic block) even amount to 95%. Manhattan routing fabrics themselves

Table 1. Definitions and related (standard-cell) area figures of Manhattan and multiplexer-based routing fabrics for two (LUT4 and DSP1) logic block variants. The routing resources have been chosen to enable routing of the applications listed in Table 2 and Table 4. For the DSP1 FPGA, the connectivity patterns of the routing multiplexers have not yet been fully optimized (simple copy-paste from LUT4 case) which may explain the limited 9% area savings.

		FPGA Architecture			
		LUT4		DSP1(=cluster of 4×LUT2)	
		Manhattan	mux-based	Manhattan	mux-based
routing resources per tile	#direct L1,L2,L4 horizontal tracks	0,0,2,28		8,4,8,8	
	#direct L1,L2,L4 vertical tracks	0,0,2,28		8,4,8,8	
	#tristate & pass-gate switches	140 & 120		72 & 90	
	#routing & connection muxes		16 & 10		36 & 48
configuration bits per tile	#logic block bits	17	17 (0 %)	27	27 (0 %)
	#routing bits	280	72 (-74 %)	317	226 (-29 %)
area consumption per tile	normalized area	1.000	0.397 (-60 %)	1.000	0.911 (-9 %)
	routing area	0.948	0.345 (-64 %)	0.867	0.778 (-10 %)
	logic block area	0.052	0.052 (0 %)	0.133	0.133 (0 %)

are dominated by the massive amount of tri-state and pass-gate switches, and associated configuration bits, in the (output-) connection and switch boxes. Unfortunately, the utilization of these switches is usually very low and, as shown in this paper, typically range between 3% and 10%.

Various approaches have been proposed to reduce the number of switches, and associated configuration bits in Manhattan routing fabrics. For example, in recent FPGA device families of Xilinx and Altera, unidirectional wires have been introduced next to traditional bidirectional wires to improve (area-)efficiency [1,3]. In [4], it is stated that up to 26% fewer switches are required when introducing hierarchy in Manhattan routing fabrics (according to a so-called Mesh-of-Tree approach). In the present work a simple 4-LUT logic block has been considered for which the multiplexer-based routing fabric will be shown to require up to 74% fewer routing bits and no switches at all. Alternative, non-Manhattan routing fabrics have been proposed to bring down the number of configuration bits (and area) by making use of crossbars between wire segments instead of Manhattan switches. Examples are the crossbar-based routing fabrics proposed by M2000 [5] and Leopard Logic [6] that make use of $N \times M$ and 2×2 crossbars, respectively. Like the Mesh-of-Tree Manhattan routing fabric, these crossbar-based routing

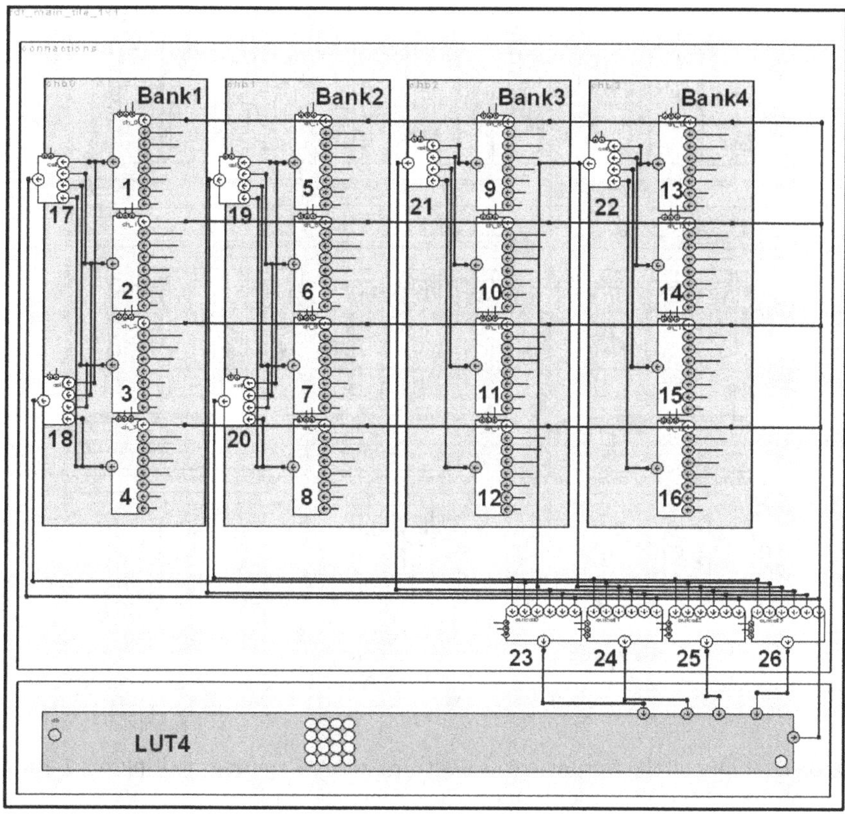

Fig. 2. Example of the multiplexer-based routing fabric in a single logic tile that contains a simple (4-input LUT) logic block. Complete cores are generated by abutment of logic tiles (and IO tiles at the core boundary) as illustrated in Figure 3.

fabrics incorporate hierarchy to improve routability and to prevent an explosion of routing resources for large FPGA arrays. However, in hierarchical routing fabrics, logic blocks that are physically close in the layout may be logically located in different hierarchical branches. Additional measures, like shortcuts or staggering [4], need to be introduced to bridge such hierarchy gaps. Such measures often will affect timing prediction and, therefore, complicate timing closure in application mapping.

This paper introduces a novel routing fabric that provides sufficient routability at relative low area cost. The work evolves from the research activities at Philips Research and NXP Semiconductors to derive area-efficient architectures for use as embedded FPGA cores. Unlike stand-alone FPGA devices, embedded FPGA cores provide more freedom for architectural optimization as the application domain is already known at FPGA core and SoC design time. Some initial results on multiplexer-based routing fabric were presented in [7]. This work further improves these results and puts the approach in a wider context.

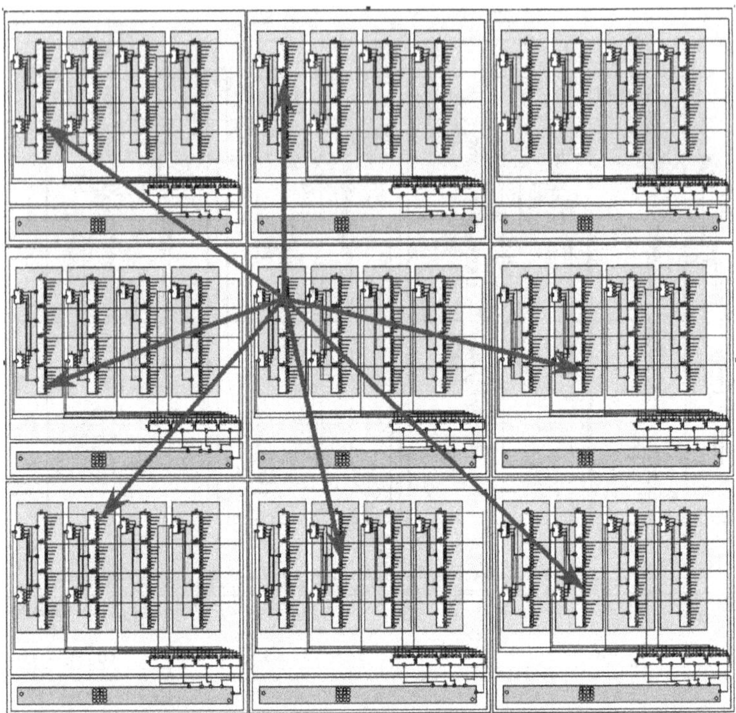

Fig. 3. Example of the output connectivity pattern of routing multiplexer 1 (in the center of the 4-LUT logic tile) to its seven neighbouring tiles

The rest of this paper is organized as follows. The novel routing fabric is illustrated in section 2, for a basic 4-LUT architecture, together with an appropriate Manhattan fabric against which it will be benchmarked. Section 3 presents the results when mapping applications from the MCNC benchmark suite to both fabrics. Here, the enhanced utilization of (area-costly) routing resources will be quantified as well as the resulting (average) cost per routed net. In section 4, the results of the implementation of the multiplexer-based routing fabrics for complex logic blocks are presented. In the section 5, a brief discussion is included on the additional (anticipated) benefits concerning performance, power, timing-closure, and on the challenge for novel place and route algorithms.

2 Routing Fabrics

This section details the multiplexer-based routing fabric connecting 4-LUTs and the Manhattan routing fabric used for comparison. Both routing fabrics have been defined using an in-house toolset of NXP Semiconductors [8] and dimensioned (e.g. the number of channel segments or routing multiplexers adapted) to enable routing of applications from the MCNC benchmark set with minimum

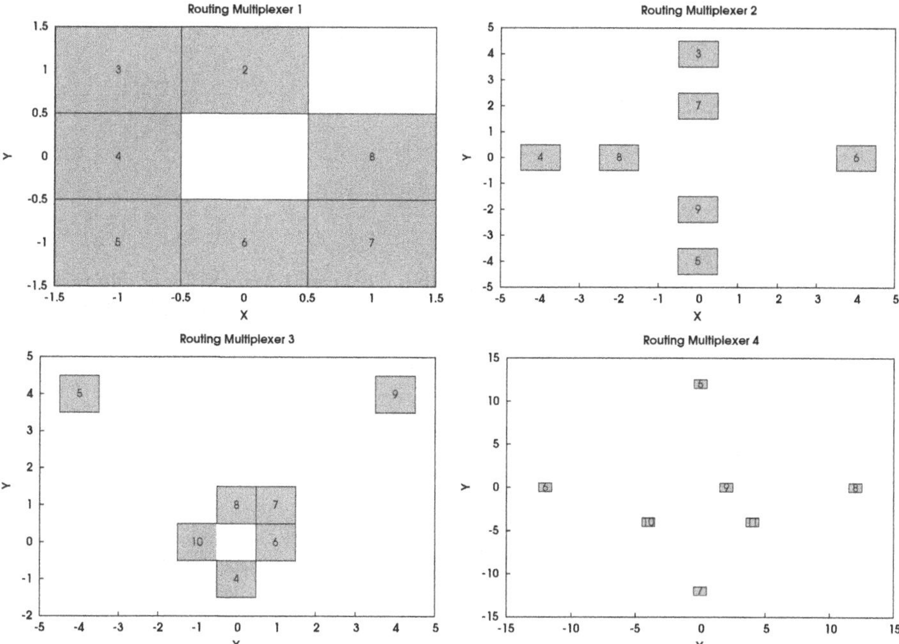

Fig. 4. Output connectivity patterns of routing multiplexers 1 to 4 (in the center 4-LUT logic tile) to, in total, 23 different surrounding tiles. The numbers indicate input channels of receiving tiles.

overhead. Table 1 depicts some main characteristics of these routing fabrics. The area numbers included in the table reveal that the multiplexer-based routing fabric can achieve routing with only 36% of the area needed by the Manhattan fabric.

2.1 Multiplexer-Based Fabric

Figure 2 depicts the multiplexer-based routing fabric for a single logic tile that contains a simple (4-LUT) logic block. The fabric shown contains 16 multiplexers (labeled 1 to 16) used for routing towards surrounding tiles. Within a tile, these routing multiplexers are connected through two layers of additional connection multiplexers, labeled 17 to 26, to all four inputs of a Look-Up-Table (4-LUT). The 4-LUT supports the functionality of any 4-input logic operation and its output is fed back to an input of all 8:1 routing multiplexers. The remaining 7 inputs of each routing multiplexer are connected to the outputs of routing multiplexers in (different) surrounding tiles. Likewise, the output of each routing multiplexer is connected to the input of routing multiplexers in 7 (different) surrounding tiles. An example of the output connectivity pattern of routing multiplexer 1 is shown in Fig. 3. The output connectivity patterns of multiplexers 2 to 4 are depicted in Fig. 4 and can be observed to partially overlap with

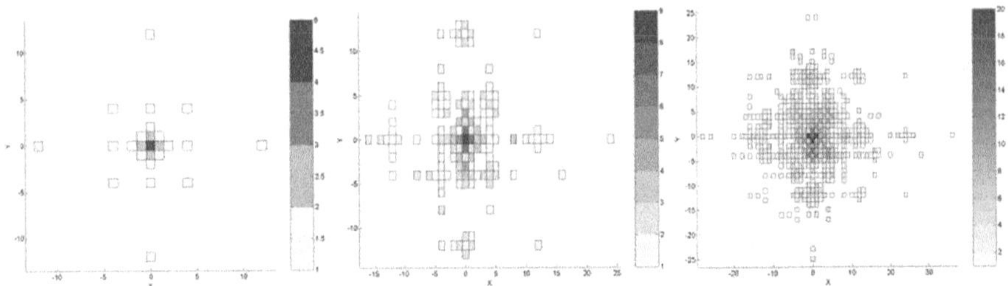

Fig. 5. Compound multiplexer-based connectivity pattern obtained by combining the individual connectivity patterns displayed in Figure 4 after (from left to right) 1-, 2-, and 3- hops. The colored indices indicate the number of paths leading to a X,Y position from routing multiplexers 1 to 4.

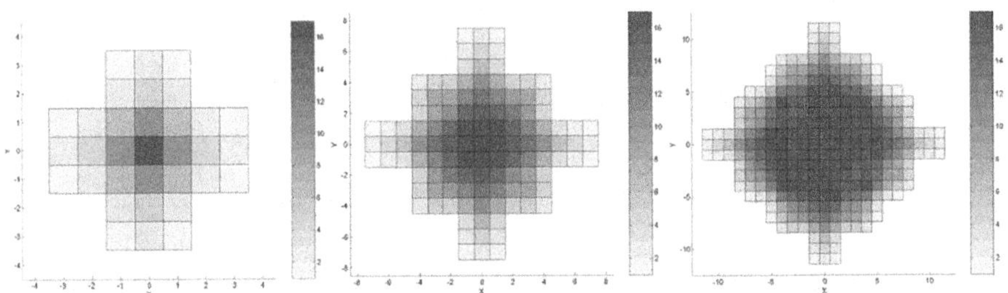

Fig. 6. Manhattan connectivity pattern after (from left to right) 1-, 2-, and 3- hops. The colored indices indicate the number of paths leading to a X,Y position using 4 horizontal and 4 vertical channels of length 4 each.

routing multiplexer 1 (in case of the orthogonal directions of multiplexer 3) and to connect to more remote tiles. For convenience, routing multiplexers 5 to 16 just replicate the output connectivity patterns of 1 to 4 although, in principle, all 16 multiplexers could have been given non-identical connectivity patterns. In Fig. 5, the combined region covered by all 16 routing multiplexers is illustrated when a going from a center 4-LUT through a first level of routing multiplexers (hop 1), a second (hop 2) and third level of routing multiplexers (hop 3).

2.2 Manhattan Routing Fabric

Figure 7 depicts a single logic tile of the Manhattan routing fabric connecting 4-LUT logic blocks and used for comparison. This fabric closely resembles that in [9] which has been argued to be beneficial for area and performance. As detailed in Table 1, the Manhattan fabric contains 28 length-4 and two length-2 segments, 140 (bidirectional) tri-state switches in the switch box, 120 pass gates in the output connection box (providing 100% 4-LUT output connectivity to all four sides), and four 30:1 multiplexers in the input connection box (providing 100% input connectivity from all four sides). Figure 6 depicts the region covered

Table 2. Mapping results of various applications onto a LUT4-based FPGA architecture implemented with a traditional Manhattan and the novel multiplexer-based routing fabric. As depicted in Table 1, the latter routing fabric reduces the total area by 60%. Applications are from the MCNC benchmark set.

Benchmarks					Manhattan				Mux-based		
Name	total #LUT4	total #nets	rel. % of 2-term nets	Core size #tiles	segment utilization	switch utilization	avg. area per net [μm^2]	avg. area per 2-term net [μm^2]	mux utilization	avg. area per net [μm^2]	avg. area per 2-term net [μm^2]
tseng	1047	1099	55 %	33×33	26 %	5 %	3305	1408	49 %	1057	365
ex5p	1064	1072	55 %	33×33	37 %	8 %	4102	1535	60 %	1351	427
apex4	1261	1271	65 %	36×36	37 %	7 %	3960	1495	58 %	1305	420
misex3	1397	1411	76 %	38×38	34 %	7 %	3798	1395	55 %	1253	397
diffeq	1497	1561	63 %	39×39	27 %	5 %	3257	1575	52 %	1105	394
alu4	1522	1536	83 %	40×40	31 %	6 %	3602	1557	52 %	1194	389
seq	1750	1791	75 %	42×42	37 %	7 %	3803	1620	57 %	1241	405
apex2	1878	1916	74 %	44×44	36 %	7 %	3856	1656	56 %	1260	414
s298	1931	1935	98 %	44×44	29 %	6 %	3424	1456	48 %	1137	364
dsip	1370	1599	71 %	54×54	16 %	3 %	3412	1481	28 %	1155	370
bigkey	1707	1936	70 %	54×54	19 %	4 %	3379	1435	31 %	1054	359
frisc	3556	3576	71 %	60×60	40 %	8 %	4046	1688	57 %	1271	422
elliptic	3604	3735	66 %	61×61	34 %	6 %	3615	1664	53 %	1160	416
spla	3690	3706	79 %	61×61	43 %	9 %	4214	1660	61 %	1467	415
des	1591	1847	72 %	63×63	17 %	3 %	3629	1417	24 %	1099	354
pdc	4575	4591	77 %	68×68	47 %	10 %	4474	1834	64 %	1542	459
ex1010	4598	4608	70 %	68×68	37 %	7 %	3773	1739	57 %	1257	435
avg.	2238	2305	72 %	49×49	32 %	6 %	3744	1566	51 %	1230	400

by this fabric when going from a center 4-LUT onto the first level of adjacent wires (hop 1), onto a second level of wires (hop 2, connected to the first level by switches), and onto a third level of wires (hop 3). Comparison of Fig. 5 and Fig. 6 shows that the multiplexer-based routing fabric may span a relative large XY region (per hop) and, moreover, provides off-diagonal connections. These characteristics prove beneficial for routability of the applications.

3 Results and Discussion

Table 2 presents the MCNC mapping results for the Manhattan and multiplexer-based routing fabrics described above. To provide a fair comparison, the quality of the in-house placer and router [8] as well as the number of tiles has been kept identical when mapping each application to both fabrics. Columns 6 and 7 within Table 2 confirm that the routing resources in the Manhattan fabric are not used efficiently at all and vary between 16% and 47% utilization for the segments and even between only 3% and 10% for the switches. In contrast, the multiplexers

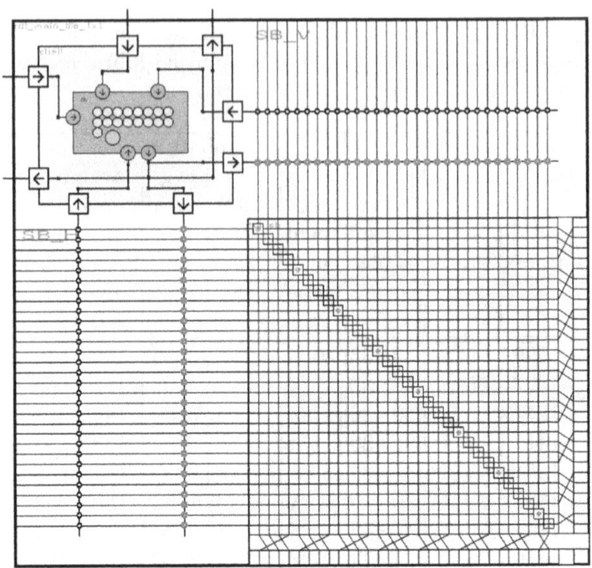

Fig. 7. Tile implementation of the Manhattan routing fabric with a 4-input LUT logic block

in the proposed fabric are used much more efficiently (between 24% and 64%). The inherent area-efficiency of the proposed routing fabric can be ascribed to its ability to route signal nets over (almost) independent channels thereby avoiding congestion. This is illustrated in Fig. 8(b) where only a single channel is required to route the indicated two-terminal net without affecting (blocking) channels at intermediate (non-producer or non-consumer) tiles. As a consequence, the number of routing channels can be kept low (e.g. 16 in the example in Fig. 2) which is a first condition for area efficiency. Second, the use of multiplexers enables to minimize the number of configuration bits (74% lower as indicated in column 5 of Table 1). Third, the use of (unidirectional) point-to-point connections enables routing of nets in all directions over all distances with a low number of hops (as indicated by column 5 in Table 3). This favors low-cost routing of especially two-terminal nets that, in practice, are dominant in most applications. Column 4 in Table 2 illustrates that, for the MCNC benchmark applications, on average 72% of all nets are two-terminal nets. In contrast, Manhattan routing fabrics typically route signal nets over tracks that do affect the routability of intermediate (non-producer or non-consumer) tiles. This can be inferred from Fig. 8(a) where the indicated two-terminal net can no longer be used to route the 4-LUT output signal of six intermediate tiles (labeled 1 to 6). Consequently, the number of tracks in a channel should not be too low and, in practice, the channel is often over-dimensioned to enhance routability. Additionally, the abundant use of switches and associated configuration bits, causes a high silicon cost per track (thus per signal net). Moreover, since these switches are not utilized efficiently

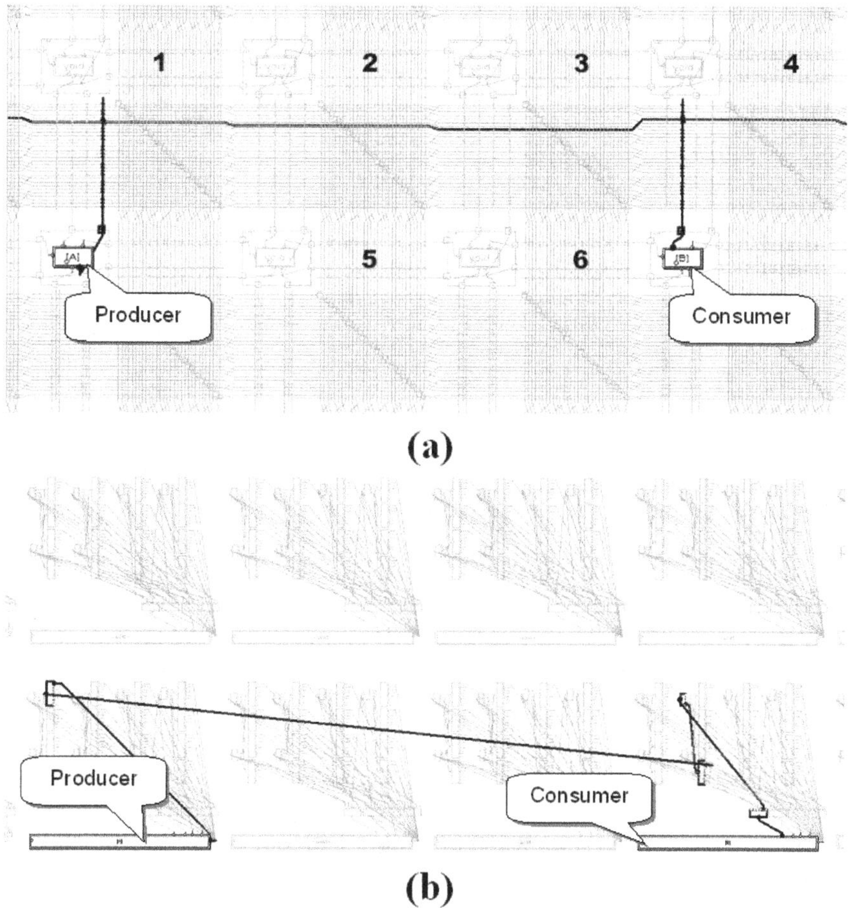

Fig. 8. Illustration of (hop 1) two-terminal connections in a Manhattan routing fabric (a) and multiplexer-based routing fabric (b)

(only 6% on average, as indicated by column 7 in Table 2). For example, the (hop 1) two-terminal net in Fig. 8 (a) requires only a single switch (and bit) at the output connect box of the producer to connect to the length 4 routing track, however, it wastes 29 output switches (and bits) to the remaining tracks. On the six intermediate tiles, another six output switches (and bits) are wasted.

Three bidirectional (back-to-back tri-state) switches (and six bits) are required to isolate the routing track. Finally, a single 30:1 multiplexer (requiring five bits) is needed in the input connection box to connect the routing track to a 4-LUT input of the consumer. The compound cost of this length 3 two-terminal net can be easily calculated based on the identified resources and the result is listed in column 3 of Table 3. The table also reflects that, due to the rigid choice of length 4 (orthogonal) tracks, longer (two-terminal) nets can be realized only by increasing the number of hops.

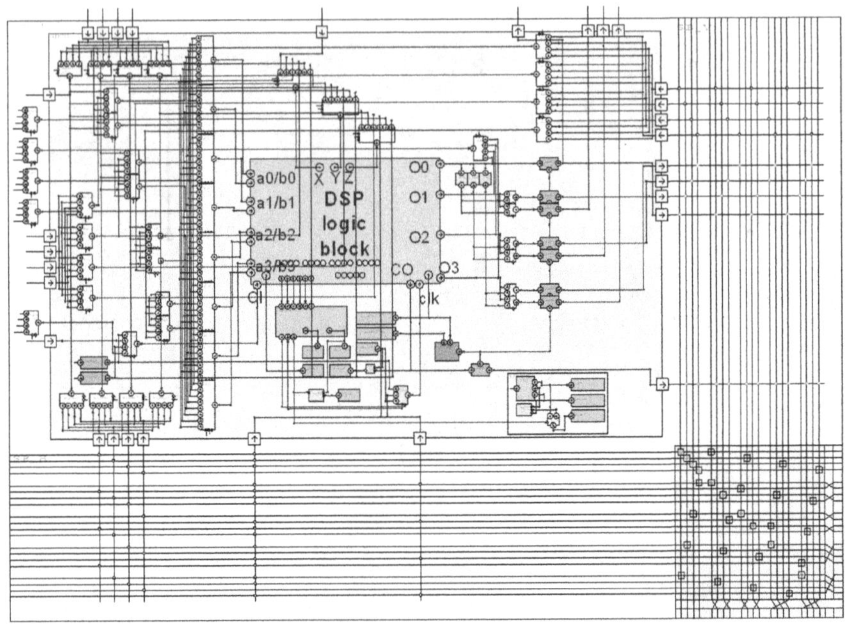

Fig. 9. Architecture of Manhattan routing fabric containing DSP logic block

Consequently, a two-terminal net of length 12 requires at least 2813 μm^2 in the Manhattan fabric, whereas, it may consume as little as 328 μm^2 for the proposed fabric. Note that the calculated costs per two-terminal nets matches the order of magnitude of the derived costs listed in Table 2 and, moreover, suggest that most two-terminal nets in both fabrics only require between 1 and 2 hops. It is important to note that it proved far from trivial to define multiplexer-based routing fabrics that are area efficient. First of all, one needs a flexible toolset capable of defining non-traditional routing fabrics and performing placement and routing exercises [8]. In addition, only "smartly" chosen connectivity patterns resulted in area-efficient fabrics. It proved rather difficult to define these patterns up-front as the point-to-point connections between routing multiplexers may be defined in all directions over all possible distances. So far, three "connectivity rules" have been defined. First, orthogonal directions should be (slightly) favored over non-orthogonal directions. These experiments used placement and routing algorithms that are based upon bounding-box cost functions. Such algorithms are known to favor orthogonal connections and, therefore, perform well for existing Manhattan routing fabrics (for which these algorithms have been developed). Second, connectivity patterns should favor short point-to-point connections. Finally, short, medium, and long point-to-point connections should be heavily interchanged. In general, if we define the set of coordinate pairs (x, y) reachable from any initial tile after n hops as $\{X; Y\}^n$, than multiplexer-based routing solves the

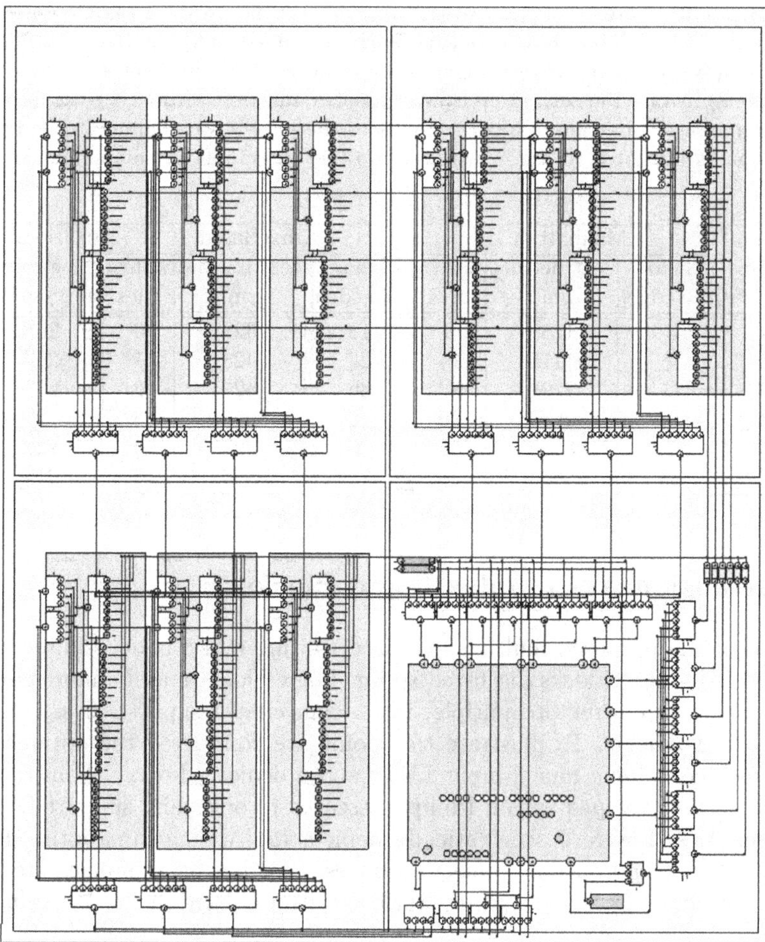

Fig. 10. Architecture of multiplexer-based routing fabric containing DSP logic block

optimization criteria $| \{X;Y\}^n | \rightarrow$ max together with $X_{\max} - X_{\min} \rightarrow$ max and $Y_{\max} - Y_{\min} \rightarrow$ max at lower area cost than Manhattan routing as long as these connectivity rules are followed. Still, the problem of finding the connectivity patterns $\{X_n, Y_n\}$ for every multiplexer $1 \ldots n$ together with suitable value for n is NP-complete.

It should be mentioned that in the current implementation of the multiplexer-based routing fabric, connections of a tile located close to a core edge are simply omitted (and thus non-available for routing) when extending across that core edge. In principle, these connections should be redirected (folded or mirrored) but, since experiments on oversized cores indicated no real changes in mapping results, no effort has been spend on the edge connections in this study.

Table 3. Modeled area cost per two-terminal net for the 4-LUT FPGA architectures with Manhattan and mux-based routing fabrics (detailed in Table 1). The underlying models simply add up the areas of the routing resources (multiplexers, switches, configuration bits) involved in setting up two-terminal connections. Note that the maximum length Lmax listed in column 5 corresponds to the mux-based channel in the positive x-direction as indicated in Fig. 5 whereas in other directions the maximum length is shorter.

#Hubs	Manhattan			Mux-Based			Ratio area per net
	Lmax [tile edge]	cost per net [μm^2]	#thru tiles	Lmax [tile edge]	cost per net [μm^2]	#thru tiles	mux/switch
1	3	1253	6	12	328	0	26%
2	7	1773	14	24	428	1	24%
3	11	2293	22	36	527	2	23%
4	15	2813	30	48	627	3	22%
5	19	3333	38	60	727	4	22%
6	23	3854	46	72	826	5	21%

4 Extension to Complex Logic Blocks

The use of the proposed multiplexer-based routing fabric is not limited to the simple 4-LUT logic blocks discussed so far. Logic blocks may be more complex and comprise a cluster of multiple, intra-connected N-input LUTs, equipped with dedicated logic. To illustrate this point, we considered the options for a logic block containing four 2-input LUTs and a dedicated carry chain that has been recently developed within Philips Research to optimally support DSP applications [10]. Figure 9 schematically depicts the Manhattan routing fabric, including input and output connection boxes, as it has been implemented on a recent test chip [10]. Some routing fabric details are listed in the 5th column of Table 1.

Table 1 also lists some details of an alternative multiplexer-based routing fabric that is schematically depicted in Fig. 10. The routing fabric strongly resembles the 4-LUT multiplexer-based fabric depicted in Fig. 2 but contains more routing and connection multiplexers to achieve routing of the increased number of functional inputs (11) and outputs (5) of the DSP logic block. For convenience, the 36 routing multiplexers are grouped into nine identical banks of four multiplexers each. The connectivity patterns of the four routing multiplexers within a bank simply replicate those derived for the 4-LUT case (displayed in Fig. 4 and Fig. 5) and no further optimization has been attempted that might lead to a further reduction in routing and/or connection multiplexers. Despite this non-optimality, the multiplexer-based routing fabric already requires 29% fewer configuration bits and 10% less routing area compared to its Manhattan alternative (see Table 1). The multiplexer-based routing fabric is (tuned to be) capable of routing the applications listed in Table 4. Again, routing resources are found to be used more efficiently compared to the Manhattan fabric although, for practical reasons, the utilization statistics could not be generated exhaustively

Table 4. Application mapping results for a DSP-tuned FPGA architecture with Manhattan and multiplexer-based routing fabrics. As depicted in Table 1, the latter routing fabric consumes (at least) 9% less area. Unlike the 4-LUT results in Table 2, heavy usage of the low-cost direct (point-to-point) connections in the Manhattan fabric (like in routing the asu8 and des56 benchmarks) can cause the average area per two-terminal net to become lower than in the multiplexer-based fabric.

Benchmark					Manhattan		Mux-based	
Name	#CLBs	#nets	% of 2-term nets	Core size #tiles	avg. area per net [μm^2]	avg. area per 2-term net [μm^2]	avg. area per net [μm^2]	avg. area per 2-term net [μm^2]
Viterbi	153	641	35%	8×18	916	793	747	665
asu8	381	1661	80%	17×17	799	482	764	596
des56	594	1987	66%	24×24	987	613	790	625

at present. However, columns 6 and 8 in Table 4 implicitly demonstrate the enhanced efficiency as, on average, multiplexer-based nets can be routed at lower silicon cost compared to Manhattan nets.

5 Conclusions

This paper presents first results on multiplexer-based routing fabrics that offer sufficient routability at significant lower silicon cost compared to common Manhattan routing fabrics. For a fabric connecting basic (4-LUT) logic blocks, area savings of 60% have been demonstrated for the MCNC benchmark set. This saving is derived from the standard-cell area involved when implementing both fabrics in a given CMOS node but does not include layout considerations. Based on previous layout experiences [10], we feel confident that the order of magnitude in area savings will not change significantly after layout. Key in achieving area efficiency is in optimizing the connectivity pattern between the logic blocks that, at present, requires a rather time-consuming empirical (trial-and-error) approach. So far, three connectivity rules have been identified, which (when implemented with an appropriate cost function in our semi-automated architecture exploration flow) could provide further optimizations and reduce the effort. The potential for a fabric connecting complex logic blocks is illustrated as well and the reported 10% in area savings is considered an upper boundary as it has been obtained without optimization of connectivity patterns. Although this paper focuses on area efficiency, multiplexer-based fabrics potentially offer timing-closure, performance and power benefits as well. The frequent use of pass gates in the switch boxes of Manhattan routing fabrics, each replacing two back-to-back tri-state drivers for area reasons, is known to complicate timing closure when routing applications. In practice, due to timing-closure problems and the inherent area overhead, configurable logic runs at lower speeds than (non-configurable) standard-cell logic. Since pass gates are excluded in multiplexer-based fabrics and, moreover, heavy pipelining of signal paths is possible at low cost (by adding by-passable latches to the multiplexer outputs with limited area cost), timing- predictability, timing-closure and performance should improve. Moreover, since the number of configuration bits is significantly lower in multiplexer-based fabrics, the static power dissipation will be lower as well. Future work will be required to quantify these anticipated performance and power benefits. Finally, the results presented in this paper have been derived using traditional place and route algorithms that are based on bounding-box cost functions. These algorithms typically have been developed and optimized for Manhattan-like routing fabrics and, for example, favor the abundant orthogonal connections. Since multiplexer-based routing fabrics allow for connections to be defined in all directions and over all possible distances, alternative (non-bounding box) algorithms may lead to further routing fabric optimizations. First trials with algorithms favoring spherical (and shorter) connections look promising and will be further explored.

References

1. Lemieux, G., Lewis, J.: Design of Interconnection Networks for Programmable Logic. Kluwer Academic Publishers, Dordrecht (2004)
2. Ahmed, E., Rose, J.: The effect of LUT and cluster size on deep-submicron FPGA performance and density. IEEE Transactions on Very Large Scale Integration (VLSI) Systems 12(3), 288–298 (2004)
3. Lemieux, G., et al.: Directional and single-driver wires in FPGA interconnect. In: Proceedings of the IEEE International Conference on Field-Programmable Technology, pp. 41–48 (2004)
4. DeHon, A., Rubin, J.: Design of FPGA Interconnect for Multilevel Metallization. IEEE Transactions on VLSI systems 12(10), 1038 (2004)
5. M2000 US6594810 patent: Reconfigurable Integrated Circuit with a Scalable Architecture
6. Leopard Logic, US6940308 patent: Interconnect Network for a Field Programmable Gate Array
7. Danilin, A., Bennebroek, M.: Multiplexer-Based Routing Fabric for Reconfigurable Logic. In: Proceeding of the International Conference on Field Programmable Logic and Applications 2007, pp. 27–29 (August 2007)
8. Danilin, A., Bennebroek, M., Sawitzki, S.: A novel toolset for the development of FPGA-like reconfigurable logic. In: Proceeding of the International Conference on Field Programmable Logic and Applications 2005, August 24–26, pp. 640–643 (2005)
9. Betz, V., Rose, J., Marquardt, A.: Architecture and CAD for Deep-Submicron FPGAs. Kluwer Academic Publishers, Dordrecht (1999)
10. Bennebroek, M., Vranken, K., Danilin, A.: Stuck-At Fault Testing of FPGA Cores using Standard Test Pattern Generation Tools. In: Proceedings of the 11th IEEE European Test Symposium (2006)

Part V

Real-Time Architectures

A Predictable Simultaneous Multithreading Scheme for Hard Real-Time

Jonathan Barre, Christine Rochange, and Pascal Sainrat

Institut de Recherche en Informatique de Toulouse,
Université de Toulouse - CNRS, France
{barre,rochange,sainrat}@irit.fr
http://www.irit.fr/TRACES

Abstract. Simultaneous multithreading (SMT) processors might be good candidates to fulfill the ever increasing performance requirements of embedded applications. However, state-of-the-art SMT architectures do not exhibit enough timing predictability to allow a static analysis of Worst-Case Execution Times. In this paper, we analyze the predictability of various policies implemented in SMT cores to control the sharing of resources by concurrent threads. Then, we propose an SMT architecture designed to run one hard real-time thread so that its execution time is analyzable even when other (non critical) threads are executed concurrently. Experimental results show that this architecture still provides high mean and worst-case performance.

1 Introduction

These last years, the complexity of embedded software has grown exponentially. As an example, it is now expected that next-generation upper class cars will include as much as 1GB binary code [1]. The explosion of the software size is due to the implementation of more and more functionalities, either to improve safety (e.g. anti-lock braking system), to augment the conveniences for the users (e.g. automatic control of windscreen wipers) or to address environmental issues (e.g. control of gas emissions).

In the same time, it is not desirable to increase the number of computing nodes at the same pace because this might raise difficulties concerning interconnections among others. Then one solution is to integrate several tasks in a single computing node, as supported by the Automotive Open System Architecture (AUTOSAR) and Integrated Modular Avionics (IMA) initiatives.

To support multitasking, it seems unavoidable that high-performance processors, like those now found in desktop computers, will more and more often be used in embedded systems. We feel that simultaneous multithreading (SMT) cores [16] might be good candidates, especially when tasks of different criticality levels are to be executed on the same node. However, high performance processors are generally incompatible with the predictability requirements of hard real-time applications. Actually, the state of the art in the domain of Worst-Case Execution Time computation cannot handle properly some mechanisms

U. Brinkschulte et al. (Eds.): ARCS 2008, LNCS 4934, pp. 161–172, 2008.

designed to improve instruction parallelism, e.g. speculative execution. Thread parallelism adds new difficulties and we feel that it cannot be safely analyzed by static WCET estimation techniques unless the hardware is designed for predictability. This is what this paper deals with.

We propose a WCET-aware architecture for a processor implementing simultaneous multithreading. This architecture is aimed at being able to execute *one* thread with hard real-time constraints in parallel with less critical threads. The issue is that the timing behavior of the hard real-time thread must be predictable through static analysis so that it can be proved that it will always meet its deadlines. The solution resides in carefully selecting/designing the instruction distribution and scheduling policies that control the sharing of internal resources between concurrent threads.

We are aware that some applications would require that *several* threads with hard real-time constraints be executed on the same processing node. Our architecture provides timing predictability for a *single* critical thread, but it can be considered as a first step towards designing an architecture that can handle several critical threads.

The paper is organized as follows. In Section 2, we give some background information on simultaneous multithreading. In particular, we review the resource distribution and scheduling strategies proposed in the literature and implemented in commercialized SMT processors. Section 3 describes the architecture that we propose to execute a real-time thread with a predictable Worst-Case Execution Time, in parallel with non real-time threads. Experimental results are provided and discussed in Section 4. Section 5 reviews related work and we conclude the paper in Section 6.

2 Simultaneous Multithreading and Timing Predictability

Simultaneous multithreading (SMT) processors execute several threads concurrently to improve the usage of hardware resources (mainly functional units) [16]. Concurrent threads share common resources: instruction queues, functional units, but also instruction and data caches and branch predictor tables. In this paper, we focus on the pipeline resources (we leave the issues related to caches and branch prediction for future work).

Two kinds of pipeline resources should be distinguished: *storage* resources (instruction queues and buffers) keep instructions for a while, generally for several cycles, while *bandwidth* resources (e.g. functional units or commit stage) are typically reallocated at each cycle [14]. The sharing of storage resources is controlled both in terms of space and time: there are several possible policies to distribute the resource entries among the active threads (*distribution* policies) and to select the instructions that will leave the resource at each cycle (*scheduling* policies). Space sharing does not make sense for bandwidth resources since they are reallocated on a cycle basis. Depending on their distribution and scheduling schemes, the sharing of resources can be a major source of indeterminism to the timing behavior of a thread.

In this section, we describe the most common distribution and scheduling policies (either in research or in industrial projects) and we highlight the predictability problems that may arise when considering a hard real-time thread executing along with arbitrary threads on an SMT processor.

2.1 Resource Distribution Policies

The most flexible scheme for distributing the entries of a resource (e.g. an instruction queue) among the threads is the *dynamic distribution* policy under which any instruction from any thread can compete for any free entry.

This policy was the first considered in academic research. The dynamic distribution policy was implicitly retained to maximize the resource usage (which is the primary objective of simultaneous multithreading), ensuring that any resource would be used if any thread needed it. However, since there is no limit on the number of resource entries that can be held by a thread, some threads might undergo starvation when the all the resource entries are used by other threads. When starvation may happen depends on the respective behaviors of the concurrent threads. Considering a real-time thread, it cannot be guaranteed that one of its instructions that would require an entry in a dynamically-distributed resource get it immediately and the time it might have to wait before being admitted by the resource cannot be bounded (unless very pessimistically). Hence, with dynamic distribution, the worst-case execution time of a thread cannot be estimated due to the high variability of the delays to gain access to shared resources. This policy is therefore not suitable for hard real-time applications.

The *dynamic distribution with threshold* policy was designed to minimize the risks of starvation. Now each thread cannot retain more slots in a resource than a given threshold (usually a percentage of the resource capacity, greater than one over the number of threads). A single thread cannot monopolize all the entries. This policy is used to control the instruction schedulers in the Pentium 4 Hyper-Threading architecture [13].

In the context of hard-real time applications, dynamic distribution with threshold still has an unpredictable nature: it cannot be determined whether a thread will be allowed to hold as many resource entries as the threshold since some entries might be used by some other threads. Then it might be delayed to get an entry in a storage resource even if it has not reached its threshold and this delay cannot be upper bounded. Hence, it is not possible to derive an accurate WCET estimation for a real-time thread.

The distribution of resources can also be *static*: each resource is partitioned and each thread has a private access to one partition. This completely prevents starvation and ensures a fair access to the common resources to all threads. The performance may not be optimal in this case since some threads may be slowed down due to a lack of resource while other threads might underuse their partition. Static partitioning is widely used to share instruction queues among threads in SMT implementations [9][13], except in the out-of-order parts of the pipeline (like the issue queues of the Power5 and the schedulers queues of the

Pentium 4). This is probably because a partitioned queue is easier to implement than a dynamically shared queue.

Static resource distribution is naturally the most adequate to hard real-time system since it is fully deterministic. Actually, each thread is granted a given amount of resources which it cannot exceed and which cannot be used by another thread. Then the behavior of this thread with regards to statically-partitioned resources does not depend on surrounding threads.

2.2 Scheduling Policies

Besides to their distribution policy, shared resources are also controlled by a scheduling policy that arbitrates between threads to select the instructions that can leave the resource and go forward in the pipeline. Possible schemes are overviewed in the next section.

The most common scheme is the very simple *Round-Robin* (RR) policy. It gives each thread its opportunity in turn in a circular way, regardless of the behavior of the other threads. One should distinguish the *optimized round-robin* policy (O-RR) that skips the turn of a thread that has not any ready instruction (or an empty thread slot) from the *strict round robin* (S-RR) algorithm that might select an idle thread. As RR is completely oblivious of what happens in the processor, it is reputed to exhibit moderate performance, in contrast with context-aware policies.

Considering hard real-time applications and WCET calculation, S-RR is a very predictable policy. It is very easy to determine when the instructions of a real-time thread will be selected, since it is fixed that the thread can be selected every $1/n$ cycles if the processor is designed to handle up to n active threads. The O-RR algorithm slightly impairs predictability but the delay between two successive active turns for a thread can still be upper-bounded. The access from almost all the statically-shared queues to downstream resources is controlled by an O-RR policy in the Intel Pentium 4 [13] and by an S-RR strategy in the IBM Power5 [9].

The *icount* policy is another possible strategy that is widely considered for scheduling the fetch queue in academic projects [2][3][5]. It is based on dynamic thread priorities which are re-evaluated at each cycle to reflect the number of instructions of each thread present in the pre-issue pipeline stages (the highest priorities are assigned to the threads that have the fewest instructions in these stages). Instructions of several threads can be fetched simultaneously, with the constraint that the thread with the highest priority is satisfied first. Several variants of the *icount* strategy have been proposed in the literature: they use some counters related to each thread as a basis for updating thread priorities. For example, the *brcount* policy [17] considers the number of branches in the pre-issue stages while the *drca* policy is based on the resource usage [5]). Unfortunately, priority-based thread scheduling makes the timing behavior of one thread dependent on the other active threads. Hence, *icount* and parented policies cannot be used in the context of a hard real-time thread requiring WCET calculation.

Another policy, that we call the *parallel* scheme, equally partitions the bandwidth among all the active threads by selecting the same number of instructions for each thread. This means that all threads can have instructions progressing in the pipeline at every cycle. As far as we know, this policy in only used in the IBM Power5 to select instructions for commit [9]. Each core of this processor is a 2-thread SMT that can commit a group of instructions from each thread at each cycle. This policy is fully deterministic as the progression of one thread is independent from the other threads.

3 A Predictable SMT Architecture

Our objective is to design a multithreaded (SMT) architecture that makes it possible to analyze the Worst-Case Execution Time of real-time tasks. As a first step, we propose an SMT processor where *one* hard real-time thread can run along with other non critical threads. The hard real-time thread should execute with no interference with the other threads to exhibit an analyzable timing behavior. In the same time, performance should be preserved for the other threads so that SMT benefits are not cancelled by our modifications in the architecture.

3.1 Basic Pipeline Structure

To illustrate our approach, we consider the basic SMT pipeline structure shown in Figure 1. In the fetch stage (IF), instructions of one thread are read from the instruction cache and stored in the fetch queue (FQ). There, they wait to be selected for decoding (ID), after what they enter the decode queue (DQ). After renaming (RN), they are allocated into the reorder buffer (ROB). The EX (execution) stage selects instructions with ready inputs and an available functional unit from the ROB and issues them to functional units. Instructions from the same thread might be executed *out-of-order* to improve instruction-level parallelism. Terminated instructions are finally read from the ROB by the CM (commit) stage and leave the pipeline.

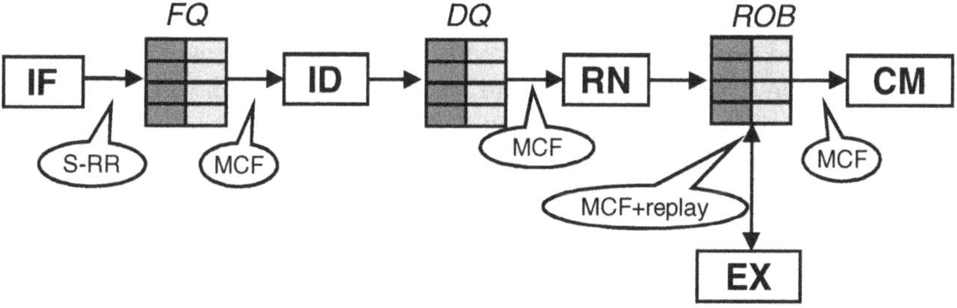

Fig. 1. A time-predictable SMT pipeline

3.2 Resource Distribution Policy

To achieve timing predictability, we statically partition each storage resource (i.e. instruction and decode queues and the reorder buffer). As discussed in the previous section, only static partitioning can make the timing behavior of a real-time thread analyzable. This is illustrated in Figure 1 where a capacity of two active threads is assumed: the fetch and decode queues and the reorder buffer are statically-distributed in two partitions, one for each thread.

3.3 Thread Scheduling

At each cycle, the IF stage fetches a sequence of instructions from a single thread:, the thread to be fetched is selected according to an S-RR policy.

As said previously, the fetch queue is statically partitioned. We must now specify the algorithm implemented to select the instructions to be decoded among those stored in the fetch queue. To have the hard real-time thread (also referred to as *hrt-t* in the following) processed in a way that does not depend on concurrent threads, we consider a partial fixed-priority scheme, where instructions from *hrt-t* are selected in the first place. If there are less *hrt-t* instructions in the fetch queue than the decode bandwidth, instructions from the non critical threads are selected on an O-RR basis. We will refer to this scheme as the *Most-Critical-First* (MCF) scheduling policy.

After decoding, instructions enter the partitioned decode queue. They are selected for renaming using the predictable MCF strategy described above. Once renamed, instructions are stored in the statically-partitioned reorder buffer where they wait for their input operands. When an instruction is ready, it becomes eligible for being issued to a functional unit. Besides to the intra-thread instruction scheduling policy (e.g. instructions are selected on an oldest-first basis), the thread scheduling policy has to arbitrate between the threads that have some ready instructions. As far as the hard real-time thread (*hrt-t*) is concerned, the delay for one of its ready instructions to be selected must not depend on concurrent threads. To achieve this, we complement the most-critical-first scheduling with a *Replay* scheme. When an *hrt-t* instruction is ready for execution, three situations can be observed:

- if the required functional unit is free, the instruction can be issued immediately;
- if the required functional unit is already allocated to an instruction that also belongs to the hard real-time thread, the execution is delayed. However, this is statically analyzable since it only depends on the thread own behavior.
- if the required functional unit is used by an instruction from a non critical thread, this instruction is squashed from the functional unit and switched back to the ready state in the reorder buffer. This means that it will have to be issued again later on. The functional unit is then immediately allocated to the *hrt-t* thread. Due to the MCF scheduling, this situation can only happen when a non critical thread executes an operation with a latency greater than one cycle in a non pipelined functional unit (in our example core, this only concerns divisions and loads/stores).

Finally, terminated instructions are selected for commit using a Most-Critical-First scheme that ensures timing predictability for the hard real-time thread.

4 Performance Evaluation

4.1 Simulation Methodology

We carried out the experiments reported in this paper using a cycle-level simulator developed as part of the OTAWA framework [6]. OTAWA is dedicated to WCET calculation and includes several utilities among which a cycle-level simulator built on SystemC. The simulator models generic processor architectures where each pipeline stage is seen as a box that reads instructions from an input queue, processes them by applying a set of predefined actions, and writes them to an output queue. Each queue is parameterized with a distribution policy and a scheduling policy. This timing simulator is driven by a functional simulator automatically generated from the PowerPC ISA description by our GLISS tool[1].

4.2 Processor Configuration

For the experiments, we have derived our predictable SMT architecture from a 4-way superscalar core, i.e. each stage is 4-instruction wide. The number of simultaneous threads has been fixed to 2 or 4 threads.

We have considered a perfect (oracle) branch predictor and a perfect (always hit) data cache. While we did not model the instruction cache (and in particular the related inter-thread interferences), we have considered a random 1% instruction miss rate, with a 100-cycle miss latency.

Table 1 gives the main characteristics of the pipeline. The queues are statically partitioned into 2 or 4 (number of threads). In the experiments, we consider two architectures: (a) the *baseline* core implements the O-RR scheduling policy for all the resources except for the issue to the functional units where instructions are selected on an oldest-first basis, independently of the thread they belong to; (b) the *WCET-aware* architecture is the one we designed to be time-predictable and implements our MCF policy together with the Replay scheme.

4.3 Benchmarks

A workload is composed of two or four threads compiled into a single binary code (this is because our functional simulator can only handle a single address space). The source code of each thread is embedded in a function call and the corresponding program counter is initialized at the entry point of this function. To maximize the possible inter-thread interferences, we have considered concurrent threads executing the same function. The different functions used in the experiments reported here are listed in Table 2 (their source code comes from the SNU-RT suite[2], a collection of relatively simple tasks commonly executed on hard real-time embedded systems).

[1] `http://www.irit.fr/Gliss`

[2] `http://archi.snu.ac.kr/realtime/benchmark`

Table 1. Baseline configuration

Parameter		Value
Pipeline width		4
Fetch queue size		16
Decode queue size		16
Reorder buffer size		16
Functional unit latencies	MEM (pipelined)	2
	ALU1	1
	ALU2	1
	FALU (pipelined)	3
	MUL (pipelined)	6
	DIV (pipelined)	15

Table 2. Benchmarks functions

Function	Comments
`fft1k`	Fast Fourier Transform
`fir`	FIR filter with Gaussian number generation
`ludcmp`	LU decomposition
`lms`	LMS adaptative signal enhancement

All executables were compiled using `-O` directive that removes most of useless accesses to memory while keeping the code algorithmic structure (which allows performing the flow analysis on the source code).

4.4 Experimental Results

To serve as a reference, we have simulated each thread in parallel with dummy threads, i.e. threads that do not execute any instruction nor allocate any dynamically-shared resource and, therefore, do not interfere with the main thread. All the storage resources were considered as partitioned. Raw results (execution time of the main thread, expressed in cycles, measured on the baseline, unpredictable architecture) are given in Table 3. The execution time of the reference thread is always longer with 4 threads than with 2 threads because the overall capacity of the resources is the same in both cases. Then, in the 4-thread configuration, each thread has smaller private partitions.

Table 3. Reference execution times

	2 threads	4 threads
`fft1k`	1 239 147	2 384 030
`fir`	25 022	47 897
`ludcmp`	4 165	8 205
`fft1k`	390 815	752 858

Table 4 shows how the same threads execute on the baseline (unpredictable) SMT architecture when they are concurrent to other (identical) threads. The reported execution times are those of the last completed threads: all the other threads have a lower execution time. In each case, we indicate the increase in the execution time over the reference measurements reported in Table 3.

Table 4. Execution times in the unpredictable SMT core

	2 threads	**4 threads**
fft1k	1 345 598 *+8.6%*	3 009 002 *+26.2%*
fir	26 548 *+6.1%*	60 691 *+26.7%*
ludcmp	5 068 *+21.6%*	10 686 *+30.2%*
lms	420 161 *+7.5%*	951 210 *+26.3%*

Table 5. Percentages of instructions delayed by concurrent threads

		delays (# cycles)					
		0	**1-5**	**6-10**	**11-20**	**21-30**	**>30**
fft1k	*2 threads*	93.93%	4.18%	1.25%	0.58%	0.04%	0.02%
	4 threads	94.50%	5.29%	0.09%	0.11%	0.00%	0.00%
fir	*2 threads*	92.93%	5.88%	0.76%	0.38%	0.02%	0.03%
	4 threads	96.66%	3.16%	0.09%	0.09%	0.00%	0.00%
ludcmp	*2 threads*	89.32%	9.83%	0.19%	0.43%	0.04%	0.19%
	4 threads	98.88%	1.01%	0.08%	0.04%	0.00%	0.00%
lms	*2 threads*	92.16%	7.08%	0.47%	0.24%	0.03%	0.03%
	4 threads	96.91%	2.89%	0.09%	0.11%	0.00%	0.00%

As expected, the global execution time for two or four "real" threads is higher than the execution time of one thread executed in parallel with dummy threads. This is due to threads competing for accessing dynamically-shared resources. Table 5 gives an insight into how often and how long instructions from one thread are delayed due to instructions from concurrent threads. The numbers indicate the percentage of instructions that have been delayed by n cycles to get a resource (physical register or functional unit). It appears that about 10% of the instructions are delayed by a concurrent thread in a 2-thread core. Note that some instructions undergo severe delays (some delays as long as up to 90 cycles have been observed).

The results achieved with our predictable core (with the *Most-Critical-First* scheduling policy and the *Replay* scheme) are shown in Table 6. Again, the execution times are those of the last completed thread. They do not concern the hard real time thread that exhibits, *in all cases*, the same execution time as

Table 6. Execution times in the predictable SMT core

	2 threads	4 threads
ff1k	1 867 441 *+38.8%*	3 503 297 *+16.4%*
fir	37 401 *+40.9%*	68 023 *+12.1%*
ludcmp	5 302 *+4.6%*	12 012 *+12.4%*
lms	520 369 *+23.8%*	1 001 526 *+5.3%*

the one given in Table 3. The performance loss (in terms of execution time increase) against the baseline SMT architecture is indicated in each case.

Naturally, the scheduling schemes that we implemented to insure timing predictability for one critical thread do degrade performance. However, the loss is moderate: 27% on a mean for a 2-thread core and 11.6% for a 4-thread core. The reason why the loss is higher for the 2-thread core is that, in that case, a quarter (instead of a half) of the statically-partitioned resources is dedicated to the real-time thread. Then roughly 25% (instead of 50%) of the instructions are prioritized at the expense of the other 75% (50%). This lets more opportunities for non-critical instructions to execute normally.

5 Related Work

Crowley and Baer [7] consider analyzing an SMT processor using a widely used approach for WCET computation (namely the IPET technique [11]). They express all the possible thread interleavings within the ILP (Integer Linear Programming) formulation of WCET computation. Naturally, the size of the generated ILP specification grows exponentially with the size of the threads and, unless considering very simple tasks (with few flow control), the problem cannot be solved in a reasonable time. This assessment is at the root of our work on predictable SMT architecture: we believe that the interleaving of threads must be controlled at runtime (i.e. by the hardware) to make it efficient and deterministic so that it can be taken into account when estimating the worst-case execution times of tasks with strict deadlines. Other works aim to make the timing behavior of threads more predictable through the use of appropriate thread scheduling strategies at the system level. Lo *et al.* [12] explore algorithms used to schedule real-time tasks on an SMT architecture. However, they do not take into account the possible interferences between active threads inside the pipeline and their effects on the worst-case execution times. In [10], Kato *et al.* introduce the notion of Multi-Case Execution Time (MCET): it is computed from the different WCETs of the considered thread when it runs along with different concurrent threads. We feel that the number of different possible WCET values for a thread might be considerable as soon as each thread exhibits a large number of possible execution paths (then the number of possible interleavings with other threads might be huge). This is why we believe that these works require a predictable architecture (like the one we propose in this paper) to get valid results.

In [8], the goal is to preserve as much as possible the performance of specified prioritized threads, while still allowing other threads to progress. This goal is close to ours except that it does not insure timing predictability and thus is not appropriate in a strict real-time context. Some architectural schemes have been proposed by Carzola *et al.* [2][3][4] to guarantee a quality of service for a set of threads. This solution mainly targets soft real-time tasks and is out of the scope of our work. The CarCore processor [18] features simultaneous multithreading with two specialized pipelines: one for data processing instructions and one for memory accesses. Instructions from four active threads can process in parallel in the pipelines. This architecture can support *one* critical thread through a priority-based instruction scheduling policy. Contrary to our architecture, the CarCore processor cannot execute instructions out of order.

6 Conclusion

Higher and higher performance requirements, related to an ever increasing demand for new functionalities, will make it unavoidable to use advanced processing cores in embedded systems in the near future. Multithreaded cores might be good candidates to execute several tasks of different criticality in parallel. However, current simultaneous multithreading processors do not exhibit enough timing predictability to fit certification requirements of critical applications. Actually we feel that the thread interleaving cannot be handled by usual static analysis techniques. This is why we think that the solution does reside in the design of specific hardware.

We have proposed a predictable SMT architecture where the policies implemented to control the sharing of internal resources among threads are designed to allow a predictable execution of a single hard real-time thread concurrently with less critical other threads. All the storage resources (instruction queues and buffers) are statically-partitioned and low-level thread scheduling is done using a *Most-Critical-First* strategy that gives priority to the hard real-time thread. This is complemented by the *Replay* scheme that ensures that an instruction of the critical thread cannot be delayed by an instruction of a non-critical thread for accessing a functional unit.

Experimental results show that, while the hard real-time thread executes as fast as if it was alone in the pipeline, the performance loss for the other threads is moderate. It is less than 12% for a 4-thread predictable SMT core.

As future work, we intend to address some issues that were ignored in this preliminary study, like the strategy for sharing the instruction and data caches, as well as the branch predictor, so as to maintain full timing predictability for the critical thread. We will also investigate solutions that would allow the concurrent execution of several critical threads.

References

1. Broy, M., et al.: Engineering Automotive Software. Proceedings of the IEEE 95(2) (2007)
2. Cazorla, F., et al.: QoS for High-Performance SMT Processors in Embedded Systems. IEEE Micro 24(4) (2004)
3. Cazorla, F., et al.: Predictable Performance in SMT Processors. In: ACM Conf. on Computing Frontiers (2004)
4. Cazorla, F., et al.: Architectural Support for Real-Time Task Scheduling in SMT Processors. In: Int'l Conf. on Compilers, Architecture, and Synthesis for Embedded Systems (CASES) (2005)
5. Cazorla, F., et al.: Dynamically Controlled Resource Allocation in SMT Processors. In: 37th Int'l Symposium on Microarchitecture (2004)
6. Cassé, H., Sainrat, P.: OTAWA, a Framework for Experimenting WCET Computations. In: 3rd European Congress on Embedded Real-Time Software (2006)
7. Crowley, P., Baer, J.-L.: Worst-Case Execution Time Estimation for Hardware-assisted Multithreaded Processors. In: HPCA-9 Workshop on Network Processors (2003)
8. Dorai, D., Yeung, D., Choi, S.: Optimizing SMT Processors for High Single-Thread Performance. Journal of Instruction-Level Parallelism 5 (2003)
9. Kalla, R., Sinharoy, B., Tendler, J.: IBM Power5 Chip: A Dual-Core Multithreaded Processor. IEEE Micro 24(2) (2004)
10. Kato, S., Kobayashi, H., Yamasaki, N.: U-Link: Bounding Execution Time of Real-Time Tasks with Multi-Case Execution Time on SMT Processors. In: 11th Int'l Conf. on Embedded and Real-Time Computing Systems and Applications (2005)
11. Li, Y.-T. S., Malik, S.: Performance Analysis of Embedded Software using Implicit Path Enumeration. In: Workshop on Languages, Compilers, and Tools for Real-time Systems (1995)
12. Lo, S.-W., Lam, K.-Y., Kuo, T.-W.: Real-time Task Scheduling for SMT Systems. In: 11th Int'l Conf. on Embedded and Real-Time Computing Systems and Applications (2005)
13. Marr, D., et al.: Hyper-Threading Technology Architecture and Microarchitecture. Intel Technology Journal 6(1) (2002)
14. Raasch, S., Reinhardt, S.: The Impact of Resource Partitioning on SMT Processors. In: 12th Int'l Conf. on Parallel Architectures and Compilation Techniques (2003)
15. Tuck, N., Tullsen, D.: Initial Observations of the Simultaneous Multithreading Pentium 4 processor. In: 12th Int'l Conf. Parallel Architectures and Compilation Techniques (2003)
16. Tullsen, D., Eggers, S., Levy., H.: Simultaneous Multithreading: Maximizing On-Chip Parallelism. In: 22nd Int'l Symposium on Computer Architecture (1995)
17. Tullsen, D.,et al.: Exploiting Choice: Instruction Fetch and Issue on an Implementable Simultaneous Multithreading Processor. In: 23rd Int'l Symposium on Computer Architecture (1996)
18. Uhrig, S., Maier, S., Ungerer, T.: Toward a Processor Core for Real-time Capable Autonomic Systems. In: IEEE Int'l Symposium on Signal Processing and Information Technology (2005)

Soft Real-Time Scheduling on SMT Processors with Explicit Resource Allocation

Carlos Boneti[1], Francisco J. Cazorla[2], Roberto Gioiosa[2], and Mateo Valero[1,2]

[1] DAC, Universitat Politècnica de Catalunya
{cboneti,mateo}@ac.upc.es
[2] Barcelona Supercomputing Center
{francisco.cazorla,roberto.gioiosa,mateo.valero}@bsc.es

Abstract. Several software or hardware approaches have been proposed to reduce the execution time variability of SMT processors. Software solutions rely on profiling the schedulable tasks to determine the effects of resource sharing over their performance, while the hardware approaches consider a fixed small number of tasks, avoiding the global system-scheduling problem. Both approaches lack of generality or do not take into account architectural details.

This work targets the scheduling of soft real-time tasks on an explicit resource allocation processor, where the system is able to enforce hardware allocation decisions. We propose a simple extension to the *Earliest Deadline First* scheduler: *Resource Aware EDF*. RA-EDF uses resource allocation mechanisms to ensure at least the minimum amount of resources needed by a task to meet its deadline. It yields improvements on every case when compared to previous task schedulers: 8% better on average and up to 18%, requiring no additional profiling.

1 Introduction

SMT processors adapt a superscalar front-end to fetch from several threads while the back-end is shared. They have high throughput but poor performance predictability. The scheduling of a task set in such processors involves two main steps as shown in Figure 1 (a). In a first step, known as *workload selection* [10], the Operating System (OS) scheduler selects a set of N tasks from the task set of M tasks, where N is the number of contexts of the SMT processor and M is usually greater or equal than N. This set of N tasks is called the *workload*. Next, the OS passes the workload to the architecture. In a second step, known as *resource sharing*[10], the SMT internal resource allocation mechanism determines how resources are distributed among threads, and how the threads are prioritized at a hardware level. In current processors this resource allocation mechanism is limited to the instruction fetch policy, like icount [19] or FLUSH++ [1] , while the first step is performed roughly every time slice (typically between 1 and 100ms), the second step occurs every cycle.

The key issue in the interaction between OS and a traditional SMT system is that the OS only assembles a workload of N tasks while it is the processor that

U. Brinkschulte et al. (Eds.): ARCS 2008, LNCS 4934, pp. 173–187, 2008.

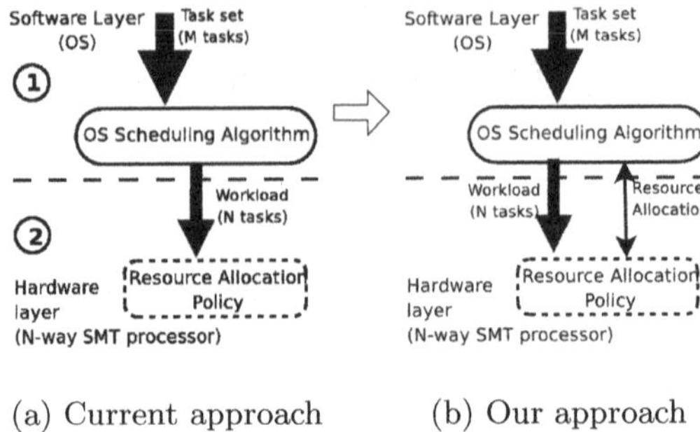

(a) Current approach (b) Our approach

Fig. 1. Collaboration between the OS job scheduler and the SMT hardware: steps required to schedule a task set in classical SMT processors

decides how to execute this workload, implicitly by means of its internal resource allocation policy. Hence, there are two different schedulers working, without any collaboration with each other, and part of the traditional responsibility of the OS "disappears" into the processor, sometimes reverting software priorities or simply disregarding them. Consequently, the OS may not be able to guarantee time constraints on the execution of a thread if that thread is running concurrently with other threads, even though the processor has sufficient resources to do so. In order to deal with this variability, several hardware (resource sharing policies) and software approaches have been proposed [2] [3] [4] [6] [10] [15].

In this paper we address the problem of scheduling a task set in a SMT system from the software and hardware layers in a collaborative way. Our proposal allows better control of the underlying hardware resources (like the issue queues or the registers) by the scheduling algorithm, increasing the task scheduling success rate. Assuming that the Worst Case Execution Time (WCET) is given, for every task, our mechanism does not require any additional profiling.

The original Earliest Deadline First (EDF) [12] algorithm only aims to determine the order in which threads should be executed. This is not enough if the task set is scheduled on an SMT processor due to the execution time variability of threads. We developed and evaluated a new scheduling algorithm, called RA-EDF (Resource-Aware EDF), that uses the hardware support proposed in [3]. RA-EDF, in addition to determine the execution order of threads, determines the amount of resources to give to co-scheduled threads. We provide EDF with knowledge of the processor resources and instruct it in how to split resources among threads in order to meet their deadlines. This increases the success rate when scheduling tasks, outperforming state-of-the-art scheduling algorithms. The proposed scheduler algorithm obtains better results on every case when compared to the previous proposed task schedulers: 8% average improvement, and up to 18% on success rate.

This paper is structured as follows: Section 2 presents some background on real-time scheduling and the related work; Section 3 explains our proposal; Section 4 presents our experimental setup while Section 5 provides the experimental results; finally Section 6 is devoted to the conclusions.

2 Background and Related Work

In this paper we focus on real-time SMT scheduling for independent tasks. In this case real-time systems are characterized by a group of tasks, called a *task set*. For each task, the scheduler knows three main parameters: first, the *period* (p_i), that is, the interval at which new instances of a task are ready for execution. Second, the *deadline* (d_i), that is, the time before which an instance of the task must complete. For simplicity, the deadline is often set equal to the period resulting into an implicit-deadline system [7] [9]. This means that a task has to be executed before the next instance of the same task. Third, the *Worst Case Execution Time* ($WCET_i$) is an upper bound of the time required to execute any instance of the task, which should never be exceeded (for single threaded executions). The WCET is known a priori and is not considered profiling.

In soft-real time scheduling, many algorithms (e.g., EDF [12] or LLF [5]) have been used to schedule a task set in single-threaded systems. However, these algorithms are no longer sufficient on SMT processors, since the execution time of a thread is unpredictable when this thread is scheduled with other threads. The high variability of SMTs implies that a real-time job scheduler for SMT processors is much more complex and challenging than for single-threaded processors.

2.1 Workload Composition

In [10] the authors make a detailed space design exploration of scheduling algorithms. From the many proposed algorithms, the best one is GLOB_SYM_US, while a second algorithm, called GLOB_NOSYM_US presents the best relation between performance and complexity. GLOB_SYM_US is actually a hybrid implementation that defaults to GLOB_NOSYM_US when at least one task has $U_i > \frac{N}{2N-1}$, being U_i the utilization of a task τ_i and N the number of available hardware contexts, otherwise, it defaults to GLOB_SYM_PLAIN. The latter extends EDF selecting first the task with earliest deadline, and then, for the other N-1 tasks, assign the tasks in order to maximize the symbiosis factor of the running task set, which is defined in [16] as:

$$symbiosis\ factor = \sum_{i=1}^{N} \frac{\text{realized IPC of } \tau_i}{\text{single-threaded IPC of } \tau_i} \tag{1}$$

Here, IPC (Instructions per Cycle) is used as a measure of performance. Hence, the higher is the symbiosis factor, the better should be the processor pipeline utilization and, therefore, the higher the gain of throughput due to the SMT. This algorithm is tuned to give the best processor utilization. Note, however, that this requires the profiling of every N-way task combination (from the task set of M tasks) in order to find task sets with best symbiosis, which leads to a number of profiles equal to $C_r(M, N) = \frac{(M+N-1)!}{N!(M-1)!}$. For instance, with our 10 benchmarks, we needed to profile 55 different combinations. If, instead of 10, we had 50 different benchmarks, we would need to profile 1275 different combinations. Besides, if we took into consideration that the IPC of a workload may change depending on the offset of the running threads, the profiling complexity would explode. Running all the combinations of the MediaBench benchmarks (as shown in the Table 2), in our hardware configuration, yielded a maximum symbiosis of 1.70, a minimum of 0.94 and an average of 1.40.

GLOB_NOSYM_US (also called EDF_US [18]) extends EDF by giving higher priority to tasks with utilization greater than $\frac{N}{2N-1}$ (deadlines are set to $-\infty$ and ties are broken arbitrarily).

2.2 Resource Allocation

Several hardware mechanisms have been proposed in order to bias the execution of a thread in a given workload with different degrees of success. In [17] an extension to the *icount* fetch policy is proposed by including handicap numbers that reflect the priorities of jobs. Although this mechanism is able to prioritize threads to some extent, running times of jobs are still hard to predict, making this approach still unsuited for real-time constraints.

In [3] we proposed several mechanisms that allow the OS to establish the amount of resources to give to the critical thread, controlling in this way the interaction among threads, and the slowdown suffered by each thread in SMT mode. The difference among these mechanisms is the information required from the application: the higher the information used by the hardware mechanism, the better the results, and the more complex the mechanism is. However, in that paper we did not propose any scheduling algorithm. That is, the responsibility of determining the amount of resources to give to each thread so that it meets its deadline is left to the OS.

To our knowledge, there is no work aimed to bind the OS prioritization to the hardware priorities in such a holistic level. Either resource aware hardware or software schedulers were proposed. In this work, we aim to extend a software scheduler in order to show that making this bridge is not only possible, but also profitable and desirable. We developed a simulation environment that allows us to use a larger number of software threads than available hardware contexts, we evaluated costs of context switches and implemented different system schedulers, binding the task priorities to the hardware allocation.

Such scheduler can be implemented in any explicit resource aware processor, or even on SMT processors featuring priority control. However, for this research we chose to use a simulated environment, as the use of a real system would imply on the need for a deep characterization of the prioritization impact on different workload and, therefore, would be out of the scope of this research.

3 Our Approach

In this paper we propose a scheduling policy that takes profit of SMT in-processor resource allocation mechanisms to guarantee better schedulability. Our mechanism allows a closer collaboration between the scheduling algorithm and the SMT hardware. This tight collaboration shows many advantages: First, it achieves better success rate than all the proposals previously explained in the Section 2. Second, no additional profiling, other than the WCET estimation, is required from applications to carry out the scheduling task, assuming that there is an estimate of the Worst Case Execution Time (WCET) of the tasks. Furthermore, when shared resources cannot be controlled by software, it is often the case that the internal hardware prioritization mechanism goes on the opposite direction of the OS priorities, for instance, giving fetch priority of the task with lesser OS priority. Our mechanism fully avoids this situation, as it binds the OS priorities to the hardware mechanism. Our new scheduling algorithm uses the hardware support we proposed in [3], which we call *LVP* or *Low-Variability Performance*. We start by explaining in detail the LVP mechanism.

The basis of the hardware mechanism proposed in [3] is to partition the hardware resources between the threads running on an SMT and reserve a minimum fraction of the resources for a designated *Most Critical Thread* (MCT), enabling it to meet its deadline. We proposed two hardware resource allocator denominated *static* and *dynamic* LVP (Low Variation Performance), which differ on what information the hardware mechanism expects to receive from the OS [1]. In the *static* approach, it is assumed that the OS job scheduler provides a resource allocation that is fixed for an entire period. While in the *dynamic* approach, it provides the target IPC for the MCT. In this approach the resource allocator can dynamically vary the amount of resources dedicated to the critical thread, therefore it was called *dynamic*. The Predictable Performance (PP) hardware, proposed in [4] differs from the *dynamic* LVP version as it receives the percentage of the performance the thread must be run. That is, it takes into account different program phases, being able to dynamically scale both resource allocation and the thread IPC. We chose to implement our algorithm with the *static* LVP version of the hardware. We do not implement the *dynamic* LVP or the PP hardware approach because, although they provide better results, they are more complex and have lower applicability than the *static* LVP.

When the WCET of a task is determined, it is assumed that this task has full access to all the underlying platform resources. However, when this task runs with other tasks in a multithreaded environment, it only uses a certain fraction of the resources. When the amount of resources given to a thread is reduced, its performance may decrease as well. The relation between the amount of resources allocated to a program and the performance is different for each program and may vary for different inputs of the same program. In [3] we observed that in an SMT system the relation between the amount of resources given to a thread and its *relative performance* [2] follows a "super-linear" relation. That is, if we reserve X% of resources to a given thread its relative performance is greater or equal to X% of its performance when having all the resources. We also observed

[1] Recall that in [2],[3] and [4] we only focus on the hardware part and do not deal with the workload composition problem.

[2] The relative performance is the IPC that a thread has when it is given X% of SMT resources, with respect to its performance when it is run with all the resources. It ranges between 0 and 1.

that the main shared resources to take into account are the physical registers, the fetch bandwidth, and the instruction window. The proposed hardware splits the shared hardware resources among running threads as indicated by the OS job scheduler. That is, it allows the OS to specify the amount of resources to use by each thread.

Our scheduling algorithm uses the hardware support proposed in [3] to take profit of this relation. When the OS level job scheduler wants to execute a critical task τ_i, given its $WCETst_i$ (Worst Case Execution Time in Single Thread mode) and a deadline d_i, it simply computes the allowable performance slowdown that, initially, is represented by, $S_i(0) = \frac{WCETst_i}{d_i}$, and instructs the hardware to reserve, for that hardware context, a percentage of the resources equivalent to $S_i(0)$[3]. For such a value of $S_i(0)$, each instance of this job should finish before its deadline, supposing that the real execution time of this instance is its $WCETst_i$. Hence, $\frac{T_i}{S_i(0)} = \frac{d_i}{WCETst_i} \cdot WCETst_i = d_i$. Refer to Section 3.1 to further analysis on the allowable slowdown calculation. We adapted the EDF [12] algorithm in order to use this hardware support and called this new scheduling algorithm RA-EDF. The acronym stands for Resource-Aware Earliest Deadline First.

The proposed method uses global scheduling: tasks are not bound to contexts of an SMT and can be executed in any of the available contexts. For each workload we evaluate the *Most Critical Thread* (MCT) that is the thread with the highest priority according to the scheduling algorithm under study. The MCT is evaluated every time the running workload changes (whenever there is a context-switch on a context). Therefore, at any given moment, there will be exactly one thread running as MCT (also said that this thread has the MCT status) and as we use a 2-context SMT, another as LPT (low priority thread).

3.1 The RA-EDF Scheduler

This algorithm improves the normal EDF scheduler [12] in order to make it resource aware. It adds the concept of a most critical thread (MCT) and a lower priority thread (LPT) running together in the SMT and it is aware of the sharing of hardware resources across the processor contexts.

RA-EDF starts filling contexts, putting first the task with the closest deadline and, therefore, the highest priority. This task is considered to be running as the most critical thread (MCT). Then, the second closest deadline will occupy the second hardware context, being the second highest priority task or, to keep the notation of [3], the LPT. The MCT will receive an amount of resources large enough to guarantee its deadline, i.e., $RA(0) = S_i(0)$, while the LPT will receive the rest of the available resources. This logic can be easily expanded to a n-way multithreaded processor as long as the first thread receives an amount larger or equal to the resources needed to reach its deadline, while the other threads can be considered as LPT and share the remaining resources.

[3] $S_i(t)$ stands for the allowed slowdown that a thread can have to still fulfill its deadline at a given instant t.

After some time, one of the following things may occur:

- The task with nearest deadline finishes its execution. In this case, the second closest deadline becomes the next deadline and, therefore, the previous LPT becomes now the MCT. The resource allocation to the MCT context is re-evaluated and the highest priority task receives the amount of resources necessary to fulfill its deadline. The next task with the closest deadline is put in the newly free context.
- The LPT finishes before the MCT. The next task with the closest deadline is put in the newly free context.

As we can see, during its execution time, a task can run as MCT, LPT or, more likely, both (note that the status are mutually exclusive). The resource allocation that the MCT receives at a given period of time ($RA(t)$) is calculated on the allowed slowdown ($S_i(t)$) that a task τ_i can take at an instant t, in order to fulfill its deadline, while the LPT runs with the remaining processor resources. The allowed slowdown is evaluated every time the running workload changes or when the scheduler runs (typically at time slices boundaries). In other words, whenever jobs are changed on any of the hardware context, the $S_i(t)$ for the thread with the nearest deadline (MCT) is evaluated or adjusted.

Conceptually the $S_i(t)$ calculation is very simple as it consists on the ratio between the Remaining Computation time for a job τ_i (RC_i) and the remaining time to its deadline (TTD_i), i.e. $S_i(t) = \frac{RC_i}{TTD_i}$. However, there are some considerations to be made on each of its factors, as we will see below.

The Time to Deadline (TTD) is always evaluated as the difference between the deadline d_i of a task τ_i and the current time t ($TTD_i = d_i - t$). However, we must take into account its range. When a task crosses its deadline boundary, the TTD_i becomes negative, invalidating the resource allocation calculation. The action taken in this case may vary according to the system and is relatively arbitrary. One may want to kill jobs that missed their deadlines, give them full priority, the minimum priority (understanding that the task is probably close to finish) or the last evaluated priority (probably very high).

The Remaining Computation time (RC_i) evaluation represents the difference between the total amount of work to be done and the one that was already done. The simplest way to represent it, given our available data would be: $RC_i = WCETst_i - running\,time$, where $WCETst_i$ represents the Worst Case Execution time, in single-thread, for a given task. However, the running time can be evaluated in few different ways. Among the many different possibilities, we present here the one that yielded the best results.

In [3], we showed that the performance for the MCT is super-linear. Recall that the MCT receives priority over the LPT when fetching instructions from the instruction cache. As a consequence, the relation among resources given to the LPT and its performance may, sometimes, be sub-linear. Based on this conclusion, we chose to evaluate the remaining computational time for a given job τ_i with different functions whether the task is running as a HPT or LPT. When running as LPT, the worst case, where the performance becomes sub-linear, is assumed. This correction basically makes that the time a thread runs as low priority accounts for less processing time than while it is running as a MCT. We believe that this is the most accurate evaluation. To summarize, the allowed slowdown for a task τ_i, is given by the following formula:

$$S_i(t) = \frac{WCET_i - \left(\sum_{\gamma=1}^{m}(\omega_\gamma * RA_\gamma) + \sum_{\gamma=1}^{l}(\omega_\gamma * (1 - RA_\gamma^f))\right)}{d_i - t} \tag{2}$$

Here, $\sum_{\gamma=1}^{m}(\omega_\gamma * RA_\gamma)$ represents all the resources that a given thread i received as a HPT, that is, the sum of all the intervals of size ω_γ ran with resource allocation RA_γ when t_i was the top priority task of the system. In addition, we have $\sum_{\gamma=1}^{l}(\omega_\gamma * (1 - RA_\gamma^f)$ as the total amount of processing done when running as LPT. f is an empirical constant aimed to reduce the total accounted resources for the LPT.

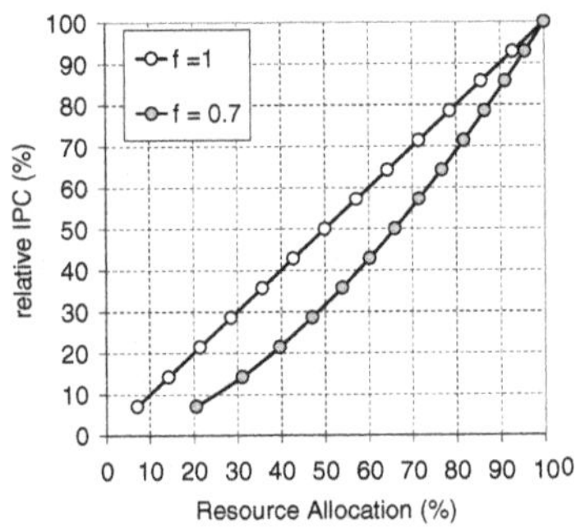

Fig. 2. Accounted performance for LPT based MCT RA

We found, based on the results of [3] and on empirical data, that 0.7 is the most appropriated value for the constant f. In Figure 2 we can see the accounted IPC for LPT when the relation between the LPT performance and resources allocated to the MCT is linear ($f = 1$) or sub-linear ($f = 0.7$). As we can see, the same amount of resources for both $f = 1$ and $f = 0.7$ translates into a lower performance accounted for the period a task was executed in LPT mode. For simplicity, we only show experimental results for that option.

The other resource evaluation mechanisms that we tried were the simpler versions of the previous formula, trying linear relation, or not even differentiating between the time run as HPT or LPT. The results shown much less flexibility and the success ratio were significantly smaller. Again, within this evaluation, the only way that RC_I can be negative is after a task misses its deadline.

We also observed that, for task sets with many tasks of relatively distant deadlines, the allowed slowdown can be very significant, giving less than half of the resources to the MCT. As we understand that, in these cases, there is no sense on giving less than 50% of the resources to the thread that is, by definition, the highest priority of the workload, we artificially constrain the Minimal Resource Allocation ($MinRA$) as 0.5. Hence, $0.5 \leq RA(t) \leq 1.0$ for the RA version of our proposed algorithm. Therefore, the MCT resource allocation at a given moment is expressed as follows: $RA(t) = \max(MinRa, S_i(t))$

It is also very important to observe that, even if the $S_i(t)$ calculation may seem complex, it is done in software, by the OS job scheduler and the above described sums are simply implemented as accumulators that are only updated when the resource allocation for the MCT changes (because of a context-switch, for instance) and the entire value of $S_i(t)$ is only evaluated for the MCT.

3.2 Example

Consider a set of 4 tasks with the deadlines, WCETs, and utilization as shown in the Table 1. In a first step, the scheduler chooses the task τ_1, the task with closest deadline. It becomes the MCT. The operating system (OS) also chooses to run, at lower priority, τ_3, which is the task with second closest deadline. The OS finally assigns a RA to the MCT. It is set to the $MAX(S_1, 0.5)$ and S_1 is calculated as $S_1 = \frac{1-0}{5-0} = 0.2$. Therefore, the MCT receives $RA = 0.5$.

Table 1. Hypothetical task set

Task	WCET	Deadline	Utilization	Task	WCET	Deadline	Utilization
τ_1	1.0	5	0.20	τ_2	0.5	7	0.07
τ_3	4.0	6	0.67	τ_4	2.0	8	0.25

Assume that, at a given instant, say $\Upsilon = 1.25$, τ_1 finishes. τ_3 becomes the task with the closest deadline and the MCT. The context where τ_1 was running, receives now τ_2. S_3 is calculated as $\frac{4-(0+(1.25*(1-0.5^{0.7}))}{6-1.25} = 0.74$, $RA = MAX(0.74, 0.5) = 0.74$. This workload executes until the instant $\Upsilon = 3.8$, when τ_2 finishes. τ_4 starts to run on the free context and the new RA for τ_3 is calculated as follows: $RA = MAX(S_3, 0.5)$ where $S_3 = \frac{4-((2.55*0.76)+(1-0.5^{0.7}))}{6-3.8} = 0.76$. This behavior repeats during the entire execution time.

4 Methodology and Experimental Environment

In this section we describe the experimental methodology used to evaluate the performance of the proposed and the previous scheduling algorithms. Our experimental setup is similar to the experimental setup shown in [6]. This section covers the definition of the task set, metrics, and the architecture simulator.

4.1 Task Sets and Metrics

In this paper, we use the MediaBench benchmark suite [11]. We compose task sets with 2 different sizes: 4 and 12 tasks randomly chosen from the MediaBench benchmarks shown in Table 2. Since in our experiments we use a two-way SMT, it is a reasonable choice, as the 2-task scheduling defaults to no scheduling need

Table 2. MediaBench benchmarks used in this paper. (encoders and decoders have the same input)

Benchmark name	Media	Language	WCET for a 1GHz proc.	Benchmark name	Media	Language	WCET for a 1GHz proc.	input
adpcm_c	speech	C	1.6772 ms	adpcm_d	speech	C	1.4599 ms	clinton.pcm
epic_c	image	C	17.8306 ms	epic_d	image	C	6.1524 ms	test_image.pgm
gsm_c	speech	C	55.9323 ms	gsm_d	speech	C	50.8701 ms	clinton.pcm
g721_c	speech	C	39.7142 ms	g721_d	speech	C	18.1077 ms	clinton.pcm
mpeg2_c	video	C	34.9833 ms	mpeg2_d	video	C	2.5358 ms	test2.mpeg

(as they don't need to be multiplexed between the two hardware contexts) and significantly larger task sets (say of hundreds of tasks), would take too long (weeks) to simulate on a cycle accurate OS/architecture simulator. Right now, one 12-task simulation takes around 6 to 10 hours to execute alone.

For a given task τ_i the *utilization* is defined as $U_i = WCETst_i/p_i$, where $WCETst$ is the Worst Case Execution Time (WCET) of the task in single-thread mode and p_i is the period of the task. As shown in [6], for a task set the *scalar utilization (SU)* is defined as the sum of the utilization of each of its tasks. In other words, given a task set with M tasks:

$$SU = \sum_{i=1}^{M} \frac{WCETst_i}{p_i} \tag{3}$$

The term *serial utilization* is also used in [10] with the exact same meaning. In this work, we will use the two terms interchangeably.

We evaluate the performance of each scheduling algorithm under different scenarios of increasing difficulty. We vary the scalar utilization from 1.0 to 2.6 with a step of 0.2, for a total of 9 scenarios. We do not present the results for scalar utilization higher than 2.6 as, even if they were simulated, they fail to add any new information: the processor is already saturated with a 2.6 serial utilization. For each task set size and scalar utilization (SU) we created 50 task sets. Thus, for each scheduling algorithm we ran 900 simulations (2 task set sizes, times 50 task sets, times 9 scalar utilization). As evaluation metric we use the *Success Rate*, which measures how many task sets are successfully scheduled. We consider that a task set is successfully scheduled when all tasks in that task set finish before their deadline.

4.2 Simulator

We use a trace driven SMT simulator derived from *smtsim* [19]. The simulator consists of our own trace driven front-end and an improved version of smtsim's back-end. It allows executing wrong path instructions by using a separate basic block dictionary that contains all static instructions.

Our baseline instruction fetch policy is *icount* [19]. Instructions are decoded and renamed to track data dependencies. When an instruction is renamed, it is allocated an entry in the window or issue queues (integer, floating point and load/store) until all its operands are ready. Each instruction also allocates one Re-Order Buffer (ROB) entry and a physical register in the register file. ROB entries are assigned in program order and instructions wait in this buffer until all earlier instructions are resolved. When an instruction has all its operands ready, it reads its source operands, executes, writes its results, and finally commits.

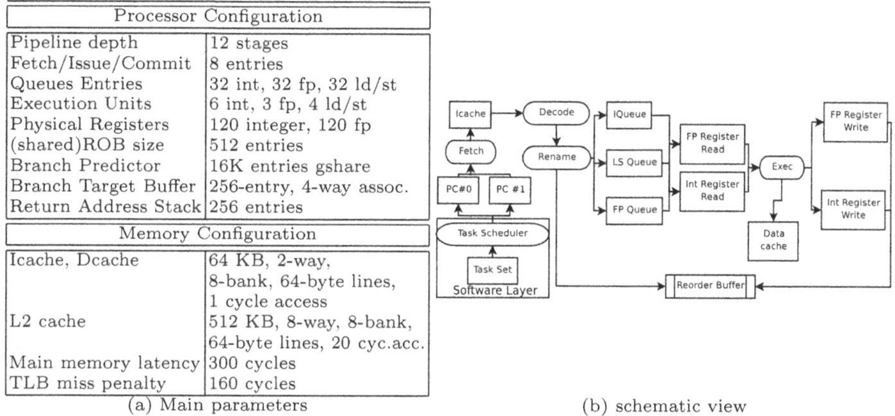

Processor Configuration	
Pipeline depth	12 stages
Fetch/Issue/Commit	8 entries
Queues Entries	32 int, 32 fp, 32 ld/st
Execution Units	6 int, 3 fp, 4 ld/st
Physical Registers	120 integer, 120 fp
(shared)ROB size	512 entries
Branch Predictor	16K entries gshare
Branch Target Buffer	256-entry, 4-way assoc.
Return Address Stack	256 entries
Memory Configuration	
Icache, Dcache	64 KB, 2-way, 8-bank, 64-byte lines, 1 cycle access
L2 cache	512 KB, 8-way, 8-bank, 64-byte lines, 20 cyc.acc.
Main memory latency	300 cycles
TLB miss penalty	160 cycles

(a) Main parameters

(b) schematic view

Fig. 3. Baseline configuration

We use an aggressive configuration, shown in Figure 3(a): many shared resources (issue queues register, functional units, etc.), out-of-order execution, wide superscalar, and a deep pipeline for high clock frequency. These features cause the performance of the processor to be very unstable, depending on the mix of threads. Thus, we evaluate our proposals on an unfavorable scenario. If those proposals work in this hard configuration, they will work better in narrower processors with fewer shared resources. Figure 3 (b) gives a schematic view of our processor while Figure 3 (a) shows our baseline configuration.

To be able to validate the system scheduling, we adapted the simulator, allowing it to receive an input of μ traces ($\mu > \eta$) and multiplex them over the η processor contexts in a way similar to the operating system (OS) task-scheduler. The context-switches are commanded by the task scheduling algorithm and can be timely dependent (say, every 10 or 20ms) or after the execution of a task instance (on a period), according to the scheduler characteristics.

Every context-switch clears the pipeline of the affected context, flushing the active instructions. We also chose to be conservative concerning the memory impact of this switch and assumed the worst case concerning the memory footprint of the task running on the physical context. Therefore, we flush the cache and completely invalidate TLB entries for a context after a context switch, as it is done in some real processors [13]. The evaluation of the Worst Case Execution Time (WCET) in single-thread mode takes into account this overhead. Another key reason for clearing the cache is that the traces may have equal physical addresses, because they were not generated at the same time. In that case, extra care must be taken in order to avoid false hits on the cache after multiplexing some successive traces.

5 Experimental Results

Figure 4 shows the number of successfully scheduled task sets for the different scheduling algorithms. We present the aggregated results for the two set sizes shown in the Experimental Environment Section (4.1). Individually, for either 4 or 12-tasks sizes, RA-EDF yields an average improvement of 8% when compared to the EDF. Due to space constraints, the charts for the individual sizes are not shown.

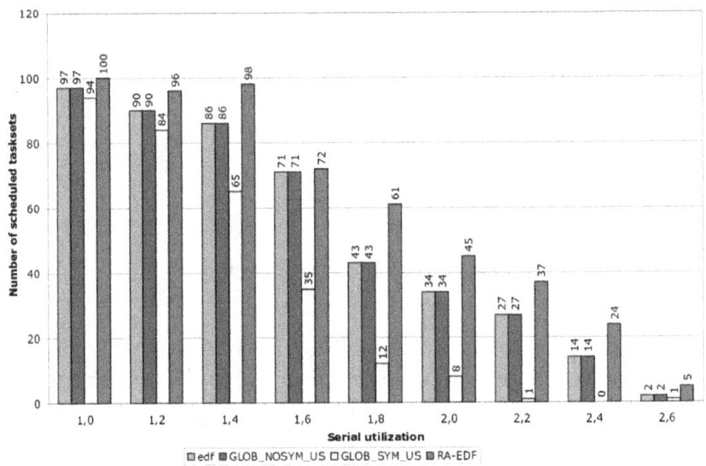

Fig. 4. Number of successfully scheduled task sets for different serial utilizations and scheduling algorithms (aggregated results for 4- and 12-tasks task sets: 100 task sets in total)

The first thing to note is the unexpected behavior of GLOB_SYM_US and GLOB_NOSYM_US. For the GLOB_NOSYM_US, recall that its behavior only differs from the EDF for tasks presenting utilization superior to $\frac{N}{2N-1}$. The percentage of these tasks in our task sets is only of 11.3%, and therefore, the results of this algorithm are very similar to those of the EDF. In average, RA-EDF is 8% better than GLOB_NOSYM_US.

For GLOB_SYM_US, our results are quite different from the results of the authors. We think that it is due to the fact that we use a different scenario and a different metric (in [10], the authors consider that a task set is not schedulable when more than 5% of the tasks in the task set are missed). For our scenario, in average, RA-EDF yields results 26% better than the GLOB_SYM_US.

Moreover, one may observe that some task sets miss even when $SU = 1.0$. This occurs because of priority inversion problems. The first two cases occurred when *adpcm_c* was running with *epic_d*. As we can see in the Table 3 (task set 1) the default *icount* policy prioritizes *epic_d*, in order to increase the overall processor throughput, disregarding the fact that *adpcm_c* had a closer deadline (due to the lack of collaboration between the OS and the processor schedulers). For the third case, shown in the Table 3 (task set 2) the same problem occurs: *epic_d* was the task with the closest deadline and was scheduled with *epic_c*, of lesser priority. Internally, *icount* policy prioritized the latter in order to increase the overall throughput. Observe that the *symbiosis* factor for these cases are larger than one, meaning that scheduling those tasks together gives a higher throughput than in single thread. This also explains why GLOB_SYM_US failed in the same cases.

Table 3. Benchmark interactions without explicit resource allocation

Task set 1:

Bench.	IPC Alone	IPC Both	Rel. IPC
adpcm_c	4.181	1.281	0.306
epic_d	1.642	1.333	0.812

Symbiosis factor: 1.118

Task set 2:

Bench.	IPC Alone	IPC Both	Rel. IPC
epic_d	1.642	0.787	0.479
epic_c	3.175	1.912	0.602

Symbiosis factor: 1.081

Furthermore, EDF is not optimum when scheduling on a SMT processor, just like on a multiprocessor system, anomalies like the Graham anomaly [8] or the Dhall effect [14] may occur.

Another interesting fact is that, even if the 4- and 12-task simulations follow the same trend of behavior, the 12-task sets yield better success rates. That can be explained by the fact that 12-task task sets generally present tasks with much lower individual serial utilization, being easier to accommodate a larger individual slowdown (traded for a global throughput increase).

As we can see in the Figure 4, our EDF-based algorithm is better than the others in all cases. Comparing to the original EDF algorithm, the RA-EDF has, in average, 8% higher success rate[4]. The higher improvement is 18% with a serial utilization (*SU*) of 1.8. In addition, RA-EDF successfully schedules task sets when others fail because of priority inversion, as it is able to explicitly control the resource allocation to the task with the highest priority.

We should observe that there is no case in which our proposed algorithm has lower success rate than any of the others. Furthermore, using this resource aware scheduling algorithms eliminates the priority inversion problems. That is, in contrast to normal SMT processors, where the hardware scheduler (fetch priority mechanism) and the OS scheduler are not aware of each other, there is no case where a lesser priority thread consumes more resources than the higher priority one. In addition, our solutions do not require profiling of the tasks to schedule. For future work, we plan to expand this technique to an N-way SMT machine: keeping one MCT and many LPT would make it feasible.

[4] Recall that we consider a task set successfully scheduled when there is no missed deadline.

Another key observation is the fact that we used a very aggressive WCET estimate. The closer is the WCET to the average execution time, the harder will it be to schedule the task set, as there will be close to zero extra time on normal execution. On real systems, WCET are normally an upper bound on the execution time, and, therefore, even more task sets would be scheduled on the common case. Considering a soft real-time scenario, using this slack between the WCET and the "expected execution time" would be, on some cases, an acceptable situation.

6 Conclusions

Current embedded systems require increasingly high throughput rates. To reach those rates, current embedded processors use features similar to the ones used in the high-performance processors. However, the use of these features impacts the performance predictability and creates new problems for real-time system. SMT processors are a clear example of this new trend. SMTs provide higher throughput with reduced costs but make harder the problem of computing the worst case execution time, generating task interference or even giving most of the shared hardware resources to a task with lower priority when multiple tasks are running on different hardware threads.

In this paper, we propose a new scheduling algorithm, the RA-EDF, to circumvent those problems. It is resource aware and does not require any profiling. Through a special hardware support proposed in [3], RA-EDF is able to control the hardware resources given to co-schedule threads. This hardware allows the scheduling algorithm to control the resource allocation, which improves the success rate when scheduling tasks. Our new scheduling algorithm yields higher success rates on every case when compared to the previous proposed task scheduling algorithms. RA-EDF improves 8% on average the original EDF.

Acknowledgments

This work has been supported by the Ministry of Science and Technology of Spain under contracts TIN-2004-07739-C02-01 and TIN-2007-60625 and by the HiPEAC European Network of Excellence. Carlos Boneti is granted by the Catalonian Department of Universities, Research and Information Society (AGAUR) and the European Social Funds.

References

1. Cazorla, F.J., et al.: Improving memory latency aware fetch policies for SMT processors. In: Proceedings of the 5th ISHPC (October 2003)
2. Cazorla, F.J., et al.: Qos for high-performance SMT processors in embedded systems. IEEE micro. Special Issue on Embedded Systems 24(4), 24–31 (2004)
3. Cazorla, F.J., et al.: Architectural support for real-time task scheduling in SMT processors. CASES-2005, 166–176 (2005)

4. Cazorla, F.J., et al.: Predictable performance in SMT processors: synergy between the OS and SMTs. IEEE Transactions on Computers 55(7), 785–799 (2006)
5. Dertouzos, M.L., Mok, A.K.: Multiprocessor online scheduling of hard-real-time tasks. IEEE Trans. Softw. Eng. 15(12), 1497–1506 (1989)
6. El-Haj-Mahmoud, A., et al.: Virtual multiprocessor: an analyzable, high-performance architecture for real-time computing. In: CASES (2005)
7. Goossens, J., Macq, C.: Limitation of the hyper-period in real-time periodic task set generation. In: Teknea (ed.) Proccedings of RTS 2001, Paris, France, pp. 133–148 (2001)
8. Graham, R.L.: Bounds on multiprocessing timing anomalies. SIAM Journal on Applied Mathematics 17(2), 416–429 (1969)
9. Goossens, J., Richard, P.: Overview of real-time scheduling problem. In: Proceedings of the ninth international conference on project management and scheduling, Nancy France (April 2004)
10. Jain, R., Hughes, C.J., Adve, S.V.: Soft real-time scheduling on simultaneous multithreaded processors. In: Proceedings of RTSS 2002 (2002)
11. Lee, A., Potkonjak1, M., Mangione-Smith, W.H.: Mediabench: A tool for evaluating and synthesizing multimedia and communications systems. In: 30th MICRO, pp. 330–335 (1997)
12. Liu, C.L., Layland, J.W.: Scheduling algorithms for multiprogramming in a hard-real-time environment. J. ACM 20(1), 46–61 (1973)
13. Marr, D.T., et al.: Hyper-threading technology architecture and microarchitecture. Intel Technology Journal 6(1) (February 2002)
14. Dhall, S.K., Liu, C.L.: On a Real-Time Scheduling Problem. Operations Research 26(1), 127–140 (1978)
15. Lo, S.-W., Lam, K.-Y., Kuo, T.-W.: Real-Time Task Scheduling for SMT Systems. In: RTCSA 2005, pp. 5–10 (2005)
16. Snavely, A., Tullsen, D.M.: Symbiotic jobscheduling for a simultaneous mutlithreading processor. SIGPLAN Not. 35(11), 234–244 (2000)
17. Snavely, A., Tullsen, D.M., Voelker, G.: Symbiotic jobscheduling with priorities for a simultaneous multithreading processor. In: Sigmetrics 2002 (2002)
18. Srinivasan, A., Baruah, S.: Deadline-based scheduling of periodic task systems on multiprocessors. Inf. Process. Lett. 84(2), 93–98 (2002)
19. Tullsen, D.M., et al.: Exploiting choice: instruction fetch and issue on an implementable simultaneous multithreading processor. SIGARCH Comput. Archit. News 24(2), 191–202 (1996)

A Hardware/Software Codesign of a Co-processor for Real-Time Hyperelliptic Curve Cryptography on a Spartan3 FPGA

Alexander Klimm[1], Oliver Sander[1], Jürgen Becker[1], and Sylvain Subileau[2]

[1] Institut für Technik der Informationsverarbeitung, Universität Karlsruhe (TH), Engesserstr. 5, 76131 Karlsruhe, Germany
klimm,sander, becker@itiv.uni-karlsruhe.de

[2] Daimler AG, Hanns-Klemm-Str. 45, 71034 Böblingen, Germany
sylvain.subileau@daimler.com

Abstract. This paper describes the acceleration of calculations for public-key cryptography on hyperelliptic curves on very small FPGAs. This is achieved by using a Hardware/Software Codesign Approach starting with an all-software implementation on an embedded Microprocessor and migrating very time-consuming calculations from software to hardware. Basic GF(2n)-hardware extensions are connected to work in conjunction with the Microprocessor and possible alternatives for connecting external hardware to the Microprocessor are investigated. The performance of the hardware implementations compared to their counterparts as a software approach are evaluated. Based on these results, a coprocessor is devised and optimized for performance. The system utilizes minimal resources and fits easily on a small FPGA. It allows for fast Hyperelliptic Curve Cryptography (HECC) operations while running at a very low clock speed of 33 MHz, thus making it suitable for usage in embedded systems.

Keywords: Hyperelliptic Curve Cryptography (HECC), Public Key Cryptography (PKC), reconfigurable hardware, FPGA, embedded systems.

1 Introduction

The introduction of *Public-Key Cryptography* (PKC) to embedded systems provides essential benefits for the production of system units needing to meet security requirements as well as for the logistics involved. Calculations for public-key applications on today's hardware platforms (i.e. microcontrollers) for embedded applications are very computational intensive. The resources on these platforms are also highly limited.

Neal Koblitz suggested in 1989 the usage of hyperelliptic curves for cryptographic purposes. The same level of security compared to the widespread applications of elliptic curves is achieved while using keys of comparable bit lengths. The size of the underlying finite galois fields is much smaller than of those used

U. Brinkschulte et al. (Eds.): ARCS 2008, LNCS 4934, pp. 188–201, 2008.

for elliptic curve cryptography. This makes the usage of *HECC* (hyperelliptic curve cryptography) particularly interesting for small platforms with very limited resources.

In the last couple of years implementations of HECC have been done in software [1] as well as in hardware such as FPGAs [2]. In order to achieve computational speeds suitable for real-time constrained applications, these implementations call for either very powerful general purpose processors or large FPGAs such as Xilinx's Virtex series. To minimize the usage of hardware resources as well as processor size, a hardware/software codesign-approach seems to be mandatory. The feasibility of this approach has been shown in [3], using an 8-bit microprocessor supported by a microcode instruction set coprocessor.

This paper focuses on accelerating calculations for *public-key cryptography* on *hyperelliptic curves* (HECC) on FPGAs with minimal hardware resources, i.e. Xilinx's Spartan series, by using the Xilinx's softcore processor MicroBlaze and migrating very time-consuming calculations from software to hardware.

Possible alternatives for connecting external hardware to the MicroBlaze are investigated. Hardware implementations of the underlying $GF(2^n)$-arithmetic, mainly a simple multiplication, are adapted to work in conjunction with the MicroBlaze and its interfaces. The overall performance, namely the speed of the computation in conjunction with the available hardware/software interfaces of the system, is evaluated.

Based on these results, a coprocessor is devised and optimized for performance. It allows for fast HECC operations while using minimal resources on a small FPGA.

The paper is organized as follows: In section 2, a short introduction to HECC is given. In the 3rd section the HW/SW codesign concept will be presented. This chapter includes a description of the system used for HECC, as well as the setup for the calculations' speed measurements. Also the used SW implementation and HW modules are described very briefly. In the 4th section, the results from implementation to a real Spartan3 FPGA will be discussed. The paper is closed with the conclusion and future work description in section 5.

2 Hyperelliptic Curve Cryptography

Hyperelliptic curves (HEC) are a generalization of elliptic curves (EC). Contrary to elliptic curves, hyperelliptic curves have a genus of $(g > 1)$. For efficient implementations of HECC (hyperelliptic curve cryptography) HEC's of genus $g = 2$ are targeted in this paper.

On elliptic curves an addition follows a unique geometrical mapping [4]. However for addition on HEC's the same straight forward methodology is not possible. One further abstraction has to be used - the concept of divisors.

A divisor is a formal finite sum of points on a curve (see (1)). It's degree is the sum of the coefficients m_i. The order of D on a point P_i is the integer m_i.

$$D = \sum m_i P_i \text{ in } \bar{F} \tag{1}$$

The sum of all divisors forms an additive group. D^0 is a subset of D, that includes all divisors of degree 0. Using principle divisors [5] a "Jacobian Group" curve (see 2) is defined on which addition is performed. The set of all reduced divisors on a HEC uniquely represents the Jacobian group. Solving the discrete logarithmic problem [6] on this group is the basis of security of HECC.

$$J = \frac{D^0}{P} \tag{2}$$

3 Hardware/Software Co-design

Starting point of the design was an all-software implementation of HECC (see chapter 3.2). On a PowerPC (32 Bit Processor running at 80 MHz) one scalar multiplication required 90 ms. In table 1 a comparison of execution times of one scalar multiplication in HECC is given. The implementation on the ARM7 processor has been done in [7].

Table 1. Execution times of HECC scalar multiplication in SW

Processor		Fieldsize
PowerPC 32 Bit @ 80 MHz	90 ms	2^{83}
ARM7 32 Bit @ 80 MHz	71,56 ms	2^{83}

The execution time of one scalar multiplication $k \cdot Div1$ is used as a reference for the quality of an implementation regarding speed. To gain an advantage to state of the art systems the maximum computation time of this HECC operation has to be 50 ms or less.

To achieve this goal a HW/SW co-design approach is targeted. The Xilinx's MicroBlaze 32 Bit processor on a Spartan3 FPGA is used as a target processor. Execution time of one scalar multiplication is measured and is used as a primary reference. Parts of the algorithm are migrated into hardware and the performance as well as the size of the system is evaluated successively. The evaluation's main criteria, is primarily the computational speed of the design because of the real-time requirements from the target application. Another important aspect of the evaluation is the security of the overall system. Hardware does have side-channels that might leak information to an attacker, thus compromising the system (see chapter 4.3).

Moving functionality into hardware naturally increases the amount of resources needed on the FPGA. Therefore only functionality that is used most often or needs a lot of processor-time, is implemented in hardware (see chapter 3.3). On the other hand it opens up the possibility to use different implementations for subroutines (see chapter 4.1 and [8]).

3.1 System Architecture and Components

The overall system is implemented on Spartan3-5000 FPGA. This FPGA is the biggest of the Spartan series and is only used for evaluation purposes. The choice of this FPGA has the basis that a rapid prototyping platform with this FPGA was available for real-world system integration and tests. Synthesis of the finalized design has been successfully done for a Spartan3-400 also.

Mainly the system comprises a microprocessor, crypto hardware, and a hardware timer to count clock cycles. In the following chapters the components will be described briefly.

MicroBlaze. The MicroBlaze soft-core processor is a parameterizable 32 bit RISC processor with Harvard Architecture. It has been developed specifically for usage on Xilinx Virtex and Spartan-II/3 FPGAs [9] [10]. Additional hardware can be added by connecting it via OPB (On Chip Peripheral Bus), FSL (Fast Simplex Link) and LMB (Local Memory Bus). Due to the efficient usage of FPGA resources, the processor can be clocked with up to 150 MHz. In this design the clock frequency has been limited to 33 MHz.

Hardware Timer. In order to measure the computation time of an operation a timer is required. For this issue, a simple binary counter is implemented. With every clock cycle, a register is incremented by one. This register can be accessed by the MicroBlaze via OPB. By writing a '0' into the register the timer is started. No enable signal for the counter is used, it starts counting immediately. To get the measured time, the register is read out by the MicroBlaze and the register's value is stored in the processor's internal memory for further reference.

There is a certain constant offset in the measurement due to the clock cycles needed to read out the timer's internal registers. Test cases showed that with the software driver that was used in this test scenario, the counter runs 3 additional clock cycles, while the readout command is carried out. This bias is subtracted when evaluating the result.

Cryptographic hardware. Some dedicated hardware for fast computation on Galois Field in binary representation is included into the system. These hardware implementations are directly interfaced to the MicroBlaze. The individual modules being used, are described in detail in chapter 3.3, the interfacing is described in chapter 3.4.

Communication. For debug issues and evaluation of the system, a UART Interface and an interface for external output signals are included in the system. These interfaces are exploited to transfer the calculation results to a PC for verification. The external signals are used to drive LEDs to visualize the system's status.

3.2 Software Implementation

The HECC Software implementation for a 32 Bit RISC processor provides basic operations for HECC such as GF-addition, GF-multiplication coupled with modular reduction, GF-inversion, divisor addition and divisor doubling on HEC, as well as scalar multiplication. It has been placed at our disposal by the Daimler AG in form of C-code within an ongoing joint project.

The GF-multiplication uses the *Left-to-right Comb Method* proposed in [11], using a window size of 4. For reduction of the result, the *"Fast Reduction Modulo"*-method is used (see [4], pp 55). Efficient GF-inversion in software is done by using the extended euclidean algorithm.

The methods for divisor adding and divisor doubling follow the algorithms proposed in [12]. Those operations are done in projective coordinates to save costly inversions.

The implemented scalar multiplication is based on the *"Double and Add"* algorithm (see [6]) using a variant that has a scalar in NAF (Non Adjacent Form) as input.

3.3 Algorithmic Hardware Modules

GF_MAC Unit

Only the underlying $GF(2^n)$ arithmetic of HECC is implemented in hardware, due to the fact that these calculations are performance intensive (i.e. hundreds of field multiplications per one scalar multiplication). The following hardware modules are included in the design.

Galois Field Adder (GF_ADD). A GF addition $r = a + b$ is achieved by a bitwise XOR-ing inputs a and b. The realization of this function is simple combinatorial logic using 83 XOR gates for adding two 83 bit wide input datawords. Therefore only a single clock cycle is needed for the add operation.

Galois Field Multiplier (GF_MUL). The most often used sub-operation within a scalar multiplication is the GF-multiplication. At the same time this is also one of the most time consuming parts in the software implementation. The operation $a \cdot bmodn$ is carried out by hardware GF-multiplier that has been implemented at the research group COSIC at K.U. Leuven and is used with their permission. The implementation is based on [13], a *SHIFT & ADD Algorithm* with no windowing. With binary representation of the operands a and b a multiplication is defined as:

$$a \cdot b = \left[\sum_{i=0}^{n-1} a_i \cdot 2^i \right] \cdot b \tag{3}$$

$$= a_0 b + 2a_1 b + 4a_2 b + \ldots + 2^{n-1} a_{n-1} b \tag{4}$$

If $a \cdot b > n(n$ being the field size) at step i, a reduction mod$n$ is done. This is achieved within the last clock cycle of the *SHIFT & ADD Algorithm* by adding the unique reduction polynom to the intermediate result (see chapter 3.3). The duration of one GF-multiplication is proportional to the field size. Since the finite field size is 83 bit it takes 83 clock cycles for one operation.

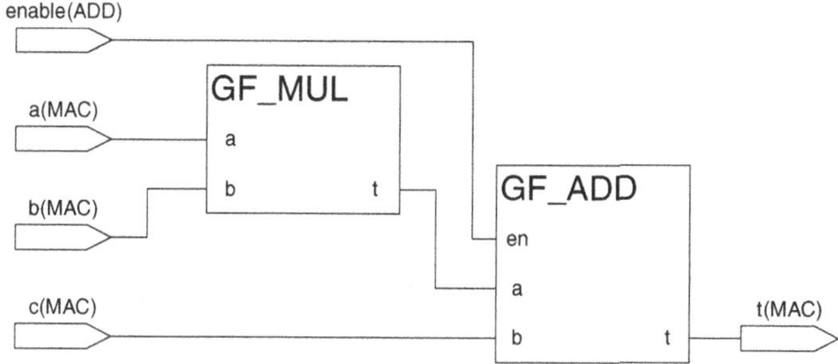

Fig. 1. GF_MAC unit

Multiply-Add Unit (GF_MAC). The GF_MAC unit is a combination of the afore mentioned modules (see figure 1). By using the enable Port on GF_ADD, it is possible to include or exclude the final addition of c into the operation. If the Adder unit is disabled the result is passed through the module immediately and input $c(MAC)$ is ignored, otherwise the addition is performed.

The GF_MAC module can be used for calculating $r = a \cdot b + c$ as well as $r = a \cdot b$. Runtime of both operations is identical. They need n clock cycles for n bit wide input data.

3.4 Co-processor Design

To exploit the modules mentioned above as a coprocessor, the interfacing to the MicroBlaze can be achieved either over OPB, FSL or LMB. The LMB (Local Memory Bus) is mainly used to interface instruction memory and data memory to the processor. Therefore this option to connect a coprocessor has not been evaluated.

In order to compare the different interfacing options and their effect on the overall computation speed, a unified structure of the coprocessor is used (see figure 2). It is not area-optimized for neither interface option, and only used for evaluation purposes. All input data is stored in internal registers. In the *"CoProcessor WorkUnit"* a simple FSM (Finite State Machine) controls the data into the GF-Hardware block, retrieves the result and puts it into an internal output register. The unit is independent of the interface that is used to connect the coprocessor to the MicroBlaze.

The *"CoProcessor InterfaceUnit"* accesses the internal registers of the WorkUnit and transfers the data to and from the main- and coprocessor. Only this unit has to be adapted to the different interfaces used on the MicroBlaze. The input operands, as well as the result, are 83 bit wide. Therefore they are divided into three 32 bit words to use the 32 bit wide interfaces of the MicroBlaze processor.

OPB Hardware/Software Interface. The MicroBlaze's OPB is a 32 bit on-chip bus that follows the IBM Core ConnectTM On-Chip Bus Standard [14]. To connect the coprocessor via OPB the module is implemented as a slave, and

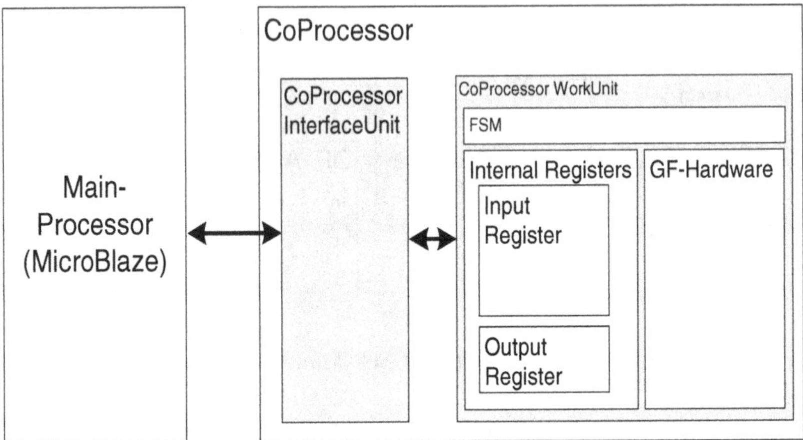

Fig. 2. Schematic view to co-processor infrastructure

the IPIF interface provided by Xilinx is used. It provides software accessible registers. C-macros are supplied to allow easy read/write access. The data is transferred into the IPIF registers by a write access via OPB using Xilinx's C-macros that are provided for the IPIF interface [10]. The registers are mapped in the *CoProcessor WorkUnit*'s internal register. The interface includes a control mechanism that checks if all required input data has been transferred and signals to the *WorkUnit*. Also it prohibits multiple write accesses to the same input register to avoid erroneous overwriting. As soon as all required data is received by the coprocessor, the data is processed. Immediately after recieving the result of the operation, the *InterfaceUnit* is cleared to receive new input data.

In the bus specification a Timeout signal is specified that aborts the read access if the slave does not react within 8 clock cycles. While data is being processed, read access by the main processor is blocked by asserting the signal IP2BUS_Toutsup. That way the Timeout signal is blocked, and the read access is prolonged until the result of the calculation is available. The processor is stalled when it is trying to read back the result before valid data is available. Since the goal is not parallelization of the algorithm but simply speeding up GF2n operations by using hardware, stalling the processor in this situation is acceptable.

Because the IPIF registers are freely addressable the transferred data words need not be transmitted in a certain order. They only have to be transferred to the correct register.

FSL Hardware/Software Interface. The MicroBlaze processor provides 8 input FSL interfaces as well as 8 output FSL interfaces. Each one is a 32 bit wide unidirectional Point-to-Point streaming (single master-single slave) interface. The communication is FIFO based (First-In-First-Out memory). It can be used to transmit data or control words. The FSL interfaces are marked by a separate bit that is propagated along with the appropriate data. By checking this bit a slave can determine if the current input is a data or a control word.

Every FSL is driven by a single master and can be read by a single slave. This enables the use of a very simple protocol. The master pushes data into the FIFO and the slaves reads it from the FIFO. To transfer data to and from MicroBlaze's memory, Xilinx provides appropriate C based macros, that supply read/write blocking mechanism, if the main processor tries to push data into an already full FIFO or tries reading an empty FIFO.

To transfer data to the coprocessor, all input operands are pushed into the *InterfaceUnit*'s FIFO. The data is immediately transferred sequentially to the *WorkUnit*'s internal registers. As before (see chapter 3.4) the operands are transmitted in groups of three 32 bit data packets. In the *InterfaceUnit* those packets are reassembled and put in the appropriate places of the registers in the coprocessor. Therefore the order of the data packets is fixed, no interleaving is permitted.

As soon as data is available in the FIFO they are moved into the internal registers. Right after the first two data words have arrived, the operation of the data is started and the result is pushed into the output FIFO of the coprocessor. When the GF_MAC unit is used, the multiplication operation is started after the first two data words have arrived. If a third data word is received it is read from the FIFO during the execution of the multiplication.

Software Drivers. To use the coprocessor all the input operands for the GF operation is put out from MicroBlaze to the coprocessor. This is done by using the appropriate C-Macros for OPB and FLS respectively. As soon as all the input data is recognized by the coprocessor (see chapter 3.4 and 3.4) it starts the computation. Immediately after the main processor has transferred the input data it polls the coprocessor's internal output register (see figure 2) until a result is available. The processor is stalled by the coprocessor until the result is valid (see chapter 3.4 and 3.4). Since the result of the coprocessors calculation is used as an input for the subsequent GF operation, stalling the processor does not prolongate the execution time. It might be possible to structure the algorithm otherwise to parallelize HW and SW computations. This has not been done in order to have a very close comparison of HW vs. SW implementation. Since Xilinx's macros are used, there is no need to write low level drivers.

The driver for OPB interfacing is only responsible for the correct mapping of input data to IPIF registers. For FSL interfacing the order of data transfers is essential and must be ensured by the driver.

All data transfers are organized through software, no interrupts are used.

4 Test and Evaluation

The modules GF_ADD, GF_MUL and GF_MAC were tested for computational speed. GF_MUL was implemented with an OPB interface as well as with a

FSL interface and was used as a benchmark to evaluate the difference in speed caused by the differences between the possible interface structures. As expected, experiments showed that the FSL interface is definitely faster than the OPB interface. All further measurements were then done with the FSL interface only since the ultimate goal is to find the fastest possible system for HECC in the investigated HW/SW codesign scenario.

GF_ADD was solely implemented as an OPB slave, since measurements of computational time for an addition in software showed that the possible speed up by using a hardware adder was probably only marginal (see chapter 4.1). Since the ratio of *speedup vs. resources* is not very satisfiable, the approach of using a hardware GF_ADD unit was not further pursued.

All measurements were done on the above mentioned test platform (see chapter 3.1). Its clock frequency was chosen with 33 MHz. An increase of the clock frequency results in a proportional speed up of the computation time. This was verified by increasing the frequency to 66 MHz. Since the modules will be implemented in an embedded system the target frequency is well below 70 MHz. The maximal frequencies of the individual modules can be found in table 2.

The duration of these computational segments have been measured:

- GF addition $(u1 + u2)$
- GF multiplication $(u1 \cdot u2)$
- GF inversion $(u1^{-1})$
- HECC DivisorAdd $(P_1 + P_2)$
- HECC DivisorDouble $(2P_1)$
- HECC scalar multiplication $(k \cdot P_1)$
- HECC Proj_to_Affine (Transformation of one divisor from projective coordinates into affine coordinates)

u: galois field element
P: divisor on an (hyper-)elliptic curve
k: scalar in binary representation

All measurements include fetching the data and transfer from internal memory, transfer to and from hardware units if required, as well as storing the processed data in internal memory again.

Table 2. Frequency of Operations

	$f_{clk,max}$	Max. propagation delay
GF_ADD	Logic only	11 ns
GF_MULT	366 MHz	—
GF_MAC	366 MHz	11 ns
MicroBlaze[1]	85 MHz	—

[1] Valid for Spartan3 FPGAs, source: Xilinx Inc. XAPP477 v.1.0.1, S.2

4.1 Timing Analysis

A first comparison was done with the basic subroutines GF addition and GF multiplication. The acceleration of one add operation using hardware support is less than 14%. Since an adder operation in software is only 3 us not much time is gained, but 83 additional XOR gates are needed. One GF multiplication has a speed up factor greater than 100. As one can see in figure 3 one MAC operation (see chapter 3.3) and one multiplication operation have identical execution time. This is due to the fact, that the third operand is transferred to the GF_MAC unit during the multiplication part of the MAC operation. The transfer is done in less than 83 clock cycles which are needed for one multiplication. No measurable communication overhead for transferring the third operand is created.

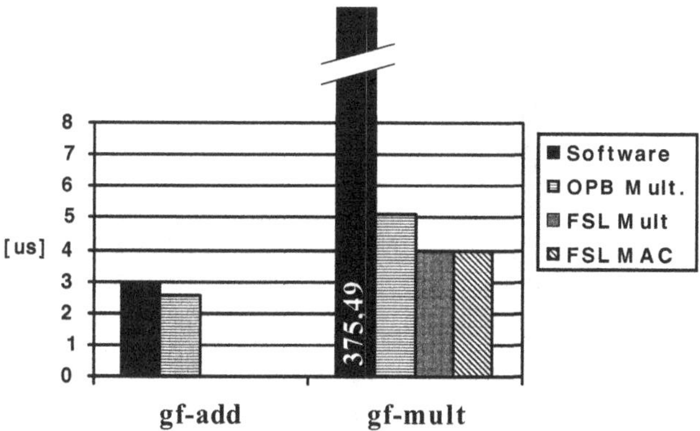

Fig. 3. Basic GF(2n) operations using hardware acceleration

As expected the FSL interface is clearly faster than the OPB interface. More than 1 us more is needed for the transfer of three 83 bit data words, consisting of three 32 bit transfers each. The communication overhead (see figure 4) is the sum of clock cycles needed to transfer data from the processor to the internal registers of the cryptohardware and the clock cycles needed to feed the data from those registers into the computational units for $GF(2^n)$ operations. Further measurements (see figure 5 and 6) show, that the difference in communication duration sums up to over 50 us for a single divisor operation and even some milliseconds for one scalar multiplication The divisor operations are all done in projective coordinates in order to save time consuming inversions. After an operation a transformation of the result from projective coordinates to affine has to be done once for the result. If this is done completely in software it needs 14,869 ms of computation time. If the GF multiplication on this algorithm is done in hardware this time frame still is 13,383 ms. About 27% of the processor time for one scalar multiplication is spent on coordinate transformation alone (see figure 6). A solution is using ITMIA (Itoh-Tsujii Multiplicative Inversion Algorithm). It can be implemented [8] by using the fast GF multiplication in hardware. Now

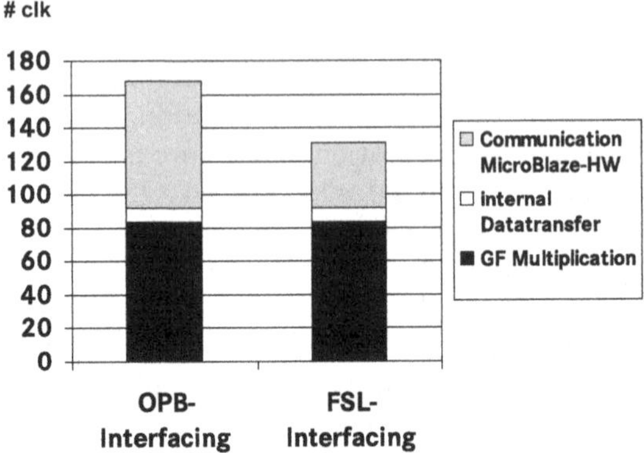

Fig. 4. Communication-Overhead OPB vs. FSL

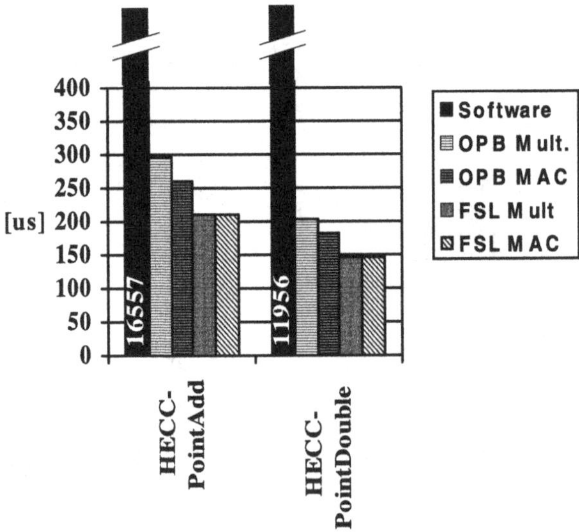

Fig. 5. Basic HECC operations in projective coordinates

one inversion needs only 0,372 ms thus lowering the overall computation time of one scalar multiplication to under 40 ms.

4.2 Area Utilization

The utilization of the hardware resources has not been optimized yet. Still the hardware extensions take up very few slices on a Spartan3 FPGA (see table 3). Although a Spartan3S5000 was used, the design fits easily on a Spartan3-500 without the need for area optimized implementation of the GF hardware extensions. Again the interfacing of hardware extension via FSL does have an

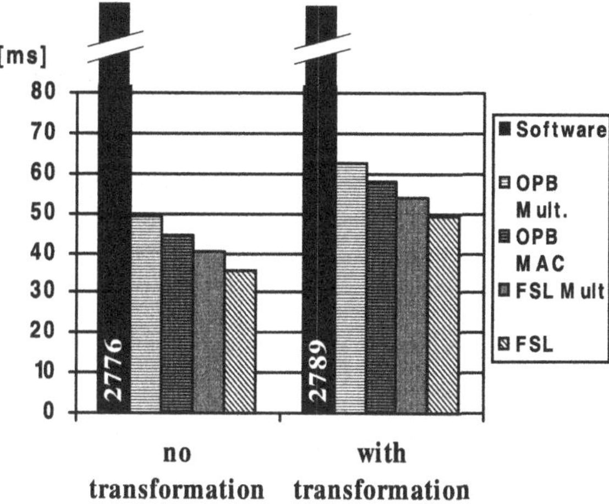

Fig. 6. Scalar multiplication

Table 3. Utilized hardware resources

Available on...	*Slices*	*FF*	*4 input LUTs*
Spartan 3S5000	33280	66560	66560
Used by...			
MicroBlaze	1020	809	1590
GF_MUL (FSL)	284	439	289
GF_MAC (FSL)	280	444	464
GF_ADD (OPB)	258	277	438
GF_MUL (OPB)	541	629	669
Counter_verylight	189	211	296

advantage over OPB interfacing. It uses much less resources. An adder is implemented in the GF_MAC unit. The whole unit including a GF adder and multiplier needs only slightly more resources as one GF adder connected via an OPB interface.

4.3 Side Channel Awareness

Moving cryptographic functionality into hardware demands the evaluation of possible attacks on the design and the overall system. Side channel attacks on hardware designs are a growing threat to embedded systems.

The FIFO in the FSL interfaces can be attacked by power analysis, since it draws comparably high currents. Also it can be localized pretty easily in the system. An attacker can therefore extract the type and sequence of operation carried out on a device. From that knowledge the secret key might be reconstructed, thus compromising the system. Therefore care must be taken to secure the system as much as possible against side channel attacks. On algorithmic level, balanced operations, key blinding, and other methods [15] can increase security against those attacks. These security measures do cost extra resources and/or computation time. Another crucial point is secure storage. This is a basic problem of all cryptographic implementations where secret information or parts of secret information is stored somewhere in the system. This information must be secured against unauthorized read and write access.

All of the above mentioned issues need to be addressed in future work.

5 Conclusion

In this paper the interfacing of software and hardware on a small Xilinx FPGA in conjunction with HECC has been evaluated. It was shown that using the FSL interface is the choice of options when interfacing a cryptographic processor to an embedded MicroBlaze processor. Even with a very crude and simple coprocessor design it is possible to speed up HECC operations enough to be used in embedded systems with the time constraints well under 0,2 seconds per one scalar multiplication. At the same time not many resources on the FPGA are used, due to the HW/SW codesign. The bottleneck of such an implementation is still the communication between main processor and coprocessor. Reducing the amount of data being transferred between those two will give an even greater benefit in computation time and is being investigated. In conclusion, HECC on very small FPGAs is feasible within fairly tight time constraints and using minimal resources on these devices, thus making it very interesting for embedded systems that need security features based on cryptography.

References

1. Sakai, Y., Sakurai, K.: On the practical performance of hyperelliptic curve cryptosystems in software implementation(special section on discrete mathematics and its applications). IEICE transactions on fundamentals of electronics, communications and computer sciences 83(4), 692–703 (2000)
2. Wollinger, T., Paar, C.: Hardware architectures proposed for cryptosystems based on hyperelliptic curves
3. Batina, L., et al.: Hardware/software co-design for hyperelliptic curve cryptography (hecc) on the 8051μp. In: Rao, J.R., Sunar, B. (eds.) CHES 2005. LNCS, vol. 3659, pp. 106–118. Springer, Heidelberg (2005)
4. Hankerson, D., Menezes, A., Vanstone, S.: Guide to elliptic curve cryptography. Springer, New York (2004)
5. Wollinger, T.: Computer architectures for cryptosystems based on hyperelliptic curves. Masterthesis, Worcester Polytechnic Institute, MA (April 2001)
6. Menezes, A.J., van Oorschot, P.C., Vanstone, S.A.: Handbook of Applied Cryptography. CRC Press, Boca Raton (2001)

7. Pelzl, J., Wollinger, T., Paar, C.: Special Hyperelliptic Curve Cryptosystems of Genus Two: Efficient Arithmetic and Fast Implementation. In: Nedjah, N. (ed.) Embedded Cryptographic Hardware: Design and Security, Nova Science Publishers, NewYork (2004)
8. Itoh, T., Tsujii, S.: Effective recursive algorithm for computing multiplicative inverses in gf(2m). IEEE Electronic Letters 24(6), 334–335 (1988)
9. Xilinx: Microblaze(tm) hardware reference guide. Document UG081 (2002)
10. Xilinx: Microblaze(tm) software reference guide (2002)
11. Hankerson, D., Hernandez, J.L., Menezes, A.: Software implementation of elliptic curve cryptography over binary fields. In: Paar, C., Koç, Ç.K. (eds.) CHES 2000. LNCS, vol. 1965, p. 1. Springer, Heidelberg (2001)
12. Batina, L.: Arithmetic and Architectures for Secure Hardware Implementations of Public-Key Cryptography. PhD thesis, Katholieke Universiteit COSIC (December 2005)
13. Beth, T., Gollmann, D.: Algorithm engineering for public key algorithms. IEEE Journal on Selected Areas in Communications 7(4), 458–466 (1989)
14. IBM: 64-Bit On-Chip Peripheral Bus, Architecture Specifications Version 2.1; SA-14-2528-02 (April 2001)
15. Coron, J.S.: Resistance against differential power analysis for elliptic curve cryptosystems. In: Koç, Ç.K., Paar, C. (eds.) CHES 1999. LNCS, vol. 1717, pp. 292–302. Springer, Heidelberg (1999)

Part VI

Organic Computing

A Reference Architecture for Self-organizing Service-Oriented Computing

Lei Liu, Stefan Thanheiser, and Hartmut Schmeck

Karlsruhe Institute of Technology - Institute AIFB
76128 Karlsruhe, Germany
{lei.liu,stefan.thanheiser,hartmut.schmeck}@kit.edu

Abstract. Service orientation promotes a new way to design and implement large-scale distributed applications across organizational and technical boundaries. However, it does not provide sufficient means to cope with the increasing complexity in service-oriented applications. A promising way out of this dilemma is to enable self-organization in service-oriented computing - as advocated in current research initiatives (e.g. the Organic Computing project). Self-organization helps to keep system complexity hidden from human system participants. In this paper, we propose a reference architecture to establish controlled self-organization in a service-oriented environment with respect to existing reference architectures for SOC and self-organization.

Keywords: Service-oriented Computing, Organic Computing, Self-organization, Reference Architecture, Reference Model.

1 Motivation

Today's ever paced and changing business world demands for consistent IT infrastructures potentially spanning across organizational and technological boundaries. Emerging technologies, i. e.SOC, drives further convergence of existing enterprise IT systems towards integrated enterprise-level business applications. In this context, the design paradigm *service orientation* provides basic means for constructing business logic based on distributed business capabilities from various enterprise IT systems across the Internet, which leads potentially to a tighter alignment between business and IT [1]. Utilizing service orientation in the architectural design facilitates reusability, flexibility, interoperability, and agility of IT architectures. However, this design paradigm does not address the handling of system complexity resulting e.g. from interacting elements in large quantities or changes in the system and its environment. In particular, the lack of sufficient support to explicitly predict all eventualities at runtime, e.g. by providing predefined programming models, makes human interaction with SOC-based systems more complex. Hence, human participants are still strongly involved in managing large-scale distributed systems to cope with increasing system complexity.

U. Brinkschulte et al. (Eds.): ARCS 2008, LNCS 4934, pp. 205–219, 2008.

A plausible way out of this dilemma lies in utilizing software components exhibiting the characteristic of *controlled self-organization*. Such software components are able to operate autonomously in their environment, while still being under control of human system participants. This idea of building self-organizing software components is a major objective of several academic and industrial initiatives - such as the Organic Computing research program (GI/ITG and DFG) [2] or the Autonomic Computing initiative [3]. The automation of monitoring and controlling software components establishes a range of self-x properties in the system - including self-configuration, self-protection, self-optimization, and self-healing. These self-x properties allow corresponding software components to adapt their behaviour to external preferences transparently (either from human participants or from other external systems). However, the behaviour of self-organizing technical systems can still be influenced by human participants through operational policies as well as high-level system objectives.

This paper aims at extending the view presented in [4,5,6] and refining it to a reference architecture for self-organizing SOC. In software engineering, a reference architecture serves as an architectural blueprint for constructing software systems targeting particular problem domain(s) with specific functional, behavioural, and quality attribute requirements [7]. It outlines a set of necessary software components, their externally viewable interfaces as well as interrelationships existing between them (e.g. data flows). The major effort in this paper is to infuse the design paradigm of Organic Computing into approaches of SOC to establish controlled self-organization, while keeping the system complexity hidden from human system participants. To simplify requirements analysis and to better illustrate the reference model, we chose to use Service-oriented Architecture (SOA) as a representation of SOC-based systems in this paper.

The remainder of the paper is organized as follows. Section 2 determines key design requirements to establish self-organization in a large-scale, distributed service-oriented architecture. Section 3 provides an overview of related work focusing on existing reference architectures for SOC and self-organization. Section 4 will propose a reference architecture by discussing design patterns and a high-level architecture with respect to the given design requirements. Finally, Section 5 concludes the paper and gives an outlook on our future research.

2 Key Design Challenges

SOA provides a means for building large-scale distributed applications across organization and technology boundaries by leveraging distributed business logic that may be under control of different ownership domains. Compared to traditional distributed approaches, SOA serves business demands in a more efficient and organized way by applying a set of design principles, such as service abstraction, reusability, and composability. Despite of the potential of SOA to align business and enterprise IT, SOA still exhibits a set of characteristics that make it complicated to apply self-organization to an SOA-based System. Parts of these SOA characteristics are inherited from traditional distributed paradigms;

some others are more SOA-specific. In the following, we will review the key design challenges for a reference architecture aiming at controlled self-organization in SOA.

Service autonomy. As one of the fundamental design principles for service orientation, Autonomy refers to the desired behaviour of services to be responsible for their own operational status. Therefore, services may autonomously vary their implementation, deployment, operation, and management independently of their consumers. Generally, service autonomy raises the question of how to establish proper operation status on the system level, especially in presence of possible failures in the underlying service elements.

Dependency. Dependency is a phenomenon frequently observable in service-oriented applications. It exists not only between service providers and service consumers, but also between services and their underlying environment. Generally, we can identify the following two dependency types in SOA:

Functional Dependency. In the abstract layered SOA model, services build the conjunction part between the business layer and underlying enterprise IT layers. The functional operability of a service relies on technical components from the IT layers, such as application server or database server. In turn, the proper operability of services ensures the functionality of business processes based on them. In this context, services along with business processes, applications, and infrastructural elements build a 'vertical functional link' between functionally interrelated SOA elements. All the SOA elements in the functional link are functionally dependent on each other.

Weak Dependency. Apart from functional dependencies, there are weak dependencies between system elements indirectly related to each other. Weak dependency occurs, if two independent system elements functionally depend on the same element in the system (e.g. two services running on the same application server) or if they support the same system element (e.g., a web server and a database server supporting the same Web service). Weak dependency does not play a critical role for proper operation of service-oriented applications. It is mainly used to determine the effective environment of a system element.

Decentralization and distribution. Service orientation can be regarded as an evolution of traditional distributed application concepts. It imposes decentralization by utilizing business capabilities provisioned by various distributed organizational units. From a system management point-of-view, system decentralization requires appropriate management approaches to cope with the distributed nature of service-oriented applications and to avoid situations like resource bottlenecks or single-point-of-failure.

Dynamism. SOA dynamism can partly be derived from service autonomy: the open architecture of an SOA allows for introducing/removing services as autonomous functional units to/from the system at any time. Furthermore, each service is free to adapt its behaviour autonomously to environmental changes. A similar level of dynamism can be observed in other SOA elements, in particular with respect to element variability and possible emergent behaviours on the system level. Therefore, we need approaches to deal with system dynamism - both at system level and at element level.

Heterogeneity and interoperability. The IT landscape for service-oriented applications is heterogeneous with respect to the variety of elements on the application layer and infrastructure layer in the abstract SOA model - different platforms, different technologies, different capabilities. Although the standard-based interactions help to reduce the impact of heterogeneous technologies on the SOA-based system, this characteristic remains a challenge for designing generic self-organizing approaches managing the system.

Robustness. The desirable reference architecture has to keep the balance between *optimal* and *suboptimal but robust* solutions. As aforementioned, a self-organizing solution for service-oriented applications has to face a dynamic and decentralized system. Both characteristics make it difficult to ensure the overall optimal behaviour of the solution, which can only exist in a static and centralized environment. In contrast to such optimal but strongly restricted behaviour in a service oriented environment we prefer a self-organizing solution exhibiting potentially suboptimal but robust behaviour.

Scalability. A service-oriented application may scale from simple applications leveraging a few services to large-scale enterprise-level applications involving a set of back-end systems such as CRM, ERP. Hence, a solution for enabling self-organization in SOA has to be able to deal with various scalability levels of the targeted service-oriented application.

Transparency. This characteristic refers to the willingness of an autonomous SOA element to reveal information about itself and to accept external operational objectives. The background for this request is the necessary collaboration between interrelated components at runtime. In such a scenario, a component can decide autonomously if it is willing to reveal its internal information and how to reveal it. Depending on the different degrees of willingness, we can generally distinguish between *fully-transparent* - if an element reveals its (consolidated) internal information to each SOA system element and is ready to cooperate with any other element, *partly-transparent* - if an element only reveals part of its internal information e.g. to elements with functional dependency, and *non-transparent* - if an element acts as a black box without exposing any internal information except the predefined service messages.

3 Related Work

A reference architecture provides architectural patterns for building software systems targeting certain problem domains. In recent years several organizations have worked on various reference models as well as reference architectures for SOA and self-organizing applications to establish a common understanding on designing and implementing such systems.

3.1 Service-Oriented Computing

Several reference models and reference architectures exist in the context of service-oriented systems. W3C has worked on the foundation for service orientation and defined Web services as well as the Web service architecture technology stack addressing how a service-oriented architecture can be built upon this stack. As work-in-progress, the technical committee from OASIS aims at conceptualizing a reference model and a reference architecture for SOA. They study the concept of SOA from another point-of-view and emphasize the various aspects in SOA and their relationships to each other.

A comprehensive reference architecture for SOA called "Service-oriented Solution Stack" (S3) is proposed by Arsanjani et al. [8]. They divide a service-oriented environment into nine independent layers. The five basic layers are from top-down the *consumers* and *business processes* layers with more consumer concerns, the *services* layer, and the *service components* and *operational systems* with more provider concerns. The other four layers cut across the five basic layers and support the aspects *integration*, *quality of service*, *information architecture*, and *governance and policies* in the environment. The S3 reference architecture addresses the management perspective with the *quality of service* layer and the *governance and policies* layer, and outlines the connection between these two layers. However, the S3 architecture is limited mainly to issues on an abstract level and does not detail both layers on the component level. Similar approaches are e.g. the integrated Service-oriented Architecture (iSOA) introduced in the Karlsruher Integrated InformationManagement (KIM) project [9] or the extended Service-oriented Architecture (xSOA) by Papazoglou [10].

3.2 Self-organization

Self-organization is a phenomenon often studied in the natural sciences, e.g. in cybernetics focusing on the circular mechanisms to control complex systems. A representative work in this research area is the viable system model (VSM) developed by S. Beer in the 1970s [11,12]. In the VSM, a viable system exhibits a set of characteristics, among other things, adaptivity, self organisation, ability to communicate, and ability to learn. The VSM targets at viable systems and has been applied successfully to various problem domains such as organization modelling. In general, the VSM encapsulates three interacting aspects of viable systems: *operation*, *control*, and *environment* of the system. The five subsystems - System 1 to System 5 - declared in the VSM cover these aspects and their relationships to one another, as illustrated in Fig. 1. All the operating components in the system are referred to System 1. In other words, System 1 may have several instances in a viable system. In the context of SOA, System 1 may contain e.g. a service providing certain business capabilities or application server supplying the hosting environment for services. Each instance in System 1 is autonomous and may operate according to its local environmental situation with limited view to the environment. To coordinate the operating components, System 2 establishes the necessary communication and provides the necessary interface to System 3, which supervises and controls all the activities in System 1 from a local perspective. So far, with System 1, 2, 3, the system is capable of dealing with immediate and internal concerns taking place in the local environment. To adapt to changes in the global environment, the VSM employs a further System 4 to control and predict the system behaviour based on information collected from global and local environments. The balance between the internal operational status and given external operational goal is guaranteed by System 5. With given operational policies, System 5 supplies and enforces logical policies to the entire system. From this point-of-view, it creates a interface for superior system to control the system behaviour externally. With System 4 and System 5, the system is capable of controlling itself based on given policies as well as on situations in the global environment. Furthermore, the VSM can be applied in a recursive manner - in other words, each System 1 may contains a viable subsystem consisting of all the 5 systems mentioned afore.

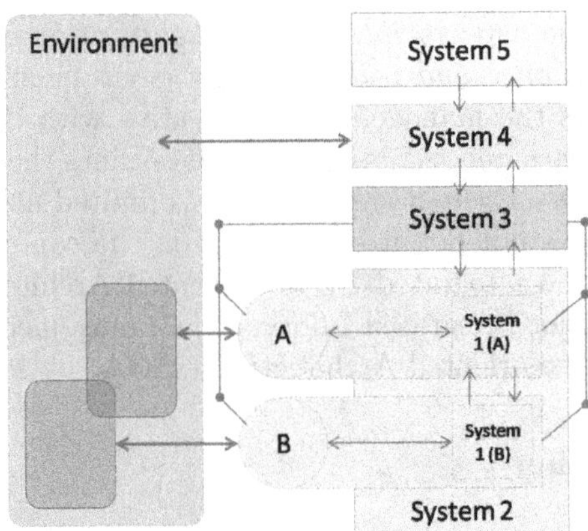

Fig. 1. The Viable System Model (VSM) [11,12]

More software centric reference architectures for self-organization are the generic Observer/Controller architecture introduced in the OC priority program [13] or the MAPE (monitor, analyse, plan, and execute) control loop from the AC initiative [14]. OC is a vision for designing technical systems to adapt to dynamically changing requirements of their environment by exhibiting various so called self-x properties - e.g. self-configuring, self-protecting, self-healing, etc. The major goal of the O/C architecture is to monitor technical systems and - if necessary - to influence their behaviour to satisfy a particular operational goal. The 'System under Observation and Control' (SuOC), which can be a large collection of interconnected active objects, makes up the basic system to be managed by the O/C architecture. The 'Observer' collects data from the SuOC and computes a status model representing the current state of the system. This status model is passed on to the 'Controller'. For taking a decision, the Controller will consult its local knowledge base to check, if an intervention is required to influence the system behaviour and which action is most appropriate. The possible decision guidance can be e.g. the reported status model, the given operational policies, as well as its experiences reflected by the action history. The action to be imposed on the SuOC can be executed by e.g. influencing the SuOC's environment, by utilizing predefined controlling interface, or by directly modifying a component's behaviour in the SuOC. Together with the SuOC, the Observer and the Controller build the basic architecture of an 'organic system'.

Rationale. All the related work discussed afore focus on self-organisation in various problem domains. However, in the context of SOC, these work cannot be applied directly to establish self-organisation in SOC. The major issues herein are the autonomous and distributed nature of SOC elements, as discussed in Section 2. The autonomy of SOC elements requires an in-depth control of their functional components. This local aspect for self-organisation is well defined by e.g. the Observer/Controller architecture of OC or the MAPE control loop of AC. However, both approaches lack efficient support to enable collaboration between related SOC elements. Decentralization in SOC and given dependencies between various SOC elements make self-organisation depend to a large extent on collaboration between SOC elements. This global aspect for self-organisation is in turn well reflected by the VSM model, i. e., by its capabilities to interact with the environment to control the system operational state. From this point-of-view, a comprehensive concept for SOC has to combine approaches for enabling self-organisation locally and on a global base. Thus, in the following sections, we introduce the reference architecture for self-organising SOA utilizing the strength of the models introduced in this section.

4 The Reference Architecture for self-organizing SOA

This section focuses on the desired reference architecture endowing SOC with self-organizing capabilities. The key design challenges addressed in the last section define the requirements for designing the reference architecture in detail. Based on these requirements, we first introduce an abstract system model for a self-organizing SOA on the meta level, before we go on discussing the structure of self-organizing elements making up the reference architecture on the component level.

4.1 An Abstract Meta Model for Self-organizing SOA

In previous work [5,6], we have applied the design principles of Organic Computing to SOA to achieve controlled self-organization with so called 'Organic SOA' (OSOA). The basic idea of this concept is to equip each SOA element in the system with an Observer/Controller (O/C) unit. This schema is applied in a multi-level way with respect to the existing functional dependencies between SOA elements. An O/C unit observes the behaviour of the corresponding SOA element and tends to control its behaviour to match given operational directives. In this way, the O/C unit can cooperate with other relevant O/C units, especially those in its immediate neighbourhood.

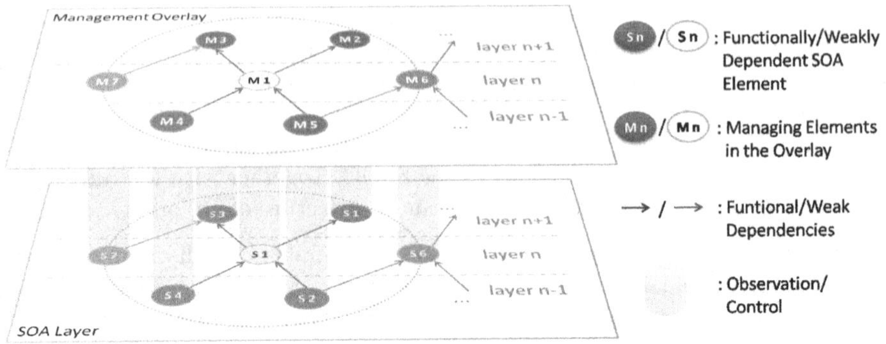

Fig. 2. Abstracted meta model for self-organizing SOA

Fig. 2 illustrates an OSOA with abstracted SOA elements and their managing elements including the aforementioned O/C unit. A similar approach is e.g. introduced by Bouajila et al. in context of System on Chip [15]. In the abstract model, each technical component in a real SOA-based application, such as a Web service or a database server is abstracted to an element in the figure with incoming/outgoing relationships to other elements. An incoming relationship indicates that the corresponding element consumes services from other elements. Analogously, an outgoing relationship indicates that the element delivers services to other elements in the system. In analogy to real world service-oriented applications, each element from the layer n can consume services from elements in layer n-1 only and deliver services to elements in layer n+1. To logically separate the management concern from the original business-centric aspect of SOA, all managing elements establishing self-organization in corresponding SOA components make up a management overlay over the existing SOA layer, as illustrated in Fig. 2. However, the overlay is not isolated from the SOA layer. It reflects the element structure in the underlying SOA layer, especially various dependency relationships between SOA elements. The mapping of relationships ensures a context-aware management of corresponding elements in the SOA layer.

Managing the underlying SOA layer is achieved by the managing elements and by their collaboration inside the overlay. In analogy to the VSM, each SOA element along with its managing element in the overlay exhibits the aspects operation, control, and environment in the OSOA. With respect to operation, each element delivers service(s) to other elements in the system in different ways - such as invoking particular business capabilities, hosting service, or platform/infrastructure support. The control of such elements is achieved by the corresponding managing element from the overlay. The environment of an SOA element is defined by the group of elements to which it maintains either functional or weak dependency relationships. In this way, an SOA element can determine its immediate neighbourhood in the system. Furthermore, the definition includes only the minimal set of interrelated elements in the system and so induces a less complex state space. Hence, this definition allows for efficient and effective coordination between the elements at runtime.

4.2 Architectural Pattern

The extraction of managing elements from the original SOA layer into a separate overlay enables a clear separation between management-centric and service-centric communication. In the overlay, communication between various managing elements allows a managing element to cooperate with other elements to manage one or more SOA elements in the underlying SOA layer.

In OSOA, each managing element has simultaneously a local and a global context. Locally, each managing element interacts with its corresponding SOA element in the underlying layer to provide self-organization capabilities. Globally, each managing element is situated in an environment consisting of elements with functional/weak dependencies. These managing elements in the neighbourhood are all potential cooperation partners at runtime. To facilitate cooperation at runtime, each managing element exposes a set of services to other managing elements in the overlay while keeping its internal autonomous behaviour unaffected. From this viewpoint, we can apply service orientation to the management overlay to get it better organized.

Furthermore, employing design principles of service orientation in the overlay keeps it flexible with respect to changes in the underlying SOA layer. Any change in the SOA layer results in change(s) to the management overlay layer. E.g., if a new element is introduced in the SOA layer, a corresponding managing element will be added to the management overlay, too. This desirable capability can be achieved e.g. by employing the service repository introduced in the W3C's Web service architecture. Furthermore, the open architecture of SOA allows integrating further services into the management overlay with particular capabilities such as a service providing decision support in case of uncertainties/conflicts between managing elements or an "information desk" service delivering a common understanding on particular vocabularies to managing elements.

Rationale. Using service orientation for building the management overlay addresses many of the architectural design challenges discussed in Section 2. Among other things, this approach addresses the following points:

- *Decentralization and distribution:* In OSOA, decentralized control of a service-oriented application is enabled by distributed managing elements organized in compliance with the same service-oriented principles. This streamlines decentralized control essentially to cope with the inherent distributed characteristics of service-oriented applications.
- *Dynamism:* A management overlay employing service-oriented design principles reveals the dynamic characteristics of SOA-based systems. Various approaches from service orientation help the management overlay to cope with the dynamism in the underlying SOA layer - such as the service registry defined in the Web service architecture or the WS-Discovery specification for discovering services.
- *Heterogeneity and interoperability:* The underlying SOA layer to be managed is heterogeneous e.g. with respect to technical platforms, supporting technologies. Service orientation resolves the heterogeneity by employing a

set of standards - such as XML, SOAP, WSDL. Applying service orientation to the management overlay ensures that the communication between managing elements in the layer can take place independently of their technical implementation.

- *Scalability:* The managing elements in the overlay reflect the structure of the underlying service-oriented application in the SOA layer. In other words, any changes in the underlying service-oriented application results in analogous changes in the overlay. This allows the management overlay to scale in accordance to the underlying system to be managed.

However, in comparison with traditional centralized management solutions and in compliance with service orientation the decentralized architecture of the overlay implies some trade-offs and limitations. Obviously, the decentralized control requires more communication and coordination efforts which may affect the performance of the system. Moreover, each managing element has only a limited view on the entire system, which may lead to suboptimal decisions with respect to centralized control. From this point of view, the management overlay is a trade-off between decentralized but robust control and centralized but restricted control.

4.3 The Managing Element in OSOA

In the previous section, we have discussed how managing elements are organized in the management overlay to enable decentralized control over the underlying SOA-based system. In this section, we focus on the internal structure of managing elements. Fig. 3 shows the managing element as a set of interacting runtime subcomponents. The component view of the managing element in the figure reflects the VSM to enable adaptive behaviour with respect to local operation and global environment. In the following, we will rely on the VSM to outline the internal structure of a managing element.

System 1 of the VSM contains all operative elements carrying out predefined business capabilities. In our model, System 1 consists of operative subcomponents - *business capabilities* and *service interface* that make up a normal service in an SOA - and the local regulatory subcomponents concerning various management aspects of operative subcomponents, e.g. *availability management*, *service-level management* and *cost management*. *Business capabilities* define functionalities the service offers to other components in the SOA, such as hosting service of a Web server or database service of a database instance. A consumer can access the *business capabilities* through the given *service interface*. The *service interface* separates the invocation aspect from the operation aspect of the *business capabilities*. This allows for defining invocation-related artefacts, such as service level agreements, without affecting the operational part. Runtime-related management aspects make up the local management part within System 1. Fig. 2 illustrates some of these aspects. These subcomponents perform low-level management operations only in the local context. They do not have any reference to e.g. the global context or other external operational directives.

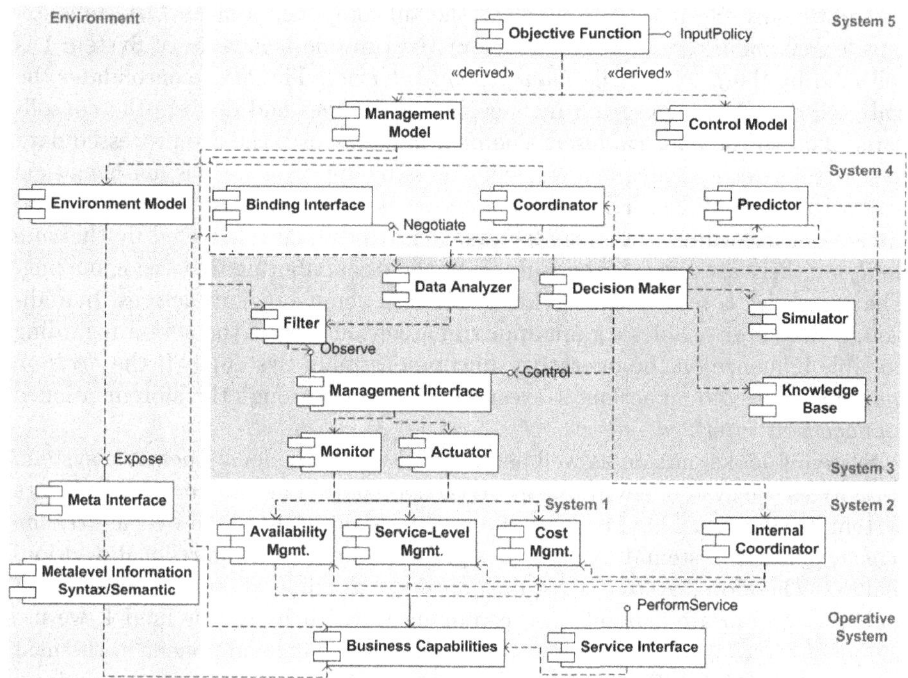

Fig. 3. Component view of a self-organizing component in OSOA with mapping to the VSM

System 2 coordinates all the operative elements as well as the low-level management subcomponents and provides a regulatory centre for them. The *internal coordinator* in System 2 coordinates the management subcomponents and takes charge of their impact on the operative system. There are certain dependencies between various management aspects. For instance, any changes in the service-level may lead to changes in cost calculation. Such dependencies are covered by the *internal coordinator* for the consistency across all the aspects.

In the VSM, System 3 implies the control of System 1 and 2 by managing immediate internal activities in them. The control over System 1 is achieved by three subcomponents: *monitor*, *actuator* and *management interface*. The *monitor* employs various mechanisms such as events, log files, instrumentation APIs to gather details about the runtime behaviour of the *business capabilities*. The other subcomponent, the *actuator*, changes the runtime behaviour of the *business capabilities* by executing given actions. This may take place by e.g. changing the configuration or invoking APIs in System 1. The *management interface* provides the possibility of platform-independent access to the *monitor* and the *actuator*. Existing approaches such as the WS-Management or the Web Service Distributed Management (WSDM) specification can be applied to design the *management interface*.

Additionally, System 3 contains all the subcomponents of an O/C unit except for the *predictor*. Information about the runtime behaviour of System 1 is collected by the *filter* via the *management interface*. The *filter* consolidates the collected data based on given management objectives and delivers the consolidated data to the *data analyser*. The *data analyser* uses the pre-processed data to search for recognizable behaviour patterns by applying various mathematical or statistical methods. The *decision maker* is responsible to select appropriate actions according to various factors. Next to the data delivered by the *data analyser*, there are several other subcomponents contributing to decision making. The *knowledge base* delivers e.g. historical data about previous actions. In addition, a *simulator* enables e.g. an approximate evaluation of the action regarding possible influence on the operative subcomponents in System 1. If the *decision maker* has selected an action, it executes the action through the aforementioned *management interface*.

System 4 looks outside as well as to the future of the local operative system. It analyses the system environment on the global level and try to predict future system behaviours. This increases the quality of decisions made by the *decision maker*, because System 4 incorporates global context to support local decision-making. Therefore, System 4 requires an understanding about its environment and the appropriate capability to communicate with it. In our model, we use the *predictor* to predict the behaviour of the underlying component in the next sample time unit(s). The coordination with managing elements in the environment is carried out by the *coordinator*. In addition, the *binding interface* enables managing elements to share information as well as to set up collaborations.

Until now, we have constructed a managing element that is adaptively aware of local as well as global changes in the system. However, we still miss the aspect of controlled self-organization in the model. This aspect is realized by System 5 in the VSM. In our model, System 5 consists of the *objective function*, the *management model* and the *control model*. The *objective function* accepts policies from an external source, e.g. from a human administrator or other superior managing element. Since policies are used to influence the behaviour of the entire system, the managing element is therefore controlled by an external instance in this way. The input policies are further divided into a *management model* and a *control model*. The *management model* decides e.g. the way in which the filter collects runtime information or the way in which the data analyser should process the consolidated runtime information. The *control model* controls the *decision maker* and specifies e.g., how the various subcomponents like *data analyser*, *coordinator*, *predictor* or similar should be combined to support decision-making.

The *Environment* forms the last part in our model. In the last section, we defined the environment of a managing element as the group of all managing elements with either functional or weak dependencies. In our model, the *environment model* always contains an up-to-date system model - including the information about all related managing elements in the environment, relationships to these elements, and other meta-level information. All this meta-level information is exposed by the meta interface. The meta-level information facilitates collaboration between managing elements at runtime. In combination with other approaches such as dynamic discovery, the *meta interface* helps to keep the overlay up-to-date without any manual procedures.

Rationale. In our model, we can generally classify all the subcomponents into two groups. The subcomponents of System 1, 2, 3 establish self-organization in the local context. In addition, the subcomponents of System 3, 4, 5 facilitate the control of the underlying SOA element through coordination and collaboration with other managing elements in its immediate neighbourhood. The overall controlled self-organizing behaviour of a managing element is the result of collaboration between both groups on the higher level. The separation of local self-organization from the coordination on a higher level enables clear design of the system and increases modularity and reusability of the subcomponents.

To illustrate the functionality of the reference architecture in context of self-organization, we consider a self-healing scenario in an SOA system. Initially, a service and a business process negotiate a service-level agreement specifying service-level objectives that both of them have to follow. With the given agreement, System 5 of the service's managing element will propagate an appropriate policy to all other subsystems in order to align their behaviour. Among other things, it specifies e.g. the type of metrics to be monitored by the *filter* in System 3, how the *data analyser* has to pre-process the collected data, and how the *decision maker* can make decision based on estimated data. For example, for managing availability, the *filter* has to monitor the number of processed requests per time unit by the service. The *data analyser* then can perform time-services-analysis on the monitored data. If the *predictor* in System 4 predicts a possible violation of the SLA, the *decision maker* tries to solve the cause for it. Let's assume that the increased processing time per request is caused by low processing priority of the service in the underlying Web server. In this case, the *coordinator* will try to contact the underlying Web server specified in the environment model to increase the priority of its corresponding service. This activity is possible e.g. in combination with higher cost. If the *coordinator* can reach a new agreement with the underlying Web server, the *decision maker* does not need to perform any action in the service; otherwise it has to negotiate a new agreement with the business process again.

5 Conclusion

In this paper, we have presented a reference architecture to enable controlled self-organization in a service-oriented environment. The distributed and heterogeneous characteristics of service-oriented computing demand for comprehensive management approaches. In our reference architecture, self-organization of SOA elements is achieved by a separate management overlay observing and controlling the underlying SOA layer. In comparison to existing traditional management solutions, our reference architecture represents a generic and technology-independent approach that can be applied to each element in an SOA-based system. Furthermore, utilizing service orientation in the management overlay makes the overlay more flexible and agile.

Our future work will focus on the refinements of the reference architecture and apply the reference architecture in simulation tools to verify the design and its impact on the underlying SOA-based system. In particular, the following open questions have to be addressed:

- In this paper, we assume that each SOA element can be equipped with a corresponding management element in the management overlay. For legacy systems inside SOA, this may pose a challenge due to missing interfaces in the legacy SOA element. Therefore, it is essential to investigate how to integrate such legacy elements into an OSOA landscape.
- In the management overlay, a managing element may receive concurrent or even inconsistent instructions from other functionally dependent managing elements. In this case, mechanisms are needed to solve conflicts and, if possible, to find the most adequate solution.
- The OSOA should be controllable by external policies supplied by human system participants. Therefore, it is to investigate how the "human-machine" interaction can take place at runtime. In particular, how the human strategies and operational goals can be translated into OSOA policies.

References

1. Cherbakov, L., et al.: Impact of service orientation at the business level. IBM Systems Journal 44(4), 653–668 (2005)
2. Schmeck, H.: Organic Computing- a new vision for distributed embedded systems. In: Proceedings Eighth IEEE International Symposium on Object-Oriented Real-Time Distributed Computing (ISORC 2005), pp. 201–203. IEEE Computer Society Press, Los Alamitos (2005)
3. Horn, P.: Autonomic Computing: IBMs perspective on the state of it (2001), `http://www-03.ibm.com/industries/government/doc/content/bin/auto.pdf`
4. Liu, L., Schmeck, H.: A roadmap towards autonomic service-oriented architectures. International Transactions on Systems Science and Applications 2(3), 245–255 (2006)
5. Liu, L., Thanheiser, S., Schmeck, H.: Coping with the complexity of service-oriented computing using controlled self-organization. In: Workshop Service Oriented Computing: a look at the Inside 2007 (SOC@Inside 2007), Vienna (2007)
6. Thanheiser, S., Liu, L., Schmeck, H.: Towards collaborative coping with IT complexity by combining soa and organic computing. System and Information Sciences Notes 2(1), 82–87 (2007)
7. Kazman, R., Clements, P., Bass, L.: Software Architecture in Practice. Addison-Wesley, Reading (2003)
8. Arsanjani, A., et al.: S3: A Service-oriented reference architecture. IT Professional 9(3), 10–17 (2007)
9. KIM: The Karlsruher Integrated InformationsManagement (KIM) project (2007), `http://www.kim.uni-karlsruhe.de`

10. Papazoglou, M.P.: Extending the service-oriented architecture. Business Integration Journal 2005(FEB), 18–21 (2005)
11. Beer, S.: Brain of the Firm, 2nd edn. John Wiley & Sons, Chichester (1981)
12. Beer, S.: Diagnosing the System for Organizations. Wiley, Chichester (1985)
13. Branke, J., et al.: Organic computing - adressing complexity by controlled self-orgnization. In: 2nd International Symposium on Leveraging Applications of Formal Methods, Verification and Validation, pp. 200–206 (2006)
14. IBM: An architectural blueprint for Autonomic Computing (2005), `http://www03.ibm.com/autonomic/pdfs/AC7.pdf`
15. Bouajila, A., et al.: Organic computing at the system on chip level. In: IFIP International Conference on Very Large Scale Integration of System on Chip 2006, Springer, Heidelberg (2006)

Towards Self-organising Smart Camera Systems

Martin Hoffmann, Jörg Hähner, and Christian Müller-Schloer

Leibniz Universität Hannover
Institute of Systems Engineering, System and Computer Architecture
Appelstr. 4, 30167 Hannover, Germany
{hoffmann,haehner,cms}@sra.uni-hannover.de

Abstract. Smart Camera Systems consist of large numbers of networked cameras which can adjust their fields of view by panning, tilting and zooming. Each Smart Camera is an embedded systems that does not just capture raw video streams but also analyses video data locally using computer vision techniques. Apart from image processing tasks the second important issue is the management of such systems, e.g. camera alignment and calibration. Due to the increasing number of cameras in these systems manual administration becomes hardly feasible. Therefore, algorithms for autonomous system organisation are needed. As a basis for these algorithms, in this paper we propose a distributed system architecture which is tailored to the requirements of Smart Camera Systems. Inspired by self-organisation –a major paradigm of Organic Computing– this paper presents an algorithm relying on our distributed architecture for one important management problem in Smart Camera Systems, i.e. the spatial partitioning of an area under observation.

Keywords: Distributed Smart Cameras, self-organising, spatial partitioning.

1 Introduction

Future camera based surveillance systems, as for example used at airports and train stations, will rely on several hundreds of distributed Smart Cameras [1,2]. Smart Cameras (SCs) are capable of analysing captured video data autonomously and inform security staff in case of critical events. Current research advances in computer vision make way for cooperative scene understanding, see e.g. [3]. Therefore, Smart Cameras are able to detect for example intruders in non-public areas and acts of violence, vandalism or even terrorism [4].

This paper focuses on a self-organising system infrastructure rather than on computer vision techniques. We especially investigate SCs that are used for surveillance of large areas, e.g. aprons of airports. In order to secure these wide spaces, large numbers of spatially adjacent SCs carrying out coordinated surveillance tasks are needed. E.g., these tasks may be target tracking or object identification. An overview of past and current research projects concerned with automated scene understanding is given in Section 3. The amount of data collected by SC systems can hardly be analysed by human staff – for privacy reasons

U. Brinkschulte et al. (Eds.): ARCS 2008, LNCS 4934, pp. 220–231, 2008.

as well as due to costs arising. An SC system offers many degrees of freedom for configuration (heading and zoom setting for hundreds of cameras) so it is hardly feasible to rely on human operators only. Organic Computing [5,6] offers paradigms and algorithms that make way for the design of systems with certain self-x properties. This paper describes an algorithm for self-organisation of SC systems. Self-organisation for a single SC means, to find an optimal viewing angle to increase the overall systems performance. Therefore, an algorithm dealing with the question of how to partition an area under surveillance is subject of our current research [7]. The design of this algorithm led to questions concerning the overall system architecture.

This paper focuses two main aspects:

- the networked system architecture and SC node architecture
- a distributed algorithm (ROCAS) enabling SCs to self-organise their fields of view

ROCAS is used for the evaluation of the SC node architecture. Since large systems of SCs are not at hand for testing purposes right now, we enhanced the Network Simulator NS2 [8] to simulate our proposed architecture. The program code running inside the simulator can directly be transferred to our existing SC prototype, see [9]. Therefore, we assume simulation results to realistically reflect the characteristics of our architecture under real world constraints.

Our SCs have fixed positions but make use of their PTZ (pan/tilt/zoom) abilities to change their alignment. The distributed partitioning algorithm is a special application enabling SCs to self-organise their fields of view in order to reach a high surveillance coverage. In our distributed SC system, this is a non-trivial task since SCs do not have global but local knowledge only. Since a single point of failure is not acceptable for safety critical applications, we investigated an approach relying on fully distributed SCs.

This paper is structured as follows. At first we present our system architecture and related work. Afterwards, the Art Gallery Problem [10] will be introduced as well as its differences from the spatial partitioning problem we investigated further. In the end, we present experiments and results.

2 Architecture

The following Section consists of two parts. The description of an anticipated networked system architecture is followed by the description of a single SC node architecture.

2.1 Networked System Architecture

The left side of Fig. 1 shows the proposed system architecture. The architecture relies on ad-hoc networked Smart Cameras (SCs). A set of SCs forms a Smart Camera Sub System (SCSS). Smart Cameras are able to form clusters by electing leaders, so called SCSS gateways (SCSS GWs). These SCSS GWs are in charge of high-level tasks (alarm management, inter-SCSS communication).

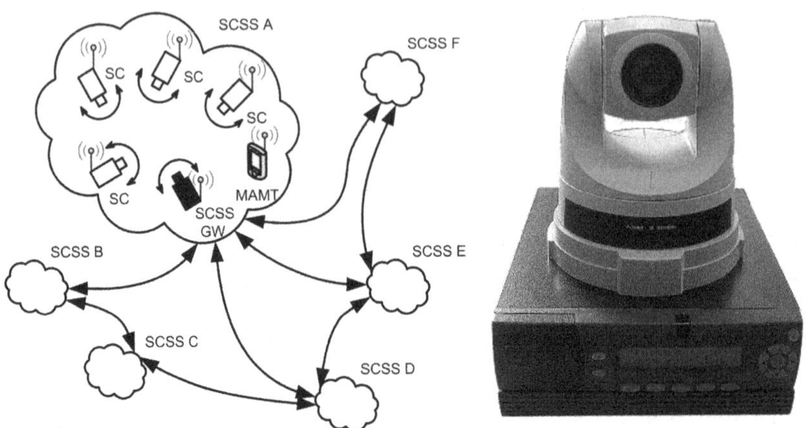

Fig. 1. Networked system architecture (left) and Smart Camera prototype (right)

Future SCs will be able to analyse scenes cooperatively. In case a predefined incident happens, an alarm is raised. This alarm is typically sent to a central control room where human operators take appropriate steps. In addition to a central control room, we propose the use of Mobile Alarm Management Terminals (MAMTs). These mobile devices are carried by patrolling security personnel. Thereby alarms can be distributed faster to nearby guards without having to wait for feedback from the control room. By not relying solely on the operator in the control room, we abolish the single point of failure of today's surveillance systems. For this paper, we investigate SCs inside a SCSS. For the current stage of our work, we assume this system to be completely decentralised. Speaking in terms of self-organisation as defined by Cakar et al. [6], we investigate *self-organisation without central control.* A detailed discussion and an algorithm allowing for self-organised spatial partitioning of SCs is introduced in Section 4.

2.2 Smart Camera Node Architecture

A picture of the SC prototype is shown in Fig. 1 on the right. The SC consists of an off-the-shelf PTZ camera and a computing unit. The computing unit is a miniature-sized, linux-based embedded PC (Pentium M running at 1.6GHz with 512MB RAM). This platform is used for the implementation of our SC node software framework. This software framework has partly been implemented and evaluated, see box I in Figure 2. Beginning from the bottom, we will shortly describe the functionality of the components. The *Sensor* used is the IP camera depicted in Fig 1. We use a combination of the open source tools VLC media player [11] and Intel's OpenCV [12] for *Image Processing.* VLC is a media player that can be used for acquiring video streams from an IP camera. The incoming data is converted by a wrapper and can then be passed on to a video filter provided by OpenCV. OpenCV is a collection of Computer Vision algorithms that enables our SC to detect faces or track objects as depicted in Fig. 4. In

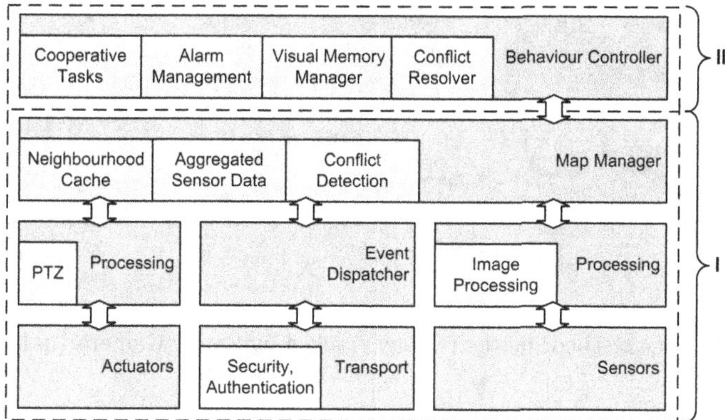

Fig. 2. Smart Camera Node Architecture; Implemented and evaluated components (I) and future enhancements (II)

our testbed, a model railway train is tracked by our SC prototype. Therefore, an extensible control library for PTZ camera movement has been implemented. Currently two different types of PTZ cameras can be used, see Fig. 3 for an UML class hierarchy. This library offers a unified interface so our SC's computing unit can be attached to various PTZ IP cameras.

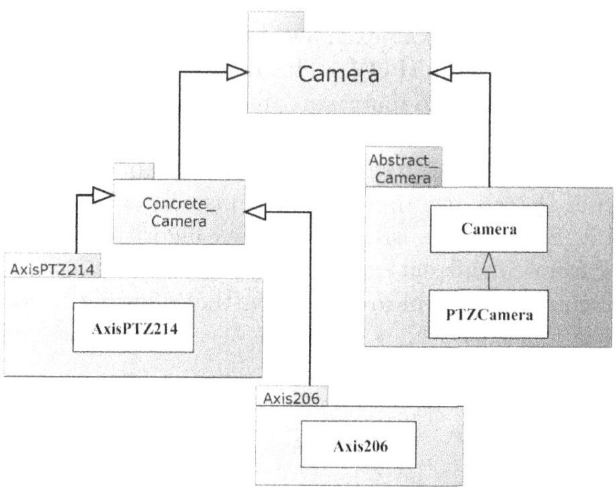

Fig. 3. Class hierarchy UML diagram of the *Processing PTZ* element

We currently use a single SC prototype to evaluate the sensor and actuator parts of our SC node architecture. Since we aim at investigation of large networks of SCs, we use a simulator for the evaluation of the remaining components.

Fig. 4. Laboratory testbed: model railway tracked by Smart Camera (indicated by an ellipse)

2.3 Using NSClick to Simulate Smart Cameras

The *Map Manager* and *Event Dispatcher* components base upon the Click Modular Router, see [13]. Click is a flexible and extensible open source program for IP based network programming. Click and our extensions can either be run inside a network simulator [9] or as a Linux kernel module on our prototype. Since there is currently no large testbed of SCs available, our implementation has been evaluated by simulation. For the simulation of large ad-hoc networks, the network simulator NS2 is used [8]. In order to reach realistic simulation results, we used a IEEE 802.11 based network as described in [14].

The *Map Manager* is in charge of holding all information provided by spatially adjacent SCs. Neighbouring nodes exchange information about their position and geometry of their field of view (FOV). This data is stored in the *Neighbourhood Cache*. The *Map Manager* also maintains *Aggregated Sensor Data*. Currently, a history of the neighbourhood cache is saved here. Future work includes event management and therefore more sensor data needs to be held by the *Map Manager*. The *Conflict Detection* component contains a distributed mutex algorithm by Maekawa [15]. By using a distributed mutex algorithm, we aim at avoiding conflicts arising from concurrent neighbouring SCs.

After introducing our system architecture, the following Sections presents a broad overview of related work.

3 Related Work

Valera et al. present an overview of past, current and future surveillance systems in [16]. They distinguish between Phase I, Phase II and Phase III systems, where Phase III systems consist of autonomous, intelligent cameras. Phase I and Phase II systems are surveillance systems as used today: hard-wired and non-intelligent, broadcasting their video streams to control rooms. In the following section, we shortly describe current research in the field of Phase III surveillance systems. According to the structure of this paper, we start presenting SC architectures first and come to algorithms in the end.

At Stanford Wireless Sensor Lab, Hengstler et al. developed so called Smart Camera Motes [17]. These motes consist of a CCD-sensor, a movement sensor and an ARM-microcontroller responsible for computing tasks. In case the movement sensor recognizes action near the Smart Mote, the CCD-sensor is activated and a set of pictures is taken and sent to a control room.

Rinner et al. are investigating Embedded SmartCams at the TU Graz [18]. They developed several SmartCam prototypes consisting of a CCD-sensor, DSPs for the analysis of captured video data and a networking unit. These SmartCams are able to cooperate in terms of tracking persons. These SmartCams are also able to detect car accidents and lost cargo. Communication interfaces are provided via IEEE 802.x Ethernet.

The PRISMATICA project was funded by the EU and aims at increasing security in public transport. [19] gives an overview of the achievements of the PRISMATICA project. Within this project, PC-based, intelligent cameras have been developed. These cameras provide far reaching data processing methods, e.g. detection of intruders standing in forbidden areas, detection of persons going in a reverse way. Results of this automated analysis are sent to a control room via wireless links. Valera et al. present a communication architectures for these intelligent cameras [16]. Field tests have been carried out in cooperation with London Underground, the Paris Metro and Newcastle International Airport.

Systems mentioned above lack several abilities with respect to a self-organising overall architecture. Velastin et. al state, this is due to the fact that "the work on intelligent distributed surveillance systems has been led by computer vision laboratories perhaps at the expense of system engineering issues", see [2]. An approach to building a reliable and scalable system is to use large numbers of inexpensive and simple nodes instead of few complex nodes.

Apart from SC architecture, this paper deals with a distributed algorithm increasing surveillance coverage. We therefore present a short overview of current research.

Strategies to increase and measure surveillance coverage are proposed by Mundhenk et al. [20]. Results published consider movement strategies of a single pan/tilt camera. Cooperation between cameras is not discussed. The visualization methods used by Mundhenk et al. have been proposed by Hew in [21]. Hew's approach of visualizing surveillance coverage by fading colors on a 2-dimensional map has been used for the visualisation of our simulation results.

Erdem et al. developed an application, that determines where to place cameras to satisfy task-specific and floor plan-specific coverage requirements, see [22]. The presented algorithms allow offline partitioning of a surveillance area under constraints and consider viewing obstacles, the viewing field of cameras and regions of special interest that need to be observable in high resolution. The 2D camera model proposed is similar to our camera model, see Sec. 2.

Our work focuses on the online partitioning of a given surveillance area, whereas Erdem et al. present a planning tool for statically configured surveillance systems. Nevertheless, offline optimisation of camera alignment needs to be considered in distributed, self-organising systems of SCs, too.

Erdems work is closely related to the Art Gallery Problem. We will shortly describe the Art Gallery Problem in the following and present distributed algorithm that aims at solving the problem of SC alignment on wide areas.

4 The Art Gallery Problem and ROCAS

In the 1970s, Victor Klee posed the question how many guards are needed to completely observe an art gallery room. Vasek Chvátal showed in 1976, that $\lfloor \frac{n}{3} \rfloor$ guards are occasionally needed and always sufficient to cover a polygon with n vertices, i.e. an n-walled room. This computational geometry problem and derivatives have thoroughly been discussed, see [10]. A related problem is the adjustment of SCs FOV in such way so that optimal surveillance coverage is reached. This problem can formally be described as follows:

Optimal partitioning of an area $\mathcal{A}$ means to find an adjustment for all SCs on $\mathcal{A}$, so that the surveillance coverage becomes maximal. Surveillance coverage is maximal in case of the overlap of SCs being minimal. An SC is characterised by a set of parameters (i.e. position and FOV). The set of all SC on $\mathcal{A}$ is $\mathcal{SC}$, i.e. the system configuration. FOV describes the mapping of an SC's FOV onto an area A, $FOV : SC \rightarrow A$. $\mathcal{FOV}$ is the union of all FOV on $\mathcal{A}$, $\mathcal{FOV}(\mathcal{SC})= \bigcup_{SC \in \mathcal{SC}} FOV(SC) \cap \mathcal{A}$. Intersection with $\mathcal{A}$ is necessary, since we are only interested in solutions leading to an optimal coverage of $\mathcal{A}$ but still accept FOV covering areas not in $\mathcal{A}$. Goal is to find $\mathcal{FOV}(\mathcal{SC}) = \mathcal{A}$. Achieving this goal requires FOV being ideally suited for the coverage of $\mathcal{A}$. Since this requirement is usually not met in practice, a system configuration coming as close as possible to cover $\mathcal{A}$ is searched.

Since finding optimal spatial surveillance coverage is a time critical task, we investigated fast and lightweight heuristics to solve this problem.

4.1 A Self-organising Approach to the Art Gallery Problem: ROCAS

The FOV of an SC can be simplified as an isosceles triangle. See Figure 5 for the 2-dimensional geometry of an SC's FOV. Each SC has a constant position $\boldsymbol{p}_i(x_i, y_i)$ and an initial value for its heading, δ_i. It also has a viewing angle α_i, and a depth of field τ_i, which is the distance between the SC and the farthest object that can be seen by the SC. In future, an SC is supposed to change its viewing angle and depth of field, but for now we assume these values to be fix. One side with the length τ_i leads from the camera to direction δ_i and the second side with same length to $\delta_i + \alpha_i$. Since it is useful to define an angle for an SC's heading, we introduce the angle β_i. $\beta_i = (\delta_i + \alpha_i)/2$ is simply the angle the SC is directly looking at.

A first version of a distributed algorithm called ROCAS has been presented in [7]. ROCAS stands for Robust Online Camera Alignment System. ROCAS makes SCs exchange information about their position, geometry and heading regularly. Each SC calculates the overlap between its own FOV and all the neighbouring SCs *FOV*. A fast polygon clipping library is used for calculation of spatial overlap, see [23]. In case overlap can be minimised, an SC tilts to the nearest angle where overlap is minimal. Therefore, the SC iteratively increases its heading β about ω ($1°$ in the experiments) and calculates the resulting overlap with neighbouring SCs. See Algorithm 4.1 for an overview of how ROCAS works.

Due to the local optimisation approach oscillations may occur in the system: a set of SCs may periodically carry out slight changes. Therefore, strategies to avoid this unwanted emergent behaviour of the system are needed. A first approach is to prevent SCs to carry out non-significant changes to β by setting up a threshold ($3°$ in the experiments). Future work contains investigation of more elaborate mechanisms.

Algorithm 1. Overview of the ROCAS algorithm

for $0° < \beta < 360°$
oldoverlap ← *overlap*
$\beta \leftarrow \beta + \omega$
overlap ← *calculate overlap with all neighbours*
if *oldoverlap* > *overlap*
minimise overlap by changing own heading
send new geometry to neighbours
end if
end for

This algorithm allows Smart Cameras to take over the cooperative task of partitioning an area under surveillance. This cooperative task serves as an evaluation example for the node architecture we presented in Section 2.
Future work includes further investigation on cooperative tasks. E.g., Smart Cameras are expected to be able to track objects cooperatively. An anticipated approach will be introduced shortly in the following.

5 Towards Object Tracking: SOM-Based Algorithm

Taking the SC system as a structure of units exchanging information and reacting in dependence of stimuli and neighborhood shows that it has certain affinity to SOMs (Self-Organising Maps). Teuvo Kohonen described SOMs as a subtype of artificial neural networks expedient for visualising low-dimensional views of high-dimensional data, see [24]. We applied the concept of SOMs to our SC partitioning problem. For our arrangement of SCs, the SOM's input dimension is 2D - as is the output dimension. Equivalent to the neurons, we take SCs as iterative, competitive learning entities. A first goal is to achieve high coverage of the entire area by the SCs. This happens during a training process with adapted input signals, which are located in a defined input space. The input space in general is bounded by a rectangle or another simple shape. In practice, these shapes depend on floorplans of buildings or maps of the area under surveillance.

The possible input space is reduced to this area, where every point can be observed by at least one camera. A significant difference to SOMs is that the input space is adjusted by the training process, too. The input space is intended to deliver signals that are not located in any FOV at that time. By using equally distributed stimuli, an high surveillance coverage is achieved. In future, the SOM based approach will be extended to target tracking. Objects to be tracked can be interpreted as stimuli for the SOM-based recursive regression progress. SCs in viewing range of a stimulus adjust their FOV in such way so that one SC directly focuses the stimulus. Other SCs move their headings slightly towards the stimulus. In Figure 5, the SC at $\boldsymbol{p}_2$ will directly focus $\boldsymbol{p}_k$ whereas the SC at $\boldsymbol{p}_1$ will move only slightly towards $\boldsymbol{p}_k$. Implementation and evaluation of this approach is part of our future work.

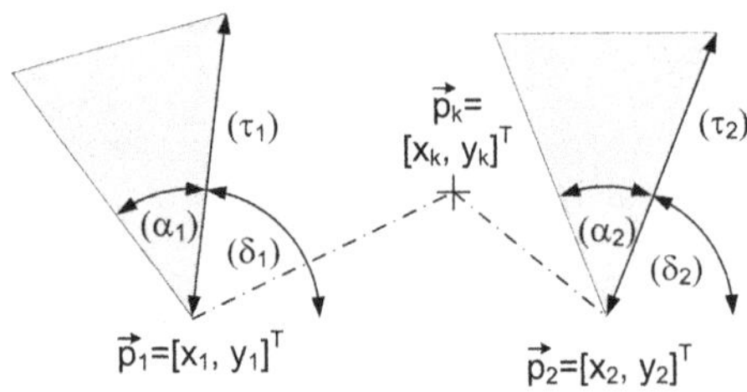

Fig. 5. Two Smart Cameras and a stimulus

6 Experiments and Results

The experimental setup consists of SCs observing a wide area without any viewing and communication obstacles. For this purpose, SCs are ideally positioned in a grid. Such scenarios can be found at aprons of airports or public transport depots. A number of eight to 80 SCs forming a grid is therefore analysed in detail. The density of nodes is kept constant, i.e. the observed area increases with the number of SCs (75m by 100m for eight SCs to 250m by 300m for 80 SCs). SCs communicate using ad-hoc communication similar to IEEE 802.11 WLAN. Communication range is larger than the viewing range and we expect a communication range of 160m in outdoor scenarios [14]. Metrics applied for the measurement of the algorithm's quality are the surveillance coverage as a fraction of the optimum and the message complexity per node. Simulation has been carried out for a loss-free as well as for a lossy communication channel. The lossy communication channel drops 20% (equally distributed over time) of all packets that are sent.

Figure 6 shows how surveillance coverage is increased by ROCAS in comparison to an initial random SC alignment. ROCAS performs well even in large SC systems with up to 80 SCs. Packet loss has only slight impact on the increase of surveillance coverage. Surveillance coverage achieved is between 88% for the 80 SC scenario and up to 100% for the 8 SC scenario.

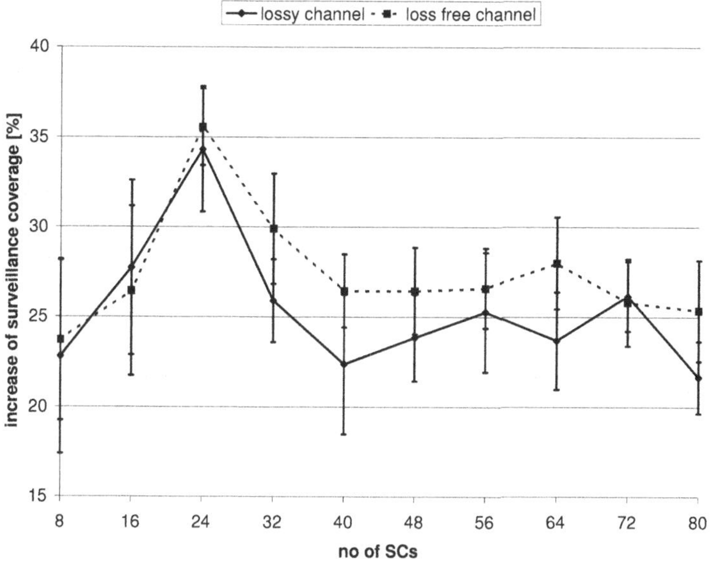

Fig. 6. Increase of surveillance coverage depending on the number of cooperating SCs

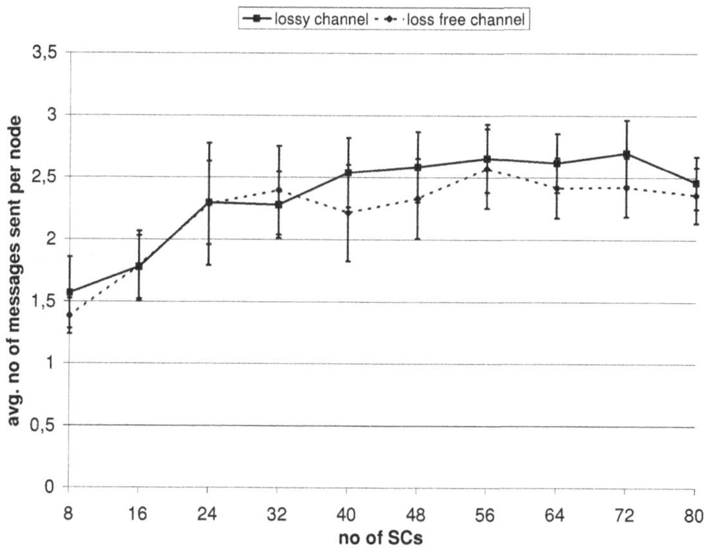

Fig. 7. Average no of messages sent per node depending on system size

Message complexity is low for both scenarios using a lossy or a loss-free communication channel respectively. Figure 7 shows, that nodes do not send more than an average number of three messages even when a lossy channel is used.

7 Conclusion

In this paper we presented an overall architecture for a Smart Camera System. Both the architecture of a single node as well as the networked system architecture have been described. A prototype and its abilities in terms of computer vision have been shown. A short overview of related work in the area of SC system architectures has been given. A sample application, the self-organised spatial partitioning of an area under surveillance has been described and evaluated. Differences and similarities to the Art Gallery Problem have been discussed. For simulation of large networks of SCs we used a network simulator and shortly described our enhancements.

Experiments have been carried out and results show, that even in a completely decentralised system SCs are able to self-organise their FOV in order to reach the highest possible surveillance coverage. The presented algorithm is robust towards a lossy communication channel as has been shown by simulation.

The decentralised architecture allows to overcome drawbacks of common surveillance systems. Apart from the distributed system scaling very well (evaluation results for networks of up to 80 SCs are presented) there is no single point of failure in our decentralised architecture. This is an important issue when safety critical environments need to be secured.

Future work on SCs includes decentralised object tracking and the support of mobile alarm management terminals. We also expect the SC system to be an ideal testbed for several Organic Computing paradigms and algorithms that allow for self-x properties and the system's dynamical adaption to changes in its environment. Therefore, the proposed SC node architecture needs to be enhanced.

References

1. Quaritsch, M., et al.: Autonomous Multi-Camera Tracking on Embedded Smart Cameras. EURASIP Journal on Embedded Systems (2007)
2. Velastin, S., Remagnino, P.: Intelligent Distributed Video Surveillance Systems (Professional Applications of Computing). Institution of Engineering and Technology (2006)
3. Wolf, W.: Distributed Peer-to-Peer Smart Cameras: Algorithms and Architectures. In: ISM 2005: Proceedings of the Seventh IEEE International Symposium on Multimedia, Washington, DC, USA, p. 178. IEEE Computer Society Press, Los Alamitos (2005)
4. Cupillard, F., Brémond, F., Thonnat, M.: Automated scene understanding for airport aprons. In: Measuring Behavior, Wageningen The Netherlands (2005)
5. Schmeck, H.: Organic computing-vision and challenge for system design. In: PARELEC, p. 3 (2004)
6. Çakar, E., et al.: Towards a quantitative notion of self-organisation. In: IEEE Congress on Evolutionary Computation (2007)
7. Hoffmann, M., Hähner, J.: ROCAS: A robust online algorithm for spatial partitioning in distributed Smart Camera systems. In: Proceedings of ICDSC 2007, IEEE Computer Society Press, Los Alamitos (2007)

8. Web: The Network Simulator - NS2, `http://www.isi.edu/nsnam/ns/`
9. Neufeld, M., Jain, A., Grunwald, D.: Nsclick: bridging network simulation and deployment. In: MSWiM 2002: Proceedings of the 5th ACM international workshop on Modeling analysis and simulation of wireless and mobile systems, pp. 74–81. ACM Press, New York (2002)
10. O'Rourke, J.: Art gallery theorems and algorithms. Oxford Univ. Press, New York (1987)
11. Web: VideoLAN - VLC media player, `http://www.videolan.org/`
12. Web: OpenCV, `http://www.intel.com/technology/computing/opencv/`
13. Kohler, E., et al.: The click modular router. ACM Trans. Comput. Syst. 18(3), 263–297 (2000)
14. Xiuchao, W.: Simulate 802.11b Channel within NS2. Technical report, School of Computing, National University of Singapore (2005)
15. Maekawa, M.: An algorithm for mutual exclusion in decentralized systems. ACM Trans. Comput. Syst. 3(2), 145–159 (1985)
16. Valera, M., Velastin, S.A.: Intelligent distributed surveillance systems: A review. IEE Proceedings - Vision, Image, and Signal Processing 152(2), 192–204 (2005)
17. Hengstler, S., Aghajan, H.: A Smart Camera Mote Architecture for Distributed Intelligent Surveillance. In: Working Notes of the International Workshop on Distributed Smart Cameras (DSC) (2006)
18. Bramberger, M., et al.: Distributed Embedded Smart Cameras for Surveillance Applications. Computer 39(2), 68–75 (2006)
19. Velastin, S.A., et al.: PRISMATICA: A multi-sensor surveillance system for public transport networks. In: IEE International Conference on Road Transport Information and Control, 2004, pp. 19–25. IEE (2004)
20. Everist, J., et al.: Visual surveillance coverage: strategies and metrics. In: Casasent, D.P., Hall, E.L., Röning, J. (eds.) Intelligent Robots and Computer Vision XXIII: Algorithms, Techniques, and Active Vision. Proceedings of the SPIE, vol. 6006, pp. 91–102 (2005)
21. Hew, P.C.: Visualisation of Surveillance Coverage by Latency Mapping. In: Pattison, T., Thomas, B. (eds.) Australian Symposium on Information Visualisation (invis.au 2003), Adelaide, Australia, ACS. CRPIT, vol. 24, pp. 11–16 (2003)
22. Erdem, U.M., Sclaroff, S.: Automated camera layout to satisfy task-specific and floor plan-specific coverage requirements. Comput. Vis. Image Underst. 103(3), 156–169 (2006)
23. Vatti, B.R.: A generic solution to polygon clipping. Comm. of the ACM 35(7), 56–63 (1992)
24. Kohonen, T.: The self-organizing map. Proceedings of the IEEE 78(9), 1464–1480 (1990)

Using Organic Computing to Control Bunching Effects

Oliver Ribock[1], Urban Richter[2], and Hartmut Schmeck[2]

[1] oliver@ribock.de
[2] Karlsruhe Institute of Technology – Institute AIFB
76128 Karlsruhe, Germany
{urban.richter,hartmut.schmeck}@kit.edu

Abstract. In this paper, the well-known emergent phenomenon of bunching as appearing in lift group traffic control systems is taken as a technical scenario for validating the generic observer/controller architecture which has been designed as part of an anticipated organic framework - providing generic toolbox mechanisms to observe, analyse, and control emergent behaviour in self-organising systems. In particular, we show how to control and prevent global, collective, unwanted behaviour of groups of lifts, based on observations of the local behaviour of lift cabins.

1 Introduction

Today's technical systems are becoming increasingly complex. Future systems will consist of a multitude of complex soft- and hardware components, which interact with each other to satisfy global system functional requirements. This trend bears the risk of more and more breakdowns and other unexpected behaviour. Organic Computing (OC) is driven by the vision of addressing the challenges of complex distributed systems by making them more life-like (organic), i. e. endowing them with abilities such as self-organisation, self-configuration, self-repair, or adaptation. This can only be achieved by giving the system elements adequate degrees of freedom, some kind of awareness of their current situation, and the ability to provide appropriate responses to dynamically changing environmental conditions. In self-organising systems this may result in an emergent global behaviour, which can have positive as well as negative effects. Therefore, we need an observer/controller architecture, which allows for monitoring essential parameters of the self-organising system and for providing adequate reactions to control the – sometimes completely unexpected – emerging global behaviour.

Self-organising systems bear several advantages over classical, centrally controlled systems: The failure of a single component should not cause a global malfunction, the system should be able to adapt to changing circumstances and much more. As a result, self-organisation is viewed to be a means of reducing the *complexity* of computer systems. Nevertheless, self-organising systems are complex systems themselves. However, the user does not have to manage this

U. Brinkschulte et al. (Eds.): ARCS 2008, LNCS 4934, pp. 232–244, 2008.

complexity as, to a far extent, the system manages itself, that means the *externally visible complexity* is reduced.

But self-organisation and emergent phenomena also give rise to new problems unknown in classical technical systems. As global emergent behaviour usually is a non-linear combination of local behaviour both potential design directions turn out to be highly non-trivial tasks: For a top-down approach it is hard to deduce adequate local rules from a desired global behaviour, and in a bottom-up design, quite often it remains unclear how to characterise how the local rules map to global behaviour, see [1].

1.1 Controlled Self-organisation

Computer systems should not simply self-organise, they should use self-organisation to achieve a certain externally provided goal. Furthermore, the system has to be capable to deal with (unanticipated) emergent behaviour and to adapt to changing environmental requirements. Although OC systems will have certain degrees of freedom for autonomous adaptivity, there remains the necessity of potential intervention by a human user or operator. Therefore, OC systems are assumed to support controlled self-organisation. This requires a range of methods for monitoring and analysing the system performance and for providing appropriate control actions whenever necessary. The generic observer/controller architecture as specified in [2,3] promises to provide the necessary components for satisfying all these demands. Similar to the MAPE cycle (Monitor, Analyse, Plan, and Execute) of Autonomic Computing (see [1]), a closed control loop is defined to keep the properties of the system within preferred regions, working as follows: Observe certain attributes of the system and act according to an evaluation of the observation (which might include the prediction of future behaviour); if the current situation does not satisfy the requirements, take action to direct the system back into its desired range; observe the effect of the intervention and take further action, if necessary.

Although the observing and controlling process is executed in a continuous loop, the system under observation and control is assumed to be able to run autonomously even if the observer and controller are not present. This allows for autonomous operation and for carefully applied control as well, making sure that the system always acts in the desired way. In [4] three different architectural variants are suggested: central (one observer/controller for the whole system), distributed (an observer/controller for each subsystem), and multi-level (one observer/controller for each subsystem as well as one (or more) for higher observer/controller levels). In particular, for larger and more complex systems it will be necessary to build hierarchically structured observer/controller systems instead of trying to manage the whole system with one observer/controller.

In this paper, the concepts of OC are applied to the technically oriented scenario of a group of self-organising lifts. The effects of applying an observer/controller architecture are carefully analysed and shown to lead to an improved performance. The paper is structured as follows: In Sect. 2 we introduce our test scenario of a group of self-organising lifts. Methods for analysing and evaluating their performance are described in Sect. 3. This is followed by an explanation of simple control mechanisms in Sect. 4, and a presentation of first experimental results in Sect. 5 validating the generic observer/controller architecture. The paper concludes with a summary and a discussion of future work.

2 Lift Group Control

Beginning in 1975 the use of *microprocessors* with programmable features has changed the lift operational controllers dramatically. Over the years many features have been incorporated in lift systems to answer especially the demands of high-rise buildings. In practice, under certain conditions, (simple) lift group control systems will exhibit a phenomenon called bunching. While ideally, different lifts should arrive at a floor with a certain separation time, under heavy traffic load conditions the lifts tend to *synchronise* and serve the floors at unequal intervals in form of a wave. In an extreme case the lifts behave like a huge, single lift with the capacity equal to the sum of the individual lifts. This phenomenon is called bunching.

The probably most common definition of bunching is given by Al-Sharif and Barney [5]: *"When the time interval between cars leaving the main terminal is not equal, bunching occurs and degrades the performance of the lift system. [...] A typical case of bunching can be seen in lift systems when the lifts start following each other (or even frog-leaping), as they answer adjacent calls in the same direction. This has a detrimental effect on passenger waiting time. The ultimate case is when all the lifts in the group move together, acting effectively as one huge lift with a capacity equal to the summation of the capacities of all the lifts in the group."* Bunching is defined by [6] and [7] in a very similar way. Hence, to detect bunching effects the departure intervals at an arbitrary floor are monitored and if lifts do not arrive at a floor with a certain separation time equal to an average interval, then the lifts tend to synchronise and we call this bunching. As bunching itself cannot be expected beforehand and its occurrence cannot be predicted from the system description, it is considered as an emergent phenomenon and it affects system performance.

2.1 Bunching Effects

Usually, the performance of lift traffic control systems is measured in terms of the *average waiting time (AWT)* of the passengers (other performance measures are possible, but not considered in this paper). Under the assumption of Poisson distributed arrival rates, it can be shown that best system performance is achieved for constant inter-arrival times of the lifts. Since every deviation from the equal distribution leads to a lower system performance, lift traffic control systems are trying to maintain an equal distribution of the lifts throughout the building.

How does bunching actually arise? Referring to the example from [8] we imagine two buses b_1, b_2 serving a route of length l containing two stops s_1, s_2. The route is in form of a loop and both buses circle around the loop clockwise in the same direction. The two stops are *equally distributed* over the loop, i. e. the distances between them are in each case half of the loop: $h_1^\star = [s_1, s_2] = \frac{l}{2}$ and $h_2^\star = [s_2, s_1] = \frac{l}{2}$. The buses travel at the same speed, and it takes for both buses the same time $t^\star$ to travel from one stop to the other, i. e. the inter-arrival times t_{12} and t_{21} between buses b_1 and b_2 (or between b_2 and b_1, respectively) at stop s_1 or s_2 are equal to $t^\star$. To minimise the AWT, buses depart from the stops at equal time intervals $t^\star$, i. e. they maintain a distance of $t^\star$ or $\frac{l}{2}$, respectively.

Caused by a random event as for example an old person who takes longer to alight, b_1 falls slightly behind schedule and is delayed. Now the distances among the buses are shifted a little bit: b_2 seems to *chase* b_1, and b_2 will arrive earlier than b_1 at the next stop. As a constant passenger arrival rate is assumed, there will be more people waiting for b_1 than for b_2 at the next stop. Now b_1 has to spend more time than on average on picking up the passengers whereas b_2 saves time at every stop (since more passengers need more time to board). As a result, b_2 will catch up and pretty soon (with decreasing t_{12} or t_{21}) the two buses will travel in a convoy which increases waiting times of the passengers.

This scenario can easily be adopted to lift traffic control where events like holding the door open to let another passenger board causes delays within the schedule and the lifts to bunch. The common objective is to keep lifts in the group as far apart as possible during usual traffic conditions. Within the example stated above, bunching is clearly a self-aggravating situation that after a slight incentive develops on its own.

2.2 Experimental Environment

Our lift group scenario is simulated using the *REcursive Porous Agent Simulation Toolkit (Repast)*[1] and hence written in Java. A group of lifts is serving passengers which arrive at different floors within a building at a user-defined rate. The number of lifts, the number of floors, and some other parameters can be chosen freely. The different strategies of the lifts – how they serve the different calls – are described in the following. Unlike classical lift control systems, which are controlled centrally, here the lifts act in a fully autonomous and self-organised way. In the simulation, bunching effects are easily produced accompanied by an increasing AWT of the passengers. A brief overview of substantial characteristics of the simulation model is given below.

Type of the building and traffic pattern: The building consists of one lobby and an arbitrary number of floors. The lobby is the lowermost floor of the building, where passengers start during up-peak and arrive during down-peak. Every floor of the building is equal in terms of relevance for the passengers and the lifts. We assume identical passenger arrival rates for all floors including the lobby. Up-peak traffic in the morning rush hour, where every lift is filled up in the lobby with passengers and stops at many different upper floors, or down-peak

[1] http://repast.sourceforge.net

traffic, which shows a reversed situation, many arrival floors and one destination, are ignored.

Lift system: The number of lifts in a group can be chosen as desired, however, values should range between two to eight. Eight is the maximum number of lifts efficiently operating together in a group in practice, referring to [7].

Passenger arrival model: During normal inter-floor traffic passengers arrive at an arrival rate following the *Poisson distribution*: the time from one passenger arrival to the next is based on an average passenger arrival rate $\gamma = \frac{average\ number\ of\ passengers}{ticks}$ that specifies how many passengers arrive on average in the system per simulation tick (e. g. 4 persons/second). This time is independent of the time elapsed since the last arrival. On passenger arrival, both the floor where the passenger arrives as well as the target floor are chosen randomly. The choice is based on a *(discrete) uniform distribution*, i. e. one floor is chosen out of all floors with the same probability.

Lift strategies: A lift follows its currently assigned strategy, which is a sequence of simple decisions resulting in an order to be executed. We have investigated different strategies, but in the following we focus only on the default strategy: within this strategy the lifts serve the *hall calls* on all floors sequentially in travelling direction. Hall calls represent a floor where passengers are waiting to be served and the calls are registered by passengers from outside the lift by activating the up or down buttons. The destination floors are registered by the passengers after they entered the car, therefore, these calls are called *car calls*. Instead of serving the calls using a strategy like *first come first serve*, the calls are sorted by floors for each travelling direction and the lifts serve those floors with an active call in their travelling direction one after another. If there is no further active call in the current direction, they will serve the next call in the opposite direction, and, if the list of calls is empty they will remain at the current floor. Furthermore, a lift is not affected by the behaviour of the other lifts in the group, because there exists no communication between them. In contrast to classical lift control, our lifts are not supervised by a central authority. Every lift acts on its own, as if it would be the sole lift in the system, serves passengers according to the described strategy, and *decides* by itself which call is served. Replacing the central control authority constitutes a *paradigm shift* from central to distributed lift control.

3 Quantitative Measures of Bunching

Measuring the extent of bunching quantitatively is quite essential in order to compare the performance of different systems and be able to take appropriate countermeasures. Al-Sharif has published several articles concerning the bunching of lifts and in particular its measurement. He focuses on *up-peak* traffic conditions. However, the insights gained from the observation of bunching at up-peak can be adopted to general traffic conditions.

Al-Sharif's measure is derived directly from the lift system behaviour. He defines an ideal behaviour of the lift system under no bunching conditions, calculates the deviation from the ideal state and uses this deviation as an indicator for bunching (see [5,9] for more details). The ideal behaviour of a lift system is defined as the departure of the lifts from the main terminal at equal time intervals $INT = \frac{RTT}{N}$ at which RTT is the round trip time, which is the time in seconds for a single lift trip around a building from the time the lift doors open at the main terminal, until the doors reopen, when this lift has returned to the main terminal floor, and N is the number of lifts in the group. The time between lift number i and lift number $i+1$ is defined as $t_{i,i+1}$ which, in the ideal case, should equal $\frac{RTT}{N}$. Thus the deviation of $t_{i,i+1}$ from the ideal behaviour can be expressed as $(t_{i,i+1} - \frac{RTT}{N})$. Since positive as well as negative deviations are equally harmful, the absolute value is taken: $\left|t_{i,i+1} - \frac{RTT}{N}\right|$. The sum of all these differences between the lifts in the group serves as an indication of the system's deviation from ideal performance.

The value of RTT is continuously measured during the operation and thus adapting to changes in the system (for example changes in the passenger arrival rate). Using normalisation the value of the bunching coefficient lies between 0.0 and 1.0 where 1.0 represents full bunching.

The general idea of quantifying the bunching effect is to define the ideal lift system behaviour in terms of ideal parameter values and to compare these ideal values to the actual parameter values obtained by observation. The deviations from the ideal values indicate the current amount of bunching present in the lift system. This essentially follows Al-Sharif's definition and an approach introduced in the United States patent number 5447212 [10]. This patent is based on the same general thoughts as introduced by Al-Sharif, but measures the current spacing between the lifts instead of the departure intervals at the main terminal. The distances can be evaluated easily by counting the number of floors lying between lifts with respect to their travelling direction.

3.1 An Observer for Lift Group Systems

In our simulation the group of lifts is augmented with an observer/controller architecture following the generic model [2,3]. The system under observation and control is formed by the lifts travelling in the building and the passengers waiting at the floors and travelling in the lifts. However, the passengers are neither controlled by the controller nor are they monitored by the observer (fixed arrival rates are used for inter-floor traffic). The task of the observer is to monitor the system in real-time and generate the system parameters based on the current system state.

The only observed parameters are lift positions and lift travelling directions. Parameters as the number of floors or the number of lifts are already taken into account in the lift strategies. Hall or car calls are not observed, either.

During pre-processing, basic computations are performed like calculating the distances between the lifts by transforming the current lift positions in the building. Using the circle representation of the bus example above we calculate for each lift l_i the distance d_i to its next lift l_{i+1}.

Subsequently, the current bunching value is measured within the data analysing step by comparing the current situation to the ideal situation. Ideally, the lifts are perfectly distributed throughout the building. Thus, in an ideal case, consecutive lifts are separated by a constant distance $d^\star = \frac{2F-2}{N}$ with F being the number of floors. In order to compare the current situation with ideal conditions, the absolute deviations of the distances d_i from the ideal distance $d^\star$ are accumulated. By normalising with respect to the worst possible value of D the current bunching value BV is obtained:

$$D = \sum_{i=1}^{N} |d_i - d^\star| \tag{1}$$

$$BV = \frac{D}{D_{worst}} = \frac{D}{(N-1) \cdot d^\star + |(2F-2) - d^\star|} \tag{2}$$

Finally, in the aggregating step, the obtained BV is filtered and smoothed with the *exponential moving average* to reduce the effects of noise. This smoothing method is very similar to the standard moving average, except that it puts greater emphasis on more recent values.

4 Methods to Cope with Bunching

As bunching has negative effects on performance, various strategies for coping with this effect have been suggested. We refer to [7] for more information and just sum up some main ideas:

To achieve a uniform distribution of the lifts throughout the building, the lifts are dispatched from the main terminal at equal intervals with *early* lifts waiting longer than *late* lifts before their departure. The effect, however, is a decrease in handling capacity, since lifts are waiting unproductively at the lobby.

Another relatively simple but very drastic approach is the idea of *zoning* and *spotting* of the lifts. Zoning is used mainly at up-peak where bunching has occurred to the greatest extent. The idea of zoning is to let the lifts serve only certain floors of the building: For example, in a group of six lifts let three of them serve the lower and three the upper floors. Spotting is a similar approach designating each lift to serve a limited number of floors, only.

Another idea to reduce the effects of bunching is to assign hall calls to lifts with regard to the expected result of bunching (which has to be measured/estimated somehow). By calculating the *estimated arrival time* of the lifts (the time required to travel from a lift's current position to a hall call), the hall calls are assigned to maintain an equal spacing of the lifts. A problem within hall call allocation arises from the uncertain destinations of the boarding passengers. Therefore, some modern lift control systems provide means for the passenger to register their destination outside the lifts before entering. Based on this information the passengers are grouped with respect to their destinations and then assigned to lifts (i. e. the passengers have to enter their assigned lift).

The presented provisions differ in their *dependence on the actual traffic pattern*. E. g. at normal inter-floor traffic, zoning shows very poor performance as the passenger travel time is unnecessarily increased without reducing the AWT. Hence, it should be beneficial for the performance of the lift system, if the controller recognised the current traffic pattern as soon as possible to safely initiate actions which could be harmful if applied in an improper situation. This is one reason why controlling the lift by a central authority is a very demanding task, in particular, if more information is available, the state space of the system increases, and an optimal routing strategy has to be found in real-time. Instead of developing another even more sophisticated central control strategy, we investigate the idea of applying a control strategy based on the ideas of OC.

4.1 A Controller for Lift Group Systems

After the observer has finished evaluating the current system state, the controller becomes active. The controller decides whether the measured situation satisfies the system objectives. The decision is based on the bunching value only, and the situation is considered undesirable if this value surpasses a certain predefined threshold. If the controller decides to intervene, two different control strategies may be triggered. We should mention that it is the goal to keep the self-organising nature of the system and to interfere only slightly with the individual lift control. Thus, we do not intend to implement orders like *lift A, go to floor 5* within the control strategies. Instead, we focus on interventions which influence the lift behaviour indirectly. An example for such an indirect intervention would be the hiding of the hall call at floor 4 from lift A and thus making lift A travel directly to floor 5.

To maintain an equal spacing of the lifts the controller should restore the initial situation. The controller has two possible (abstract) ways to intervene: it could accelerate delayed lifts and/or slow down early lifts. A lift is considered to be delayed, if the distance to the next lift in travelling direction is significantly higher than the average distance. The basic idea behind both implemented strategies is to accelerate delayed lifts. By passing a hall call we accelerate a lift, and this lift saves time compared to the other lifts and finally speeds up.

Strongintervention: This strategy accelerates lifts by making them blind with regard to hall calls. A blind lift will not serve any hall calls in the building and will thus stop less frequent. Instead of blinding only one lift, several lifts are blinded simultaneously, or can be blinded partially. At first, the controller sorts all lifts l_i with respect to their decreasing distance d_i to the next lift in travelling direction. Now, the controller blinds half of the lifts having the most distance ahead, i. e. the lifts $l_1, \ldots, l_{\lceil N/2 \rceil}$ (with N being the number of lifts), with decreasing intensity (we assume w. l. o. g. that $(l_1, \ldots, l_N)$ is the sorted sequence). The amount of blindness $b(l_j)$, which is assigned to the lifts, is defined as follows:

$$b(l_j) = \begin{cases} 1 - (\frac{1}{\lceil N/2 \rceil} \cdot (j-1)) & \text{if } j \leq \lceil N/2 \rceil \\ 0 & \text{else} \end{cases} \tag{3}$$

The blindness $b(l_j)$ of a lift determines the probability of serving a hall call, e. g. a lift being 50% blind will pass a hall call with a probability of 50%. In other words, a fully blind lift will *deliver* all remaining passengers in the lift without picking new passengers up.[2] On the one hand this process could be regarded as hiding hall calls from a lift and therefore as a manipulation of the perception of a lift's environment. On the other hand, this represents a change of a lift's decision rules, since a blind lift does not distinguish between the separate hall calls, i. e. its behaviour can be described in form of a changed strategy. Therefore, it seems plausible to consider strongIntervention as manipulating (a parameter of) the decision rules of the lifts. As drawbacks of this strategy we see that there is no distinction between the hall calls – they are all treated in the same way and waiting times of the passengers are not taken into account. Another point regards the fact that always half of the lifts are blinded (if the controller is active). Hence, it is possible that more lifts than necessary are set as blind and this might lead again to an increase of the AWT.

Softintervention: This strategy is more sophisticated, performing relatively precise interventions. Within this strategy, acceleration is performed by hiding a hall call from a certain lift. Consequently, this lift will not serve the hidden hall call but pass it. Hence, the next hall call in travelling direction of a delayed lift is hidden in order to accelerate this lift. This procedure is performed for several delayed lifts at a time. It is important to realise that in this case only specific calls are hidden from a lift in contrast to treating all hall calls in the same manner as in strongIntervention.

Therefore, this strategy is clearly an approach of changing the lift's perception of its surrounding. Certain hall calls are hidden from some lifts without altering the environment (the hall calls are only hidden, but they exist further on) or changing the decision rules of the lift. The decision rules are not modified, only their input changes due to the hiding of calls. This means the behaviour of a lift being influenced by the controller cannot be expressed in form of a lift strategy showing equivalent behaviour. On the contrary, when softIntervention is active, the lifts' general strategy is not changed; they rather react to a feigned neighbourhood.

It also has to be kept in mind that the current implementation of the controller forms only a very basic realisation of the generic concept. Neither self-optimising abilities nor learning methods that enable self-adaptation have been implemented or investigated.

5 Experimental Results

We have used the simulation to find out whether the two strategies succeed in reducing the emergent behaviour of bunching within the lift system. We examined the influence of controller and system parameters on the system behaviour

[2] Serving a car call and a lift has to stop on a floor where passengers are waiting then it is possible that these passengers enter the lift.

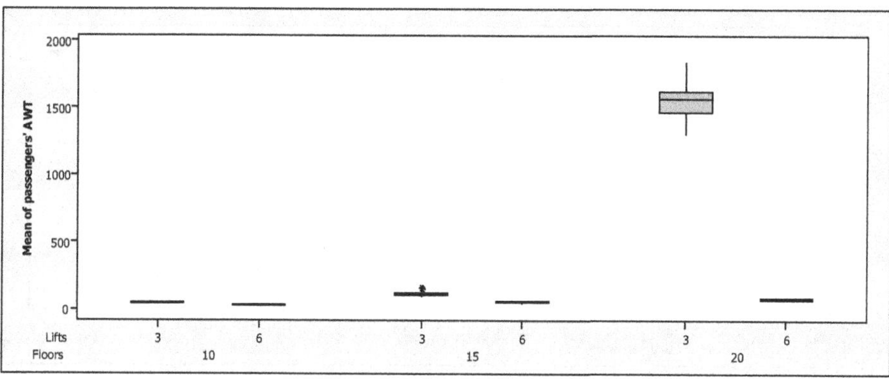

Fig. 1. Preliminary investigations of parameters that influence the system behaviour in scenarios with 3 or 6 lifts, 10, 15, or 20 floors, and a traffic intensity of 0.6

(e. g. the choice of different control strategies). In addition, we have checked the correlation of the bunching value to the AWT, which could give us an indication of the quality of the bunching measurement with regard to representing the amount of bunching.

Preliminary Investigations: Initially, several preliminary investigations have been carried out to find reasonable levels for the parameters. To determine the influence of the parameters on the system, we have calculated how all main factors as well as all possible subsets of factor combinations affect the response by use of regression models. As stated before, we chose the AWT of the passengers during a simulation run as the response variable. That means, a lower response corresponds to a better system performance.

The impact of variations of the number of floors, the number of lifts, and the traffic intensity is as intuitively estimated. Increasing the number of floors or the arrival rate results in a higher AWT. In contrast, more lifts lead to a lower AWT. There is also interdependence among the number of floors and the traffic intensity. If both are raised/lowered simultaneously, the AWT responds stronger than at unilateral deviation. On the whole, the lift system shows intuitive response to variations of the building parameters. Their interactions have heavy influence on the system and most likely superpose the other effects (e. g. a scenario of 3 lifts, 20 floors, and a traffic intensity of 0.6 shows a collapsing behaviour, see Fig. 1). Hence, we performed another analysis based on the results of the initial factorial experiment to get a better overview of the influence of the controller strategy, the threshold of bunching for activating the controller, and the interactions between strategy and threshold.

Effectiveness of the Control Strategies: The overall effectiveness of the control strategies was tested by varying the threshold of bunching for activating the controller. The simulation has been executed with a fixed scenario of 3 lifts, 10 floors, and a traffic intensity of 0.6. Obviously, a threshold of 0.0 means

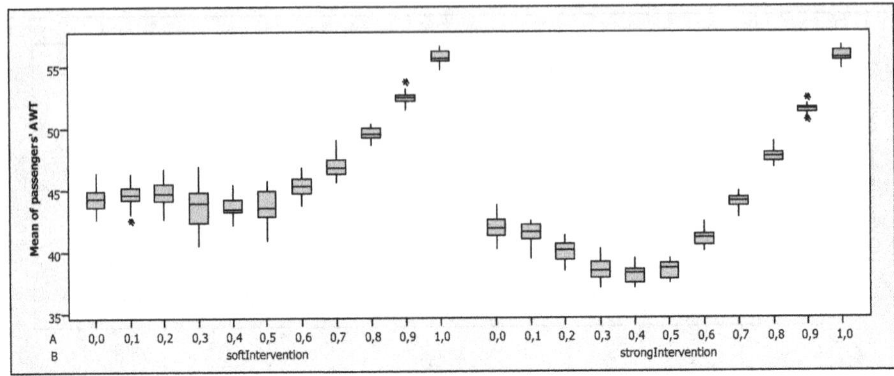

Fig. 2. Effect of varying the threshold of bunching when the controller gets active (A) on the AWT for both control strategies (B)

that the controller is always active while a threshold of 1.0 corresponds to a completely deactivated controller.

The results of the runs are shown in Fig. 2. Since the choice of the controller strategy has no effect in the case of an inactive controller, a threshold of 1.0 results in the same AWT for each strategy. The system performance is always superior with an activated controller compared to an inactive controller. Differences are visible with respect to the extent of the advantage in terms of AWT. A lower threshold results in a lower AWT. However, when the controller is always activated (threshold equal to 0.0), the AWT increases again for both strategies. Most likely, this is caused by passing hall calls unnecessarily at low bunching conditions. As a result, the affected passengers have to wait longer without any positive effect for the system, as the bunching is already at a low level. Additionally, the strategy strongIntervention shows better results than softIntervention. Regardless, we can conclude that the controller should not be always active, because this increases the AWT compared to an on demand activation.

Examination of the Bunching Value: A correct representation of the bunching level by the bunching value is crucial for our work since all controller interventions are based on it. Therefore, we examined the bunching value with respect to its quality to represent bunching within the lift system. Verifying the quality of the bunching value is done by comparing the actual bunching with the measured bunching in terms of the bunching value. However, quantifying the current level of bunching is a difficult task, since we know no other means to measure it. Therefore, we use a different approach and compare the bunching value with the performance of the lift system expressed in AWT of the passengers.

The underlying idea is that varying controller parameters will alter the effectiveness of the controller which mainly changes the level of bunching within the lift system. A resulting different bunching level will in turn affect AWT. In other words, varying controller parameters changes bunching which in turn changes the AWT. Thus, there will be a verifiable connection between the bunching value and the AWT, if the bunching value *works*. Hence, we calculated the correlation between mean bunching value and AWT between different simulation runs differing by controller parameter variations. Within this analysis, a Pearson's correlation coefficient of above 97% could be observed, which indicates a strong relationship between the mean bunching value and the AWT. Thus the bunching value as defined in this paper can be considered as a valid indicator.

6 Conclusion and Outlook

This paper investigated the potential of applying concepts of OC to a scenario of a group of self-organising lifts, showing a macroscopic behaviour that depends on local rules only. The lifts synchronise, move up and down together, and show the emergent effect of bunching. Providing feedback and decision capabilities to this group of lifts we have shown that bunching can be observed and prevented autonomously with respect to a global objective function. We have used a metric based on ideas of [10,11] to detect bunching effects. For controlling the lifts we have implemented two simple methods that modify the perception of the environment and thus affect the local behaviour of the lifts.

Our experimental results validate the idea of using the generic observer/controller architecture to modify the environmental parameters of the system under observation and control without modifying the local rules of the lift cabins directly. This led to significant improvements in the performance of the lift group system. Future work will focus on the following topics:

1. Endowing the controller with adaptation capabilities as designated in the generic architecture it should be able to recognise and react to different traffic patterns. Our investigations have focused only on inter-floor traffic, but it seems to be interesting whether bunching is the correct measurement to characterise the effectiveness of the group behaviour during up-peak or down-peak phases (this requires an extended observation model).
2. We have done first investigations of integrating a prediction module into the observer that computes the bunching value with respect to history data. We expect a better performance of observer and controller functionalities, but this could not be verified so far.

Acknowledgement. We gratefully acknowledge the financial support by the German Research Foundation (DFG) within the priority programme 1183 Organic Computing. We are especially indebted to Moez Mnif and Christian Müller-Schloer, both from Leibniz Universität Hannover, and Jürgen Branke, Universität Karlsruhe (TH), for their valuable suggestions. Also, we thank Christoph Pickardt for his work on a lift simulation that serves still as our testbed of investigations.

References

1. Kephart, J.O., Chess, D.M.: The Vision of Autonomic Computing. IEEE Computer 36(1), 41–50 (2003)
2. Richter, U., et al.: Towards a generic observer/controller architecture for Organic Computing. In: Hochberger, C., Liskowsky, R. (eds.) INFORMATIK 2006 – Informatik für Menschen! GI-Edition – Lecture Notes in Informatics (LNI), vol. P-93, pp. 112–119. Köllen Verlag (2006)
3. Branke, J., et al.: Organic Computing – Addressing complexity by controlled self-organization. In: Margaria, T., Philippou, A., Steffen, B. (eds.) Proceedings of the 2nd International Symposium on Leveraging Applications of Formal Methods, Verification and Validation (ISoLA 2006), Paphos, Cyprus, pp. 200–206 (2006)
4. Çakar, E., et al.: Towards a quantitative notion of self-organisation. In: Proceedings of the 2007 IEEE Congress on Evolutionary Computation (CEC 2007), Singapore, pp. 4222–4229 (2007)
5. Al-Sharif, L.R., Barney, G.C.: Bunching factors in lift systems (2). Report 754, Control Systems Centre, Control Systems Centre, UMIST, Manchester (1992)
6. Barney, G.C.: Elevator Traffic Handbook: Theory and Practice. Spon Press (2003)
7. Strakosch, G.R.: The Vertical Transportation Handbook, 3rd edn. John Wiley & Sons, New York (1998)
8. Sheffi, Y.: Poker and random bunching. The Tech 126(50), 5 (2006)
9. Al-Sharif, L.R.: Bunching in lift systems. In: Barney, G.C. (ed.) Proceedings of the 5th International Conference on Elevator Technologies (Elevcon 1993), IAEE conference series, Vienna, Austria (1993)
10. Powell, B.A.: Measurement and reduction of bunching in elevator dispatching with multiple term objection function (USP 5447212) (1995)
11. Al-Sharif, L.R.: Bunching in lifts...: Why does bunching in lifts increase waiting time? Elevator World 11, 75–77 (1996)

Part VII
Computer Architecture

A Generic Network Interface Architecture for a Networked Processor Array (NePA)

Seung Eun Lee, Jun Ho Bahn, Yoon Seok Yang, and Nader Bagherzadeh

536 Engineering Tower, Henry Samueli School of Engineering
University of California, Irvine, CA 92697-2625, USA
{seunglee,jbahn,ysyang,nader}@uci.edu

Abstract. Recently Network-on-Chip (NoC) technique has been proposed as a promising solution for on-chip interconnection network. However, different interface specification of integrated components raises a considerable difficulty for adopting NoC techniques. In this paper, we present a generic architecture for network interface (NI) and associated wrappers for a networked processor array (NoC based multiprocessor SoC) in order to allow systematic design flow for accelerating the design cycle. Case studies for memory and turbo decoder IPs show the feasibility and efficiency of our approach.

Keywords: Network-on-Chip (NoC), Interconnection Network, Network Interface, Networked Processor Array (NePA), Multiprocessor System-on-Chip (MPSoC).

1 Introduction

In order to meet the design requirements for computation intensive applications and the needs for low-power and high-performance systems, the number of computing resources in a single-chip has been enormously increased. This is mainly because current VLSI technology can support such an extensive integration of transistors and wires on a silicon. As a new SoC design paradigm, the Network-on-Chip (NoC) [1][2][3][4] has been proposed to support the integration of multiple IP cores on a single chip. In NoC, the reuse of IP cores in plug-and-play manner can be achieved by using a generic network interface (NI), reducing the design time of new systems. NI translates packet-based communication into a higher level protocol that is required by the IP cores by packetizing and depacketizing the requests and responses of the cores. Decoupling of computation from communication is a key ingredient in NoC design. This requires well defined NI that integrates IP cores to on-chip interconnection network to hide the implementation details of an interconnection.

In this paper, we focus on the architecture of NI in order to integrate IP cores into on-chip interconnection networks efficiently. We split the design of a generic NI into master core interface and slave core interface. First, we present an NI architecture for an embedded RISC core. Then, an application specific wrapper for a slave IP core is introduced based on the NI. In order to implement

U. Brinkschulte et al. (Eds.): ARCS 2008, LNCS 4934, pp. 247–260, 2008.

a wrapper, we start by choosing application-specific parameters and writing an allocation table for architecture description. The allocation table is used for the configuration of the modular wrapper and for the software adaptation. The main contributions of this paper are a description of a generic NI architecture which allows to accelerate the design cycle and a proposal of a systematic design flow for an application specific interface.

This paper is organized as follows. Section 2 introduces an example of networked processor array (NePA) platform and related works in NI. The prototype of NI for OpenRISC interface is addressed in Sections 3. Section 4 describes a modular wrapper for a generic NI and presents case studies based on the proposed design flow. Finally, we conclude with Section 5.

2 Background

2.1 Networked Processor Array (NePA)

Since the focus of this paper is on developing a generic NI to support plug and play architecture, a simple mesh based NoC architecture is assumed. As shown in Fig. 1, NePA platform has a 2-dimensional $m \times n$ processor array with mesh topology. Each router communicates with its four neighbors and each core is connected to a router using an NI. The packet forwarding task follows a simple, adaptive routing, that uses a wormhole switching technique with a deadlock- and livelock- free algorithm for 2D-mesh topology [4]. The packet structure, shown in Fig. 2, includes two major fields. One is the destination address $(\Delta x, \Delta y)$ field to indicate the destination node in the head flit. The address of the destination node is represented by the relative distance of horizontal and vertical direction,

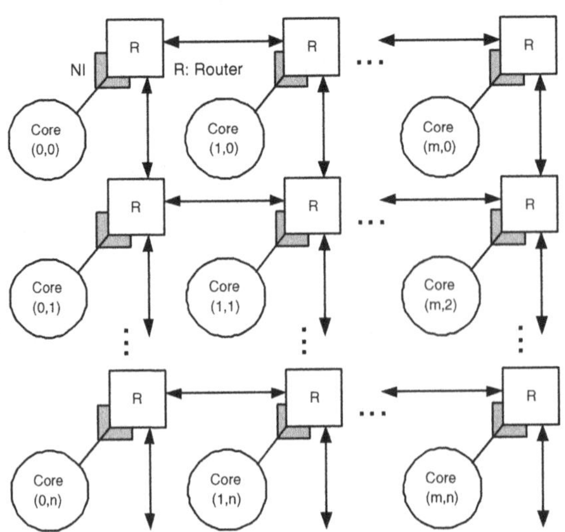

Fig. 1. A NePA architecture with mesh topology

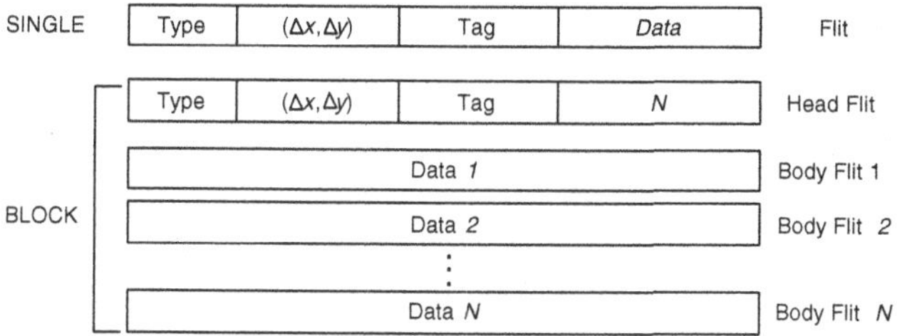

Fig. 2. Message structure

so it is updated after each transition. The second field consists of a tag and the number of data to be exchanged. The body flits deliver data to the destination IP core.

2.2 Related Works

Since most of the published works have focused on the design of novel network architecture, there has been relatively little attention to NI design. Bhojwani and Mahapatra [5] compared three schemes of paketization strategy such as software library, on-core and off-core implementation, and related costs in terms of latency and area are projected, showing trade offs in these schemes. They insisted that a hardware wrapper implementation has the lowest area overhead and latency. Bjerregaard et. al. introduced Open Core Protocol (OCP) compliant NIs for NoC [6][7][8][9] and Radulescu presented an adapter supporting DTL and AXI [10]. While standard interface has the advantage of improving reuse of IP cores, the performance is penalized because of increasing latency [7]. Baghdadi proposed a generic architecture model which is used as a template throughout the design process accelerating design cycle. Lyonnard defined parameters for automatic generation of interface for multiprocessor SoC integration [11]. However, they limited the embedded IP cores to CPUs (ARM7 and MC68000) [12]. The designs of wrapper for application specific cores still lack generic aspects and only tackle restricted IP cores. This paper investigates the actual design of NI for NePA and presents systematic design flow for arbitrary IP cores. The long-term objective is to develop a tool that automatically generates an application specific wrapper accepting as inputs the IP core interface specifications.

3 Network Interface Architecture

In the current prototype of NI, we limit the processing elements (PE) to Open-RISC cores. A tile consists of an adaptive router [4], a network interface, Open-RISC and program/data memory as shown in Fig. 3. Some parameters are needed to build a packet header for sending/receiving data over a network. These parameters are given by the PE (OpenRISC).

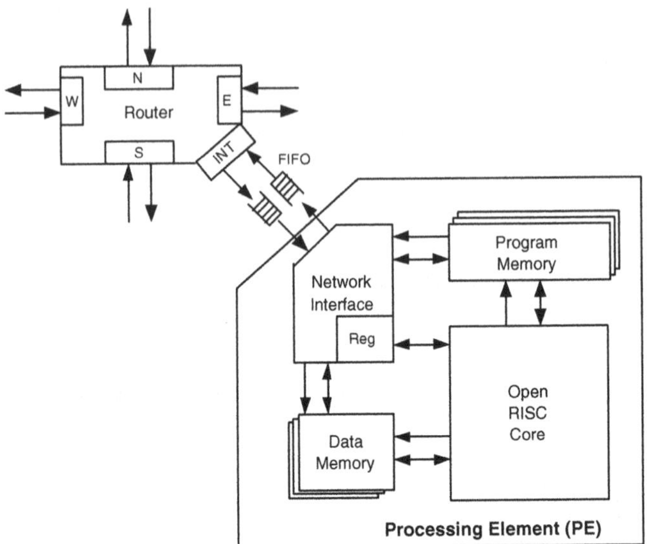

Fig. 3. A NePA tile architecture

3.1 Design of Network Interface

NI consists of a packetization unit (PU), a depacketization unit (DU) and PE interface (see Fig. 4). NI is located between a router and a PE, decoupling the communication and computation. It offers a memory-mapped view on all control registers in NI. That is, the registers in NI can be accessed using conventional bus interface. In this prototype, the parameters required to manage NI are given by OpenRISC. Table 1 shows the registers details. With this interface model, a simple implementation can be accomplished. All of the register accesses are done by bus interface and BLOCK data transfer can be handled by the DMA controller. DMA controller manages BLOCK data transfer from/to the internal memory by controlling *sReadAddrReg*, *rWriteAddrReg* and the given number of transferred data (this can be from the lower 16-bits of *rDataReg* or *sDataReg* for receiving and sending, respectively). In order to achieve high performance, all operations are completed in one cycle.

Packetization Unit. The packetization unit (PU) builds the packet header and converts the data in the memory into flits. PU consists of a header builder, a flit controller, a send DMA controller and registers. The header builder forms the packet header based on the information provided by registers such as destination address, data ID, number of body flits and service level. DMA controller generates control over the address and read signal for the internal memory by referring the start address of the memory (*sReadAddrReg*) and the number of data (*sDataReg*) for BLOCK data/program transfer. Flit controller wraps up the head flit and body flits into a packet.

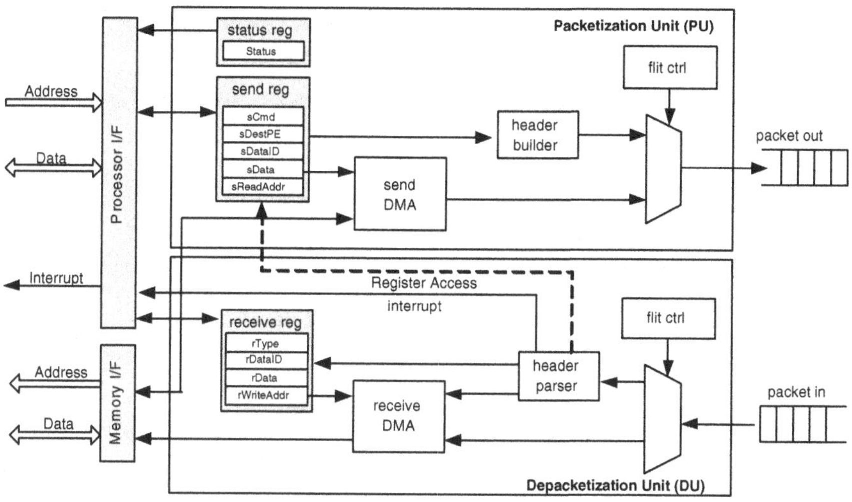

Fig. 4. NI (network interface) block diagram

Table 1. Register Definition of the Network Interface

Name	width	R/W	Offset	Description
sCmdReg	8	W	0x00	command value
sStatusReg	4	R	0x04	status register
sDestPEReg	8	W	0x08	dest_PEaddr of the corresponding packet
sDataIDReg	16	W	0x0C	data_ID /cmd_opcode
sDataReg	32	W	0x10	SINGLE: data/ operand BLOCK: number of flits
sReadAddrReg	32	W	0x14	start address of the sending data
rTypeReg	8	R	0x20	MSB 8 bit of header flit
rDataIDReg	16	R	0x24	data_id/ cmd_opcode of the received packet
rDataReg	32	R	0x28	SINGLE: data/ operand BLOCK: number of flits
rWriteAddrReg	32	W	0x2C	start address for storing BLOCK data

Depacketization Unit. The depacketization unit (DU) performs the receiving data from interconnection network. DU includes a flit controller, a header parser, a DMA controller and registers. The flit controller selects head flit from a packet and passes it to the header parser. The header parser extracts control information from the head flit such as address of source PE, number of body flits, and specific control parameters. Also, it asserts an interrupt signal to the OpenRISC core to get the local memory address for the packet. DMA controller automatically writes the body flit data into the internal memory by accessing *rWriteAddrReg* assigned by OpenRISC.

Program 1. Send SINGLE Packet from OpenRISC

```
write sDestPEReg (destination address)
write sDataIDReg (data id/op code)
write sDataReg (data)
write sCmdReg (command)
```

Program 2. Send BLOCK Packet from OpenRISC

```
write sDestPEReg (destination address)
write sDataIDReg (data id/op code)
write sDataReg (number of data)
write sReadAddrReg (start address of data)
write sCmdReg (command)
```

Program 3. Receive Packet to OpenRISC

```
read rTypeReg
if SINGLE then
  read rDataIDReg
  read rDataReg
else
  read rDataReg
  write rWriteAddrReg (start address of data)
endif
```

3.2 Programming Sequence

Both sending and receiving packets are performed by accessing the corresponding registers. Program 1 shows the programming sequence for OpenRISC core to initiate a SINGLE packet. For sending a SINGLE data/command packet, all the required parameters such as *dest_PEaddr*, *data_ID/cmd_Opcode* and corresponding 32-bit data are set to the associated registers. Finally, when the exact value of MSB 8-bit for the current transmission is set into *sCmdReg*, a complete SINGLE packet is generated by the NI, and injected into the network. For sending a BLOCK packet (Program 2), *sReadAddrReg* is used for the NI to access the internal memory. Latency for SINGLE and BLOCK transmission in NI are 4 and 5 cycles, respectively.

When a SINGLE packet arrives at the node, NI generates an interrupt. Simultaneously the necessary parameters are parsed from the received packet and stored into the associated registers. At the interrupt service routine (Program 3), each stored parameter is accessed by the internal PE. When *rDataReg* is accessed, all the procedures for the current packet is assumed to be complete. On the other hand, for receiving a BLOCK packet, the only difference is to set the corresponding write address (*rWriteAddrReg*) for internal memory access. The NI will use this as the write address for storing the following data into the internal memory. All the operations for receiving data are initiated by the corresponding interrupt generated by the NI. Latency to copy an incoming packet into internal memory is 5 cycles as shown in Program 3.

Table 2. Physical Characteristics

	NI	8-depth FIFO
Voltage	1.0V	1.0V
Frequency	719 MHz	1.8 GHz
Area	18,402 μm^2	17,428 μm^2
Dynamic Power	7 mW	10 mW
Leakage Power	184 μW	161 μW

3.3 Physical Characteristics

The NI was implemented using $Verilog^{TM}$ HDL and a logic description of our design has been obtained by the synthesis tool from the *Synposys*^{TM} using *TSMC* 90nm technology. Table 2 summarizes the physical characteristics of the NI and FIFO. The *Synopsys*^{TM} tool chain provided critical path information for logic within the NI and FIFO up to 719MHz and 1.8GHz, respectively. NI including two FIFOs has an area of approximately 0.053mm^2 (NI Area + FIFO Area × 2) using the 90nm technology. The *ARM11 MPCore*^{TM} and *PowerPC*^{TM} *E405*, that provide multi CPU designs, occupies 1.8mm^2 and 2.0mm^2 in 90nm technology, respectively [13][14]. If the NI was integrated within a NePA, the area overhead imposed by the NI would be negligible.

4 Generic Network Interface (NI)

Since NePA requires application optimization, different application specific cores may be attached to interconnection network with minimum redesign of the specific interfaces. In the remaining parts of this paper, we classify the possible IP cores for PE and define the parameters for wrapper in the context of the classification. Moreover, we provide a modular wrapper which can be configured at design time.

4.1 Classification of IP Cores for PE

A node in NePA is a specific CPU or IP core (memory, peripheral, specific hardware). We can classify IP cores into two categories: master (active) and slave (passive) IP cores (see Fig. 5). Only the master IP cores can initiate a data transfer over the network and the slave IP cores respond to requests from master IP cores.

Master IP Core. A master IP core initiates communication over interconnection network and controls NI by accessing the associated registers. It sends data packet over the network to be processed by another core and requests for packets to be sent from the other core.

A master IP core can be easily integrated into NoC using current NI architecture because it has the ability to access internal registers in the NI. A wrapper

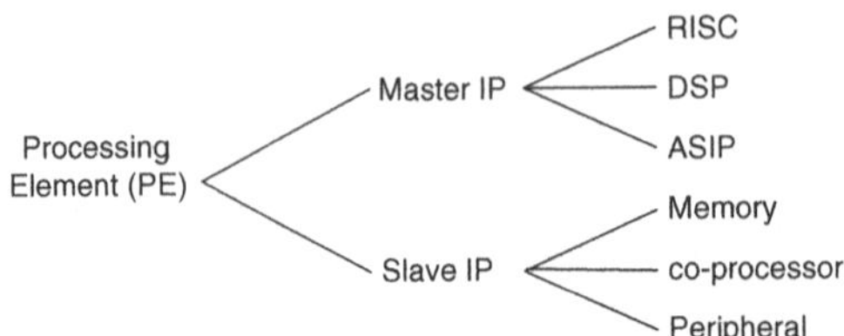

Fig. 5. Classification of IP cores

translates the protocol between IP core and NI. A master IP core is characterized with the following parameters for the purpose of a wrapper design:

- Processor type (RISC, DSP, ASIP, etc.)
- Architecture (Von Neumann, Harvard)
- BUS type (x80 system, 68 system, etc.)
- Memory size and memory map
- BUS configuration (width, data/address interleaving, endian, etc.)

For instance, a wrapper for master IP core should translate different protocols to the NI protocol according to the bus type. Architecture defines the number of interface ports and memory size determines the address width. If there is mismatch in data width, additional logic is required to adjust the data width.

Slave IP Core. A slave IP core can not operates by itself. It receives data sent over network from other cores, processes the data, and sends computed result over the network to another core. Memory, stream buffers, peripherals and co-processors (DCT, FFT, Turbo decoder, etc.) are classified as slave IP cores. Following parameters represent the characteristic of a slave IP core for a wrapper design:

- IP type (memory, co-processor, peripheral, etc.)
- Number of control signals
- Memory size and memory map
- Internal register map
- Set of control output signals (busy, error, done, re-try, interrupt, etc.)
- Data interface (serial/parallel, big/little endian, burst mode, interleaved data, etc.)

4.2 Modular Wrapper for Slave IP Cores

A slave IP core is not able to write registers in a current prototype of NI in order to indicate a destination node or to set command register. With small modification in the NI, these registers can be accessed by other cores through networks, updating the register values. This is easily realized using the predefined instruction set which access these dedicated registers (see dotted line in Fig. 4). The opcode and operand of an instruction are located at *Tag* and *Data* fields in

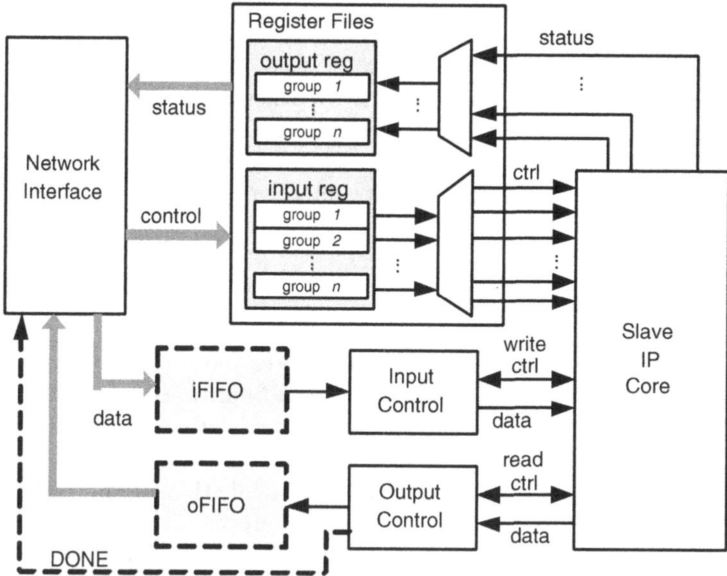

Fig. 6. Micro-architecture of a modular wrapper for a slave IP core

the SINGLE packet, respectively. *Type* field indicates that the packet contains an instruction for NI control. The instruction decoder in the header parser fetches opcode and operand from a packet and updates the internal send registers. For instance, the core (0,0) can set *sDestPEReg* in NI (2,1) to 0x01 in order to forward the computed results of core (2,1) to core (2,2) by injecting the following packet into the network.

Type **NI access**	$(\Delta x, \Delta y)$	*Tag* **Opcode**	*Data* **Operand**
SINGLE	0x21	write (*sDestPEReg*)	0x01

There are two signal groups, control and data signals, in a slave IP core. The input control signals initialize and manage a slave IP core. Also, a slave IP might generate status signals to indicate its internal state (busy, error, done, etc.) or to request special services (re-try, interrupt, etc.) for specific operations.

Fig. 6 shows the micro-architecture of a modular wrapper for a slave IP core interface. The input control signals are grouped by their functionality and then assigned to the application specific registers in the wrapper. These registers are accessed by NI using SINGLE packet to initialize the control signals which are allocated to dedicated signals and fed to the slave IP core completing initialization. Status signals have specific functions. For instance, the *error* signal requires special services such as generating trap to another PE or stop the operation of the slave IP core. The *done* signal initiates communication to another PE to transmit the results of the slave IP. These status signals need dedicated logic for each signal. There are a set of status signals and associated control logic to generate the controller for status signals.

Input data for a slave IP core is sent by other cores through network and NI translates the incoming packet for the slave IP core. There are differences in data width between the IP core and flit. In order to handle this mismatch, we present two operation modes for the data interface:

- **Unbuffered Mode:** data is exchanged in data stream without intermediate buffer.
- **Buffered Mode:** data is saved in the intermediate buffer temporarily.

In data interfacing, either unbuffered or buffered mode can be adopted. There are trade offs in network utilization, latency, and hardware overhead. Choosing appropriate interface mode is determined by an application designer and strongly depends on the characteristic of an application. Some cores support reading input data and writing output data concurrently, while they are processing. If the bus width of a core is less than a flit width, the interface is completed in the unbuffered mode removing the intermediate FIFOs in Fig. 6. The unbuffered mode could waste the available bandwidth of the network since it might not utilize the MSB parts of a flit. Other cores start execution after receiving all the input data in a local memory. Similarly, the result of processing is saved in memory and injected into network after completing the processing of data. Wrappers for these cores are designed in the buffered mode adding the intermediate FIFOs in Fig. 6. While the buffered mode operation increases network utilization by packing and unpacking data into a flit according to the data width, it requires additional FIFOs and packing/unpacking logic. The input and output controllers generate signals for the slave IP core completing data exchanges. The input controller reads data from the NI or FIFO and writes data to the slave IP core. On the contrary, the output controller reads data from the slave IP core and passes data to the NI or FIFO. In designing input and output controllers, designer should keep track of the specification of an IP core such as timing, data rate, etc.

For the systematic design flow, we define an allocation table for our wrapper design as shown in Table 3. Each line contains the specific parameters of an IP core for a wrapper design. *TYPE* defines the type of IP core whether it is master or slave. The input control signals are mapped to the *iControl* and the number of *iControl* depends on the number of input control signals in the IP core. The index i is used to access the internal register files using the specific instruction. Similarly, *oControl* reflects the status signals from the IP core. *Mode* defines the type of data transmission such as unbuffered and buffered mode. *iData* and *oData* are used to describe the interface signals to the IP core in order to complete data exchanges between NI and IP cores. The allocation table will be used for the configuration of the wrapper and for the programming model through the network.

Table 3. Allocation Table for Wrapper Design

Name	Description
TYPE	type of IP core (master/slave)
iControl i	map for ith input register
oControl i	map for ith output register
Mode	type of data transmission (Unbuffered/Buffered)
iData	signals for input data
oData	signals for output data

Table 4. Allocation Table for Memory and Turbo Decoder

Name	MEMORY	TURBO DECODER
TYPE	SLAVE	SLAVE
iControl 1		BSIZE[15:0]
2	NONE	PHYMODE[1:0], RATE[2:0], IT[4:0]
3		THRESHOLD[7:0], DYN_STOP
oControl 1	NONE	EFF_IT[4:0]
Mode	Unbuffered	Buffered
iData	DIN, ADDRESS, WE(I), CS(I)	D[15:0], DEN(I), DBLK(I), DRDY(O)
oData	DOUT, ADDRESS, OE(O), CS(I)	Q[1:0], QEN(O), QBLK(O), QRDY(I)

4.3 Case Studies

In this section, we show example design flows for a memory and a turbo decoder. We first generate the allocation table for the specific IP cores as shown in Table 4 and present the detail architecture for wrappers based on the modular wrapper.

A wrapper for a memory. Memory elements are important resources in computing systems. Memory cores are embedded in the system in order to maintain data during processing and are shared among a number of processing elements. We assume synchronous SRAM model for the memory core. The core type is slave and there are no control signals for initialization or status monitoring. By assuming the data width to be 64-bits (the same with the flit width), data interface is realized in the unbuffered mode removing the FIFOs between NI and memory. The prototype NI already has the interface to memory core, generating address and control signals. Memory core is integrated in the NePA by wiring to the prototype NI.

In order to access the memory core through the network, a master IP core should activate the node which contains the memory core. In case of writing, the base address is set to the desired value by sending SINGLE packet to the node which contains *WRITE* instruction to the *rWriteAddrReg* register in the NI. Then, BLOCK data is sent to the the memory core (Program 4). For read operation, four registers in the NI are accessed through the network setting destination address, base address of read operation, number of data, and command register. After updating the command register (*sCmdReg*), the NI automatically

Program 4. Write to the memory core through network

```
SINGLE: write (rWriteAddrReg) // set start address
BLOCK: write (Data) // send data to memory
```

Program 5. Read from the memory core through network

```
SINGLE: write (sDestPEReg) // set return PE address
SINGLE: write (sReadAddrReg) //set read address
SINGLE: write (sDataReg) // set number of read data
SINGLE: write (sCmdReg) // initiate read packet
```

reads the data from the memory and sends the data to the destination node (Program 5).

A wrapper for a Turbo decoder. Demands on high data rate in portable wireless applications make error correcting techniques important for a communication system. An error correction technique known as Turbo Coding has a better error correction capability than other known codes [15]. In this paper, turbo decoder [16] used in wireless systems, either in the base station or at terminal side, is embedded in NePA. The core is a stand-alone turbo decoder operating in a block by block process. The core type is slave and there are six signals which are used for initialization and mode selection. We map the input control signals to three groups which are accessed by a packet. The status signal is mapped to a output control signal group. Since we adopt the buffered operation mode, the FIFOs are inserted in the modular wrapper.

The input controller unpacks 64-bits incoming flits into 16-bits input data and generates control signals (DEN and $DBLK$). It also observes the signal $DRDY$ in order to monitor the state of the core. The output controller packs 2-bits output into 64-bits flit and forwards the flit to the output FIFO. The

Program 6. Initialize the turbo decoder through network

SINGLE: write (iControl 1) // set *iControl1* value
SINGLE: write (iControl 2) // set *iControl2* value
SINGLE: write (iControl 3) // set *iControl3* value
SINGLE: write (sDestPEReg) // set return PE address
SINGLE: write (sReadAddrReg) // set address to oFIFO
SINGLE: write (sDataReg) // set number of data

Program 7. Write to the turbo decoder through network

```
SINGLE: write (rWriteAddrReg) // set address to iFIFO
BLOCK: write (Data) // write data to iFIFO
```

Program 8. Read from the turbo decoder through network

SINGLE: write (sDestPEReg) // set return PE address
SINGLE: read (oControl 1) // read *oControl1* value
SINGLE: write (sCmdReg) // initiate read packet

data communication is completed by NI accessing the FIFOs. In addition, the output controller generates *DONE* signal to notify that decoding of one block is completed. The *DONE* signal updates the *sCmdReg* and the NI starts to send a packet to the destination node automatically reading the output FIFO.

Before starting turbo decoding, the decoder is initialized by sending packet which access the input control signals (Program 6). We also set up the destination node (*sDestPEReg*) that receives the results of turbo decoding. The read address (*sReadAddrReg*) is set to the output FIFO and the number of data (*sDataReg*) is fixed to the block size.

In order to feed data to the turbo decoder, the write address (*rWriteAddrReg*) is set to the input FIFO and BLOCK data is sent to the turbo decoder (Program 7). Internal state of the decoder is accessed using the output control register (*oControl 1*) as shown in Program 8.

5 Conclusions

In this paper, we proposed the network interface architecture and modular wrapper for NoC. The NI decouples communication and computing, hiding the implementation details of an interconnection network. For a generic NI, we have classified the possible IP cores for PE and introduced an allocation table for a wrapper design. The allocation table is used for the configuration of the modular wrapper and for the software adaptation. The case studies in memory and turbo decoder cores demonstrated feasibility and efficiency of the proposed design flow. In addition to being useful for designing NI, the proposed design flow can be used to generate wrapper and NI automatically.

References

1. Dally, W.J., Towles, B.: Route packets, not wires: On-chip interconnection networks. In: Proc. of the DAC 2001, pp. 684–689 (2001)
2. Tabrizi, N., et al.: Mars: A macro-pipelined reconfigurable system. In: Proc. CF 2004, pp. 343–349 (2004)
3. Lee, S.E., Bagherzadeh, N.: Increasing the throughput of an adaptive router in network-on-chip (noc). In: Proc. of the CODES+ISSS 2006, pp. 82–87 (2006)
4. Lee, S.E., Bahn, J.H., Bagherzadeh, N.: Design of a feasible on-chip interconnection network for a chip multiprocessor (cmp). In: SBAC-PAD 2007: Proc. of the 19th International Symposium on Computer Architecture and High Performance Computing, pp. 211–218 (2007)
5. Bhojwani, P., Mahapatra, R.: Interfacing cores with on-chip packet-switched networks. In: Proc. of the VLSID 2003, pp. 382–387 (2003)
6. Bjerregaard, T., et al.: An ocp compliant network adapter for gals-based soc design using the mango network-on-chip. In: Proc. of the 2005 Int'l Symposium on System-on-Chip, pp. 171–174 (2005)
7. Ost, L., et al.: Maia: A framework for networks on chip generation and verification. In: Proc. of the ASP-DAC 2005, pp. 49–52 (2005)
8. Stergiou, S., et al.: xpipes lite: A synthesis oriented design library for networks on chips. In: Proc. of the DATE 2005, pp. 1188–1193 (2005)

9. Bhojwani, P., Mahapatra, R.N.: Core network interface architecture and latency constrained on-chip communication. In: Proc. of the ISQED 2006, pp. 358–363 (2006)
10. Radulescu, A., et al.: An efficient on-chip ni offering guaranteed services, shared-memory abstraction, and flexible network configuration. IEEE Trans. Computer Aided Design of Integrated Circuits and systems 24(1), 4–17 (2005)
11. Lyonnard, D., et al.: Automatic generation of application-specific architectures for heterogeneous multiprocessor system-on-chip. In: Proc. of the DAC 2001, pp. 518–523 (2001)
12. Baghdadi, A., et al.: An efficient architecture model for systematic design ofapplication-specific multiprocessor soc. In: Proc. of the DATE 2001, pp. 55–62 (2001)
13. ARM: Arm11 mpcore, `http://www.arm.com`
14. IBM: Ibm powerpc 405 embedded core, `http://www.ibm.com`
15. Vucetic, B., Yuan, J.: Turbo codes: Principles and applications. Kluwer Academic Publishers, Dordrecht (2000)
16. TurboConcept: High speed wimax convolutional turbo decoder, `http://www.turboconcept.com`

Constructing Optimal XOR-Functions to Minimize Cache Conflict Misses

Hans Vandierendonck and Koen De Bosschere

Dept. of Electronics and Information Systems (ELIS)/HiPEAC, Ghent University,
St.-Pietersnieuwstraat 41, B-9000 Gent, Belgium
{hans.vandierendonck,koen.de.bosschere}@elis.ugent.be

Abstract. Stringent power and performance constraints, coupled with detailed knowledge of the target applications of a processor, allows for application-specific processor optimizations. It has been shown that application-specific reconfigurable hash functions eliminate a large number of cache conflict misses. These hash functions minimize conflicts by modifying the mapping of cache blocks to cache sets.

This paper describes an algorithm to compute optimal XOR-functions, a particular type of hash functions based on XORs. Using this algorithm, we set an upper bound on the conflict reduction achievable with XOR-functions. We show that XOR-functions perform better than other reconfigurable hash functions studied in the literature such as bit-selecting functions.

The XOR-functions are optimal for one particular execution of a program. However, we show that optimal XOR-functions are less sensitive to the characteristics of the execution than optimal bit-selecting hash functions. This again underlines that XOR-functions are the best known hash functions to implement reconfigurable hash functions.

1 Introduction

The design of embedded systems is strongly dominated by power and performance constraints. To maximize performance and minize power to the fullest extent, it is necessary to apply application-specific optimizations to the processor. The optimizations that are applied depend on the executing program: the optimizations act differently for different programs. In the context of caches, attention has been drawn to application-specific reconfigurable hash functions to minimize conflict misses.

The literature focusses on two types of reconfigurable hash functions: bit-selecting functions and XOR-functions. Bit-selecting functions determine each set index bit by selecting one of the address bits. XOR-functions involve some computation: each set index bit is the XOR of a subset of the address bits. The conventional modulo-power-of-2 indexing belongs to both categories.

A particular sub-class of XOR-functions, namely permutation-based functions where the XOR is performed on at most 2 address bits, are particularly interesting to implement reconfigurable hash functions in hardware, yielding circuitry that is less complex than that of reconfigurable bit-selecting functions [1].

U. Brinkschulte et al. (Eds.): ARCS 2008, LNCS 4934, pp. 261–272, 2008.

Although XOR-functions require less hardware support than bit-selecting functions, the problem remains of constructing hash functions that minimize the number of conflict misses. A heuristic algorithm for constructing XOR-functions is described in [1,2]. It is, however, very hard to state how good a heuristic algorithm actually is if it is not known what the optimum is. To close this gap, we present an optimal algorithm for computing XOR-functions. With this algorithm, we further reduce the number of conflict misses and we can evaluate how near to optimal the heuristic algorithm is.

The optimal XOR-function is optimal with respect to one particular execution of a program by nature of the algorithm. The same property is true for the heuristic algorithm: the estimates are valid only for a single run of a program. In practice, however, the hash functions should work properly across multiple program executions. We show that optimality is lost due to changing the program's input data set, but the net conflict reduction of applying a hash function remains impressive. Furthermore, the optimal XOR-function removes more conflicts than a heuristically constructed XOR-function, regardless of the input data set.

The remainder of this paper is organized as follows. Section 2 describes related work. The optimal algorithm is explained and illustrated in Section 3. It is evaluated in Section 4 and the paper concludes with Section 5.

2 Background and Related Work

XOR-functions are generally represented by a matrix [3,4]. When n address bits are mapped onto m set index bits ($m < n$), then the XOR-function is a $n \times m$ binary matrix. The bit in column c and row r is 1 if the r-th address bit is included in the XOR computing the c-th set index bit.

Permutation-based functions are a subset of the XOR-functions that obey spatial locality [4]. Their matrix representation is characterized by a diagonal of ones, and otherwise zeroes, in the lower m rows. In a 12×6 permutation-based function, only the cells with a dot can be chosen freely:

$$H = \begin{bmatrix} 0\,0\,0\,0\,0\,1 \\ 0\,0\,0\,0\,1\,0 \\ 0\,0\,0\,1\,0\,0 \\ 0\,0\,1\,0\,0\,0 \\ 0\,1\,0\,0\,0\,0 \\ 1\,0\,0\,0\,0\,0 \\ \cdot\;\cdot\;\cdot\;\cdot\;\cdot\;\cdot \\ \cdot\;\cdot\;\cdot\;\cdot\;\cdot\;\cdot \\ \cdot\;\cdot\;\cdot\;\cdot\;\cdot\;\cdot \\ \cdot\;\cdot\;\cdot\;\cdot\;\cdot\;\cdot \\ \cdot\;\cdot\;\cdot\;\cdot\;\cdot\;\cdot \\ \cdot\;\cdot\;\cdot\;\cdot\;\cdot\;\cdot \end{bmatrix} . \tag{1}$$

Note that the rows are numbered from the top down (the top row involves address bit 0) and the columns are numbered from right to left.

Permutation-based functions are non-overlapping with bit-selecting functions, except for the conventional modulo-power-of-2 indexing that belongs to both classes of functions.

Reconfigurable hash functions are implemented in hardware by adding a small amount of configuration memory and a multiplexer to every address line of the cache memory [5,1]. The multiplexer selects one out of a set of address bits. The select input of the multiplexer is stored in the configuration memory. As the configuration remains fixed during long periods of time, the multiplexer introduces marginable latency [5].

Reconfigurable permutation-based functions can be implemented with less hardware than reconfigurable bit-selecting functions, provided that the number of inputs per XOR is restricted to 2 [1]. This implies that, in the example above (Equation 1), only one of the dots in a single column can be 1. Note that allowing more inputs per XOR-gate allows small additional reductions of the conflict misses, but the complexity of the hardware implementation of the reconfigurable XOR-functions increases strongly [1].

Several algorithms have been described to optimize hash functions to a particular program execution. Most of these are profile-based approaches that analyze reuse edges in the memory access stream [6,5,1]. Another algorithm analyzes only the strides [7]. The algorithm of Patel *et al* [5] computes an optimal bit-selecting function. It is a guide to our algorithm for optimal XOR-functions.

3 Optimal Algorithm for XOR-Functions

We present an algorithm for computing optimal XOR-functions. The algorithm achieves simultaneous simulation of all hash functions in a given class by cleverly encoding the conflict miss count for each hash function in a symbolic expression. The algorithm combines the reuse-edge analysis of [1] with the symbolic modeling of conflict miss counts of [5].

3.1 Definitions

The execution of a program is represented by a trace of memory accesses. The trace length is denoted N. Each memory access refers to an address. Addresses are denoted in bold, e.g. $\mathbf{a}$. The i-th address in the trace is $\mathbf{a}_i$ for $0 \leq i < N$.

3.2 Data Reuse and the Structure of the Algorithm

Caches exploit temporal locality [8]: each cache block is typically used multiple times during a given time span. This *reuse* makes temporarily storing the cache block in a local memory efficient.

Reuse behavior in a memory access trace can be analyzed using *reuse edges* [9,10]. The reuse edge points from one access to a cache block to the previous access in the trace relating to the same cache block. The position of this access in the trace is denoted $r(i)$, so there is an edge from i to $r(i)$. Note that $r(i)$ is undefined if the i-th address in the trace is the first access to a cache block. The actual reuse of the block depends on the cache blocks accessed in the portion of the trace that is covered by the reuse edge. If any of these cache blocks maps to the same set of the cache as the current cache block, then it displaces the current cache block from the cache.

These observations lead to the following structure of an algorithm for constructing hash functions [1,2]. The algorithm analyzes the memory access stream one memory access at a time. If the currently analyzed cache block has not been accessed before (it is not possible to construct a reuse edge), then a compulsory miss occurs [8].

If a reuse edge exists, it marks the set of cache blocks that can intervene in the reuse of the current block: If any of these cache blocks map to the same cache set as the current block, then a conflict miss occurs for the current block. This rule can be used to decide if a conflict miss occurs for a particular hash function. The optimal algorithm uses this rule to compute the set of hash functions where a conflict miss occurs. In principle, one can iterate over all hash functions and over all blocks spanned by the reuse edge to compute this set of hash functions. A more appropriate solution is obtained by symbolically modeling the set of hash functions incuring a conflict miss. This symbolic model is built on the *miss conditions.*

3.3 Recapitulation of Miss Conditions for Bit-Selecting Functions

The set of hash functions incurring a conflict miss for particular reuse edge is denoted by a symbolic expression. The symbolic expression contains unknowns describing the hash function. In the case of bit selecting functions, the unknowns describe the bits that are selected by the hash function. For an n-bit address, there are n boolean variables $y_0, \ldots, y_{n-1}$. Variable y_i is true when address bit i is selected by the hash function.

The symbolic expression for the set of hash functions incuring a conflict miss is built in two steps. First, we define the *direct conflict pattern DCP* [5]. $DCP_{i,j}$ expresses whether the addresses $\mathbf{a}_i$ and $\mathbf{a}_j$ are mapped to the same set index:

$$DCP_{i,j} = \bigwedge_{k=0}^{n-1} (\gamma_k \; y_k)'$$

where $\gamma_k = 1$ when the k-th address bits of $\mathbf{a}_i$ and $\mathbf{a}_j$ are equal. The rationale is that, for a conflict miss to occur, the set indices of $\mathbf{a}_i$ and $\mathbf{a}_j$ must be equal. This happens when the hash function selects only address bits that are equal in $\mathbf{a}_i$ and $\mathbf{a}_j$.

The total conflict pattern CP_i accumulates the occurence of a conflict miss across all accessed blocks spanned by a reuse edge. A conflict miss occurs for the reuse edge if one or more of the accessed blocks cause a direct conflict:

$$CP_i = \bigvee_{j=r(i)+1}^{i} DCP_{i,j}$$

where $r(i)$ is the position in the trace of the previous use of the block accessed at position i in the trace.

A total conflict miss count (CMC) is computed for the whole trace. The CMC evaluates to the total number of conflict misses for any hash function:

$$CMC = \sum_{i=0}^{N} CP_i$$

The boolean values 0 and 1 in CP_i are reinterpreted as arithmetic 0 and 1 in the equation above.

3.4 Miss Conditions for Permutation-Based Functions

Hash functions have different degrees of freedom, so they are described using a different set of variables. The degrees of freedom for an n-to-m permutation-based hash function are the unknown bits in the matrix representation (Equation 1), so there are $m(n-m)$ boolean variables $y_{i,j}$ with $0 \leq i < m$ and $m \leq j < n$. Variable $y_{i,j}$ is 1 if there is a 1-bit on row i and column j in the matrix model of the XOR-functions (Equation 1). It is 0 otherwise. Note however that we need an additional restriction on the variables $y_{i,j}$ variables: at most one of the variables $y_{i,j}$ for $m \leq j < n$ and i fixed can be one, as we allow only 2-input XORs.

The DCP is a little more complex in the case of permutation-based hash functions. Let us consider only the k-th set index bit for the moment. The k-th set index bit is the XOR of address bit k with one of the address bits $m, \ldots, n-1$, or none of these bits. The k-th set index bits of $\mathbf{a}_i$ and $\mathbf{a}_j$ differ when one of the address bits k and the selected bit differ, but not both (property of the XOR). The extra bit differs between $\mathbf{a}_i$ and $\mathbf{a}_j$ when $\bigvee_{l=m}^{n-1} \gamma_l \; y_{k,l} = 1$, so we can write the DCP for permutation-based functions:

$$DCP_{i,j} = \bigwedge_{k=0}^{m-1} \left(\gamma_k \oplus \left(\bigvee_{l=m}^{n-1} \gamma_l \; y_{k,l} \right) \right)' \qquad (2)$$

3.5 BDD and ADD Data Structures

As in [5] we represent the direct conflict pattern (DCP) and total conflict patterns (CP) using binary decision diagrams (BDD) [11]. The conflict miss count (CMC) evaluates to an integer and is represented by an arithmetic decision diagram (ADD) [12].

The BDDs and ADDs turn out as relatively simple symbolic expressions in the case of bit-selecting functions. Therefore, a straightforward encoding into BDDs is used: the BDD is a binary tree, where an internal node at any level of the BDD tests the value of one of the boolean unknowns and branches two-ways. Each terminal node corresponds to a hash function. The path from the root of

```
Let n = length of vectors
Let a_i = block address of reference i
Let CMC = conflict miss count, initially all
zeroes

for each reference i in program trace do
    if a_i was accessed before then
        CP_i = 0
        for each a_j on stack above a_i do
            compute DCP_{i,j}
            CP_i = CP_i ∨ DCP_{i,j}
        od
        move a_i to top of stack
        CMC = CMC + CP_i
    else    /* compulsory miss */
        push a_i on stack
    fi
od
```

Fig. 1. The profiling algorithm

the BDD or ADD to the terminal node tells what bits are selected by the hash function by the y_i variables that are 1.

The BDDs and ADDs for XOR-functions are more complex and BDD/ADD computation time dominates the algorithm. We optimize the size of the BDD using the constraint that at most one of the variables $y_{i,j}$ is 1, where $m \leq j < n$ and i fixed.

The BDD/ADD is an m-level tree where each level of the tree corresponds to one of the columns of the hash function. The BDD branches $(n - m + 1)$-ways at each level. $(n - m)$ branches correspond to XORing the fixed address bits with one of the address bits $m, \ldots, n - 1$, in which case exactly one of the $y_{i,j}$ variables is 1, with i equal to the level in the tree. The $(n - m + 1)$-th branch corresponds to the case where the fixed bit is not XORed with any other address bits: all $y_{i,j}$ variables are 0.

The structure of the BDD and ADD is illustrated in Figure 2. Here, $n = 4$ address bits are hashed into $m = 2$ bits. The top level of the tree selects between the possible cases for the hashed bit 0 (column 0 in the matrix representation). The possible cases are: (i) XOR address bit 0 with address bit 2 ($y_{0,2} = 1$), (ii) XOR address bit 0 with address bit 3 ($y_{0,3} = 1$) or (iii) do not XOR address bit 0 with any other address bit ($y_{0,2} = 0$ and $y_{0,3} = 0$).

3.6 The Algorithm

The algorithm is presented in Figure 1. Some optimizations are useful to speedup the algorithm.

The total conflict pattern is computed over the list of blocks that are spanned by a reuse edge. It is not uncommon that this list contains many duplicates.

Table 1. Computation of DCPs and CPs on an example trace

Conflict pair	DCP	CP
1100-0100	$y'_{0,3}y'_{1,3}$	$y'_{0,3}y'_{1,3}$
0100-1101	$y_{0,3}y'_{1,3}$	
0100-1100	$y'_{0,3}y'_{1,3}$	$y'_{1,3}$
0100-1001	$(y_{0,2} + y_{0,3})y'_{1,2}y'_{1,3}$	$(y_{0,2} + y_{0,3})y'_{1,2}y'_{1,3}$
1100-0100	$y'_{0,3}y'_{1,3}$	
1100-1001	$y_{0,2}y'_{1,2}$	
1100-1101	0	$y_{0,2}y'_{1,2} + y'_{0,3}y'_{1,3}$

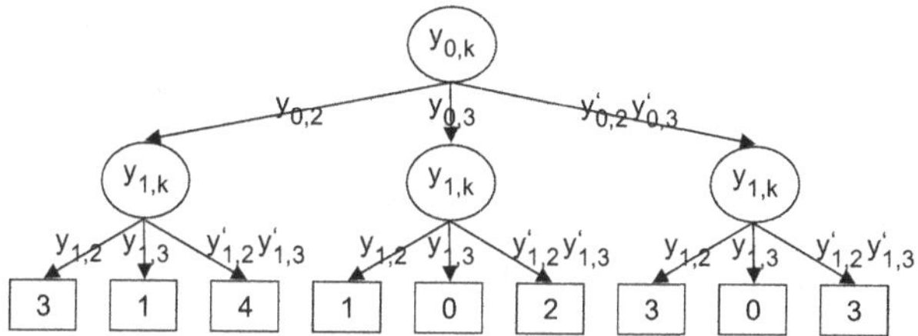

Fig. 2. The ADD computed for the example

Constructing the DCP for each of these duplicates is a waste of time, as the total conflict pattern ORs all these DCPs.

Filtering out duplicates from the list of blocks is straightforward when using a stack. The stack is ordered such that more recently used blocks are placed above less recently used blocks.

The DCP degrades to a special case if it is computed for a pair of addresses where only the m low-order address bits differ, In this case, XORing the low-order address bits with high-order bits cannot solve the conflict, because the operation performed on the low-order address bits (toggle or not toggle) is the same for both addresses. This can also be seen by setting all $\gamma_l = 0$ with $m \leq l < n$ in Equation 2.

3.7 Example

We present a simple example to illustrate the analysis of conflict misses and the construction of the ADD. We assume that 4 address bits are mapped to 2 set index bits ($n = 4$, $m = 2$). The ADD has 2 levels ($m = 2$). Each node branches 3-ways ($n - m + 1 = 3$). Furthermore, we assume that a program accesses following block addresses: 12, 4, 12, 13, 4, 9, 4, 12. The computation of the DCPs and CPs is illustrated in Table 1.

The CMC for this example is shown in Figure 2. There are two optimal hash functions in the example, achieving zero conflict misses. These hash functions can be constructed by tracing the path from the root node of the ADD to the terminal node. They are:

$$H_0 = \begin{bmatrix} 0\,1 \\ 1\,0 \\ 0\,0 \\ 1\,1 \end{bmatrix} \qquad H_1 = \begin{bmatrix} 0\,1 \\ 1\,0 \\ 0\,0 \\ 1\,0 \end{bmatrix}$$

4 Experimental Evaluation

We characterize the algorithm for optimal XOR-functions using benchmarks from the PowerStone [13], MediaBench [14] and MiBench [15] suites. Many of the PowerStone benchmarks are trivial. We use them to make a comparison to prior work [5,6]. The other benchmarks are run with large data sets when available. The benchmarks are compiled for the SA-110 ARM processor by the ARM C compiler using optimization level 2. They are simulated using the PowerAnalyzer simulator (`http://www.eecs.umich.edu/~panalyzer/`).

We compute hash functions for demand-fetching data caches with sizes of 1 KB, 4 KB and 16 KB. The cache block size is 32 bytes. All caches are direct mapped.

Optimal bit-selecting functions are computed using the algorithm of Patel *et al* [5]. Heuristic XOR-functions are computed from a profile that is measured as in [1]. Then, a XOR-function is proposed by randomly generating a large number of XOR-functions and estimating their performance using the profile information. The number of randomly generated XOR-functions is determined emperically and it was found that 10000 functions is sufficient to obtain high-quality XOR-functions [2].

4.1 Minimizing Conflict Misses

XOR-functions obtained using heuristics remove more conflict misses than bit-selecting functions [1]. We evaluate first if optimally determined XOR-functions provided an added benefit over heuristic XOR-functions. Table 2 shows the misses per kilo-uop incurred in the different cache configurations, averaged over the PowerStone benchmarks. Optimal bit-selecting functions incur fewer misses than conventional modulo indexing, heuristic XOR-functions incur still fewer misses and optimal XOR-functions incur the fewest misses of all. This behavior

Table 2. Misses per kilo-uop averaged over the PowerStone benchmarks

Hash	1 KB	4 KB	16 KB
modulo	21.32	8.63	2.03
bit-select	18.17	7.64	1.88
heur. XOR	16.35	6.87	1.78
opt. XOR	16.21	6.79	1.76

Table 3. Misses per kilo-uop for the 4 KB cache and the PowerStone benchmarks

Bench-mark	modulo index	bit-select	heur. XOR	opt. XOR
adpcm	4.07	4.07	1.40	1.40
bcnt	79.80	17.30	17.30	17.30
blit	202.74	27.91	27.91	25.28
compress	14.77	14.77	11.62	11.60
crc	1.70	1.62	1.62	1.62
des	10.60	10.60	8.97	8.73
engine	3.87	0.03	0.03	0.03
fir	0.20	0.16	0.16	0.16
g3fax	2.24	2.24	0.68	0.68
jpeg	4.56	4.56	4.02	4.01
pocsag	1.44	0.96	0.96	0.96
qurt	1.88	1.88	1.88	1.88
ucbqsort	6.63	0.26	0.26	0.26
v42	17.94	17.74	16.73	16.50
average	8.63	7.64	6.87	6.79

is consistent across all cache configurations, although the difference between the hash functions diminishes quickly with increasing cache size.

The relative performance between the hash functions is valid too for every single benchmark. Table 3 shows the per-benchmark misses per kilo-uop for the 4 KB cache. The difference between two hashing functions can be large, i.e., it succeeds in removing conflict misses or it does not succeed. E.g. the optimal bit-selecting function for g3fax is modulo indexing incurring 2.24 misses per kilo-uop. On the other hand, a heuristically found XOR-function incurs only 0.68 misses per kilo-uop, which is also the optimum. Another example involves bcnt, where any type of hash function performs well.

4.2 Impact of Cross-Profiling

The hash functions are determined for one particular run of the benchmark, using one particular input data set. In practice, applications execute many different data sets, which may lead to a shift in the optimal hash function. We analyze the impact of the input data set using cross-profiling, i.e. we determine the hash functions using a different (smaller) data set than the data set used to present results.

Table 4 shows the misses per kilo-uop for the 4 KB cache and media benchmarks. When considering only the self-profile, we can draw the same conclusions as for the PowerStone benchmarks. The input data set, however, has a large impact on the conflict-avoidance properties of the hash function. The relative performance of the hash functions remains unaltered, underlining again the performance of XOR-functions.

Table 4. Misses per kilo-uop for the 4 KB cache and the media benchmarks

Bench-mark	modulo index	Self-profile bit-select	Self-profile heur. XOR	Self-profile opt. XOR	Cross-profile bit-select	Cross-profile heur. XOR	Cross-profile opt. XOR
susan	6.78	4.60	4.53	4.46	8.09	4.84	4.78
jpeg enc	20.12	11.94	7.03	6.95	20.12	7.67	7.42
jpeg dec	16.53	16.27	12.38	12.17	23.88	16.87	17.23
adpcm dec	1.49	1.49	0.05	0.05	1.49	0.05	0.05
adpcm enc	0.86	0.86	0.03	0.03	0.86	0.03	0.03
epic dec	4.47	4.29	3.31	3.29	4.64	3.85	3.41
mb/jpeg dec	20.63	16.89	12.76	12.25	22.16	21.03	16.95
average	13.24	9.31	6.53	6.40	14.39	8.25	7.65

The misses per kilo-uop become significantly higher when applying cross-profiling. The misses raise by 1.25 and 1.72 per kilo-uop on average for optimal and heuristic XOR-functions, respectively. The misses raise by 5.08 misses per kilo-uop for optimal bit-selecting functions, which is worse than the baseline modulo index.

XOR-functions prove to be much more resilient to changing the input data set of a program than optimal bit-selecting functions. This is not surprising since XOR-functions can be applied without knowledge of the running program too [3,16]. They eliminate conflict misses by randomizing the accesses to the cache, which works for all programs with a high conflict miss rate.

4.3 Performance Improvement

We compute the performance improvement of the hash functions on a processor model that ressembles the XScale processor. Our processor model is an inorder-issue processor that fetches 1 instruction per cycle and can issue up to 2 instructions per cycle. The branch predictor is a 128-entry bimodal branch predictor.

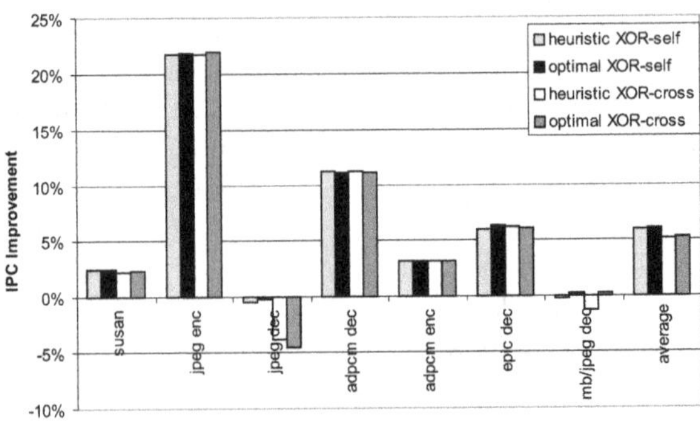

Fig. 3. IPC improvement for different XOR-functions

The memory hierarchy consists of 4 KB level-1 caches backed by memory with a 32-cycle memory access time. We assuem the same cache access latency in all configurations.

Figure 3 shows the IPC improvement of this processor when different hash functions are applied relative to the IPC of the processor with a conventional modulo index function. These results confirm the previous findings: XOR-functions improve performance by minimizing the number of conflict misses. We observe again that the choice of profiling input has an important impact on the quality of the XOR-function. Differences in conflict reduction between the heuristic and optimal XOR-functions remain present but their effect is smaller in the IPC metric than it is in the cache miss rate metric.

5 Conclusion

Reconfigurable hash functions are an application-specific processor optimization that provides large cache conflict miss reductions. We consider hash functions that are XOR-functions, but the set of allowable functions are restricted such that the XOR is performed on at most two address bits and one of the address bits is fixed. Previous work has shown that this is an interesting class of functions.

This paper presents an algorithm to compute an optimal XOR-function yielding maximal conflict miss avoidance. The algorithm models the occurence of conflict misses using symbolic expressions. Evaluating the expression for a particular hash function yields the number of conflict misses incurred by that hash function.

Our algorithm produces hash functions that reduce more conflict misses than any other algorithm described in the literature. XOR-functions halve the number of cache misses for a set of embedded benchmarks accessing a 4 KB cache.

The optimal algorithm yields XOR-functions that outperform those of heuristic algorithms by a small margin. Yet, this small margin is sufficiently large (0.60 misses/Kuop) to motivate the use of the slower optimal algorithm.

Hash function construction algorithms generally are profile-based algorithms, which make their results dependent on the input data set used during profiling. The optimal XOR-functions are less sensitive to variations in the input data set than hash functions constructed using other algorithms described in the literature.

Acknowledgments

Hans Vandierendonck is Post-Doctoral Fellow with the Fund for Scientific Research-Flanders (FWO). This research is sponsored in part by the Institute for the Promotion of Innovation by Science and Technology in Flanders (IWT), Ghent University and HiPEAC.

References

1. Vandierendonck, H., Manet, P., Legat, J.D.: Application-specific reconfigurable XOR-indexing to eliminate cache conflict misses. In: Design, Automation and Test Europe, pp. 357–362 (March 2006)
2. Vandierendonck, H.: Avoiding Mapping Conflicts in Microprocessors. PhD thesis, Ghent University (2004)
3. Rau, B.R.: Pseudo-randomly interleaved memory. In: Proceedings of the 18th Annual International Symposium on Computer Architecture, pp. 74–83 (May 1991)
4. Vandierendonck, H., De Bosschere, K.: XOR-based hash functions. IEEE Transactions on Computers 54(7), 800–812 (2005)
5. Patel, K., et al.: Reducing cache misses by application-specific re-configurable indexing. In: ICCAD 2004: ACM/IEEE International Conference on Computer-Aided Design, pp. 125–130 (November 2004)
6. Givargis, T.: Improved indexing for cache miss reduction in embedded systems. In: Design Automation Conference (2003)
7. Abraham, S.G., Agusleo, H.: Reduction of cache interference misses through selective bit-permutation mapping. Technical Report CSE-TR-205-94, The University of Michigan (1994)
8. Smith, A.J.: Cache memories. ACM Computing Surveys 14(3), 473–530 (1982)
9. Temam, O.: Investigating optimal local memory performance. In: Proceedings of the 8th International Conference on Architectural Support for Programming Languages and Operating Systems, pp. 218–227 (November 1998)
10. Vandierendonck, H., De Bosschere, K.: An optimal replacement policy for balancing multi-module caches. In: Proceedings of the 12th Symposium on Computer Architecture and High Performance Computing, pp. 65–72 (October 2000)
11. Bryant, R.E.: Symbolic boolean manipulation with ordered binary-decision diagrams. ACM Comput. Surv. 24(3), 293–318 (1992)
12. Bahar, R., et al.: Algebraic decision diagrams and their applications. In: ICCAD 1993: Proceedings of the 1993 IEEE/ACM international conference on Computer-aided design, pp. 188–191 (1993)
13. Scott, J., et al.: Designing the low-power M Core architecture. In: Proceedings of the IEEE Power Driven Microarchitecture Workshop, pp. 145–150 (June 1998)
14. Lee, C., Potkonjak, M., Mangione-Smith, W.H.: MediaBench: A tool for evaluating and synthesizing multimedia and communications systems. In: Proceedings of the 30th Conference on Microprogramming and Microarchitecture, pp. 330–335 (December 1997)
15. Guthaus, M.R., et al.: MiBench: A free, commercially representative embedded benchmark suite. In: IEEE 4th Annual Workshop on Workload Characterization (December 2001)
16. Topham, N., González, A., González, J.: The design and performance of a conflict-avoiding cache. In: Proceedings of the 30th Conference on Microprogramming and Microarchitecture, pp. 71–80 (December 1997)

Potentials of Branch Predictors: From Entropy Viewpoints

Takashi Yokota[1], Kanemitsu Ootsu[1], and Takanobu Baba[1]

Department of Information Science, Utsunomiya University,
7–1–2 Yoto, Utsunomiya-shi, Tochigi, 321–8585 Japan
{yokota, kim, baba}@is.utsunomiya-u.ac.jp

Abstract. Predictors essentially predicts the most recent events based on the record of past events, history. It is obvious that prediction performance largely relies on regularity–randomness level of the history. This paper concentrates on extracting effective information from branch history, and discusses expected performance of branch predictors. For this purpose, this paper introduces entropy point-of-views for quantitative characterization of both program behavior and prediction mechanism. This paper defines four new entropies from different viewpoints; two of them are independent of prediction methods and the others are dependent on predictor organization. These new entropies are useful tools for analyzing upper-bound of prediction performance. This paper shows some evaluation results of typical predictors.

1 Introduction

Predictors are inevitable in the state-of-the-art microprocessor cores. Prediction mechanism is essential for any speculation features in the micro-architecture. However, the effect of speculation essentially incorporates prediction accuracy. More precise prediction does better performance and vice versa.

One of the essential and fundamental properties of today's most predictors is that they predict based on the past events (i.e., history). Many prediction methods have been proposed, however, most of them discuss relative performance improvements to some typical and well-known prediction method. Until now, no one knows the possible performance of predictors, i.e., the absolute maximum. For example, assuming that predictor A performs 5% better than predictor B, we cannot discuss any more for further improvements, because we cannot know possible maximum performance.

This paper presents theoretical views on branch predictors so that we can discuss potentials of branch predictors. Our major focus is to represent information of past events and to clarify possible maximum performance of branch predictors. We introduce classical information theory originated by Shannon. Originally, an information entropy quantitatively represents essential information of the forthcoming symbol, based on the existing data.

A branch predictor intends to extract essentially the same information with Shannon's entropy, based on the past branch results. Shannon discussed relatively large set of symbols S, say the alphabet. Fortunately, a branch predictor

U. Brinkschulte et al. (Eds.): ARCS 2008, LNCS 4934, pp. 273–285, 2008.

uses a binary symbol, i.e., a branch will be taken or untaken. This one-bit symbol helps us to discuss potentials of prediction performance.

The remainder of this paper is organized as follows. We first give the overview of Shannon's information theory and describe our targeted branch predictors in Section 2. After the preliminaries, we discuss information from two aspects: entropies that are independent of prediction mechanisms (in Section 3), and entropies based on predictor organization (in Section 4). Section 5 shows evaluation results from various perspectives. Section 6 shows related work, and Section 7 concludes this paper.

2 Preliminaries

2.1 Information Entropy

This paper stands on Shannon's information entropy[1]. This subsection summarizes the fundamentals. Assume that we are discussing an entropy $H(S)$ of a Markovian information source S that produces a string of symbols. Instead of the entropy of S itself, we first discuss the augmented adjoint source of S. An n-th order augmented adjoint source of S, denoted by $\overline{S}^n$, generates n consecutive symbols. The entropy of the n-th order augmented adjoint source $H(\overline{S}^n)$ is given as the following equation:

$$H(\overline{S}^n) = -\sum_i p(S_i^n) \log_2 p(S_i^n), \tag{1}$$

where $p(S_i^n)$ represents the probability of an individual symbol S_i^n that comprises consecutive n original symbols.

$H(\overline{S}^n)$ represents information in consecutive n symbols, and it monotonically increases as n increases. Differential coefficient of $H(\overline{S}^n)$ at n shows net information of single symbol. Thus, when $(n+1)$-th order augmented adjoint entropy $H(\overline{S}^{n+1})$ is given, the n-th approximation of the entropy $H(S)$ of the objective Markovian information source is given by

$$H^n(S) = H(\overline{S}^{n+1}) - H(\overline{S}^n). \tag{2}$$

Therefore, the true value of the targeted entropy is given by limiting n to infinity:

$$H(S) = \lim_{n\to\infty} H^n(S). \tag{3}$$

The entropy $H(S)$ provides essential information of the next symbol. The entropy also presents the predictability of the forthcoming symbol.

2.2 Branch Predictors

This paper discusses performance issues in branch predictors. Our approach in this paper is to discuss generic and practical issues. To simplify the discussion

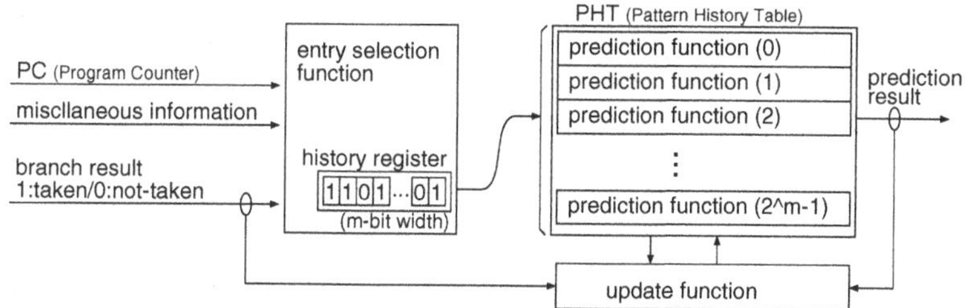

Fig. 1. Generalized organization of table-formed branch predictor

without loss of generality, we assume some typical organization and mechanisms in branch predictors.

Until now, there have been a variety of prediction methods proposed. They mainly claim their performance improvement and compete each other. Championship Branch Prediction (CBP [2,3]) hosted competitions under certain regulations, where many powerful predictors were discussed. We could analyze the state-of-the-art predictors, but it is difficult to stay in generality and fairness due to wide variations. We prefer general and fundamental discussion, instead of specific discussion on a particular predictor. General but deep discussion of fundamental predictors will give us generalized knowledge on predictors.

We specifically use table-formatted predictors as shown in Figure 1. A predictor is organized by three major functions; entry selection, prediction, and update functions. The prediction function includes one or more sub-functions, where each prediction function is basically independent from each other. The entry selection function selects an appropriate prediction function according to the given selection rule. Update function updates the prediction function. Following the conventions in two-level predictors, we use m bits of 'history register' (HR for short) as a result of selection function to point one of the prediction functions. We also use 'pattern history table' (PHT) that is an aggregation of prediction functions. Each entry of PHT consists of a prediction function. We use bimodal (`bimode`)[4], two-level (`2level`)[5], gshare (`gshare`)[6], and perceptron (`perceptron`)[7,8] branch predictors. All of them follow the simple organization shown in Figure 1.

`bimode`, `2level` and `gshare` differ in selection function; `bimode` uses a simple hash function of program counter, `2level` uses the latest m results of branch execution, and `gshare` uses the exclusive-or result of branch history and program counter. However, they typically use the same prediction function, i.e., a two-bit saturation counter that counts the number of 'taken' results. If the result is untaken, the counter is decremented.

`perceptron` uses hash function of program counter as its selection function. Its prediction function is distinguishing; it is based on a neural-network Perceptron. Each prediction function makes use of the latest h branch results and corresponding h weight values. Each weight value w_i is a signed integer with an arbitrary length, say 8 bits. The predictor calculates the weighted sum: $s = \sum_i w_i \cdot b_i$

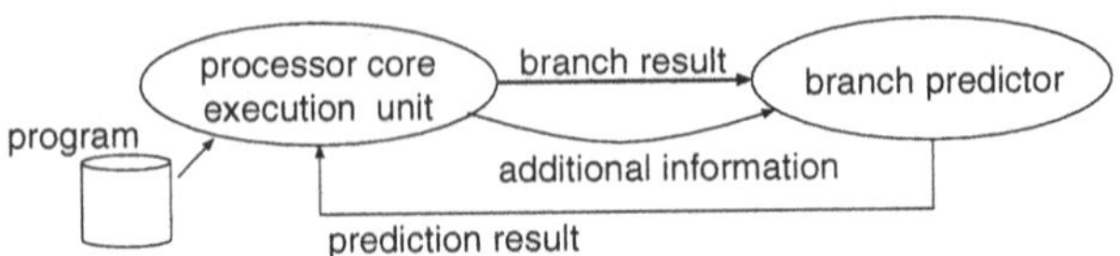

Fig. 2. Processor core as an information source to branch predictor

where b_i is 1 if the corresponding branch result is 'taken' and $b_i = -1$ otherwise. If the resulting sum s is positive, 'taken' is predicted, otherwise 'untaken' is predicted. Each PHT entry consists of a set of weight values. Update function modifies each of weight values according to the prediction result (hit or mishit).

3 Entropies Independent of Prediction Mechanisms

Section 2.1 discusses information in a string of symbols that are generated sequentially. We can apply the discussion to a string of branch results by simple substitution of 'branch results' for 'symbols.' And, by careful observation of program execution but prediction mechanisms, we offer the following two entropies.

3.1 Execution Unit as Information Source

First viewpoint is an execution unit in a processor core. As the processor execute a program, branch instructions are executed according to the program. The execution unit explicitly generates branch results so that the results are used for prediction in the branch predictor. Figure 2 illustrates it.

We can discuss entropy for the series of branch results. We consider Markovian information source B, i.e., the execution unit. By considering n consecutive branch results, we can define n-th order augmented adjoint information source $\overline{B}^n$. By simple application of Section 2.1, we can define the entropy of the n-th order augmented adjoint source $H(\overline{B}^n)$, and the n-th approximation of the targeted entropy $H(B)$, i.e., $H^n(B)$. The essential entropy $H(B)$ is given by limiting n to infinity as Equation (3). We call the new entropy **Branch History Entropy** (BHe).

3.2 Branch Instructions as Information Sources

Another viewpoint is individual branch instruction. Each branch instruction has its *own* branch history. Thus, we can define an entropy for each branch instruction. We consider that each branch instruction is a Markovian information source I_i. By applying the original entropy definition given in Section 2.1, we can define the entropy of i-th branch instruction, $H(I_i)$. Overall entropy is given as the average of $H(I_i)$, i.e., $H(I) = \frac{1}{N_b}\sum_i n_i{\cdot}H(I_i)$ where n_i is the execution count

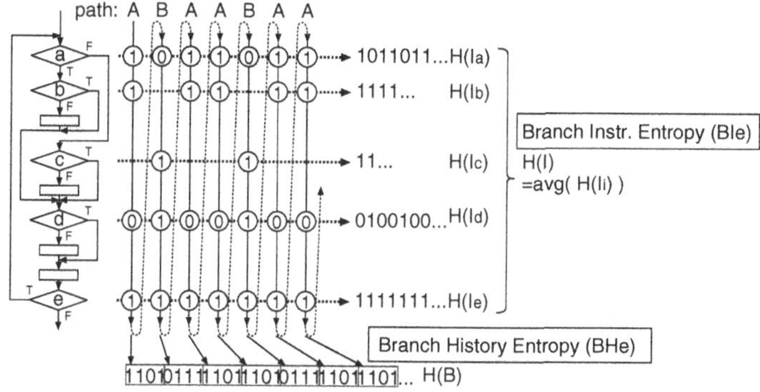

Fig. 3. Example path repetition and BHe, BIe entropies

of the i-th branch instruction and N_b is the total number of branch executions. We call the entropy **Branch Instruction Entropy** (BIe).

3.3 Fundamental Properties of Proposed Entropies

These entropies have a common important feature: they are independent of any prediction mechanisms. They represent essential information that is extracted through the program execution, i.e., they represent program behavior.

BHe represents information only from the branch history. This means that BHe shows the certainty degree of the forthcoming branch result, with no any additional hints. The branch history itself contains no information on individual branch instruction but sequence of branch results. In practical situations, a string of branch history often shows a particular execution path.

On the other hand, BIe is basically defined for each branch instruction. It essentially does not represent 'execution path' information, but it represents the local regularity of program behavior.

We claim that BHe represents information of *global* history, and BIe shows *local* (or *per address*) history information. We will discuss further with a practical example.

As an example situation, assume that a loop has two frequently-executed paths A and B that show branch history '1101' and '0111,' respectively. These paths are regularly executed as simple repetition of A→A→B. Figure 3 shows BHe and BIe in such situation. Solid vertical arrows show loop iterations and circles designate branch instructions and their branch decisions. Each horizontal dotted line shows per-address branch history at the corresponding instruction.

Executed paths are recorded in the BHe trace. Each BIe trace shows local history at the corresponding branch instruction. In this example, high regularity in path execution reflects the regularity of the local history. This observation tells us that BHe and BIe are not strictly orthogonal but correlated at a considerable level.

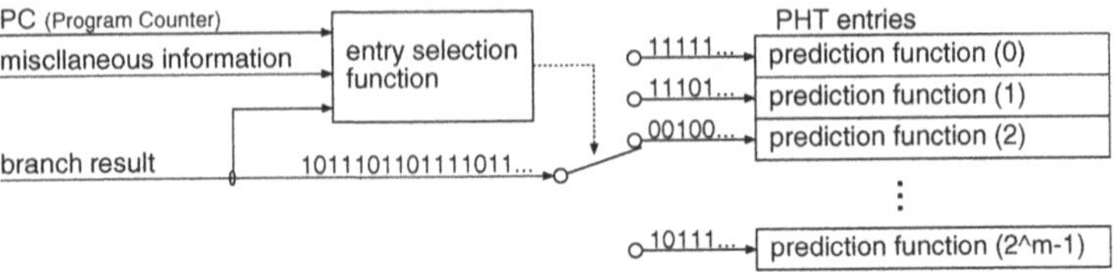

Fig. 4. Flow of branch result information

4 Entropies in Predictor Organization

4.1 Information to Each Prediction Function

We will enter specific discussion on fundamental organization of predictors as given in Section 2.2. A string of branch results, originated by the processor core, inherently contains the first-order information. We can consider that the information flows along the predictor organization. Figure 4 illustrates the flow. The information is first poured into the 'entry selection function' and it reaches individual entry of PHT, i.e., a prediction function. The original information is divided and only a segment of information is delivered into each prediction function.

This observation drives us to different entropy definition. Each prediction function has its own information of branch results, on which we can define entropy. Similarly to the Branch Instruction Entropy discussion, we can define entropy of each prediction function. Input sequence to a prediction function E_i has entropy $H(E_i)$. The overall entropy is given by the average of $H(E_i)$, i.e., $H(E) = \frac{1}{N_e} \sum_i e_i \cdot H(E_i)$ where e_i is the reference count of the i-th prediction function E_i and N_e denotes the total number of references to PHT. We call the entropy **Table Entry Entropy** (TEe).

4.2 Information in Imbalanced References

TEe represents net information at each effective prediction function, however, we cannot know how many prediction functions effectively operate. In general, when a program uses a small number of prediction functions, the program has small *working-set* and high levels of prediction performance can be expected. But the working-set does not always represent prediction performance, because a program may have large working-set with high predictability. In other words, we need another metric that represent the net usage of prediction functions in order to represent program behavior adequately.

We define **Table Reference Entropy** (TRe). TRe represents effective number of active entries. Following to the discussion in the previous section, e_i is the number of references to i-th prediction function, and N_e is the total number of PHT references. $r_i = e_i/N_e$ shows the probability of reference on the i-th prediction function (entry). Table Reference Entropy is given by $H(R) =$

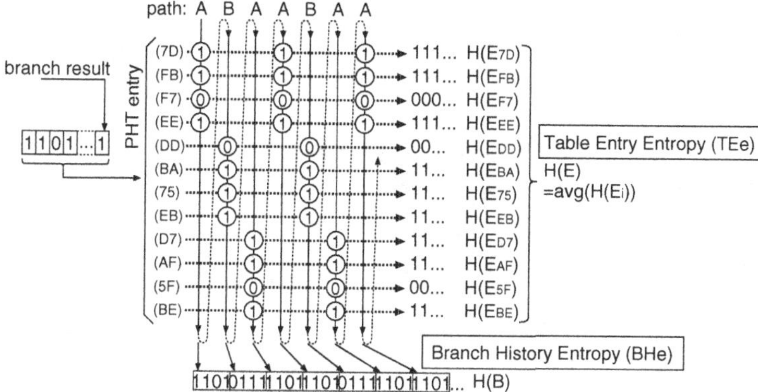

Fig. 5. Example path repetition and BHe, TEe entropies

$-\sum_i r_i \log_2 r_i$. The first-order information bifurcates at the entry selection function, and some portion of the original information is lost. TRe compensates this.

4.3 Discussion

TEe and TRe have different standpoints, but their origin is common, i.e., the first-order branch information. TEe shows the practical information poured into each prediction function, i.e., 'per-predictor' information. This is very likely to BIe as a (quasi-)orthogonal measure to BHe. Low TEe means that each predictor input has low information and, thus, the predictor is ease to predict.

Figure 5 shows the same example with Figure 3, but the figure shows sequences of branch history at each prediction function. The first-order information is delivered to individual PHT entry, which is prediction function, similarly to individual branch instruction. Most paths contain several or more lengths of branch history, thus, the first-order information is delivered to more destinations than those in the BIe condition. However, we can expect lower information entropy, thus higher prediction accuracy, from this entropy.

We can further discuss TEe and TRe entropies under the specific branch prediction mechanisms given in Section 2.2. `bimode` and `perceptron` predictors use a hash function of program counter. If these predictors have sufficient PHT entries, most of active entries correspond to their own branch instructions and, thus, TEe is very close to BIe. If only a limited number of instructions dominate, TRe becomes low.

In `2level` predictors, history register (HR) shows the latest m branch results. Since TRe is based on the values of HR, the entropy is just the same as m-th order augmented adjoint source entropy, i.e., $H(\overline{S}^m)$ given by Equation (1).

`gshare` predictor uses an XOR'ed value of branch history and program counter. This scatters the use of PHT entries. Thus, TRe shows wide variations of local history at branch instructions.

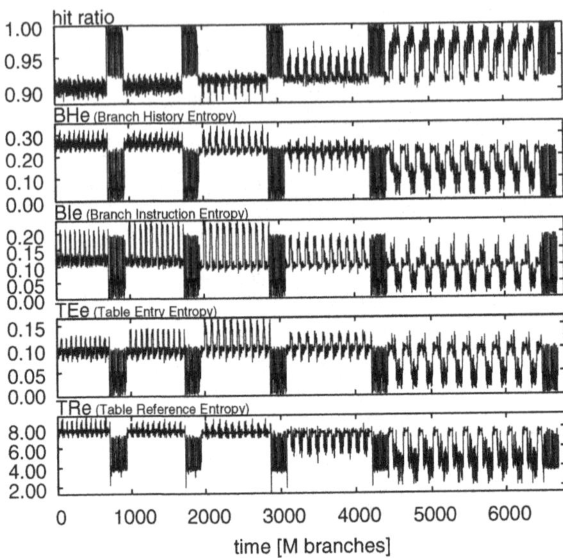

Fig. 6. Time sequence plot of prediction hit ratio, BHe, BIe, TEe and TRe

5 Evaluation

5.1 Evaluation Environment

We extended the `sim-bpred` simulator in the SimpleScalar toolset[9] so that our defined entropies are measured. We also implemented the perceptron predictor in `sim-bpred`. PISA instruction set was used. Some programs in SPEC CPU2000[10] benchmark are compiled by gcc 2.7.2.3 PISA cross compiler. The benchmark set has variety of problem size: we used 'train.'

Entropies and prediction hit ratio are measured in every 1,000,000 (1M) branches time-window. Size of the time-window is important for accuracy of the measured entropy. Although more samples produces more precise results, long time-window may bury important characteristics of 'phases' in program execution. We consider the 1 million branch time-window is proper[7,8].

Predictors use the same size of PHT entry, $2^{12} = 4096$ entries, thus HR is 12-bit width. Theoretical entropy definition (Equations (2) and (3)) is not practical, because actual $H(\overline{S}^n)$ does not smoothly increases as n increases. We measured 14-, 15-, 16-, 17-, and 18-th order augmented adjoint entropies and the essential entropy is calculated by the least-square method of these five entropies.

5.2 Potentials of Branch Predictors

We firstly show time-sequence curves of predictor hit ratio and some of proposed entropies in Figure 6. We can find that these curves are considerably correlated to each other. We will discuss potentials of branch predictors by analyzing correlations in detail.

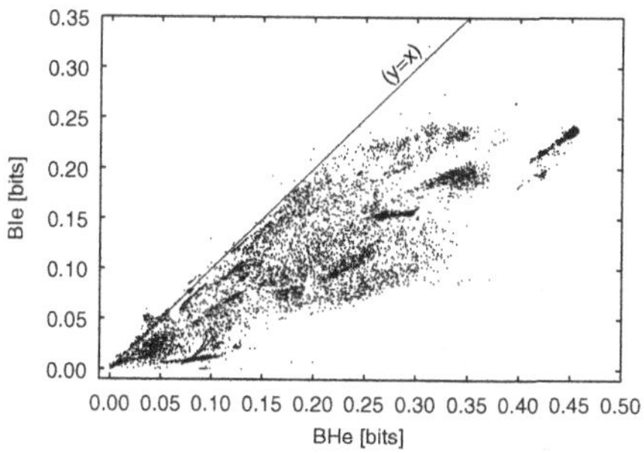

Fig. 7. Correlation between BHe and Ble

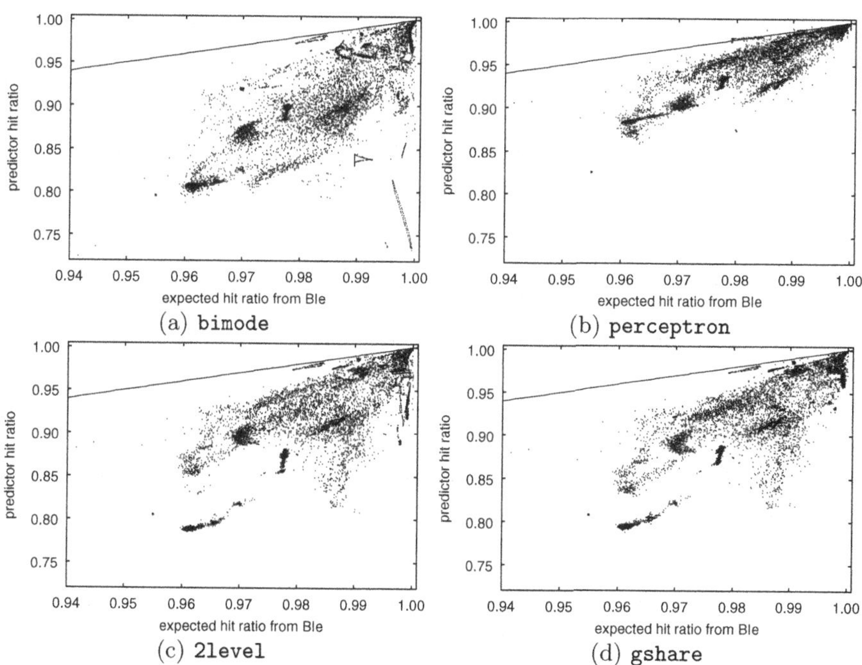

Fig. 8. Expected hit ratio from Ble and predictor hit ratio

As discussed in Section 3.3, BHe and Ble have different standpoints, but they are not always orthogonal. Figure 7 shows the correlation between BHe and Ble. Each dot shows BHe and Ble at the corresponding time-window. Dots widely scatter, but clear correlation is observed.

The important fact is that most dots are below the $y = x$ line. This means that BHe is larger than Ble at most measured points. Since BHe and Ble correspond global and local history, respectively, this result says that local history shows higher level of regularity, i.e., higher predictability, than global history.

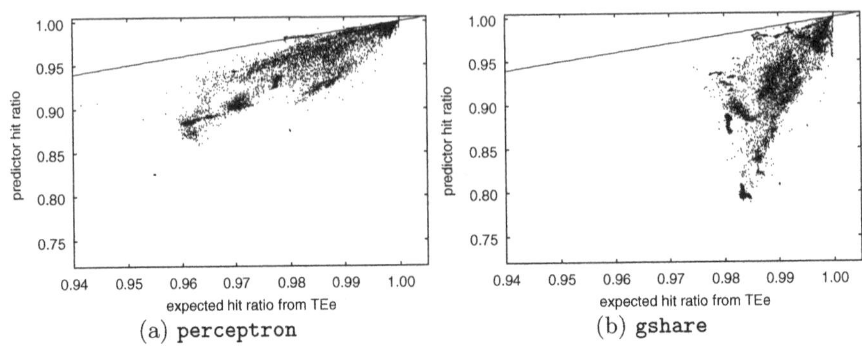

(a) perceptron (b) gshare

Fig. 9. Expected hit ratio from TEe and predictor hit ratio

Essential entropy definition for binary-event system is given by the original information entropy; $f(p) = -p\log_2 p - (1-p)\log_2(1-p)$, where p denotes the probability of the event. When an entropy value ε is given, we can estimate the originated probability p by the inverse function of $f(p)$, $f^{-1}(\varepsilon)$. We call the estimated probability **expected hit ratio** in this paper.

Table 1. Summary of prediction hit ratios and expected hit ratios from proposed entropies

benchmark	actual hit ratios				expected hit ratios			
	bimode	2level	gshare	perceptron	BHe	BIe	TEe (2level)	TEe (gshare)
(CINT2000)								
164.gzip	.9241	.9370	.9363	.9467	.9702	.9853	.9893	.9890
175.vpr(pl)	.8963	.8720	.8812	.9333	.9532	.9777	.9782	.9808
175.vpr(rt)	.8707	.9013	.8965	.9110	.9402	.9720	.9847	.9837
176.gcc	.9134	.9098	.9140	.9760	.9758	.9890	.9890	.9892
181.mcf	.8959	.9382	.9261	.9468	.9723	.9806	.9905	.9892
197.parser	.8939	.9203	.9252	.9509	.9601	.9837	.9894	.9912
254.gap	.9359	.9475	.9519	.9799	.9832	.9927	.9937	.9942
255.vortex	.9769	.9318	.9642	.9976	.9881	.9989	.9949	.9967
256.bzip2	.9824	.9820	.9841	.9877	.9913	.9937	.9947	.9956
300.twolf	.8123	.7979	.8042	.8902	.9108	.9636	.9758	.9839
(CFP2000)								
168.wupwise	.8556	.9275	.9540	.9859	.9874	.9962	.9990	.9994
171.swim	.9913	.9926	.9941	.9972	.9963	.9976	.9978	.9979
172.mgrid	.9745	.9755	.9754	.9807	.9791	.9811	.9846	.9860
173.applu	.7569	.9719	.9736	.9985	.9899	.9986	.9991	.9993
177.mesa	.9829	.9861	.9876	.9930	.9965	.9985	.9984	.9987
179.art	.9071	.9911	.9910	.9916	.9959	.9980	.9985	.9986
183.equake	.8839	.9660	.9763	.9801	.9881	.9937	.9980	.9981
188.ammp	.9659	.9787	.9800	.9854	.9820	.9905	.9922	.9931
301.apsi	.9727	.9707	.9833	.9925	.9845	.9919	.9915	.9925

Figure 8 shows correlation of the expected hit ratio by BIe and actual prediction hit ratio. Similarly to Figure 7, each dot represents expected hit ratio by BIe and predictor's performance (hit ratio) at the corresponding time-window. Each graph in the figure shows the $y = x$ line. The line represents performance criterion: dots located above the line show that the predictor performs beyond expectation. In Figure 8 cases, no predictor exceeds the criteria and the $y = x$ line shows potential performance.

Expected hit ratio can also be derived by other entropy metrics; BHe and TEe. These entropies also show similar graphs to that of BIe. Figure 9 shows TEe results of `perceptron` and `gshare` predictors. Note that expected hit ratio by BIe shows a generic criterion that is independent of predictor organization, and that expected ratio by TEe shows a specific potential.

Actual and expected hit ratios in each application are summarized in Table 1. Each fraction shows an average value throughout the whole execution of the corresponding application. In most applications except `255.vortex`, TEe is the best in expected hit ratio. Practically, TEe values show potentials of predictors. Note that BIe values are very close to those of TEe; their difference is less than 1 percent in most applications. However, populations of those entropies are very different: population of BIe is the number of executed branch instructions in the time-window, and TEe population scatters according to the changes in history register. As a typical example of `164.gzip`, populations of BIe and TEe are about 100 and 1,000, respectively. This means that, in actual programs, branch instructions act very regularly as well as prediction functions.

6 Related Work

Major contribution of this paper can be described in two perspectives; first one is quantitative representation of program behavior from a sequence of branch results, and the other one is estimation of potential prediction performance.

Many researches have concentrated to imbalanced feature in program execution. Tyson et al.[11] show some imbalanced feature in taken/untaken sequences of branch results. They show four typical cases; long consecutive takens, long consecutive untakens, a small number of untakens in long consecutive takens, and other patterns. Kise et al.[12] discuss a new predictor based on extremely biased branches. Such classifications help prediction, but no quantitative discussions are made on imbalanced features.

Periodicity is possibly a quantitative measure of program behavior. Freitag et al.[13] proposed Dynamic Periodicity Detector (DPD) by examination of sequences of data values that appear during program execution. Fourier Analysis Branch (FAB) predictor, proposed by Kampe et al.[14], uses the Fourier coefficients for representing periodicity for branch prediction purpose. Periodicity offers quantitative representation, however, it does not show essential information.

Mudge and Chen et al.[15,16] present limits in the prediction performance based on prediction using the Partial Matching (PPM) method. They use m-th order Markov predictor and underlying idea is very similar to ours. Driesen et al.[17,18] discuss limits of indirect branch prediction from a different point of view from that used in this paper. Jha et al.[19] also use a Markovian model to represent an optimal prediction mechanism for a given history length. Vintan et al.[20] discuss prediction limits based on unbiased branches. Idealistic predictors discuss substantial limits on prediction performance in Championship Branch Prediction competitions (CBP [2,3]). These researches are not successful for quantitative representation of regularity/randomness features in program execution, as our defined entropies do. Our preliminary results are found in [21,22,23]. Our approach to the limits on prediction is unique in its theoretical and quantitative approach based on information entropy.

7 Concluding Remarks

Prediction performance essentially relies on the nature of past events. Thus, modern predictors enter detailed discussion to effectively extract useful information on prediction. But theoretical limit on prediction performance was unclear.

This paper introduces information entropy concept to clarify theoretical limits in branch prediction. Our approach has two aspects: one is independent of prediction methods and the other one is dependent on predictor organization. We proposed two entropies, BHe and BIe, to represent *global* and *local* features in branch history. Furthermore, we defined TEe and TRe entropies for typical table-formatted predictors. BHe, BIe and TEe entropies can derive expected prediction performance, i.e., limits on prediction. BHe and BIe show prediction limits by global and local history, respectively. TEe shows theoretical limits on the predictor organization.

Potentials in branch prediction are calculated on a time-window basis. This offers a detailed criterion for program execution phases as well as applications themselves. Evaluation results reveal the potentials are high and we have still large rooms to improve prediction performance.

Acknowledgments. This research was supported in part by Grant-in-Aid for Scientific Research ((B)18300014, (C)19500037) and Young Scientists ((B)17700047) of Japan Society for the Promotion of Science (JSPS), and by Eminent Research Selected at Utsunomiya University.

References

1. Shannon, C.E.: A mathematical theory of communication. Bell System Technical Journal 27, 379–423, 623–656 (1948)
2. The 1st JILP Championship Branch Prediction Competition (2004), `http://www.jilp.org/cbp/`
3. The 2nd JILP Championship Branch Prediction Competition (2006), `http://camino.rutgers.edu/cbp2/`
4. Smith, J.E.: A Study of Branch Prediction Strategies. In: Proc. 8th Int'l Symp. Computer Architecture, pp. 135–148 (May 1981)

5. Yeh, T.-Y., Patt, Y.N.: Two-Level Adaptive Branch Prediction. In: Proc. 24th ACM/IEEE Int'l Symp. Microarchitecture, pp. 51–61 (November 1991)
6. McFarling, S.: Combining Branch Predictors, Technical Report TN–36, Digital Equipment Corp., Western Research Laboratory (June 1993)
7. Jiménez, D.A., Lin, C.: Dynamic Branch Prediction with Perceptrons. In: Proc. 7th Int'l Symp. High-Performance Computer Architecture, pp. 197–206 (January 2001)
8. Jiménez, D.A.: Piecewise Linear Branch Prediction. In: Proc. 32nd Annual Int'l Symp. Computer Architecture, pp. 382–393 (2005)
9. SimpleScalar LLC, `http://www.simplescalar.com/`
10. Standard Performance Evaluation Corporation, SPEC CPU2000 V1.3 (2004), `http://www.spec.org/cpu2000/`
11. Tyson, G., Lick, K., Farrens, M.: Limited Dual Path Execution, Technical Report CSE–TR–346–97, University of Michigan (1997)
12. Kise, K., et al.: The Bimode++ Branch Predictor Using the Feature of Extremely Biased Branches. IPSJ SIG Techical Report 2005(7), 57–62 (2005)
13. Freitag, F., Corbalan, J., Labarta, J.: A Dynamic Periodicity Detector: Application to Speedup Computation. In: Proc. 15th Int'l Parallel and Distributed Processing Symp. (April 2001)
14. Kampe, M., Stenstrom, P., Dubois, M.: The FAB Predictor: Using Fourier Analysis to Predict the Outcome of Conditional Branches. In: Proc. 8th Int'l Symp. High-Performance Computer Architecture, pp. 223–232 (February 2002)
15. Chen, I-C.K., Coffey, J.T., Mudge, T.N.: Analysis of Branch Prediction via Data Compression. In: Proc. 7th Int'l Conf. Architectural Support for Programming Languages and Operating Systems, pp. 128–137 (October 1996)
16. Mudge, T., Chen, I.-C., Coffey, J.: Limits to Branch Prediction, Technial Report CSE–TR–282–96, University of Michigan (February 1996)
17. Driesen, K., Hölzle, U.: Limits of Indirect Branch Prediction, Technical Report TRCS97–10, Computer Science Department, University of California, Santa Barbara (June 1997)
18. Driesen, K., Hölzle, U.: Multi-stage Cascaded Prediction, Technical Report TRCS99–05, Computer Science Department, University of California, Santa Barbara (February 1999)
19. Jha, S., Lu, Y., Clarke, E.: Formal Analysis of Branch Prediction Algorithm, Technical Report, Computer Science, Carnegie Mellon University (1998)
20. Vintan, L., et al.: Understanding Prediction Limits Through Unbiased Branches. In: Jesshope, C., Egan, C. (eds.) ACSAC 2006. LNCS, vol. 4186, pp. 480–487. Springer, Heidelberg (2006)
21. Yokota, T., et al.: Entropy Properties in Program Behaviors and Branch Predictors. In: Proc. 18th IASTED Int'l Conf. Parallel and Distributed Computing and Systems, pp. 448–453 (November 2006)
22. Yokota, T., Ootsu, K., Baba, T.: Introducing Entropies for Representing Program Behavior and Branch Prediction Performance. In: Proc. 2007 Workshop on Experimental Computer Science, ACM digital library (June 2007)
23. Yokota, T., Ootsu, K., Baba, T.: Proposal of Entropies for Representing Program Behavior and Branch Prediction Performance. IPSJ Transactions on Advanced Computing Systems (to appear)

Author Index

Lecture Notes in Computer Science

Sublibrary 1: Theoretical Computer Science and General Issues

For information about Vols. 1–4598
please contact your bookseller or Springer

Vol. 4934: U. Brinkschulte, T. Ungerer, C. Hochberger, R.G. Spallek (Eds.), Architecture of Computing Systems - ARCS 2008. XI, 287 pages. 2008.

Vol. 4927: C. Kaklamanis, M. Skutella (Eds.), Approximation and Online Algorithms. X, 289 pages. 2008.

Vol. 4921: S.-i. Nakano, M.. S. Rahman (Eds.), WALCOM: Algorithms and Computation. XII, 241 pages. 2008.

Vol. 4919: A. Gelbukh (Ed.), Computational Linguistics and Intelligent Text Processing. XVIII, 666 pages. 2008.

Vol. 4917: P. Stenström, M. Dubois, M. Katevenis, R. Gupta, T. Ungerer (Eds.), High Performance Embedded Architectures and Compilers. XIII, 400 pages. 2008.

Vol. 4910: V. Geffert, J. Karhumäki, A. Bertoni, B. Preneel, P. Návrat, M. Bieliková (Eds.), SOFSEM 2008: Theory and Practice of Computer Science. XV, 792 pages. 2008.

Vol. 4904: S. Rao, M. Chatterjee, P. Jayanti, C.S.R. Murthy, S.K. Saha (Eds.), Distributed Computing and Networking. XVIII, 588 pages. 2007.

Vol. 4878: E. Tovar, P. Tsigas, H. Fouchal (Eds.), Principles of Distributed Systems. XIII, 457 pages. 2007.

Vol. 4875: S.-H. Hong, T. Nishizeki, W. Quan (Eds.), Graph Drawing. XIII, 402 pages. 2008.

Vol. 4873: S. Aluru, M. Parashar, R. Badrinath, V.K. Prasanna (Eds.), High Performance Computing – HiPC 2007. XXIV, 663 pages. 2007.

Vol. 4863: A. Bonato, F.R.K. Chung (Eds.), Algorithms and Models for the Web-Graph. X, 217 pages. 2007.

Vol. 4860: G. Eleftherakis, P. Kefalas, G. Păun, G. Rozenberg, A. Salomaa (Eds.), Membrane Computing. IX, 453 pages. 2007.

Vol. 4855: V. Arvind, S. Prasad (Eds.), FSTTCS 2007: Foundations of Software Technology and Theoretical Computer Science. XIV, 558 pages. 2007.

Vol. 4851: S. Boztaş, H.-F.(F.) Lu (Eds.), Applied Algebra, Algebraic Algorithms and Error-Correcting Codes. XII, 368 pages. 2007.

Vol. 4848: M.H. Garzon, H. Yan (Eds.), DNA Computing. XI, 292 pages. 2008.

Vol. 4847: M. Xu, Y. Zhan, J. Cao, Y. Liu (Eds.), Advanced Parallel Processing Technologies. XIX, 767 pages. 2007.

Vol. 4846: I. Cervesato (Ed.), Advances in Computer Science – ASIAN 2007. XI, 313 pages. 2007.

Vol. 4838: T. Masuzawa, S. Tixeuil (Eds.), Stabilization, Safety, and Security of Distributed Systems. XIII, 409 pages. 2007.

Vol. 4835: T. Tokuyama (Ed.), Algorithms and Computation. XVII, 929 pages. 2007.

Vol. 4783: J. Holub, J. Žďárek (Eds.), Implementation and Application of Automata. XIII, 324 pages. 2007.

Vol. 4782: R. Perrott, B.M. Chapman, J. Subhlok, R.F. de Mello, L.T. Yang (Eds.), High Performance Computing and Communications. XIX, 823 pages. 2007.

Vol. 4771: T. Bartz-Beielstein, M.J. Blesa Aguilera, C. Blum, B. Naujoks, A. Roli, G. Rudolph, M. Sampels (Eds.), Hybrid Metaheuristics. X, 202 pages. 2007.

Vol. 4770: V.G. Ganzha, E.W. Mayr, E.V. Vorozhtsov (Eds.), Computer Algebra in Scientific Computing. XIII, 460 pages. 2007.

Vol. 4769: A. Brandstädt, D. Kratsch, H. Müller (Eds.), Graph-Theoretic Concepts in Computer Science. XIII, 341 pages. 2007.

Vol. 4763: J.-F. Raskin, P.S. Thiagarajan (Eds.), Formal Modeling and Analysis of Timed Systems. X, 369 pages. 2007.

Vol. 4759: J. Labarta, K. Joe, T. Sato (Eds.), High-Performance Computing. XV, 524 pages. 2008.

Vol. 4746: A. Bondavalli, F. Brasileiro, S. Rajsbaum (Eds.), Dependable Computing. XV, 239 pages. 2007.

Vol. 4743: P. Thulasiraman, X. He, T.L. Xu, M.K. Denko, R.K. Thulasiram, L.T. Yang (Eds.), Frontiers of High Performance Computing and Networking ISPA 2007 Workshops. XXIX, 536 pages. 2007.

Vol. 4742: I. Stojmenovic, R.K. Thulasiram, L.T. Yang, W. Jia, M. Guo, R.F. de Mello (Eds.), Parallel and Distributed Processing and Applications. XX, 995 pages. 2007.

Vol. 4739: R. Moreno Díaz, F. Pichler, A. Quesada Arencibia (Eds.), Computer Aided Systems Theory – EUROCAST 2007. XIX, 1233 pages. 2007.

Vol. 4736: S. Winter, M. Duckham, L. Kulik, B. Kuipers (Eds.), Spatial Information Theory. XV, 455 pages. 2007.

Vol. 4732: K. Schneider, J. Brandt (Eds.), Theorem Proving in Higher Order Logics. IX, 401 pages. 2007.

Vol. 4731: A. Pelc (Ed.), Distributed Computing. XVI, 510 pages. 2007.

Vol. 4728: S. Bozapalidis, G. Rahonis (Eds.), Algebraic Informatics. VIII, 291 pages. 2007.

Vol. 4726: N. Ziviani, R. Baeza-Yates (Eds.), String Processing and Information Retrieval. XII, 311 pages. 2007.

Vol. 4719: R. Backhouse, J. Gibbons, R. Hinze, J. Jeuring (Eds.), Datatype-Generic Programming. XI, 369 pages. 2007.

Vol. 4711: C.B. Jones, Z. Liu, J. Woodcock (Eds.), Theoretical Aspects of Computing – ICTAC 2007. XI, 483 pages. 2007.

Vol. 4710: C.W. George, Z. Liu, J. Woodcock (Eds.), Domain Modeling and the Duration Calculus. XI, 237 pages. 2007.

Vol. 4708: L. Kučera, A. Kučera (Eds.), Mathematical Foundations of Computer Science 2007. XVIII, 764 pages. 2007.

Vol. 4707: O. Gervasi, M.L. Gavrilova (Eds.), Computational Science and Its Applications – ICCSA 2007, Part III. XXIV, 1205 pages. 2007.

Vol. 4706: O. Gervasi, M.L. Gavrilova (Eds.), Computational Science and Its Applications – ICCSA 2007, Part II. XXIII, 1129 pages. 2007.

Vol. 4705: O. Gervasi, M.L. Gavrilova (Eds.), Computational Science and Its Applications – ICCSA 2007, Part I. XLIV, 1169 pages. 2007.

Vol. 4703: L. Caires, V.T. Vasconcelos (Eds.), CONCUR 2007 – Concurrency Theory. XIII, 507 pages. 2007.

Vol. 4700: C.B. Jones, Z. Liu, J. Woodcock (Eds.), Formal Methods and Hybrid Real-Time Systems. XVI, 539 pages. 2007.

Vol. 4699: B. Kågström, E. Elmroth, J. Dongarra, J. Waśniewski (Eds.), Applied Parallel Computing. XXIX, 1192 pages. 2007.

Vol. 4698: L. Arge, M. Hoffmann, E. Welzl (Eds.), Algorithms – ESA 2007. XV, 769 pages. 2007.

Vol. 4697: L. Choi, Y. Paek, S. Cho (Eds.), Advances in Computer Systems Architecture. XIII, 400 pages. 2007.

Vol. 4688: K. Li, M. Fei, G.W. Irwin, S. Ma (Eds.), Bio-Inspired Computational Intelligence and Applications. XIX, 805 pages. 2007.

Vol. 4684: L. Kang, Y. Liu, S. Zeng (Eds.), Evolvable Systems: From Biology to Hardware. XIV, 446 pages. 2007.

Vol. 4683: L. Kang, Y. Liu, S. Zeng (Eds.), Advances in Computation and Intelligence. XVII, 663 pages. 2007.

Vol. 4681: D.-S. Huang, L. Heutte, M. Loog (Eds.), Advanced Intelligent Computing Theories and Applications. XXVI, 1379 pages. 2007.

Vol. 4672: K. Li, C. Jesshope, H. Jin, J.-L. Gaudiot (Eds.), Network and Parallel Computing. XVIII, 558 pages. 2007.

Vol. 4671: V.E. Malyshkin (Ed.), Parallel Computing Technologies. XIV, 635 pages. 2007.

Vol. 4669: J.M. de Sá, L.A. Alexandre, W. Duch, D. Mandic (Eds.), Artificial Neural Networks – ICANN 2007, Part II. XXXI, 990 pages. 2007.

Vol. 4668: J.M. de Sá, L.A. Alexandre, W. Duch, D. Mandic (Eds.), Artificial Neural Networks – ICANN 2007, Part I. XXXI, 978 pages. 2007.

Vol. 4666: M.E. Davies, C.J. James, S.A. Abdallah, M.D. Plumbley (Eds.), Independent Component Analysis and Signal Separation. XIX, 847 pages. 2007.

Vol. 4665: J. Hromkovič, R. Královič, M. Nunkesser, P. Widmayer (Eds.), Stochastic Algorithms: Foundations and Applications. X, 167 pages. 2007.

Vol. 4664: J. Durand-Lose, M. Margenstern (Eds.), Machines, Computations, and Universality. X, 325 pages. 2007.

Vol. 4661: U. Montanari, D. Sannella, R. Bruni (Eds.), Trustworthy Global Computing. X, 339 pages. 2007.

Vol. 4649: V. Diekert, M.V. Volkov, A. Voronkov (Eds.), Computer Science – Theory and Applications. XIII, 420 pages. 2007.

Vol. 4647: R. Martin, M.A. Sabin, J.R. Winkler (Eds.), Mathematics of Surfaces XII. IX, 509 pages. 2007.

Vol. 4646: J. Duparc, T.A. Henzinger (Eds.), Computer Science Logic. XIV, 600 pages. 2007.

Vol. 4644: N. Azémard, L. Svensson (Eds.), Integrated Circuit and System Design. XIV, 583 pages. 2007.

Vol. 4641: A.-M. Kermarrec, L. Bougé, T. Priol (Eds.), Euro-Par 2007 Parallel Processing. XXVII, 974 pages. 2007.

Vol. 4639: E. Csuhaj-Varjú, Z. Ésik (Eds.), Fundamentals of Computation Theory. XIV, 508 pages. 2007.

Vol. 4638: T. Stützle, M. Birattari, H. H. Hoos (Eds.), Engineering Stochastic Local Search Algorithms. X, 223 pages. 2007.

Vol. 4630: H.J. van den Herik, P. Ciancarini, H.H.L.M.(J.) Donkers (Eds.), Computers and Games. XII, 283 pages. 2007.

Vol. 4628: L.N. de Castro, F.J. Von Zuben, H. Knidel (Eds.), Artificial Immune Systems. XII, 438 pages. 2007.

Vol. 4627: M. Charikar, K. Jansen, O. Reingold, J.D.P. Rolim (Eds.), Approximation, Randomization, and Combinatorial Optimization. XII, 626 pages. 2007.

Vol. 4624: T. Mossakowski, U. Montanari, M. Haveraaen (Eds.), Algebra and Coalgebra in Computer Science. XI, 463 pages. 2007.

Vol. 4623: M. Collard (Ed.), Ontologies-Based Databases and Information Systems. X, 153 pages. 2007.

Vol. 4621: D. Wagner, R. Wattenhofer (Eds.), Algorithms for Sensor and Ad Hoc Networks. XIII, 415 pages. 2007.

Vol. 4619: F. Dehne, J.-R. Sack, N. Zeh (Eds.), Algorithms and Data Structures. XVI, 662 pages. 2007.

Vol. 4618: S.G. Akl, C.S. Calude, M.J. Dinneen, G. Rozenberg, H.T. Wareham (Eds.), Unconventional Computation. X, 243 pages. 2007.

Vol. 4616: A.W.M. Dress, Y. Xu, B. Zhu (Eds.), Combinatorial Optimization and Applications. XI, 390 pages. 2007.

Vol. 4614: B. Chen, M. Paterson, G. Zhang (Eds.), Combinatorics, Algorithms, Probabilistic and Experimental Methodologies. XII, 530 pages. 2007.

Vol. 4613: F.P. Preparata, Q. Fang (Eds.), Frontiers in Algorithmics. XI, 348 pages. 2007.

Vol. 4600: H. Comon-Lundh, C. Kirchner, H. Kirchner (Eds.), Rewriting, Computation and Proof. XVI, 273 pages. 2007.

Vol. 4599: S. Vassiliadis, M. Bereković, T.D. Hämäläinen (Eds.), Embedded Computer Systems: Architectures, Modeling, and Simulation. XVIII, 466 pages. 2007.